Early Education
Curriculum

A Child's Connection to the World

SECOND EDITION

Early Childhood Education

providing lessons for life

www.EarlyChildEd.delmar.com

Early Education Curriculum

A Child's Connection to the World

SECOND EDITION

Hilda L. Jackman

Professor Emerita
Brookhaven College
Dallas County Community College District

Africa • Australia • Canada • Denmark • Japan • Mexico • New Zealand • Philippines
Puerto Rico • Singapore • Spain • United Kingdom • United States

NOTICE TO THE READER

Delmar Staff
Business Unit Director: Susan L. Simpfenderfer
Executive Editor: Marlene McHugh Pratt
Acquisitions Editor: Erin O'Connor Traylor
Development Editor: Melissa Riveglia
Executive Production Manager: Wendy A. Troeger
Project Editor: Amy E. Tucker
Production Editor: Eileen M. Clawson/Sandra Woods
Technology Project Manager: Kim Schryer
Executive Marketing Manager: Donna J. Lewis
Channel Manager: Nigar Hale

Cover Design: TDB Publishing Services
Illustrations: Laurent Linn

Library of Congress Cataloging-in-Publication Data

Jackman, Hilda L.
  Early education curriculum : a child's connection to the world. / Hilda L. Jackman. — 2nd ed.
     p. cm.
Includes bibliographical references and index.
  ISBN 0-7668-0919-6
  1. Early childhood education—United States—Curricula. 2. Curriculum planning—United States. 3. Interdisciplinary approach in education—United States. 4. Early childhood education—Activity programs—United States. I. Title.
  LB1139.4 .J33 2000
  372.19—dc21
                                                                                              00-030719

Brief Contents

Contents

PART TWO Discovering and Expanding the Early Education
Curriculum 57

Chapter 3 Language and Literacy 59

Preface

Many changes are taking place as we enter the twenty-first century—new research, rapidly advancing technology, changing family relationships, and violence in our communities. All this affects the families we serve. Nevertheless, the focus of early childhood educators remains the same: *the children*. We should listen to the children and concentrate our efforts on their needs, abilities, interests, and cultural diversity as we plan our curriculum.

In this second edition, interconnecting philosophies are emphasized. The first advocates that curriculum is *child-centered and child-directed*, that it is sensitive to, and supportive of, the development of young children, individually and in a group, emphasizing acceptance of all children. This includes acceptance of diversity, individual differences, and special needs. The second focus is *process*. The text suggests leading adult students through the same process as the children. This encourages experimentation, self-control, and the building of a positive self-image ("I can do it myself!"). The third philosophy recognizes the importance of *cultural context* in the development and learning of young children. Growing up as members of families and communities, children come to us with rich backgrounds of cultural experiences. The fourth belief advocates developing a learning environment that invites *creativity*. This provides opportunities for unevaluated discovery and activity, while promoting acceptance and respect for one another's creations. The fifth concept involves reciprocal *relationships between teachers and families*. Positive communication between home and school is crucial to providing a consistent and beneficial experience for young children. Each of these philosophies allows children to make choices and is nourished by play.

All chapters of the text are separate and complete, while at the same time connecting to other chapters to form curriculum as a whole for children from infancy to age eight. This allows each instructor to use the chapters in any sequence. This approach is helpful in meeting the individual needs of the teacher, the student, and ultimately the children.

This book is designed for a beginning student as well as an experienced teacher looking for fresh ideas or insights. It can be used by those in early education curriculum courses, in mini/fast-track courses, and in workshop/seminar courses for continuing education of teachers. It is also applicable for students working toward the Child Development Associate credential.

The text is divided into two parts. Part One, Creating the Environment that Supports Curriculum and Connects Children, presents the elements of the foundation of early education curriculum. Chapter 1, Starting the Process, presents strategies for organizing instruction, with emphasis on developmentally, individually, culturally, and creatively appropriate practices; the importance of play in the lives of children; the planning process; ways to include diverse ages, groupings, and individual differences; and communication with parents. Chapter 2, Creating Curriculum, offers examples of curriculum models and programs; explains the process of curriculum development, including multicultural, anti-bias, and special needs considerations, space arrangement of indoor and outdoor environments, determining concepts and skills, themes, specific lesson and activity plans, and a plan of assessment and evaluation based on different ages and individual differences. Both chapters end with an afterview, key terms, exploration activities, references, and additional readings and resources.

Part Two, Discovering and Expanding the Early Education Curriculum, explores each curriculum area in depth, taking into consideration the individual child, group of children, process of setting up appropriate environments, special subject content, and integration of all curricula. Each chapter presents developmentally appropriate activities for each age group and encourages self-esteem and creativity development. The content chapters offer guidance tips for teachers, multicultural/anti-bias activities, an afterview, key terms, exploration assignments, references, and additional readings and resources.

Chapter 3 Language and Literacy
Chapter 4 Literature
Chapter 5 Puppets
Chapter 6 Dramatic Play and Creative Dramatics
Chapter 7 Art
Chapter 8 Sensory Centers
Chapter 9 Music and Movement
Chapter 10 Math
Chapter 11 Science
Chapter 12 Social Studies

Examples of early education room arrangements and lesson plans are included in Chapter 2. Flannelboard characters, puppet patterns, lesson plan worksheets, and additional resources for teachers are included in the appendices. Key terms have been highlighted in the text and are defined in the glossary.

The *Instructor's Manual and Test Bank* to accompany *Early Education Curriculum: A Child's Connection to the World* includes guidelines for student observation of, and participation with, children, chapter summaries and competencies, topics for class discussions, student activity worksheets for each chapter, and chapter tests.

NEW FEATURES OF THE SECOND EDITION

This edition has been updated and revised to include:

- Current practices, trends, and approaches used by early childhood educators.
- Recommendations and position statements of professional organizations, such as the National Association for the Education of Young Children (NAEYC), National Council of Teachers of Mathematics (NCTM), International Reading Association (IRA), and the Music Educators National Conference (MENC).
- A full color insert reflecting guidance techniques to support a developmentally appropriate classroom community, infancy to age eight.
- Special needs considerations and accommodations in early childhood settings.
- Additional references, readings, resources, and Internet Web sites. *Internet Disclaimer:* The author and Delmar make every effort to ensure that all Internet resources are accurate at the time of printing. However, due to the fluid, time-sensitive nature of the Internet, Delmar cannot guarantee that all URLs and Web site addresses will remain current for the duration of this edition.
- Examples of curriculum models and programs.
- Expanded children's literature selections, including books to nurture inclusion.
- An in-depth interview with *Sesame Street's* "Rosita."

This text is designed to provide additional assistance as you continue to make a difference in the lives of young children, their families, and the early childhood profession.

Dedication

This book is lovingly dedicated to the men in my life: my husband, PHIL, and my two sons, STEPHEN and LARRY

. . . and to my nephew, JARED, who keeps me connected to the ever-changing world of children.

Acknowledgments

My sincere appreciation is extended to the many individuals, especially the children, who have encouraged, supported, and assisted me in the writing of the second edition of *Early Education Curriculum: A Child's Connection to the World*.

Special recognition must go to my son, **Laurent Linn**, for his wondrous illustrations that show his love and understanding of children and that give depth and meaning to what I have tried to communicate in words.

I am most appreciative to **Jo Eklof** and **Bea Wolf**, my friends and colleagues, whose musical creativity and commitment to and respect of children and the world we live in is expressed in their songs and writings.

To the charming **Carmen Osbahr** and **"Rosita"** and to the gracious **Caroll Spinney, Big Bird,** and **Oscar the Grouch** of *Sesame Street*, I gratefully acknowledge your contributions to Chapter 5.

Additional thanks I extend to **Janet Galantay, Shirley Smith,** and **Nita Mae Tannebaum** for their comments, contributions, and support.

My most special appreciation goes to my husband, **Phil Jackman,** for his love, patience, encouragement, and participation in this project. Without him, this book would not have been possible.

To my son, **Stephen Linn,** who is always there with much-needed additional support and reassurance from Nashville, a heartfelt "thank you."

My thanks go also to **Erin O'Connor Traylor** and the entire staff at Delmar.

And finally, I appreciate the time, effort, and contributions my reviewers have given to me. Thanks to:

Alice D. Beyrent, MEd
Chair, Early Childhood Education
Hesser College
Manchester, New Hampshire

Andrew D. Carroll, EdD
Professor of Early Childhood Education and Reading
Georgia Southwestern College
Americus, Georgia

Sandra Enders, MEd
Instructor
San Antonio College
San Antonio, Texas

Vicki C. Milstein, MS
Instructor in Education
Wheelock College
Canton, Massachusetts

Steven Reuter, PhD
Professor, Curriculum and Instruction
Mankato State University
Mankato, Minnesota

Marilyn Toliver, PhD
Professor, Early Childhood Education
John A. Logan College
Carterville, Illinois

Deborah Tulloch, EdD
Associate Professor of Education
College of Saint Elizabeth
Morristown, New Jersey

About the Author

Hilda Jackman has been working with children and families for over forty years. Through her involvement in children's theatre and children's television, as an early childhood teacher and administrator, and as coordinator-professor of Brookhaven College's child development–early childhood program, she has maintained her commitment to the field of early childhood. Since retiring from college teaching, Hilda continues to present workshops and staff development seminars, consult, and stay active in NAEYC, Texas AEYC, and other professional organizations.

To the Student

Welcome to the world of early education. I am glad you are here. Our profession needs caring, committed individuals to encourage and support children through their early years.

Each of you has a different reason for wanting to be in an early childhood classroom. Some of you are just beginning. Others are experienced teachers. No matter what type of program or what age group you work with, it is important that you understand the development of young children, help them connect with the changing world of their families, and promote developmentally appropriate practices in early education environments and curriculum.

This text is designed to be a practical guide to help you develop a curriculum appropriate for young children. Terminology is often a problem when discussing early education. Throughout this text, the terms are those used by the National Association for the Education of Young Children and most early childhood professionals. Early education, early childhood education, and early childhood *all* refer to the child from birth to age eight and the programs designed especially for these children.

Your experiences with young children are most important to your academic and professional development. I encourage you to use this curriculum text to stimulate your own creativity and knowledge of children. Mix and match, add to, and redesign the ideas and activities presented. Take the time to enjoy the uniqueness of each individual child, as well as the group of children, as they explore and interact with the curriculum.

It is also important to remember that professional ethics and confidentiality are concerns that are inseparable from all observation and participation activities. It is crucial that you deal with each child and/or adult without prejudice or partiality and refrain from imposing your own views or values upon children or adults.

I hope this text will prove helpful to you as you strive to make a difference in the lives of young children and their families. We are all in this profession together, and, like the children, we too are growing and developing.

PART ONE

Creating the Environment that Supports Curriculum and Connects Children

I stand outside the classroom, teacher,

At the doorstep to the world.

I want to see it all,

To hear and feel and taste it all.

I stand here, teacher,

With eager eyes and heart and mind.

Will you open the door?

Janet Galantay
(Reprinted with permission)

Starting the Process

■ OVERVIEW

A child's world is fresh and new and beautiful, full of wonder and excitement. . . . If a child is to keep alive his inborn sense of wonder. . . . [H]e needs the companionship of at least one adult who can share it, rediscovering with the child the joy, excitement, and mystery of the world we live in.

These words of Rachel Carson (1956) express so well what we, as students and teachers in early education, want to accomplish. To be that special adult requires enthusiasm, interest, and genuine caring about children, as well as commitment, training, experience, and knowledge about child development and how children learn. Becoming that special adult requires that we honor the uniqueness of each child and the child's family.

The child must be at the center of all we do. As you read this text, its focus on making the environment and the curriculum child-centered will be apparent. Each chapter extends this philosophy by applying developmentally appropriate, integrated curriculum philosophies. Included are ideas to enhance instruction and activities that respect a child's culture, language, and learning style.

■ EARLY CHILDHOOD EDUCATION

It is common for educators of young children to use the terms *early childhood, early childhood education,* and *early education* interchangeably. This text follows this practice. Early childhood education refers to the programs and settings that serve young children from birth through the eighth year of life (Bredekamp & Copple, 1997). Children receiving early education may attend drop-in, half-day, full-day, and before- and after-school programs that are publicly or privately funded in family child-care homes, churches, child-care centers, schools, and other community settings.

The actual number of young children enrolled in group education experiences is rising. The Children's Defense Fund research (1998) tells us

In 1973 approximately 30 percent of mothers with children under age 6 were in the work force, as were more than 50 percent of mothers of school-age children. By 1997 these percentages had grown to 65 percent and 77 percent respectively. . . . Every day 13 million children—including 6 million infants and toddlers—are in child care.

■ DEVELOPMENTALLY APPROPRIATE PRACTICE

During these important years of birth to eight, a child's physical, intellectual, emotional, and social growth should be supported within the home, child-care facility, school, and community. Each child learns and develops differently. The philosophy of developmentally appropriate practice promotes this thinking and is identified by the National Association for the Education of Young Children (NAEYC) as

the outcome of a process of teacher decision making that draws on at least three critical, interrelated bodies of knowledge: (1) what teachers know about how children develop and learn; (2) what teachers know about the individual children in their groups; and (3) knowledge of the social and cultural context in which those children live and learn. (Bredekamp & Copple, 1997)

Developmentally appropriate early education recognizes the social nature of learning, and it values cultural and linguistic diversity. Also included is the understanding that children need an environment that allows them to interact at their own level of development with a minimum amount of adult direction. Because developmentally appropriate classrooms are not only age/stage appropriate but also individually appropriate, they will not all look alike. This child-centered approach establishes educational experiences that take into consideration a child's way of perceiving and learning and develops curriculum with a child's point of view (Gordon & Williams Browne 2000). Kostelnik, Soderman, and Whiren (1998) explain, "The essence of developmental appropriateness is not simply what we do, but how we think—how we think about children and programs; what we value children doing and learning; how we define effectiveness and success."

Child Development and Learning

First, let us focus on what is developmentally occurring with young children, the variations in their development, and their developmental process for learning.

Infants and Toddlers. The early months of infancy are crucial in creating a foundation for all areas of development. Infants are actively involved with their world. They explore with all their senses (seeing, hearing, tasting, smelling, and feeling) and are acutely aware of their environment. "Their sense of belonging and ability to understand their world grow when there is continuity between the home and child care setting" (Bredekamp & Copple, 1997). Infants and the significant adults in their lives establish very special relationships that involve getting to know each other and adjusting to each other. What adults do can modify how infants behave (Wilson, 1995).

Infants learn about their surroundings by physically moving around, through sensory exploration, and by social interaction. As they are learning, the sight of the adult who feeds, holds, and comforts the infant is reinforced when that adult shows pleasure in caring for the infant. Emotional attachment develops as the child learns to expect that special person to make him feel good. The infant then seeks more contact with that adult. Even after crawling and walking have begun, the child frequently asks to be held.

Children in their second year of life grow and learn rapidly. This is a time for development in mobility, autonomy, and self-help skills. They try many tasks that are often too difficult for them. At this time, the safety of the environment is critical. As a teacher, you should expect this newfound independence and allow for trial and error. Children love to repeat and use these new skills over and over again (Essa, 1999).

Appropriate teaching techniques require the building of trust between the children and the teacher, and between the children and their environment. This can only develop if there are safe, consistent, and child-centered surroundings that encourage success for both children and teacher.

Three-, Four-, and Five-Year-Olds. Three-year-olds have a distinct period of development with added skills and challenges. They are anxious to try new things but get frustrated when they cannot do what they set out to do. They engage in more extensive conversations; and although they can play along with other children, they often find it difficult to cooperate in a game. Teachers of three-year-olds need to respect their growing skills and competencies without forgetting just how recently they were acquired.

Four-year-olds are full of enthusiasm and high energy. The ability to do more things without help, along with increased large and small muscle control, allows the children to develop a greater self-confidence. Children of this age enjoy learning to do new things and like to have an adult's attention. At the same time, because they are so eager to learn and learn so fast, they can use a higher level of language (more and bigger words) than they really understand.

Essa (1999) explains, "Peers are becoming important. Play is a social activity more often than not, although fours enjoy solitary activities at times as well." As a teacher, when you interact with these active children, you will be bombarded with questions. Sometimes they will insist on trying to do things that are too difficult for them. Help them find many things that they *can do*. Observe the children and set up the environment to match their skills.

Five-year-olds are becoming more social; they have best friends and also enjoy playing with small groups of children. Their use of language, especially vocabulary, continues to grow along with the understanding that words can have several meanings. Experimentation with language is evident at this age.

Fives are more self-controlled, but family and teacher have the most influence on how they behave. They take responsibility very seriously and can accept suggestions and initiate action. With the increase of large and small muscle abilities, five-year-olds can run, jump, catch, throw, and use scissors, crayons, and markers easily.

Exploration of the environment is important to these children. They are learning about the world and their place in it. They act on their own and construct their own meaning. Each of their actions and interpretations is unique to them. They are developing an understanding of rules, limits, and cause and effect. The teacher's role is to allow all this to happen, while at the same time creating the appropriate environment, encouraging curiosity, and learning along with the children.

Six-, Seven-, and Eight-Year-Olds. The body growth of six-to-eight-year-olds is slower but steadier, and physical strength and ability are important to them. These children are able to think and learn in more complicated ways, both logically and systematically.

The language and communication development in these primary-grade children is dramatic. They move from oral self-expression to written self-expression. "During these years, children's receptive vocabulary increases not just by listening but by reading, and their expressive vocabulary expands from spoken to written communication" (Bredekamp & Copple, 1997). They are becoming more independent and have strong feelings about what they eat, wear, and do. The six-to-eights are extremely curious about their world, and they actively look for new things to do, to see, and to explore. They are making new friends, and these peers play a significant role in their lives as they take into consideration the viewpoints of others.

Seefeldt and Barbour (1998) tell us, "They're developing the ability to see things from another perspective and are able to be more emphatic. At the same time, they're very sensitive and their feelings get hurt easily." As these primary-age children try out their new independence, they need teachers' and parents' guidance, affection, encouragement, and protection as much as, if not more than, ever.

Note: The additional references, readings, and resources listed at the end of this chapter offer additional in-depth information on the developmental process.

Individual Strengths, Interests, and Needs

Now let us examine individual appropriateness, which involves adapting an early childhood environment to meet a child's cultural and linguistic needs, as well as his individual strengths and interests. This includes providing each child with the time, opportunities, and resources to achieve individual goals of early education. The teacher should support a positive sense of self-identity in each child. It is important for a teacher to provide many opportunities for teacher-child interaction. Individual appropriateness should not result in the lowering of expectations.

It is important to include opportunities for interacting with the child's family as well. Gestwicki (1999) says it clearly:

> *Developmentally appropriate practice does not approach children as if they were equal members of an age grouping, but as unique individuals. . . . This knowledge [of specific uniqueness] primarily comes through relating and interacting with children and also their parents, who are important resources of knowledge about their children. Developmentally appropriate practice is based on parents' active involvement both as resources of knowledge and as decision makers about what is developmentally appropriate for their children.*

Including parents in the program will encourage their support and provide you more insight into their child.

By observing young children, gathering data about who they are, and developing awareness of their strengths, interests, and needs you are starting to build a child-centered curriculum. You'll discover that children benefit from being treated as individuals while being part of a class community. For curriculum and environments to be developmentally appropriate, they must be individually appropriate.

Social and Cultural Contexts

Early childhood educators are now recognizing the importance of cultural context in the development and learning of young children. Growing up as members of a family and community, children learn the rules of their culture—explicitly through direct teaching and implicitly through the behavior of those around them (Bredekamp & Copple, 1997). "Rules of development are the same for all children, but social contexts shape children's development into different configurations" (Bowman, 1994). To affirm these differences and similarities, an early education environment should encourage the exploration of gender, racial, and cultural identity, developmental abilities, and disabilities. To eliminate **bias**—any attitude, belief, or feeling that results in unfair treatment of an individual—and to create an **anti-bias** atmosphere, you need to actively challenge prejudice and stereotyping. **Prejudice** is an attitude, opinion, or idea that is preconceived or decided, usually unfavorably. **Stereotype** is an oversimplified generalization about a particular group, race, or sex, often with negative implications (Derman-Sparks, 1989).

Children with learning, behavioral, or physical disabilities should be included in early childhood classrooms for at least a part of the day. "Just as knowledge of individual variation must be used in making decisions about typically developing children, so too must knowledge of typical child development be used in providing services for children with disabilities or developmental delays" (Bredekamp & Copple, 1997). (Multicultural/anti-bias and special needs considerations are discussed more fully in Chapter 2.)

Individual appropriateness requires the teacher/adult to try to put herself in the place of the child in the classroom. It means asking questions, such as:

- What would make the environment comfortable for infants, toddlers, preschoolers, early school-age children, or children with ability differences?
- What kind of adult support would be appropriate?
- What is planned to encourage parent participation?
- What is being done to develop a child's sense of trust, sense of self, and feeling of control over the environment?
- What should be happening to encourage positive self-concept development?
- What would I see if I were at the child's level?
- What kind of activities, supplies, and materials should be available?
- What is occurring to support a child's need for privacy or "alone time"?

In answering these questions, take into account what is known about how young children develop and learn, and match that to the content and strategies they encounter in early education programs. Being reflective and carefully listening to what children have to say is also important. As we continue through this text, the activities discussed in all curriculum areas will be developmentally appropriate with an emphasis on meeting the needs of *all* children.

A child *needs* to be appreciated by the teacher and other significant adults. He needs to experience an environment that reflects back to the child an awareness of and appreciation for his individual and cultural differences. The results of these positive influences will stay with the child for a lifetime.

Creative Appropriateness

Many times we hear people say that adults have to be retaught to be imaginative. Some ask why creativity dims with age. Others believe that the years between two and six are the crucial ones in which creativity develops and, if not cultivated then, is very hard to rekindle later in life.

Clark (1997) believes

Some have used creativity synonymously with giftedness; some have limited it to feelings and affective development; some believe that creativity must be expressed in a product; and others define only the spark or insight as the entire process. A more accurate definition would include an interaction of all of these ideas.

For those of us in early education, Catron and Allen (1999) offer another point of view: ". . . [T]he development of creativity is an integral component of a spontaneous play environment, and the potential for creative development is inherent in all developmental areas." (Chapter 6 expands this concept.)

It is important that as teachers we understand the intrinsic quality of creativity. We should offer encouragement by providing opportunities for it to be expressed and by showing that we genuinely value its expression. **Creativity** is the process of doing, of bringing something new and imaginative into being. Creativity can be destroyed by a teacher who does not appreciate the creative act or the child who expresses the act.

Mayesky (1998) helps us understand that "Teachers who allow children to go at their own pace and be self-directed in a relaxed atmosphere are fostering creative development. . . . The learning environment must also welcome exploration by elimination of conditions providing stress, and too strict time limits. . . ."

In this text the importance of the *process* is often expressed. As it relates to creativity, the process is crucial. In fact, *the process is more important than the product.* With this in mind, the teacher's role is to:

- Celebrate and value each child's creativity
- Understand that there is no right or wrong way of doing things, only possibilities
- Recognize that all children are creative to some degree, and some children are more creative than others
- Recognize that some children are more creative in one area than another
- Provide extended, unhurried time for children to explore and create (creativity does not follow the clock)
- Arrange an appropriate classroom space for children to leave unfinished work to continue the next day
- Encourage children to engage in creative processing as they manipulate and play with objects, while remembering it may not result in a finished product
- Introduce children to new materials and techniques
- Supply extensive, imaginative, wonderful collections of resource materials that might be bought, found, or recycled
- Offer encouragement for, and acceptance of, a certain amount of messiness, noise, and freedom
- Continue to experiment and test alternatives to determine what is best for your children and your classroom situation
- Understand that creative expression should flow through the entire curriculum

(Adapted from Edwards & Springate, 1995; Mayesky, 1998; and Schirrmacher, 1998.)

■ IMPORTANCE OF PLAY

From playing Peek-A-Boo to playing bridge, from pedaling a tricycle to catching a fish, adults and children alike love to play. While play is indeed fun for all of us, it has a special role in childhood. Play is essential for children to learn. (McCracken, 1987)

Play is at the core of developmentally appropriate practice. **Play**—a behavior that is self-motivated, freely chosen, process oriented, and enjoyable—is a natural activity for children. It allows them the opportunity to create, invent, discover, and learn about their world. It provides children joy and understanding of themselves and others.

As with all aspects of early childhood growth and development, young children go through a series of stages in the development of play. Each new experience offers opportunities for play exploration. Some types of play are characteristic of children at identifiable stages, but children can use many of these stages in varying degrees of sophistication as they get older.

Developmental Stages of Play

Unoccupied behavior usually occurs during infancy and early toddlerhood. A child occupies herself by watching anything of momentary interest. Sometimes the child may not appear to be playing at all.

Onlooker play is sometimes observed in young toddlers or in children introduced to new situations. This play focuses on the activity rather than the environment. Onlookers place themselves within speaking distance of the activity. Although passive, they are very alert to the action around them.

Solitary play surfaces first for a toddler. The child actually engages in play activity alone at home but is within "earshot" of mother or another adult. In an early education setting, the child plays independently without regard to what other children are doing.

Parallel play can be observed in the older toddler and young three-year-old. A child this age is playing for the sake of playing. This child is within "earshot" and sight of another child, and can be playing with the same toy but in a different way. Parallel play is the early stage of peer interaction, but the focus is on the object rather than another child.

Associative play finds the three- and four-year-old playing with other children in a group, but he drops in and out of play with minimal organization of activity. Two or three children use the same equipment and participate in the same activity, but each in his own way.

Cooperative play is organized for some purpose by the four-year-old and older child. This type of play requires group membership, and reflects a child's growing capacity to accept and respond to ideas and actions not originally her own. Group play (social play) is the basis for ongoing relationships with people and requires sharing of things and ideas, organizing games and activities, and making friends. Another aspect of cooperative play is the emphasis on peers and moving away from the importance of adults in the life of a child (Parten, 1932). The six- to-eight-year-old extends cooperative and symbolic play to include detailed planning and rule making. Leadership roles begin to emerge as play becomes serious.

Symbolic or dramatic play is observable in a young child by the way he uses objects and images. The use of the environment represents what is important to the child at that moment. This type of play allows the child to imitate realities of people, places, and events within his experiences. Superhero fantasy play is considered a type of symbolic play for a child. (Chapter 6 of this text discusses in-depth dramatic play and creative dramatics for young children.)

According to Maxim (1993)

The patterns of play enjoyed in infancy develop into new patterns as children grow older and participate in play experiences. But the earlier patterns do not disappear as new behaviors emerge, and the new patterns are not just enhancements of the earlier ones. They bring maturity to children's play as new experiences are encountered.

Play allows a child to:

- Use large and small muscle skills
- Express feelings
- Develop the use of the senses
- Talk and share ideas
- Concentrate and develop attention/interest span
- Increase intellectual activities and problem solve

■ Exercise the imagination and creativity
■ Have uninterrupted time to experiment and explore
■ Practice various types of behavior
■ Develop a positive self-concept

Teachers have a responsibility to help children develop in their use of play. We also should convey to parents the importance of play in the lives of young children. Play can be a valuable means of gauging a child's developmental progress. This information, in turn, can be communicated to parents. Other teacher responsibilities are to:

■ Respect and encourage individual differences in play abilities
■ Have patience with children and give them time to learn new play skills
■ Introduce activities and materials appropriate for each child's age and stage of development
■ Take a sincere interest in learning discoveries
■ Encourage cooperation
■ Take time to listen to children as they play and to observe how each child plays, what he plays with, who he plays with, and what the child *can* do

Childhood play has a key role in the development of self and identity. Understanding this, you can help the children in your care develop to their fullest potential. As you continue through the chapters of this text, you will find specific examples of how curriculum planning and implementation influence and strengthen childhood play.

■ PROCESS OF PLANNING

Planning and scheduling are important in early education classrooms, including those with infants and toddlers. Detailed information about this process will follow in Chapter 2, but it is important to explore several guidelines at this point.

As teachers of young children, consider the following:

■ Long-range planning includes setting up goals and objectives. **Goals** help describe the general overall aims of the program. **Objectives** are more specific and relate to curriculum planning, schedules, and routines. Seefeldt and Barbour (1998) suggest, "The goals you select will be based on the nature of the children you teach, the values and goals of the community in which the children live, and your own values."
■ Goals and objectives should involve developmentally, individually, culturally, and creatively appropriate practices. They should consider the physical, intellectual, social, and emotional development of the children you are teaching.
■ The center or school in which you teach can offer a long-range plan that will help you see where you and the children fit into the total program.

Schedules and Routines

The schedule and routine components of planning can help create a framework of security for young children. The format becomes familiar to them, and they welcome the periods of self-selected activities, group time, outdoor play, resting, eating, and toileting. The establishment of trust that grows between teacher and parent is based on consistent daily contact and the well-being of the children.

All early childhood programs include basic timelines, curricula, and activities that form the framework of the daily **schedule**. The events that fit into this time frame are the **routines**. The secret of classroom management is getting the children used to routines.

- *Arrival* provides interaction time for the teacher, parent, and child. It also offers a smooth transition from home. This early morning ritual reinforces the trust, friendship, and consistency necessary to young children and their families.
- *Departure* at the end of the day should also offer a relaxed transition for the child and family. This is another time for sharing positive feedback with the parents and provides a consistent routine for the child.
- *Mealtimes and snacks* are some of the nicest moments of the day when teachers and children sit down and eat together. "Snacks and meals are pleasant when they are orderly enough to focus on eating and casual enough to be a social experience" (Feeney, Christensen, & Moravcik, 1996). Self-help skills are developed as well when children pour their own juice and milk and help themselves family-style during meals. If children bring food from home, teachers need to give the parents culturally sensitive and nutritionally sound guidance concerning what food is appropriate for the children to bring.
- *Diapering and toileting* are routines that are ongoing throughout the day as needed. The development of toileting skills and handwashing occurs as the young child matures. Adult handwashing and disinfecting diapering surfaces to prevent disease are other important daily routines.
- *Rest or naptime* runs smoothly if teachers make the environment restful, soothing, and stress free. Consistency in how this routine is handled each day provides security to the children. The use of soft music, dim lights, and personal books or blankets encourages children to rest or sleep on their mats or cots. Older children need a short rest-time too. Sitting quietly with a book offers a quiet period during the day.
- *Transitions,* such as cleanup, prepare the environment for the next activity. These times are part of your lesson plan and should be based on the developmental needs of the children. (A complete discussion of transition activities is included in Chapter 2.)
- *Activity time* offers children a large block of time to self-select from a variety of activities. "A wide variety of well-planned activities should reinforce the objectives and theme of the curriculum. Each day's activities should also provide multiple opportunities for development of fine and gross motor, cognitive, creative, social, and language skills" (Essa, 1999). In addition, appropriate times for small and large group activities, along with a balance of active and quiet activities, should be provided.
- *Outdoor activities* offer children many opportunities for growth and learning. To be developmentally appropriate, outdoor play requires the same planning, observation, and evaluation as indoor activities (Brewer, 1998). Large blocks of outdoor time should be scheduled and planned daily.

Figures 1–1, 1–2, and 1–3 are examples of infant, toddler, and three- to five-year-old schedules and routines appropriate for early education programs. Figure 1–4 illustrates how routines can be teachable moments in an environment for young children.

INFANTS

(3–18 months)
Very Flexible Schedule and Routines

7:30–9:00	Arrival
	Greet parents and infants
	Put away bottles, food, diaper supplies
	Spend individual time holding and talking to each child
8:00–9:00	*Younger infants:* Individual cereal, fruit, formula, or juice
	Young infants have individual schedules that include feeding, diapering, and sleeping
9:00	*Older infants:* Snack
9:30–11:00	Younger infants: Individual formula, juice, or water
	Individual play on floor, movement exercise, outdoor play, or walk in stroller
	Talk to each child throughout the day
	Older infants: Individual or group play, visit toddler playground, walk around center, or play in indoor playroom, read books, dramatic play, manipulatives, art, music and movement, finger plays
11:00	*Older infants:* Lunch with formula, milk, juice, or water
	Talk to individual child
11:30–12:30	Cleanup and prepare for naps: Lights dimmed, soft music, quiet play
12:30–2:00	Naptime
	Younger Infants: Talk to and play quietly with infants who are awake or have teacher-aide take noisy infants with toys to play in the hallway, indoor playroom, or outdoor area
2:00–3:30	Quiet play with books and toys as infants awaken
	Younger infants: Individual formula, juice, or water; soft snacks
	Older infants: Snack
3:30–4:30	Individual play, group activities, outdoor play, walks
4:30–5:30	Prepare for going home
	Younger infants: Individual formula, juice, or water
	Talk to parents

Diaper Changes: As needed after snacks, after lunch, before and after naps, before departure, and changing of soiled diapers anytime during the day.

FIGURE 1–1 An example of a daily schedule and routines for a group of infants.

TODDLERS

(18 months to 3 years)
Flexible Schedule and Routines

7:30–8:00	Greet children and parents, free play (children choose activities)
8:00–8:50	Center activities (art, manipulatives, blocks, dramatic play), spend individual time with each child or small group activity
8:50–9:00	Cleanup with song or poem or special individual time
9:00–9:30	Bathroom time (wash hands, change diapers, toileting, etc.), talk to each child Snack and time for washing hands and face
9:30–10:30	Outdoor play
10:30–10:40	Bathroom time (wash hands, change diapers, toileting), talk to each child
10:40–11:20	Center activities Guided exploration Large group activity of a story, finger plays, language activities, or music
11:20–11:25	Bathroom time to wash hands for lunch
11:25–11:45	Lunch
11:45–12:00	(If applicable, afternoon teacher arrives and both teachers are together until all children are either napping or resting.) Bathroom time
12:00–2:30	Quiet time with books and music while children finish in bathroom and get on their cots for naptime or rest
2:30–3:00	Wake-up time (put away cots, toileting, diaper change, washing, put on shoes), free play
3:00–3:15	Snack
3:15–3:30	Group time with story, song, flannelboard, or other language activity
3:30–4:30	Outdoor play, individual time with each child
4:30–4:45	Bathroom time
4:45–5:30	Quiet activities (books, puzzles, music), individual time with each child, playing games, singing, talking; prepare to go home

Note: This daily schedule is flexible, depending on the needs of the children and the weather.

FIGURE 1–2 An example of a daily schedule and routines for a group of toddlers.

PRESCHOOLERS and KINDERGARTNERS

(three-, four-, and five-year-olds)
Daily Schedule and Routines for Full Day Class

7:30–8:30	Arrival and free play, children can visit another room or have individual time with teacher
8:30–9:00	All centers are open for activity time Small groups rotating inside and outside play or continuation of centers
9:00–9:15	Toileting and washing hands for snacks
9:15–9:30	Snack
9:30–9:45	Group time
9:45–10:15	Centers and individual time with teacher
10:15–10:30	Cleanup to go outside
10:30–11:30	Indoor or outside play, walks, or small groups
11:30–11:45	Toileting, washing hands Any of the following activities: share time on cots with books, pictures (two children to a cot), quiet conversation or relaxing on cots, listening to music, finger plays, songs, stories, or sitting on carpet squares and reading books
11:45–12:15	Lunch
12:15–12:30	Finish lunch, toileting, washing hands, get settled on cots with story record or story the teacher will read
12:30–12:45	Quiet time transition, resting, and quiet music
12:45–2:30	Naptime or rest, with provisions made for children who wake early or cannot sleep
2:30–3:00	Wake-up time, fold and put away blankets, put on shoes, toileting, get ready for snack
3:00–3:15	Snack
3:15–3:45	Centers or individual time with teacher
3:45–4:00	Cleanup and transition activity
4:00–4:15	Group time
4:15–5:15	Indoor or outside play or small groups
5:15–5:30	Any of the following activities: quiet activities, table games, stories, songs, music Get ready to go home

Note: This schedule is flexible and subject to change. The needs of children and the weather will affect changes.

FIGURE 1–3 An example of a daily schedule and routines for a group of multi-age children.

ROUTINES ARE TEACHABLE MOMENTS

Eating Teaches Health:

Introduction to new and different foods, good nutritional habits

Eating Teaches Social Skills:

How to manage oneself in a group eating situation, focusing on eating and conversing; acceptable mealtime behavior and manners

Eating Teaches Fine Motor Skills:

Pouring; handling spoons, forks; serving self; drinking, eating without spilling

Eating Teaches Independence Skills:

Finding and setting one's place, serving self, making choices, cleaning up at snack and lunch times

Eating Teaches Individual Differences:

Likes/dislikes; choices of food; fast/slow pace of eating

Resting/Sleeping Teaches Health:

Personal care skills; relaxation habits; internal balance and change of pace; alternating activity to allow body to rest

Resting/Sleeping Teaches Independence Skills:

Preparing own rest place; selecting book/toy; clearing bed after rest

Dressing Teaches Independence Skills:

Self-awareness: size of clothes, comparisons between clothes for girls and boys, younger and older, larger and smaller children, and children in and out of diapers or training pants

Self-esteem: caring for one's own body; choosing one's own clothes

Dressing Teaches Fine Motor Skills:

How to manage snaps, buttons, zippers; handling all garments; maneuvering in and out of a snowsuit or jacket, matching hands and feet with mittens and boots or shoes

Toileting Teaches Emotional Skills:

Self-awareness: body functions, comparisons between boys and girls, learning the names and physical sensations that go with body functions

Self-identity: what girls/boys do

Self-esteem: caring for one's own body without guilt, fear, shame

Human sexuality: in a natural setting, promotes healthy attitudes toward the body and its functions; that adults can be accepting, open, and reassuring about the body and its care

FIGURE 1–4 Every routine can be used as an opportunity for learning. (Gordon & Williams Browne, 2000)

■ COMMUNICATION WITH PARENTS

It is the teacher's responsibility to keep the lines of communication open to families. It is the family's responsibility to be involved with their child's teacher and child-care center or school. "Reciprocal relationships between teachers and families require mutual respect, cooperation, shared responsibility and negotiation of conflicts toward achievement of shared goals" (Bredekamp & Copple, 1997).

Positive communication between home and school is crucial to providing a consistent and beneficial experience for young children. "Just as the teacher deals with each child as a unique individual by employing a variety of teaching guidance methods, so must a flexible approach be maintained in communicating with families to meet their individual requirements" (Essa, 1999).

Teachers and other staff members in early childhood settings should be responsive to cultural and language differences of the children and their families. Affirming and supporting diversity includes being perceptive about differences in caregiving, feeding, and other practices (Wortham, 1998).

Here are some suggestions for communicating with parents:

- Provide a daily infant report (Figure 1–5).
- Provide a daily or weekly toddler report (Figure 1–6).
- Create bulletin boards with information regarding health and safety issues, parent meetings, guest speakers, community resources and referrals, and tips for parents.
- Provide parent letters discussing the goals, objectives, theme, and classroom activities. Offer suggestions for activities parents can do with children at home to extend or emphasize classroom experience.
- Encourage parents to share with you what they know about their children and what is important to them as parents.
- Encourage parents to visit the classroom.
- Conduct parent-teacher conferences that focus on the accomplishments and needs of the individual child and that ensure privacy and confidentiality for the family.
- Provide multilingual written communications as needed.
- Provide opportunities for parents to volunteer.

INFANT DAILY REPORT

Child's Name: _____ Date: _____ Teacher: _____

BOTTLES:	Fluid	Ounces	Time
	_____	_____	_____
	_____	_____	_____
	_____	_____	_____
	_____	_____	_____
	_____	_____	_____

FOODS:	Type	Amount	Time
	_____	_____	_____
	_____	_____	_____
	_____	_____	_____
	_____	_____	_____
	_____	_____	_____

DIAPERING:
(Check indicates
diaper change.)

_____	_____		_____
_____	_____		_____
_____	_____		_____

NAPS:

_____ to _____

_____ to _____

_____ to _____

ACTIVITIES:

ITEMS NEEDED FROM HOME:

COMMENTS:

FIGURE 1–5 An example of an infant daily report.

TODDLER DAILY REPORT

Child's Name: _____ Date: _____ Teacher:_____

(*Note:* Weekly menu is posted on parent bulletin board.)

MORNING SNACK: Child Ate: well (   )   fair (   )

LUNCH: Child Ate: well (   )   fair (   )

AFTERNOON SNACK: Child Ate: well (   )   fair (   )

NAP: _____

ACTIVITIES:

ITEMS NEEDED FROM HOME:

COMMENTS:

FIGURE 1–6 An example of a toddler daily report

AFTERVIEW

An early childhood program should be based on fulfilling the developmental needs of children. It should be planned to meet each child's physical, intellectual, social, and emotional growth. Understanding the interrelationships among development, learning, and experiences is essential to provide the highest quality care and education for young children.

The program should be founded on the assumption that growth is a sequential process, that children pass through stages of development, and that children learn through their play and by actively participating in the learning experiences offered. It should adapt to the developmental, individual, and cultural differences of the children.

As teachers, we need to offer age, individually, and creatively appropriate experiences and activities for each child. We should assist each child in growing to his fullest potential by recognizing each stage of development; by providing an environment that encourages the success of each child; by respecting the culture, language, and special needs of each child; and by welcoming family participation in the program.

As we plan for children and their families, we are saying: Welcome! This environment is safe and appropriate. We care, we will listen, we will share, and we will nurture you and recognize your uniqueness.

KEY TERMS

anti-bias

associative play

bias

cooperative play

creativity

developmentally appropriate
    practice

dramatic play

early childhood education

goals

objectives

onlooker play

parallel play

play

prejudice

routines

schedule

solitary play

stereotype

symbolic play

unoccupied behavior

EXPLORATIONS

1. Plan a personal set of career goals, and discuss which "career path" you are considering or are involved with at this time. Discuss what or who influenced you to make the decisions.

2. Select an early education classroom and choose a child to observe for at least one hour. Put yourself in "the child's place" and try to experience, as she does, the classroom and the interactions with the other children and the teacher. Describe in writing what the child did during your observation (objective/factual). Focus especially on the child's interaction with the teacher. What did you learn from this observation about children, the teacher, and yourself (subjective/opinion)?

3. Think about your experiences with a teacher or teachers during your early years in school. Give an example in which the teacher encouraged your creativity. What about the teachers you had in junior high school? High school? How do you feel about your creativity now? What are some of the things you do to express your creativity? What will you do or what are you doing as a teacher to set up a creatively appropriate environment for young children?

4. Visit a child-care facility and talk to the director or lead teacher. Is there a written philosophy statement? What are the goals of the program? Are they aware of the National Association for the Education of Young Children's Developmentally Appropriate Practice and Anti-Bias Curriculum? In your opinion, what did you observe that was developmentally appropriate? Give specific examples.

5. Visit an early childhood program. Select a classroom and look at its daily schedule and the routines within the schedule. Obtain a copy, if possible. Are the schedule and routines developmentally appropriate? Do they consider the needs of all the children? Explain your answers. Would you change anything? Why or why not?

REFERENCES

Bowman, B. (1994). The challenge of diversity. *Phi Delta Kappan, 76*(3), 218–225.

Bredekamp, S., & Copple, C. (Eds.). (1997). *Developmentally appropriate practice in early childhood programs* (Rev. ed.). Washington, DC: National Association for the Education of Young Children.

Brewer, J. (1998). *Introduction to early childhood education* (3rd ed.). Boston: Allyn and Bacon.

Carson, R. (1956). *The sense of wonder.* New York: Harper & Row.

Catron, C. E., & Allen, J. (1999). *Early childhood curriculum* (2nd ed.). Columbus, OH: Merrill.

Children's Defense Fund. (1998, Yearbook). *The state of America's children.* Washington, DC: Author.

Clark, B. (1997). *Growing up gifted* (5th ed.). Columbus, OH: Merrill.

Derman-Sparks, L. (1989). *Anti-bias curriculum: Tools for empowering young children.* Washington, DC: National Association for the Education of Young Children.

Edwards, C. P., & Springate, K. W. (1995, Fall). The lion comes out of the stone: Helping young children achieve their creative potential. *Dimensions of Early Childhood, 23*(4), 24–29.

Essa, E. (1999). *Introduction to early childhood education* (3rd ed.). Albany, NY: Delmar.

Feeney, S., Christensen, D., & Moravcik, E. (1996). *Who am I in the lives of children?* (5th ed.). Columbus, OH: Merrill.

Gestwicki, C. (1999). *Developmentally appropriate practice: Curriculum and development in early education* (2nd ed.). Albany, NY: Delmar.

Gordon, A., & Williams Browne, K. (2000). *Beginnings and beyond* (5th ed.). Albany, NY: Delmar.

Kostelnik, M., Soderman, A., & Whirin, A. P. (1998). *Developmentally appropriate programs in early childhood education.* (2nd ed.). Columbus, OH: Merrill.

Maxim, G. W. (1993). *The very young* (4th ed.). New York: Merrill/Macmillan.

Mayesky, M. (1998). *Creative activities for young children* (6th ed.). Albany, NY: Delmar.

McCracken, J. B. (1987). *Play is FUNdamental* [Brochure]. Washington, DC: National Association for the Education of Young Children.

Parten, M. B. (1932). Social participation among preschool children. *Journal of Abnormal and Social Psychology, 27,* 243–269.

Schirrmacher, R. (1998). *Art and creative development for young children* (3rd ed.). Albany, NY: Delmar.

Seefeldt, C., & Barbour, N. (1998). *Early childhood education* (4th ed.). Columbus, OH: Merrill.

Wilson, L. C. (1995). *Infants and toddlers* (2nd ed.). Albany, NY: Delmar.

Wortham, S. C. (1998). *Early childhood curriculum* (2nd ed.). Columbus, OH: Merrill.

ADDITIONAL READINGS AND RESOURCES

Allen, K. E., & Marotz, L. R. (1999). *Developmental profiles: pre-birth through eight* (3rd ed.). Albany, NY: Delmar.

Casey, M. B., & Lippman, M. (1991, May). Learning to plan through play. *Young Children, 46*(4), 52–58.

Christie, J. F., & Wardle, F. (1992, March). How much time is needed for play? *Young Children, 47*(3), 28–32.

Coleman, M. (1997, July). Families and schools: In search of common ground. *Young Children, 52*(5), 14–21.

Curtis, D., & Carter, M. (1996). *Reflecting children's lives: A handbook for planning child-centered curriculum.* Saint Paul, MN: Redleaf Press.

Diamond, K. E., Hestenes, L. L., & O'Conner, C. E. (1994, January). Integrating young children with disabilities in preschool: Problems and promise. *Young Children, 49*(2), 68–75.

Dunn, L., & Kontos, S. (1997, July). What have we learned about developmentally appropriate practice? *Young Children, 52*(5), 4–13.

Fromberg, D. (1998). Play issues in early childhood education. In C. Seefeldt & A. Galper (Eds.), *Continuing issues in early childhood education* (2nd ed.). Columbus, OH: Merrill.

Fromberg, D. (1997, November). What's new in play research? *Child Care Information Exchange,* 53–56.

Jones, E., & Reynolds, G. (1992). *The play's the thing: The teacher's role in children's play.* New York: Teacher's College Press.

Kovach, B. A., & Da Ros, D. A. (1998, May). Respectful, individual, and responsive caregiving for infants. *Young Children, 53*(3), 61–64.

Manning, D., & Schindler, P. J. (1997, July). Communicating with parents when their children have difficulties. *Young Children, 52*(5), 27–34.

Pelander, J. (1997, November). My transition from conventional to more developmentally appropriate practices in the primary grades. *Young Children, 52*(7), 19–25.

Perlmutter, J. C., & Burrell, L. (1995, July). Learning through "play" as well as "work" in the primary grades. *Young Children, 50*(5), 14–21.

Spafford, C. S., Pesce, A. J. I., & Grosser, G. S. (1998). *The cyclopedic education dictionary.* Albany, NY: Delmar.

Sturm, C. (1997, July). Creating parent-teacher dialogue: Intercultural communication in child care. *Young Children, 52*(5), 34–38.

Vander Wilt, J. L., & Monroe V. (1998, July). Successfully moving toward developmentally appropriate practice: It takes time and effort. *Young Children, 53*(4), 17–24.

Watson, L. D., Watson, M. A., & Wilson, L. C. (1999). *Infants and toddlers: Curriculum and teaching* (4th ed.). Albany, NY: Delmar.

Creating Curriculum

■ OVERVIEW

As we progress through this chapter, focusing on how to create a curriculum appropriate for young children, we once again emphasize the interconnecting philosophies of this text:

1. *Curriculum* is *child-centered* or *child-initiated* while being sensitive to and supportive of the development, age, and experiences of young children individually and in a classroom community.
2. *Curriculum* provides for all of a *child's development* by planning experiences that build upon what children already know and are able to do.
3. *Curriculum* encourages children to *learn by doing* through experimentation, exploration, and discovery while building self-control and a positive self-image.
4. *Curriculum* promotes opportunities to support a child's *cultural and linguistic diversity.*
5. *Curriculum* invites *creativity* by providing opportunities for unevaluated discovery and activity while promoting tolerance and respect for each other's creation.

This chapter illustrates how we develop an early education curriculum and all it encompasses, including classroom management techniques, appropriate practices for inclusion, arrangement of indoor and outdoor space, and selection of equipment and materials. The plan of evaluation and assessment discussed at the end of this chapter will help determine if developmentally appropriate curriculum goals and content have been achieved.

The National Association for the Education of Young Children (NAEYC) and the National Association of Early Childhood Specialists in State Departments of Education (NAECS/SDE) define curriculum as "an organized framework that delineates the content children are to learn, the processes through which children achieve the identified curricular goals, what teachers do to help children achieve these goals, and the context in which teaching and learning occur" (Bredekamp & Rosegrant, 1992). Additionally, for infants and toddlers, "every experience, and every minute in the day are a part of the infant and toddler curriculum. Diapering, feeding, washing, and comforting are elements of the curriculum, as are singing, playing, watching, and moving" (Watson, Watson, & Wilson, 1999).

Curriculum is a multileveled process that encompasses what happens in an early education classroom each day, reflecting the philosophy, goals, and objectives of the early childhood program. In an early education program, the **philosophy** expresses the basic principles, attitudes, and beliefs of the center or school. **Goals**—broad, general overviews of what children are expected to gain from the program—and **objectives**—specific teaching techniques or interpretations of the goals—are designed to meet the physical, intellectual, cultural, social, emotional, and creative development of each child.

As we continue focusing on the process of curriculum development, let us remember that whatever we do, say, plan, or assess must concentrate on developing a child's positive self-esteem. Valuing each child's cultural background, experiences, interests, and abilities is critical. The "I can do it!" feelings of competence strongly influence learning ability. This is true for all children, from the youngest infant to the preschooler to the eight-year-old.

■ PROCESS OF CURRICULUM DEVELOPMENT

The *process* of curriculum development is *ongoing*. The selection of themes, projects, integrated curriculum areas, equipment, and materials is based on sound *child develop-*

ment theories reinforcing the child's current stage of development and challenging him to move toward the next stage.

As a teacher of young children, you will find many early childhood curriculum models and theories available today. It is important to identify curriculum approaches and resources that are based on the developmental and cultural needs and interests of the children in your classroom. "For our curriculum planning to be relevant and reflect the needs of our children, we should pay close attention to the children themselves and to the economic and ideological interests that compete for their childhoods" (Curtis & Carter, 1996).

Curriculum models are helpful to point out guidelines for planning and organizing experiences. However, keep in mind that no single model addresses all the developmental and cultural priorities, such as anti-bias, inclusion, emergent curriculum, and the project approach. The following overview of curriculum model examples were chosen because they continue to be identified by the early childhood profession, have been implemented in multiple locations, and "are accompanied by an extensive literature describing their educational objectives, content and structure, and assessment procedures" (Goffin, 1994). As teachers, we should continue to investigate other models and programs as well, looking for additional insights into early education curriculum.

Examples of Curriculum Models and Programs

Montessori. These programs are based on Dr. Maria Montessori's original ideas, materials, and methods designed to meet the needs of impoverished children in Italy. The Montessori method is the second curriculum model created expressly for early education (Goffin, 1994). (The first model was created by Friedrich Froebel in Germany, who began the kindergarten or "garden for children" in the mid-1800s.) In the United States today there is a wide variation and interpretation of the Montessori principles. According to Dr. Montessori's philosophy, children learn best in a child-sized environment that is stimulating and inviting for their *absorbent minds,* one that offers beauty and order. Placed in that environment, the child may choose her own work—activities that have meaning and purpose for her. "A basic premise of the Montessori philosophy is that the child copies reality rather than constructs it. From watching and then doing activities, the child organizes the world and her own thinking" (Brewer, 1998).

After the child is introduced to the Montessori materials by a guide (teacher), she is free to use them whenever she likes, for as long as she wishes, undisturbed by others. The materials are *self-correcting.* If the child makes a mistake, she can see it for herself, without the need for an adult to point out her errors. Montessori materials are also *didactic,* designed to teach a specific lesson; focused on *daily living practical tasks* to promote self-help and environmental care skills; *sensorial,* planned to encourage children to learn through using their senses; and *conceptual* or academic materials to develop the foundations of reading, writing, and math. Some examples of Montessori-type materials found in many early childhood classrooms today are:

Puzzles—self-correcting

Nesting or stacking cups, rings, or blocks—self-correcting

Rough and smooth boards and fabrics—didactic and sensorial

Containers and tops—self-correcting and practical task

Setting a table—practical task

Washing dishes—practical task

Sound or scent bottles—sensorial

Sandpaper letters and numbers—sensorial and conceptual

Measuring materials—conceptual

Head Start. These programs are the largest publicly funded educational programs for young children. They include health and medical screening and treatment, required parent participation and involvement, and comprehensive services to families. "Today there are Head Start programs in every state and territory, in rural and urban sectors, on American Indian reservations, and in migrant areas" (Essa, 1999). From its inception in 1965, Head Start has sought to provide classroom-based and most recently home-based comprehensive developmental services for children from low-income families. Head Start experience has shown that the needs of children vary from community to community and that to serve these needs most effectively, programs should be individualized, thus meeting the need of the community served and its ethnic and cultural characteristics (Head Start, 1990). Head Start programs have a low child-staff ratio, with 10 percent of the enrollment in each state available for children with special needs. Head Start provides staff at all levels and in all program areas with training and opportunities, such as the child development associate (CDA) credential and related subjects at colleges and universities.

An essential part of every Head Start program is the involvement of parents in parent education, program planning, and operating activities. Many parents serve as members of policy councils and committees and have a voice in administrative and managerial decisions, while others participate as volunteer or paid aides to teachers, social service personnel, and other staff members.

> *Many different programs have been developed and evaluated as part of Head Start, and much research in early childhood education has been undertaken in Head Start programs. Thus, Head Start has been beneficial not only to the millions of children who have attended programs but also to the profession of early childhood education. (Brewer, 1998)*

The original vision of Head Start has been improved and expanded for the new century as a model that challenges the effects of poverty and promotes physically and mentally healthy families. Head Start has a difficult challenge ahead as it protects the high quality of its original charter and meets the growing needs of a greater number of children and families. The gap between the supply of adequate, affordable care and services and the demand for it remains as wide today as it was 25 years ago (Gordon & Williams Browne, 2000; Children's Defense Fund, 1998).

Bank Street. Founded in 1916 by Lucy Sprague Mitchell, this program continues to be an important model of early childhood education in the United States. Bank Street's *developmental-interaction* method is dedicated to fostering all aspects of a child's development, not simply to promote specific learning. It also emphasizes the interaction between the child and the environment, as well as the interaction between the cognitive and affective areas of the child's development, thus underscoring that thinking and emotion are not separate but truly interactive. Mitchell and David (1992) expand on this:

> *A fundamental principle of the developmental-interaction approach is that cognitive growth cannot be separated from the growth of personal and social processes. Further, the school should be an active community, connected to the social world of which it is a part, rather than an isolated place for 'learning lessons.' This means that the school shares responsibility with children's families and with other neighborhood institutions.*

Teachers arrange the classroom environment into distinct learning centers such as math, science, art, dramatic play, and music. These centers, along with a variety of materials and experiences, relate to the ages and interests of the children in the group to encourage integrating the curriculum, making choices, taking risks, and accepting help. Teachers and children alike learn from and teach one another by building on shared experiences to develop meaningful relationships.

The Bank Street approach is considered synonymous with open education, a term encompassing programs that operate on the premise that children, provided a well-conceived environment, are capable of selecting and learning from appropriate activities. The program does not aim to teach children a lot of new concepts, but rather to help them understand what they already know in more depth. (Essa, 1999)

High/Scope. Under the leadership of David Weikert, this educational approach began in the 1960s as an intervention program for low-income, at-risk children. Today the High/Scope program serves a full range of children—preschool, elementary, and early adolescent—adapting to the special needs and conditions of their group, their setting, and their community (High/Scope Educational Research Foundation, 1999). With the revised publication of their curriculum manual, *Young Children in Action* (Hohmann, Banet, & Weikert, 1995), the High/Scope program has been successfully implemented in both urban and rural settings in the United States and around the world.

Active learning, High/Scope's central belief for all age levels, emphasizes that children learn best through active experiences with people, materials, events, and ideas. Influenced by Jean Piaget's and Lev Vygotsky's theories of cognition and social interaction, this cognitively oriented model assists children in constructing their own knowledge from meaningful experiences. Materials are organized in each activity area so that children can get them out easily and put them away independently. In this kind of environment, children naturally engage in *key experiences*—activities that foster developmentally important skills and abilities (Hohmann, Banet, & Weikert, 1995). High/Scope has also developed infant and toddler key experiences for teachers of this younger age group.

Teachers in a High/Scope program give children a sense of control over the events of the day by planning a consistent routine that allows children to anticipate what happens next. Central to this curriculum is the daily *plan-do-review* sequence in which the children, with the help of teachers, make a plan, carry it out, and then recall and reflect on the results of their chosen activities. Planning allows children to consider the what, where, when, how, and why of what they will be doing for the next time period. Doing means action, such as working with materials, interacting with other children, choosing, creating, and sharing, thus stimulating the children's thinking abilities through the application of skills to problem-solving tasks. Reviewing involves putting what one has done into words or pictures and sharing the representation with other children, teachers, or parents. Daily schedules provide for both large and small group interaction, and for the plan-do-review sequence of student-selected activities (Hohmann, Banet, & Weikert, 1995.)

Reggio Emilia. Founded thirty years ago by Loris Malaguzzi, the early childhood schools of Reggio Emilia, Italy, have captured the attention of educators from all over the world. Inspired by John Dewey's progressive education movement, Lev Vygotsky's belief in the connection between culture and development, and Jean Piaget's theory of cognitive development, Malaguzzi developed his theory and philosophy of early childhood education from direct practice in schools for infants, toddlers, and preschoolers.

In Reggio Emilia the city-run educational system for young children now includes twenty-one schools for children ages 3 to 6 years, as well as fourteen infant/toddler centers for children 4 months to 3 years of age. Children from all socioeconomic and educational backgrounds attend the program, and special needs children are given first priority for enrollment in the schools (Gandini, 1993).

The Reggio Emilia approach is based on a comprehensive philosophy encompassing:

■ The respectful image of children as being highly competent to grow and develop their potential by constructing knowledge through explorations, self-expression, and social interaction.

■ The interdependence of teacher, parent, and child, each succeeding in relation to each other.

■ The community's commitment to providing a school environment that is designed and built to honor children's rights to a comfortable, aesthetically inviting place to learn and play. The school has a *piazza* (open square) that serves as the center of activity. Around this hub is a combination of spaces filled with materials, objects, tools, and toys to support children's interests. "Reggio Emilia teachers refer to the environment as *our third teacher*" (New, 1993).

■ The main concepts of *emergent curriculum* and *projects* that develop from children's ideas, activities, and curiosities, sometimes planned and sometimes accidental.

The teachers in Reggio Emilia are partners and collaborators in learning with the children and parents. The teachers become skilled observers of children in order to plan in *response to the children*. Each group of children is assigned co-teachers. There is no lead teacher or director of the school. A *pedigogista*, a person trained in early childhood education, meets with the teachers weekly. Every school has an *atelierista*, who is trained in the visual arts, working closely with teachers and children. *The hundred languages of children* is the term teachers use in referring to the process of children depicting their understanding through one of many symbolic languages, including drawing, sculpture, dramatic play, and writing. Teachers and children work together to solve any problems that arise. Children stay with the same teacher and group of children for three years (Albrecht, 1996; Gandini, 1993; New, 1993).

Bredekamp (1993) concludes that "The approach of Reggio Emilia educators is both old and new. Fundamentally the principles of Reggio Emilia schools are congruent with the principles of developmentally appropriate practice as described by NAEYC, presumably because both sets of principles share some of the same philosophical origins."

Multicultural/Anti-bias Considerations

Each time you set up an appropriate, warm, supportive environment for young children, much of what you do is very familiar to you. At the same time, if you are exploring new ways to encompass each child's uniqueness, you may find many things that are unfamiliar to you. Exploring gender, culture, race/ethnicity, and different-abledness offers opportunities to develop new insights about yourself and the children in your care. You may feel comfortable and uncomfortable at the same time. It is important to understand that exploring and implementing a multicultural/anti-bias curriculum becomes a continuous journey of growth and change. As a teacher of young children, you should take, as one of the first steps in your exploration of multicultural education, the task of *discovering your own cultural uniqueness*. By reflecting on the culture and race/ethnicity of your family, you learn about yourself and about the culture of others as well.

Exploring your feelings about individuals who differ from you culturally, racially, or with special needs or disabilities is another step in the anti-bias curriculum development process. Discovering and coming to terms with your own feelings and attitudes will help you when these children join your group. The inclusion of all children, whether they are differently abled or not, is a supporting principle of the anti-bias rationale. Ask yourself the following questions and then evaluate yourself by asking: Which of these issues have surfaced? What have I already accomplished? On what areas do I need to work?

- What differences among people or children make me feel uncomfortable?
- Do I have strong reactions to children from certain economic backgrounds, cultures, or races?
- How do I feel when children do not conform to my expectations about appropriate or acceptable behavior?
- Do I generally tend to prefer children of one sex?
- How do I react to families who have lifestyles that are very different from my own, and do these reactions influence my relationships or feelings about their children?
- When have I experienced or witnessed bias in my life, and how did I respond?
- How did I become aware of the various aspects of my identity and culture?

The *Anti-Bias Curriculum*, developed by Derman-Sparks and the A. B. C. Task Force (1989), is a comprehensive curriculum that offers helpful guidelines, activities, and materials that create an early education environment rich in possibilities for valuing differences and similarities. "Through anti-bias curriculum, teachers enable every child to achieve the ultimate goal of early childhood education: the development of each child to her or his fullest potential."

Cech (1991) explains, "At the center of each program is the child, and at the center of each child is culture." We must be sensitive to and respectful of the cultural background of each family member. The home and the center or school should develop a partnership to enable children to make an easy transition from known to unknown. Many children today are bilingual and bicultural. We must support and retain the language and culture of the family as we add the language and culture of the early education program to each child's experiences.

As teachers we must also be aware that some cultures emphasize a child's relationship to her group with group problem solving, rather than independence, individualism, and competition. In addition, some cultures value learning by active participation, while others encourage learning by observing and listening. Therefore, we must give young children time to develop independence and accept responsibility within their own cultural framework.

> The United States is becoming more multi-cultural and more aware of its multi-cultural character. No one can afford to ignore our diversity—least of all those who live and work with children. We must prepare children to live with diversity, indeed to celebrate diversity. To do that, we must prepare ourselves. (Gonzalez-Mena, 1993)

Culture Is Learned. No one is born acculturated. You must learn the beliefs of your culture. Anthropologists and educators consider culture to be something that is learned and transmitted from generation to generation. Another dimension is the concept that culture is something that members of a group share in common. You are born to a group with rules. However, groups borrow and share with other groups. As a result, culture is ever-changing rather than static and fixed.

York (1991) believes, "Multicultural education is more than teaching information directly. It means providing a classroom that includes materials depicting people from many different places doing many different things. . . . It is also encouraging children to act, think, and talk like members of their own culture. It's helping children like themselves just the way they are." Cech (1991) explains further, "The choices the child makes form the language of that culture. . . . This cultural language may begin as early as conception, long before the child can say the word 'culture'." In infant-toddler programs how you feed, diaper, hold, talk to, and interact with each child is relevant to anti-bias curriculum. Teachers and parents should be in agreement with how these basic needs are met (Gonzalez-Mena, 1993).

Each child brings her culture into the group. Some may be from a culture different from the teacher's or that of the dominant classroom culture. Perhaps one of the children is accustomed to eating with chopsticks at home. Offering chopsticks, as well as forks and spoons, for use during lunch or snack shows that you are sensitive to the child's culture. Because the child will also be interacting with your culture, she may sometimes eat with a fork and spoon. At the same time, other children may try eating with chopsticks. This is the beginning of multicultural education in its most basic form.

Culture, then, is the sum total of a child's or family's ways of living: their values or beliefs, language, patterns of thinking, appearance, and behavior. It includes the set of rules that govern a family's behavior and are passed or learned from one generation to the next.

A multicultural/anti-bias curriculum is one that actively challenges prejudice and stereotyping and represents an opportunity for the development of mutual respect, mutual sharing, and mutual understanding. It is crucial to establish an early education environment that enables children to make connections to their reality as well as the larger world, to develop positive self-esteem, and to receive approval, recognition, and success.

Expanding learning experiences to include others helps young children develop values, respect, and a cultural sense of belonging. Suggestions for integrating multicultural/anti-bias content and materials into specific curriculum areas can be found in Chapters 3 through 12. The following guidelines, compiled from various sources (Feng, 1994; Spodek & Saracho, 1994; Gonzalez-Mena, 1993; Essa, 1999; York, 1991; Derman-Sparks, 1989), can help you provide a developmentally appropriate, multicultural/anti-bias environment for young children.

- Be sensitive to, and respectful of, each child's cultural learning style without stereotyping.
- Use differences in language and culture as a foundation for learning.
- Communicate with parents to clarify home and school values about socialization and children's cultural and racial identities.
- Involve parents in the planning and implementation of activities.
- Model acceptance and appreciation of all cultures.
- Adapt curriculum materials to make them more relevant to all your children, and offer accurate information about different cultural groups in contemporary society.
- Ensure that the environment contains abundant images that reflect diverse abilities and current racial, ethnic, gender, and economic diversity.
- Make the necessary instructional and environmental adaptations (when possible) to meet the needs of children with special needs.
- Discuss cultural, racial, physical, and language differences *and* similarities honestly with children. Children are aware of differences in color, language, gender, and physical ability at a very young age.
- Provide opportunities for children to reinforce and validate their own racial and ethnic identities. Help children develop pride in their language, and their skin, hair, and eye color. Place value on the uniqueness of each individual.
- Help children find alternative ways or words to deal with racism and racial stereotypes.

■ Focus curriculum material about cultures on similarities *and* differences, such as eating, clothing, shelters, celebrations, and music. Global awareness of similarities and differences builds understanding and respect.

■ Provide opportunities to ask children questions about the activities/materials to assess their knowledge and help them to construct new knowledge. Allow time for children to practice changing perspectives.

An anti-bias classroom can flourish regardless of the educational setting. The process, however, takes time and can only be implemented within the developmental capacities of children. For this reason, the anti-bias approach is best begun in infancy. . . . [This] approach is not an add-on; it is a way of learning that permeates every element of the curriculum, i.e., interactions and modeling, family involvement, community relation- ship, staffing, routines, and the physical environment. (Hall, 1999)

Special Needs Considerations

Recommended practices for serving young children with special needs and their fam- ilies have changed dramatically in recent years and are continuing to evolve (Davis, Kilgo, & Gamel-McCormick, 1998). Children with learning, behavioral, or physical disabilities are now included in early childhood classrooms. **Inclusion** efforts reflect the blending of practices from early childhood education and early childhood special education. Miller (1996) explains, "Inclusion means that children with special needs are totally integrated into the activity of the classroom. . . . Effective inclusion is char- acterized by its virtual invisibility. Children with disabilities are not clustered into groups of persons with similar disabilities . . . children in an inclusive classroom are children with and without disabilities."

According to Public Law 94–142, 1975 (amended to PL 99–457, 1986 and further amended in PL 102–119, 1991) children with disabilities should be placed in the *least restrictive environment*. This means an environment that is as close as possible to the environment designed for nondisabled children, while remaining appropriate for their special needs (Spodek & Saracho, 1994). The environmental arrangement requires a teacher to prepare and organize materials and activities in learning centers and make appropriate adaptations for young children with disabilities (Davis, Kilgo, & Gamel- McCormick, 1998).

In agreement with the Individuals with Disabilities Education Act (IDEA) public laws, a written IFSP—individualized family services plan—that identifies the needs and goals of young children and their families must be developed for children ages birth to three in an early childhood setting. Cook, Tessier, and Klein (1996) identify several key activities that are expected to occur in the IFSP process. These include the following:

■ In accordance with each individual state's criteria, *eligibility* must be determined for each child. This involves sharing, gathering, and exchanging information between families and staff.

■ To assist families in making choices, *assessment* of the family's resources, priorities, and concerns, as well as the child's strengths is made.

■ At a meeting, conducted in the native language of the family, *development* of the ini- tial IFSP document is accomplished. At this point, a service coordinator is desig- nated.

■ To *implement* and *monitor* the IFSP document, the service coordinator is responsible for coordinating, facilitating, and monitoring the timely delivery of early inter- vention services with a review of the IFSP every six months and a full evaluation annually.

An IEP—individualized education plan—must be written for a child with special needs over the age of three and his family, specifying learning objectives that are part of regular classroom activities and routines (Spafford, Pesce, & Grosser, 1998). "Current federal guidelines require children who will receive any special education services to be seen for a diagnostic study by members of a multidisciplinary team before services can begin" (Cook, Tessier, & Klein, 1996). How much help is provided by professionals in special education or related services depends on the needs of the children and on state and local resources (McCormick & Feeney, 1995). These specialists, together with the family and the early childhood teacher, function as a team.

Cook, Tessier, and Klein (1996) expand on what the written IEP must include:

- A statement of the child's present levels of educational performance
- A statement of annual goals and related short-term behavioral objectives
- A statement of the specific special education and related services to be provided to the child
- The extent to which the child will be able to participate in regular education programs
- The supporting services needed within the regular program
- The projected dates and duration of services
- The objective criteria and evaluation procedures

It is crucial to be aware of the special needs that families of children with disabilities have and determine how the early childhood program can help meet these needs. As a teacher, you need to be sensitive to the various reactions that parents may experience, such as grief, guilt, anger, and even disregard of their child's special need. It is important to acknowledge and accept their reactions by listening, providing practical advice, and offering information on community resources that can be of help (Essa, 1999). Services to families must be individualized with regard for their cultures, strengths, values, skills, expectations, and needs. You should help them believe that they can cope with challenges and be successful in gaining the necessary resources and services (Wolery & Wilburs, 1994).

The following suggested modifications in early education environments and teaching styles help guide us in understanding what our goals and roles should be. They are:

- To provide an inclusive educational environment in which all children can succeed
- To view each child, whether disabled or not, as an individual with unique characteristics, strengths, and needs
- To give children with special needs the opportunity to develop autonomy, independence, competency, confidence, and pride
- To recognize, encourage, and support children's individualized development across all areas of the curriculum
- To teach children with disabilities how to handle and challenge name calling, stereotypic attitudes, and physical barriers
- To teach nondisabled children how to resist and challenge stereotyping, name calling, and physical barriers directed against people with disabilities
- To implement IFSP and IEP goals through natural or modified activities found within a thematic integrated curriculum in inclusive settings
- To be responsive to individual children by using various strategies, providing a variety of materials, and planning many different learning opportunities
- To adapt room arrangements, schedules, and curricula to provide special assistance and/or special positioning of equipment, as required
- To give infants and toddlers with special needs more time and attention by reducing group size
- To provide and prepare children for realistic life experiences

- To help children develop friendships by using cooperative learning, peer tutoring, working with a partner, or small mixed group participation
- To provide environment interactions that are initiated and directed by children and in which they are highly engaged
- To develop simple classroom rules
- To support development of direct, active relationships with the families of the children by providing parent education, using IFSPs and IEPs as guides
- To remember that flexibility and patience are important and to ask for help, when necessary
- To collaborate as a team with other teachers and specialists

(Adapted from Derman-Sparks, 1989; Essa, 1999; Davis, Kilgo, & Gamel-McCormick, 1998; McCormick & Feeney, 1995; Miller, 1996; Pearce, 1996; Watson, Watson, & Wilson, 1999; and Wolery & Wilbers, 1994.)

Managing the Environment

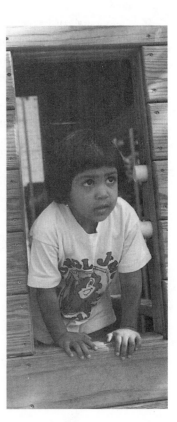

Another important ability we need to develop as teachers is managing a group of young children appropriately. Feeney, Christensen, and Moravcik (1996) explain, "You have spent many years learning to be responsible for your own behavior, but it is quite another thing to learn to manage the behavior of others—especially a group of lively young children."

Management in early education, including infant and toddler programs, is a direct result of understanding child development, establishing a philosophy, and determining goals and objectives. This includes the personal philosophy of the teacher and the overall philosophy of the early education program. Inclusion of both indoor and outdoor environments is involved. The **environment** represents all the conditions and surroundings affecting the children and adults in an early childhood setting.

A teacher spends a lot of time being a classroom manager. This requires the ability to think about and react to many things at once. The teacher's role as a supervisor and manager includes being responsible for setting up and maintaining a safe, developmentally appropriate environment, observing and listening to the children, on-the-spot training for aides and volunteers, and communicating with parents (Gordon & Williams Browne, 2000). The teacher should set clear, consistent, and fair limits for classroom and playground behavior, guide younger children toward appropriate ways to relate to others and to function in a group environment, and help older children set their own limits. Setting limits means security for young children. It is appropriate to remind children of the rules and listen when they express their feelings and frustrations. The National Association for the Education of Young Children, in the brochure *Helping Children Learn Self-Control* (1986) suggests, "The rules should be kept simple, few in number, clear, truly necessary, and reasonable for the age of the child." Whenever possible, explain the reason for the rule. For example, "The water stays in the water table so the floor will not be wet. Someone could fall on the wet floor." Remember too, as a teacher you should model good behavior. You must follow the rules you expect the children to follow.

Many times children experience intense and dramatic emotions. A part of early education management is to help children deal effectively with the outward expression of their feelings. Help the individual child identify what he is feeling, place a limit on his behavior, and give the child an appropriate outlet for that feeling. For example, "I know you are angry with Jared, but I cannot let you hit him. You may hit the playdough instead." "Use your words to tell Shirley how you feel."

Try to explain children's behavior to each other. "I think Larry wants to play with you." "I think Stephen needs to play by himself for a while." Also, try to use suggestion or redirection rather than the word *don't*. It is helpful to say "Sand stays in the sandbox," rather than "Don't throw the sand!" Tell children what you expect them to do in a positive manner.

GUIDANCE GUIDELINES FOR DEVELOPING RESPONSIBILITY AND INDEPENDENCE

- Arrange the environment to allow children access to age-appropriate toys, materials, supplies, learning centers, the restroom, etc.
- Expect children to do things for themselves, while understanding what their capabilities are. Do not expect more of them than they can give. Be patient and give the children time.
- Encourage self-help skills such as self-feeding and toileting, while planning opportunities for learning new skills, especially first attempts by children to do things for themselves. Keep in mind cultural values of independence versus interdependence.
- Give positive reinforcement for children's independent behaviors. It is the effort that counts, not the outcome.
- Offer simple yet consistent guidelines for the group and the individual child. Be sure your expectations are in line with the children's abilities and cultural expectations.

- Offer choices and then respect the child's preference and wishes. Suggest an easier or better way to do something when necessary, but leave the final decision up to the child.
- Allow and encourage children to participate in planning. Sometimes a child will come up with a better idea than the adult does.
- Allow children the privilege of learning through their mistakes without feeling guilty for having made a mistake. Be sensitive enough to know when not to help.
- Show each child that you trust and have confidence in her.
- Help each child change inappropriate behavior to appropriate behavior by using consistent, positive guidance techniques.
- Model appropriate behaviors for children so that they can be guided to attain the same behaviors.
- Avoid using words that would shame the children or cause them to doubt their competence.
- Support children when they feel frustrated and need security as they strive for independence.

FIGURE 2–1 Suggested guidance guidelines for young children.

Handle spills and mishaps as a natural part of a child's day. By saying "Janet, please get some paper towels to clean up the milk" and "I'll help you clean that up," you preserve a child's self-concept while allowing her responsibility for herself. See Figure 2–1 for suggestions on how to develop responsibility and independence.

Setting limits, anticipating, and preparing for behavior difficulties are only part of a teacher's responsibility. Ensuring safety and preventing accidents in the environment for young children must also be considered at all times and in everything we do with and for young children. Indoor and outdoor safety is essential for all children. Preparation and prevention are critical to child safety. Catron and Allen (1999) remind us, "Only when safety is ensured, needs are met, and problems are prevented or diminished can the staff turn their full attention to implementing the program goals and objectives for enhancing children's growth and development."

In Figure 2–2, Marotz, Cross, and Rush (2001) suggest a safety checklist for indoor and outdoor environments.

INDOOR AREAS

1. A minimum of 35 square feet of *usable* space is available per child.

2. Room temperature is between 68° and 85°F (20° and 29.4°C).

3. Rooms have good ventilation.
   - Windows and doors have screens.
   - Mechanical ventilation systems are in working order.

4. There are two exits in all rooms occupied by children.

5. Carpets and draperies are fire-retardant.

6. Rooms are well lighted.

7. Glass doors and low windows are constructed of safety glass.

8. Walls and floors of classrooms, bathrooms, and kitchen appear clean; floors are swept daily, bathroom fixtures are scrubbed at least every other day.

9. Tables and chairs are child sized.

10. Electrical outlets are covered with safety caps.

11. Smoke detectors are located in appropriate places and in working order.

12. Furniture, activities, and equipment are set up so that doorways and pathways are kept clear.

13. Play equipment and materials are stored in designated areas; they are inspected frequently and are safe for children's use.

14. Large pieces of equipment, e.g., lockers, piano, bookshelves, are firmly anchored to the floor or wall.

15. Cleaners, chemicals, and other poisonous substances are locked up.

16. If stairways are used:
    - A handrail is placed at children's height.
    - Stairs are free of toys and clutter.
    - Stairs are well lighted.
    - Stairs are covered with a nonslip surface.

17. Bathroom areas:
    - Toilets and washbasins are in working order.
    - One toilet and washbasin available for every ten to twelve children; potty chairs provided for children in toilet training.
    - Water temperature is no higher than 120°F (48.8°C).
    - Powdered or liquid soap is used for handwashing.
    - Individual or paper towels are used for each child.
    - Diapering tables or mats are cleaned after each use.

18. At least one fire extinguisher is available and located in a convenient place; extinguisher is checked annually by fire-testing specialists.

19. Premises are free from rodents and/or undesirable insects.

20. Food preparation areas are maintained according to strict sanitary standards.

21. At least one individual on the premises is trained in emergency first aid and CPR; first aid supplies are readily available.

22. All medications are stored in a locked cabinet or box.

23. Fire and storm/disaster drills are conducted on a monthly basis.

OUTDOOR AREAS

1. Play areas are located away from heavy traffic, loud noises, and sources of chemical contamination.

2. Play areas are located adjacent to premises or within safe walking distance.

3. Play areas are well drained.

4. Bathroom facilities and drinking fountain are easily accessible.

5. A variety of play surfaces, e.g., grass, concrete, sand are available; there is a balance of sunny areas and shady areas.

6. Play equipment is in good condition, e.g., no broken or rusty parts, missing pieces, splinters, sharp edges, frayed rope.

7. Selection of play equipment is appropriate for children's ages.

8. Soft ground covers present in sufficient amounts under large, climbing equipment; area is free of sharp debris.

9. Large pieces of equipment are stable and anchored in the ground.

10. Equipment is placed sufficiently far apart to allow a smooth flow of traffic and adequate supervision.

11. Play areas are enclosed with a fence at least four feet high, with a gate and a workable lock.

12. There are no poisonous plants, shrubs, or trees in the area.

13. Chemicals, insecticides, paints, and gasoline products are stored in a locked cabinet.

14. Grounds are maintained on a regular basis and are free of debris; grass is mowed; broken equipment is removed.

15. Wading or swimming pools are always supervised; water is drained when not in use.

FIGURE 2–2 A safety checklist for early childhood indoor and outdoor environments. (Marotz, Cross, & Rush, 2001)

Arrangement of Indoor and Outdoor Space

Arranging appropriate indoor and outdoor areas in an early education program is significant to curriculum development. This is an extension of classroom management and part of a teacher's strategy to accomplish the learning goals and objectives. The arrangement requires *planning* for each individual child and group of children, *understanding* the prior experiences and development of the children, and *supporting* the formation of trust, independence, and creativity in the children.

Teachers and children spend many hours in the classroom and on the playground. The extra time you spend to organize, plan for the needs of the children, and plan effective and efficient use of space will aid you in creating a developmentally appropriate learning environment.

Indoor Learning Environment. Children need to feel that they belong. The environment should tell the children "we care about you." For example, have a personal space or "cubbie" for each child with his name or photo. In a shared space, each child needs to know there is one place that belongs to him. Display children's art or special projects at their eye level. Reflect the interests of the children in all that you do.

The characteristics of a responsive, organized classroom offer a variety of well-defined **learning centers**, sometimes called interest centers or activity centers, where materials and supplies are combined around special groupings and common activities. These centers support children's learning and enable them to explore, experiment, and interact with the environment at their own rate of development.

Arranging and organizing the space for preschool, kindergarten, and primary classes becomes more specific and complex. The following learning centers are suggested for early education classrooms and outdoor areas (many of these can be combined or expanded):

- Books, language, and listening
- Dramatic play or home living area
- Art center
- Sensory activities with manipulatives; woodworking; cooking; water, sand, and mud play
- Blocks
- Music and movement
- Science, discovery, and nature
- Math
- Social studies/multicultural
- Computers

The learning centers involve hands-on experiences with a variety of materials. These materials and supplies have a direct correlation to a particular theme, lesson plan, or concept being introduced. Well-planned, continuous introduction and rotation of new materials stimulate interest. The learning centers make possible individual and small group instruction while providing an opportunity for the children to make choices in many different areas. The placement of the centers is important for balancing the number of noisy and quiet activities. How many of the areas are used at the same time depends on what is happening in relationship to the schedule, routines, and lesson plans. Sometimes specific learning centers may be closed to allow for expansion of other centers, for reasons relating to guidance and discipline, or because the size of the room necessitates rotation of activities. Also, the ages of the children and licensing requirements will affect the numbers and types of learning centers available in an early education setting. Chapters 3 through 12 offer specific curriculum activities and a rationale for each learning center.

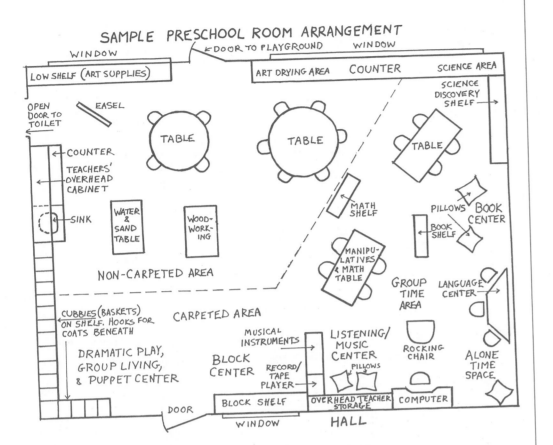

SAMPLE PRESCHOOL ROOM ARRANGEMENT

FIGURE 2–5 A suggested room arrangement diagram for preschoolers.

included dirt, water, flowers, trees, places to be alone, places to climb, places to hide, places to build, and plenty of unstructured playing time with your friends. As teachers, we have the opportunity to give the children in our care these same activities in safe, creative, stimulating, and developmentally appropriate play environments.

Criteria for Equipment, Materials, and Supplies Selection

The selection of indoor equipment (furniture and other large and expensive material), materials (smaller items such as puzzles, books, toys), and supplies (consumables such as paint, paper, glue) should be developmentally appropriate for the children in each classroom. Items must be child-size, nontoxic, aesthetically appealing, sturdy with rounded corners and edges, easy to maintain, and not easily broken. Many activities can be done on the floor, so floor covering must be "child-proof" and made of linoleum, tile, or carpeting that can take spills and hard wear. Tables can double as art, manipulative, and eating places. Both boys *and* girls need experiences with the same kind and variety of learning materials. Soft toys, big and comfy pillows, and furnishings that fit the children's size, abilities, and interests should also be included.

The Bank Street College of Education (1992) emphasizes the importance of including sensory materials in the selection for young children, especially toddlers. The use of "tactile materials (things you can feel) is a full-body experience for toddlers—they will be up to their armpits in shaving cream or finger paint and will often want to paint with their hands instead of brushes."

In the outdoor area, play structures are lower and wider for these young children who need time to climb up or down. The design, according to Frost (1992), "should

The clearly arranged spaces assist children in setting their own pace, making choices that will help them to be more self-directed, which in turn will improve their self-control. (See Figures 2–3, 2–4, 2–5, and 2–6 for suggested room arrangements for infants, toddlers, and preschoolers.) Essa (1999) tells us, "Children are more likely to follow classroom rules when the environment reinforces these: for instance, if it is important for reasons of safety that children not run inside, classroom furnishings should be arranged in a way that makes walking, rather than running, natural." For children with special needs, space supports development. Space should also meet the needs of the activity. "The kind of space that works best within an integrated curriculum format for a program that includes children with disabilities is flexible and fluid. It allows formation of interest centers, quiet corners, space for medium-size groups and whole-group activities, and widening pathways between activity areas so children with physical disabilities can have easier access to the areas" (Miller, 1996).

For infants and toddlers, a safe and healthy environment offers major activity areas designed for eating, sleeping, diapering, and playing. Caring for and playing with a few infants or toddlers at a time are the focus of these areas. Rocking chairs are a must. Babies enjoy rocking while being fed or comforted. If possible, sleeping should be in a separate room or quiet place away from active areas. These young children explore and interact with their environment through their senses; therefore, opportunities for open-ended exploration, visible and accessible materials, and safe possibilities for grasping, reaching, pushing, and pulling should be available. Mirrors add enjoyment for children during diapering and washing time. A large, sanitary floor area encourages crawling and floor play (Catron & Allen, 1999; Watson, Watson, & Wilson, 1999).

According to Lowman and Ruhman (1998), "When planning room arrangements for toddlers in group care settings there should be a basic understanding of the developmental needs of the toddler. . . . Toddlers often are the victims of the 'push-down' movement so common in many other educational settings." Developmentally appropriate toddler programs are not a scaled down version of appropriate preschool programs. For toddlers, the addition of a toileting area is necessary. Their play areas can be more specific, such as ones with blocks, books, and large and small muscle activities. They also need space where they can play alone or be onlookers as others play.

Outdoor Environment. Planning a balanced and varied outdoor environment, according to Catron and Allen (1999), "involves understanding children's perceptual motor development, incorporating outdoor activities into lesson plans, and regularly altering the outdoor environment to enhance opportunities for skill development." Planning also includes a process for developing curriculum for the outdoors in a way that parallels what teachers do indoors. Do this by putting out new props for the children to discover and respond to, keeping an eye on the evolving play, and planning for emerging developmental interests and skills (Curtis & Carter, 1996).

As a part of learning, children explore and test the environments, and so the playground, like the indoor classroom, must have limits. Fences, mandated by licensing requirements, set the parameters, and the teacher sets reasonable and appropriate rules that are consistently enforced. For example, "We sit on the slides, and come down feet first."

Safety is the first priority. At least two adults should be supervising the playground at all times. McCracken (1990) advises, "Outdoor time requires adults who are playful, have sharp senses and quick reactions, and who will closely observe children. Save reading, resting, parent conferences, team meetings, and even casual conversations with other adults for more appropriate occasions. Your attentive eyes can prevent an injury."

As you continue to plan outdoor spaces for play and learning, think back to when you were a child. What were your favorite outdoor play settings? They probably

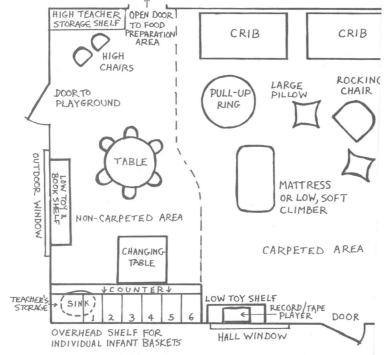

FIGURE 2–3 A suggested room arrangement diagram for infants.

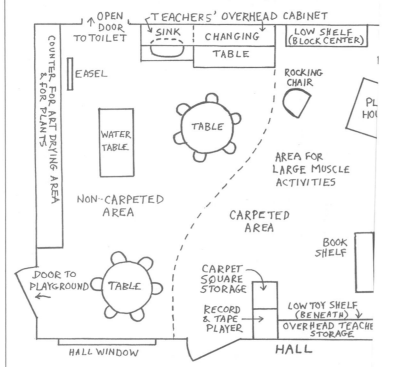

FIGURE 2–4 A suggested room arrangement diagram for toddlers.

A CHECKLIST FOR ROOM ARRANGEMENT

_____ Does your arrangement support the goals and objectives you have set up for your classroom and outdoor area?

_____ Are the learning centers well defined?

_____ Is there enough space for the activity to take place, but not too much open space to encourage running?

_____ Is each center located in the best possible place in the room? Are windows used for appropriate centers?

_____ Are water play and art centers located near water sources? Do you have hooks near your art table for children to hang up paint smocks?

_____ Are noisy and quiet centers separated?

_____ Is protection from "traffic" given to centers that need it so that traffic flow does not interrupt children's play?

_____ Can both children and teacher move about freely?

_____ Are there wide pathways available for children with wheelchairs?

_____ Is the room uncluttered but still warm and inviting?

_____ Is there clear visibility so you can see all the children?

_____ Are equipment and furniture movable and is the arrangement flexible according to changing needs? When you convert your room for lunch or nap, do you do it the same way every day to encourage your children to feel comfortable and secure?

_____ Is the furniture appropriate for the physical size of the children?

_____ Is the environment flexible to accommodate children with special needs?

_____ Are bathroom facilities convenient?

_____ Are electrical outlets available in the right place? Are they covered when not in use?

_____ Is lighting adequate?

_____ Are the materials and supplies for each center visible to and available for use by the children? Are directions clear and age appropriate?

_____ Is the number of children per center controlled? Does the arrangement or a visual clue suggest the desired number of children?

_____ Are materials limited in each center to offer choices that are not overwhelming but still offer enough materials for all?

_____ Does each center offer visual clues for placement of materials and equipment while encouraging cleanup? Are storage containers labeled with objects, pictures, photographs, or outlines of the contents?

_____ Are the learning centers organized and attractive and appropriate for young children? Do they reflect cultural diversity free of stereotyping? Do the cultures represented visually reflect the multicultural reality of the world rather than your classroom reality?

_____ Does the arrangement within the learning center promote social skills while encouraging cooperative group learning or individual learning?

_____ Is there a space for a child to have some alone time?

_____ Are pictures and bulletin boards placed at the eye level of children?

_____ Does each child have individual space for storage (cubbie)?

_____ Is the environment welcoming to parents as they enter the classroom?

FIGURE 2–6 A checklist for room arrangement in an early childhood environment.

- The Environment
- Plants and Gardening
- Animals
- Pets
- Cars, Trucks, and Buses
- Airplanes, Trains, and Tracks

Projects

A **project** is an in-depth investigation of a topic. This is usually undertaken b[y] group of children within a class, sometimes by an entire class, or individua[l] older child. This approach involves children applying skills, asking questions[,] decisions and choices, and assuming responsibility. Projects may last for a fe[w] for extended periods of time. Some examples of project work include

> *drawing, writing, reading, recording observations, and interviewing experts. The*
> *mation gathered is summarized and represented in the form of graphs, charts, diag*
> *paintings and drawings, murals, models and other constructions, and reports to*
> *and parents. In the early years, an important component of a project is dramatic p*
> *which new understanding is expressed and new vocabulary is used. (Katz, 1994)*

The first step in beginning the project process is to choose a topic, such as [ ] flowers, or the grocery store. Sometimes children have ideas for a topic, and s[ ] a teacher chooses a theme based on the children's experiences (Gandini, 1[ ] topic should allow the integration of a range of subject areas, including soci[al] science, and language arts, as well as literacy and math skills (Katz, 1994).

Progressing to the second stage involves investigating the topic based on [ ] questions and directions. This continues with exploring sites, objects, or eve[ ] project while collecting data, making observations, making models, and usin[g] resources.

In the third phase, as interest reaches its maximum point, end the [ ] reviewing what you and the children have learned and participate in a cu[ ] group activity. Throughout the project process, families act as partners in the [ ] learning. Guided by you, everyone takes an exciting exploration together.

Webs

A **curriculum web** integrates various learning activities. This visual process [ ] ibility for you and the children. You can move in different directions, desig[ ] activities that integrate various curriculum areas in special ways, and exte[ ] matic planning and/or project chosen. "Webbing" helps develop the scope[ ] tent of the theme.

To produce a thematic web, you have the choice of brainstorming a sin[g] topic by yourself, with a colleague, or with the children. Then record the i[ ] expanding web. This becomes a visual illustration of what could be included[ ] or unit or project approach to the curriculum. You can then put the elements [ ] into planned daily activities, with the children actively investigating, initia[ ] tioning, and creating. For an infant, toddler, or child with special needs, hav[ ] vidual child be the center of the theme (web) in order to plan activities for th[ ]

Figures 2–7 and 2–8 are examples of a curriculum planning web. The w[ ] Figure 2–8 is used throughout the text to demonstrate the application of lea[ ] ter activities. Another example of a thematic web can be found in Chapter 8[ ]

1) allow a wide range of movement; 2) stimulate the senses; 3) offer novelty, variety, and challenge; and 4) be safe and comfortable."

The selection of outdoor equipment and materials emphasizes safety, durability, and age appropriateness for all children. The outdoor space should contribute to physical, intellectual, creative, emotional, and social development and offer a variety of stimulation for play and exploration. The design should also offer ramps and tracks that accommodate wheelchairs and adapted vehicles, giving proper attention to slope, width, types of surface, and direct and safe accessibility to play and structures (Frost, 1992). The surfaces should offer textures and colors, such as a hard-surfaced area for games and wheeled toys, a large soft grassy area with trees, a garden area, organic loose material such as play bark/wood chips and pine bark mulch, inorganic loose material such as sand and pea gravel, and rubber or foam mats.

The following are suggestions for equipment selection:

- Permanent climbers
- Take-apart climbers for older children to rearrange
- Sturdy wooden crates and barrels
- Railroad ties surrounding sand box
- Tire swings with holes punched in several places for drainage (steelbelted tires are not appropriate)
- Slides
- Inner tubes
- Balance beam
- Tricycles, wagons, other wheeled toys
- Plastic hoops
- Rubber balls of various sizes
- Mounted steering wheel
- Sturdy cardboard boxes
- Equipment and materials that eliminate head entrapment points

You should think creatively of new ways to bring the indoor activities outside, and the outdoor activities inside, while at the same time keeping in mind the skills to be

developed: body awareness, coordination, bala
ment, encouragement of spontaneous and crea
environment, and development of positive s
Christie, & Yawkey, 1987).

■ THEMES, UNITS, PROJECTS, AN[

You will find that the core of curriculum devel
of young children, to integrate the children's n
conceptual plan for implementing goals and ol
actually *emerge* from the interests of the childr
specific time frame for the learning to unfolc
Themes, units, projects, and curriculum webs v
tered, emergent curriculum approach.

Themes and Units

Thematic curriculum is curriculum that focuses
a process for managing curriculum while ach
(Jackman, 1999; Miller, 1996). Integrated curric
approach and enables the teacher to tie in the
the children to major content areas of language
centers, music and movement, math, science, a
tion and expansion initiated by the children.

Many educators use the terms *theme* and *u*
theme as a broad concept or topic, such as '
ship," and "The Environment." This approac
activities that require active exploration, proble
concept or skill. A **unit** is a section of the curri
tant for the children to know more about and
which activities are planned. This is often offer
lar learning center.

Developing a list of themes is usually the
toward developing a lesson plan and the activ
to remain flexible and responsive to the chil
varying developmental stages and experiences
should merge play with child-directed and tea

Here are some examples of themes that ha
modified to fit any age group:

- Magnificent Me
- My Family and Me
- My Community
- Families
- Friendship
- Caring and Sharing
- The Seasons
- Weather
- My Five Senses
- Colors and Shapes in Our World
- Textures
- Things That Grow

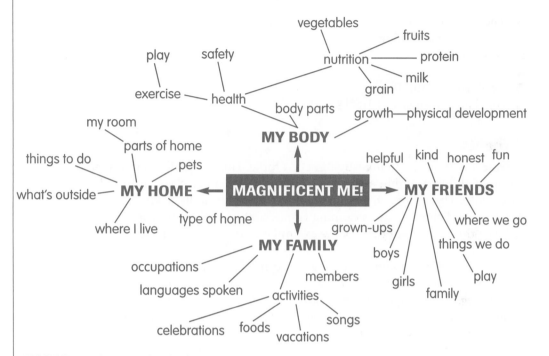

FIGURE 2–7 An example of a thematic web.

■ LESSON PLANS

The **lesson plan** is an outgrowth of theme selection, brainstorming/webbing, and selection of projects and activities. This involves making a series of choices based on the developmental stages, learning styles, and interests of the children; the goals and objectives of the program; and the availability of materials, supplies, and resources.

As you plan for the weekly, biweekly, or monthly period, think about the following:

- A classroom that is well planned, attractive, and organized provides an environment that facilitates learning and becomes a part of the learning program itself.
- It is helpful to schedule a specific teacher planning time during each week. This allows you time to reflect on your observations of the children, what is working, what needs to be changed, and what additional materials and supplies are needed.
- It is helpful to develop a planning form, such as a written lesson plan worksheet. This will clarify your thinking and aid you in articulating your rationale for what you plan to do. It can also be posted for parents, teacher-assistants, and substitute teachers to see and refer to. (See Figures 2–9, 2–10, and 2–11 for lesson plans of infants, toddlers, and preschool children. The activities included in these plans are in Chapters 3–12. Blank lesson plan worksheets can be found in Appendix A.)
- The lesson plan allows for planning the emergent curriculum theme or unit, concepts to be explored, skills to be developed, individual activities and large or small group activity times to be created, integration of the learning centers and curriculum areas, and preparation for special activities or field trips.
- It is helpful for you to develop a "things to remember" form for writing down items or materials to prepare or gather before the children arrive. It also allows you to write down ideas that come to mind to be used at another time. You will find that many new or remembered ideas come to mind during this special planning time.
- Remember to plan for "a rainy day." Unexpected events, such as bad weather, can require you to have on hand materials and supplies for new activities to be implemented at a moment's notice. A new puppet, book, game, flannelboard story, song,

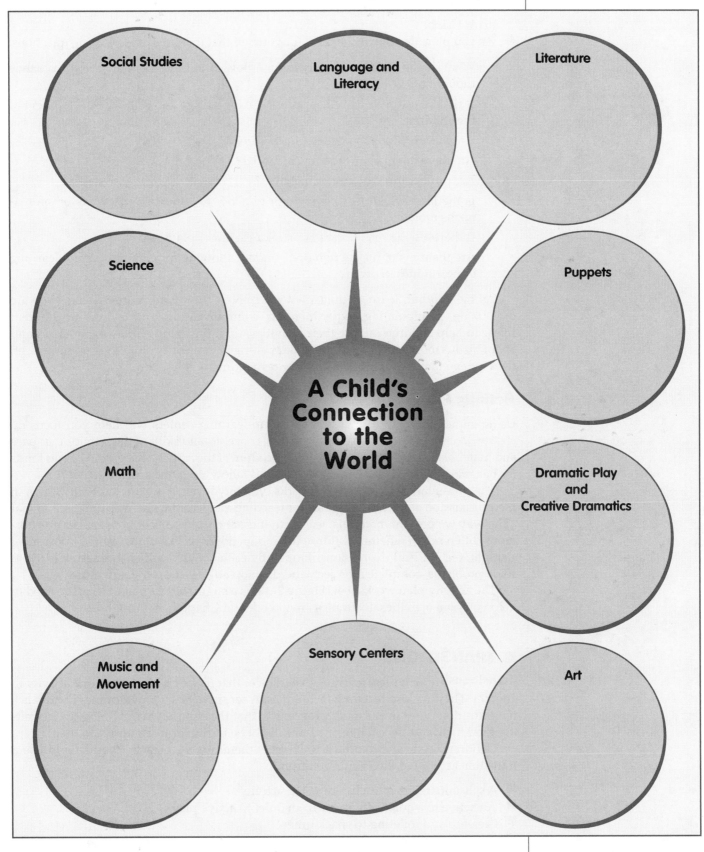

FIGURE 2–8 A curriculum planning web worksheet.

or art activity are examples of activities you can put in a special box to use for such an occasion.

■ As you plan, develop a checklist for yourself that includes the following questions:

What do the children already know? How can I build on that? What have they thought of?

Is the theme or the activity appropriate for the age and stage of development of the children?

Are the selections too general or too broad?

Are there too many or too few activities?

Are multicultural activities included?

Is the lesson plan flexible enough to allow for unexpected events or spontaneous moments?

Is there a wide selection of books, songs, finger plays, etc.?

Are the units of instruction open-ended, allowing for exploration and learning opportunities to occur?

As the children learn at their own pace about the world around them, they are organizing, manipulating, experimenting, communicating, and trying out different roles. To help children initiate their activities, trust the value of play experiences and spontaneous moments. If all of this is happening in your early childhood environment, then independent thinking and creative responding will happen.

Activity Plans

Using an activity plan format as you set up learning centers will help you focus on clearly describing the activity, the objectives, concepts, and skills of the activity, the space and materials needed, the step-by-step procedure of the activity, the guidance and limits for behavior expected, and the evaluation and follow-up of the specific activity.

The presentation of an activity works on many levels. Fortson and Reiff (1995), in their discussion of continuous goals for teaching and learning, help us understand that "The way we present materials, lead activities, and guide discussions makes an enormous difference in whether children use independent thinking and exercise powers of thought, feeling, and expression." Hopefully each activity will encourage children to solve problems, complete a project, and develop an eagerness to learn more.

The activity plan worksheet (Figure 2–12) is a suggested format that can be used to help you plan activities. Examples are included in Chapters 3 through 12.

■ TRANSITIONS

Transitions are activities/learning experiences that move children from one activity to another. They are also teaching techniques. A sensitive teacher determines in advance the transition times in the daily program so that the children avoid lining up or waiting their turn, and the change of pace will not be jarring or interruptive to them.

Children need time to adjust to change; therefore, as a teacher you should use a transition activity to direct children from

■ A self-initiated to a teacher-directed activity
■ An active to a quiet activity or from quiet to active play
■ Cleanup and toileting to snack time
■ Lunch to naptime
■ Outside to inside or inside to outside play

Sample INFANT LESSON PLAN (12–18 Months)

TEACHER(S):

DATES:

THEME: Magnificent Me!

CENTER / ACTIVITY	MONDAY	TUESDAY	WEDNESDAY	THURSDAY	FRIDAY
SENSORY: ART, MUSIC, TACTILE ACTIVITIES	Scribble with multicultural crayons. Make banana/raisin snack.	Sing "Name Song". Use large soft blocks.	Sing "If You're Happy and You Know It" with jingle bells.	Watch or chase bubbles floating to music. Play with play dough.	Cover table with white sheet & use non-toxic markers.
COGNITIVE & LANGUAGE ACTIVITIES	Sing "I Have Two Ears" and read Yellow Ball.	Show and talk about family pictures. Read My Family	Play "Pat-a-Cake" with jingle bells. Read the book Pat-a-Cake	Play "Peek-A-Boo" and read the book Peek-A-Boo.	Play "Where's ____? There s/he is!"
SMALL MUSCLE & LARGE MUSCLE ACTIVITIES	Push & pull toys	Roll ball back & forth, crawl on soft rug	Drop (wooden) clothespins into a container one at a time	Crawl up soft foam incline	Stack beanbags
SELF-AWARENESS, SELF-ESTEEM, SELF-HELP ACTIVITIES	Make faces into a mirror	Play Peek-A-Boo into mirror	"Jack Frost", fingerplay naming parts of body	Sing "Rock-a-Bye Baby" with soft babydolls.	"This is the Way We Wash Our Hands"
SPECIAL ACTIVITIES	Take stroller walk	Play on a quilt outdoors	Hang wind chimes near window or vent and listen to them.	Sing or chant "Roll the ball to ____. Roll it back to me."	Visit from grandparents (if possible)
BOOKS OF THE WEEK	Peek-a-Boo (Ahlberg), Pat-a-Cake (Kemp), Yellow Ball (Bang), I Hear (Isadora), I See (Isadora), I Touch (Oxenbury). My Family (Ostarch), Baby Says (Steptoe)				
SPECIAL NOTES	Dramatic play with soft multicultural baby dolls and blankets. Multicultural music and song tapes.				

FIGURE 2–9 An infant lesson plan worksheet.

Sample TODDLER LESSON PLAN

TEACHER(S):

DATES:

THEME: Magnificent Me!

CONCEPTS: I am special & wonderful! I'm learning to do many things.

SKILLS: Self-Help, Language, Social

DAY	LARGE GROUP ACTIVITIES	SMALL GROUP ACTIVITIES
MONDAY	Sing "I'm a Special Person and So Are You"	Practice dressing with dress-up clothes
TUESDAY	Read A Baby Just Like Me while sitting on a cozy quilt	Bathe baby dolls in warm soapy water (use no-tear baby shampoo), pat dry
WEDNESDAY	Read My Feet Wiggle toes together	Take off and sort shoes, then put your own back on
THURSDAY	Read Caps For Sale while wearing caps from dramatic play	Add caps to the pile of shoes, sort, put on, then look in the mirror
FRIDAY	Read together "Una Casita Roja (The Little Red House)"	Use small, unbreakable hand mirror "___, who do you see?"

SENSORY ACTIVITIES
Sand box toys
Colored water in water table
Play dough in various skin colors

DRAMATIC PLAY / HOME LIVING & PUPPETS
Play kitchen with dishes, aprons, dress-up clothes include hats, full-length mirror, family puppets

MOVEMENT / OUTDOOR ACTIVITIES
Chase bubbles
Push and pull toys, trikes
Climbing structure

MUSIC ACTIVITIES
Sing "Rock-a-Bye Baby" to dolls
Sing "If You're Happy & You Know It..."
Listen to multicultural music & dance.

SELF-AWARENESS, SELF-ESTEEM, SELF-HELP, ACTIVITIES
Dress self, put on shoes and caps
Serve and pour at meals

SMALL MUSCLE / MANIPULATIVE ACTIVITIES
Cut & tear paper in tactile table
Puzzles of babies & families
Small figures & doll house

ART ACTIVITIES
Scribble on sheet-covered table
Put torn paper on sticky-backed paper
Foot & hand prints with paint

LANGUAGE ACTIVITIES
"Humpty Dumpty" finger play
Discuss torn paper: color, feel, sizes
Flannel board "Una Casita Roja"

TRANSITIONS
"If your name is ___, then go to ___ (the door, etc.)"
"Name Song"

BOOKS OF THE WEEK:
Here Are My Hands. To Baby With Love. Making Friends.
Where's the Baby? On Mother's Lap. The Napping House

ACTIVITIES / NOTES:
Take a walk in the neighborhood
Visit from grandparents (if possible)
Cut up apples and eat.

FIGURE 2–10 A toddler lesson plan worksheet.

Sample PRESCHOOL-KINDERGARTEN LESSON PLAN

TEACHER(S):　　**DATES:**　　**THEME:** Magnificent Me!

CONCEPTS: I am unique, special, and part of a family

SKILLS: Prewriting, writing, measuring, graphing, problem-solving, and awareness of similarities/differences

CENTERS & ACTIVITIES	MONDAY	TUESDAY	WEDNESDAY	THURSDAY	FRIDAY
MORNING GROUP ACTIVITY	Sing "Good Morning." Introduce "My Body."	Take individual instant photos. Introduce "My Friends."	Read On the Day You Were Born. Introduce "My Family."	Make breadsticks formed in initials. Introduce "My Home."	Healthy snack chart: finish & discuss.
AFTERNOON GROUP ACTIVITY	Identify body parts and what they do.	Animal friends: share stuffed animals and/or pets	Chart birthdays of the children and family members.	Read How My Parents Learned to Eat.	Bring and share something about yourself.
LANGUAGE & LITERACY	Begin "All About Me" books.	Write about photo and put into "Me" book with photo.	Add family photo to book. Write or draw about photo.	Write class story about field trip experience.	Finish "All About Me" books and share. Finish class story.
ART	Make life-sized self-portraits.	Make thumbprint and footprint pictures.	Make puppet papercup family pop-ups.	Make kitchen gadget puppets.	Mix playdough to match skin color.
MUSIC & MOVEMENT	"Name Song" Body parts move to music.	Sing "I'm A Special Person and So Are You" and "Friends Go Marching."	Beanbag toss and Kitchen marching band	Sing "So Many Ways to Say Good Morning" and dance.	Dance in hats with streamers to music.
DRAMATIC PLAY HOME LIVING	Home living center with a full mirror and baby pictures of children.	Add phones, paper, and pencils for message taking.	Bathe baby dolls in warm sudsy water. Add stuffed animals to area.	Add a Wok and other cookware to center.	Add hats to dress-up clothes.
MATH MANIPULATIVE	Measure and record height of each child.	Graph the children's heights.	Use puzzles of family celebrations.	Gather items from home and play "What's missing?"	Estimate number of pennies in a jar, then count them.
SCIENCE & DISCOVERY	Listen to heart with stethoscope. Examine picture or model of skeleton.	Magnifying glasses to see thumbprints. Exploring shadows.	Food colors, eye droppers, and ice trays.	Weigh on scales for "Me" book. "What's That Sound?"	Magnets and what sinks, what floats?

BLOCKS
Add: people figures, animal figures, boxes, houses, cars

OUTDOOR/LARGE MUSCLE
Nature walk: obstacle course on playground Hop, run, skip, jump

TRANSITIONS
Puppet helper of the day Variations on "Name Song"

SENSORY CENTERS
Water table with warm, soapy water— Multicultural skin colored playdough. Healthy snacks "Tasting Tray"

SOCIAL STUDIES
Invite family members to visit. Field Trip to grocery store. We are all alike. We are all different.

BOOKS OF THE WEEK
My Five Senses, Big Friend, Little Friend, Mommie's Office, William's Doll

SPECIAL ACTIVITIES & NOTES

Field trip to grocery store. Children decide which healthy snacks to buy. Explain decisions.

Week-long project: Make chart or diagram re: food groups. Prepare and eat snacks. Write class story.

FIGURE 2–11 A preschool-kindergarten lesson plan worksheet.

ACTIVITY PLAN WORKSHEET

Date of activity:_____

Children's age group:_____

Number of children in this group (large group, small group, or individual activity):_____

Learning center to be used:_____

Name of Activity and Brief Description

Purpose/Objectives of Activity

(Concepts, skills, awareness, or attitudes you have designed the activity to teach or develop. Describe in measurable objectives.)

Space and Materials Needed

Procedure

(Step-by-step description of the activity. Tips for getting started: describe what you will say or do to get the children interested in the activity, and let them know what they will be doing. Describe the activity in the sequential order you will use with the children. Where will this activity take place? Plan for ending the activity. How will you help the children make a smooth transition to the next activity?)

Guidance

Establish necessary limits for behavior and boundaries of activity. Anticipate problems that may develop during this activity and consider ways to handle them.

Evaluation and Follow-Up

What was the children's response? What worked well? What didn't work? How could this activity be changed to make it effective or more appropriate? List possible activities that would extend or give practice to the objectives of this activity.

FIGURE 2–12 An activity plan worksheet

In addition, for the younger child transitions can be used to help them adjust to arriving and then separating from mommy or daddy, learning to listen, sitting down, and joining in a small group activity for a brief time. For older children transition activities can be used for getting attention, giving directions, gathering the group, and helping them understand the sequence of events or when events change without warning.

When the children get used to the schedule and routines of the day, the number of transitions used can be reduced. Children who are free to choose their play and activities will develop their own natural transitions as their interests and curiosity direct.

Examples of Transition Activities

■ Use a record or tape, or sing a song such as "The Hokey Pokey," where children can join the group as they finish with cleanup.
■ After group time, ask all children who are wearing red to stand up. Continue calling various colors until all the children are standing. Then give directions to the next activity.
■ Prepare a set of flannelboard circles with each child's name on one. Place name side down on flannelboard, and take off one at a time while saying the child's name. When the child's name is called she chooses a song, finger play, or activity for the group to do.

- Use rhythm instruments to accompany a song you are singing. Let the children take turns using these instruments. As each child finishes his turn, he chooses a learning center to go to.
- Children gather quickly when you play the autoharp, guitar, or other instrument. Let a few children strum the instrument while you are waiting for others to gather.
- Pretend that one child is the engine on a train. As that child "chugs" around the room, other children join the train by putting their hands on the shoulders of the child ahead. When all children are part of the train, then "chug" along outdoors.
- Play "Simon Says." On the last direction, Simon says, "Sit down." You are now ready for a story or other quiet activity.
- Play directional games such as "Touch your nose, turn around, sit down." Start with simple directions and get more complicated as the children are able to follow through on two and three directions.

■ PLAN OF ASSESSMENT AND EVALUATION

The process of curriculum development is one of continuous planning, implementing, assessing, and evaluating. A curriculum is planned to meet the needs of the individual children in the group by defining philosophy, goals, and measurable, meaningful objectives.

Assessment refers to the collection of information or data collecting. "Assessment is the process of observing, recording, and otherwise documenting the work children do and how they do it, as a basis for a variety of educational decisions that affect the child. Assessment is integral to curriculum and instruction" (NAEYC/NAECS/SDE, 1991).

Authentic or *performance assessment* determines the development of children through a variety of means. Puckett and Black (1999) explain:

- Authentic assessment is not a reflection of inherent capacities, but of individuals' interactions with the environment and their emerging capabilities.
- Authentic assessment celebrates development and learning.
- Authentic assessment capitalizes upon the strengths of the learner.
- Authentic assessment is embedded into the context of the ongoing developmentally appropriate curriculum.

Evaluation is the process of determining if the philosophy, goals, and objectives of the program have been met. Interpretations and decisions are made based on the collected information. Assessment and evaluation are closely related and can happen simultaneously. Gordon and Williams Browne (2000) explain further, "Evaluation is a continuous process. It is at once a definition, an assessment, and a plan. . . . In its simplest form, evaluation is a process of appraisal." Informal and formal evaluation of a program should include the indoor and outdoor environments, schedule, routines, the curriculum as a whole, themes, lesson plans, activities, performances of the children, and the teacher's role.

Observing is taking in information and interpreting it for meaning. Nilsen (2001) identifies some types of decisions the teacher makes based on observation:

- To give assistance
- To extend learning
- To discover interests
- To offer guidance
- To reflect on learning styles
- To notice physical health
- To measure progress

- To communicate with an individual child
- To communicate with parents
- To gather information for assessment and evaluation
- To further curriculum planning

The following methods for observing and recording are often used in the assessment and evaluation process:

Anecdotal record: A brief, informal narrative account describing an incident of a child's behavior that is important to the observer. It may apply to a specific child or to a group of children. Anecdotes describe the beginning and ending times of the observation, an objective, factual account of what occurred (telling how it happened, when and where it happened, and what was said and done), and the observer's subjective opinion of what was observed and why it occurred.

Checklist: A record of direct observation that involves selecting from a previously prepared list the statement that best describes the behavior observed, the conditions present, growth and development, or the equipment, supplies, and materials available. This type of observational recording helps the observer focus attention on specific behaviors or criteria. Checklists are easy to use and helpful in planning for individual or group needs.

Reflective Log or Diary: A teacher's or administrator's record of the most significant happenings, usually made at the end of the day or during an uninterrupted block of time. This includes what stood out as important facts to remember for the day, written in as much detail as possible.

Case study: A way of collecting and organizing all of the information gathered from various sources, including observations of and interviews with the child, to provide insights into the behavior of the individual child studied. Interpretations and recommendations are included. The main purposes for this detailed observational record are to discover causes and effects of behavior, for child development research, and to plan for the individual child.

Portfolio assessment: This method is based on a systematic collection of information about a child's ongoing development and the child's work gathered by both the child and teacher over time from all available sources. A portfolio is a collection of child-produced material, such as "works-in-progress," creative drawings, paintings, and dictated stories; product samples showing a child's strengths and skills; samples of a child's self-initiated "work"; teacher objectives for the child, observations and anecdotal records, developmental checklists, and parent interviews; and parents' comments. Teacher comments on each portfolio sample can help document what the child knows, can do, and how he does it. Portfolios can be a file folder or an accordion-type folder for each child (Hendrick, 1998; Batzle, 1992). Portfolio information helps the teacher "construct a well-rounded and authentic picture of each child so you are better able to plan your program, to build on individualized strengths, and to support each child's growth. . . . Because you want portfolios to be integrated into your daily program, they need to be within children's easy reach. Children enjoy looking back through their work, and browsing and reflection are important parts of this process" (Cohen, 1999).

The Early Childhood Classroom Observation from the National Academy of Early Childhood Programs Accreditation process provides a comprehensive self-study assessment for the program and the teacher. (For more information contact the Academy through the National Association for the Education of Young Children.)

AFTERVIEW

A child-centered early education environment focuses on children playing and learning. As we know, young children develop and learn in a variety of ways. As teachers we have the responsibility to understand the cultural influences and developmental characteristics of young children, to extend and support children's ideas and interests, and to provide appropriate learning activities to meet their needs. The children acquire the skills, concepts, and knowledge of the curriculum through rich and varied interaction with peers, teachers, and materials. As a teacher, you prepare and organize a developmentally, individually, and culturally appropriate classroom to provide children with a range of high-quality learning experiences. This is based on curricular goals and objectives, age-appropriate practices, children's interests, and instructional needs.

Young children entering our programs are naturally curious about their environment and are eager to explore and learn about their world. Classroom arrangements and materials directly affect children's learning and self-esteem. A developmentally appropriate classroom should give children the opportunity to select activities from a variety of centers that are interesting and meaningful. The learning centers allow the children to create situations using both the real world and their fantasy world to solve problems and express creative ideas. The selection of open-ended materials for these centers encourage children to freely explore, experiment, and create.

Effective early education classrooms involve children in multisensory and multicultural experiences in a variety of settings, including independent activities, small group activities, and large group projects. Children are encouraged to talk about and share their experiences with their peers and adults. An early education environment is truly an active one when children are engaged in learning and play.

KEY TERMS

anecdotal record	environment	philosophy
assessment	evaluation	portfolio assessment
case study	goals	project
checklist	inclusion	reflective log or diary
culture	learning centers	theme
curriculum	lesson plan	transitions
curriculum web	objectives	unit

EXPLORATIONS

1. List at least five characteristics of a developmentally appropriate, child-centered early education curriculum, and tell why each is important.

2. Interview a teacher from one of the model programs discussed in this chapter, such as Montessori or Head Start. Ask the teacher to describe the philosophy of the school; how she develops curriculum to meet the abilities, interests, and needs of the children in her class; and how she assesses or evaluates the development of the children and the program itself.

3. Keep a journal or notebook for one week on multicultural/anti-bias and inclusion activities you observed or culturally related activities that you personally experienced. List the date, event, and what you learned or experienced for each entry. Your listings can report your observations in an early education classroom; present a synopsis of articles you read in newspapers, magazines, or journals; or describe ethnic events you attended, new ethnic foods you ate, or a multicultural resource center or museum you visited in your community. Turn in your journal or notebook to your instructor, and discuss your findings with your classmates or colleagues.

4. Based on the information from this chapter and from observing in an early education classroom, create a diagram of a room arrangement for a classroom of three-, four-, and five-year-olds. Include doors, windows, furniture, sources of electricity, water, etc. Label each learning center. Use A Checklist For Room Arrangement (Figure 2–6) in this chapter to test the validity of your diagram.

5. With a classmate or colleague, select one of the themes suggested in this chapter and brainstorm a curriculum web. Describe the process you went through. Do you think you could develop a weekly lesson plan from this completed web? Explain.

REFERENCES

Albrecht, K. (1996, Fall). Reggio Emilia: Four key ideas. *Texas Child Care, 20*(2), 2–8.

Bank Street College of Education (1992). *Exploration with young children.* Mt. Rainier, MD: Gryphon House.

Batzle, J. (1992). *Portfolio assessment and evaluation.* Cypress, CA: Creative Teaching Press.

Bredekamp, S. (1993, November). Reflections on Reggio Emilia. *Young Children, 49*(1), 13–17.

Bredekamp, S., & Rosegrant, T. (Eds.). (1992). *Reaching potentials: Appropriate curriculum and assessment for young children* (Vol. 1). Washington, DC: National Association for the Education of Young Children.

Brewer, J. (1998). *Introduction to early childhood education* (3rd ed.). Boston: Allyn and Bacon.

Catron, C. E., & Allen, J. (1999). *Early childhood curriculum* (2nd ed.). Columbus, OH: Merrill.

Cech, M. (1991). *Globalchild: Multicultural resources for young children.* Menlo Park, CA: Addison-Wesley Publishing Company.

Children's Defense Fund. (1998, Yearbook.) *The state of America's children.* Washington, DC: Author.

Cohen, L. (1999, February). The power of portfolios. *Early Childhood Today, 13*(5), 31–33.

Cook, R. E., Tessier, A., & Klein, M. D. (1996). *Adapting early childhood curricula for children in inclusive settings* (4th ed.). Columbus, OH: Merrill.

Curtis, D., & Carter, M. (1996). *Reflecting children's lives: A handbook for planning child-centered curriculum.* Saint Paul, MN: Redleaf Press.

Davis, M., Kilgo, J., & Gamel-McCormick, M. (1998). *Young children with special needs: A developmentally appropriate approach.* Boston: Allyn and Bacon.

Derman-Sparks, L., and A.B.C. Task Force (1989). *Anti-bias curriculum: Tools for empowering young children.* Washington, DC: National Association for the Education of Young Children.

Essa, E. (1999). *Introduction to early childhood education* (3rd ed.). Albany, NY: Delmar.

Feeney, S., Christensen, D., & Moravcik, E. (1996). *Who am I in the lives of children?* (5th ed.). Columbus, OH: Merrill.

Feng, J. (1994). Asian-American children: What teachers should know. *ERIC Digest.* (Report No. EDO-PS-94-4) Urbana, IL: ERIC Clearinghouse on Elementary and Early Childhood Education.

Fortson, L. R., & Reiff, J. C. (1995). *Early childhood curriculum: Open structures for integrative learning.* Boston: Allyn and Bacon.

Frost, J. L. (1992). *Play and playscapes.* Albany, NY: Delmar.

Gandini, L. (1993, November). Fundamentals of the Reggio Emilia approach to early childhood education. *Young Children, 49*(1), 4–8.

Goffin, S. G. (1994). *Curriculum models and early childhood education.* Columbus, OH: Merrill.

Gonzalez-Mena, J. (1993). *Multicultural issues in child care.* Mountain View, CA: Mayfield Publishing Company.

Gordon, A., & Williams Browne, K. (2000). *Beginnings and beyond* (5th ed.). Albany, NY: Delmar.

Hall, N. S. (1999). *Creative resources for the anti-bias classroom.* Albany, NY: Delmar.

Head Start (1990). *Head Start: A child development program* [Brochure]. Washington, DC: U.S. Department of Health and Human Services.

Hendrick, J. (1998). *Total learning* (5th ed.). Columbus, OH: Merrill.

High/Scope Educational Research Foundation (1999). *Professional development programs.* Ypsilanti, MI: Author.

Hohmann, M., Banet, B., & Weikert, D. P. (1995). *Young children in action: A manual for preschool educators* (2nd ed.). Ypsilanti, MI: The High/Scope Press.

Jackman, H. L. (1999) *Sing me a story! Tell me a song! Creative curriculum activities for teachers of young children.* Thousand Oaks, CA: Corwin Press.

Johnson, J. E., Christie, J. F., & Yawkey, T. D. (1987). *Play and early childhood development.* Glenview, IL: Scott, Foresman and Company.

Jones, E., & Nimmo, J. (1994). *Emergent curriculum.* Washington, DC: National Association for the Education of Young Children.

Katz, L. G. (1994). The project approach. *ERIC Digest.* (Report No. EDO-PS-94-6) Urbana, IL: ERIC Clearinghouse on Elementary and Early Childhood Education.

Lowman, L. H., & Ruhman, L. H. (1998, May) Simply sensational spaces: A multi "S" approach to toddler environments. *Young Children, 53*(3), 11–17.

Marotz, L. R., Cross, M. Z., & Rush, J. M. (2001). *Health, safety, and nutrition for the young child* (5th ed.). Albany, NY: Delmar.

McCormick, L., & Feeney, S. (1995). Modifying and expanding activities for children with disabilities. *Young Children, 50*(4), 10–17.

McCracken, J. B. (1990). *Playgrounds safe and sound* [Brochure]. Washington, DC: National Association for the Education of Young Children.

Miller, R. (1996). *The developmentally inclusive classroom in early education.* Albany, NY: Delmar.

Mitchell A., & David J. (Eds.). (1992). *Explorations with young children: A curriculum guide from the Bank Street College of Education*. Mt. Rainier, MD: Gryphon House.

National Association for the Education of Young Children. (1986). *Helping children learn self-control* [Brochure]. Washington, DC: Author.

National Association for the Education of Young Children (NAEYC) and the National Association of Early Childhood Specialists in State Departments of Education (NAECS/SDE). (1991, March). Guidelines for appropriate curriculum content and assessment in programs serving children ages 3 through 8 (Joint Position Statement). *Young Children, 46*(3), 21–38.

New, R. S. (1993). Reggio Emilia: Some lessons for U.S. educators (Report No. EDO-PS-93-3) *ERIC Digest*. Urbana, IL: ERIC Clearinghouse on Elementary and Early Childhood Education.

Nilsen, B. A. (2001). *Week by week: Plans for observing and recording young children* (2nd ed.) Albany, NY: Delmar.

Pearce, M. (1996, September). Inclusion: 12 secrets to making it work in your classroom. *Instructor (Primary), 106*(2), 81–85.

Puckett, M. B., & Black, J. K. (1999). *Authentic assessment of the young child* (2nd ed.). Columbus, OH: Merrill.

Spafford, C. S., Pesce, A. J. I., & Grosser, G. S. (1998). *The cyclopedic education dictionary*. Albany, NY: Delmar.

Spodek, B., & Saracho, O. N. (1994). *Right from the start: Teaching ages three to eight*. Boston: Allyn and Bacon.

Watson, L. D., Watson, M. A., & Wilson, L. C. (1999). *Infants and toddlers: Curriculum and teaching* (4th ed.). Albany, NY: Delmar.

Wolery, M., & Wilbers, J. (1994). (Eds.). *Including children with special needs in early childhood programs*. Washington, DC: National Association for the Education of Young Children.

York, S. (1991). *Roots and wings*. St. Paul, MN: Redleaf Press.

ADDITIONAL READINGS AND RESOURCES

Allred, K. W., Briem, R., & Black, S. J. (1998, September). Collaboratively addressing needs of young children with disabilities. *Young Children, 53*(5), 32–35.

Baker, E., Wang, M., & Walberg, H. (1995). The effects of inclusion on learning. *Educational Leadership, 52*(4), 33–35.

Bronson, M. B. (1995). *The right stuff for children birth to 8: Selecting play materials to support development*. Washington, DC: National Association for the Education of Young Children.

Brown, W. H. (1997, Summer). Inclusion: A time to include and support young children. *Dimensions of Early Childhood, 25*(3), 3–5.

Diamond, K. E., Hestenes, L. L., & O'Connor, C. (1994, June). Integrating children with disabilities into preschool. *ERIC Digest*. (Report No. EDO-PS-94-10). Urbana, IL: ERIC Clearinghouse on Elementary and Early Childhood Education.

Edwards, C. P., Gandini, L., & Forman, G. E. (Eds.). (1994). *The hundred languages of children: The Reggio Emilia approach to early childhood education*. Norwood, NJ: Ablex Publishing.

Gestwicki, C. (1999). *Developmentally appropriate practice: Curriculum and development in early education* (2nd ed.). Albany, NY: Delmar.

Greenspan, S. I. (1998, November/December). Working with children who learn at a different pace. *Early Childhood Today, 13*(3), 27–28, 48.

Griffin, C., & Rinn, B. (1998, May). Enhancing outdoor play with an obstacle course. *Young Children, 53*(3), 18–23.

Guralnick, M. (Ed.). (1997). *The effectiveness of early intervention*. Baltimore: Paul H. Brookes Publishing Company.

Guralnick, M. (1993). Developmentally appropriate practice in the assessment and intervention of children's peer relations. *Topics in Early Childhood Special Education, 13*(3), 344–371.

Lewis, E. G. (1997, Summer). Everyone can come to school: Learning from experience. *Dimensions of Early Childhood, 25*(3), 21–25.

Pelo, A. (1997, November). "Our school's not fair!": A story about emergent curriculum. *Young Children, 52*(7), 57–61.

Reinsberg, J. (1995). Reflections on quality infant care. *Young Children, 50*(6), 23–25.

Staley, L. (1998, September). Beginning to implement the Reggio philosophy. *Young Children, 53*(5), 20–25.

Vergeront, J. (1994) *Places and spaces for preschools and primary (outdoors)*. Washington, DC: National Association for the Education of Young Children.

Walker, B., Hafenstein, N. L., & Crow-Enslow, L. (1999, January). Meeting the needs of gifted children in the early childhood classroom. *Young Children, 54*(1), 32–36.

Zeavin, C. (1997). Toddlers at play: Environments at work. *Young Children, 53*(3), 72–77.

PART TWO

Discovering and Expanding the Early Education Curriculum

A child is sunshine,

Sparkling in every step she takes.

A child is laughter,

Filling the air with sounds he makes.

A child sees beauty,

Wonder, and excitement everywhere

And freely offers

A vision of joy, to treasure, to share.

Hilda Jackman

Language and Literacy

■ OVERVIEW

As human beings, we have the desire to communicate with others. We do this in many ways. A smile communicates a friendly feeling; a clenched fist transmits anger; tears show happiness or sorrow. From the first days of life, a baby expresses pain or hunger by cries or actions. Gradually, the infant adds expressions of pleasure and smiles when a familiar person comes near. Then, the little one begins to reach out to be picked up.

A baby eventually learns the words of his parents. If the parents speak English, the baby will learn to speak English. If the baby spends a lot of time around significant adults who speak Spanish, Japanese, Hebrew, or any other language, the infant will learn the language of the people around him.

The process of learning a language is important. It is one of the most important skills a child develops. The development of oral language is a natural accomplishment. Usually, a child learns the rules of language at an early age without formal instruction. A child learns language by listening and speaking. He learns language by using it. Learning to talk, like learning to walk, requires time for development and practice in everyday situations. During the first few years of life, listening and speaking constitute a large part of a child's experience with language.

Sawyer and Sawyer (1993) explain more about language development:

Once children develop a minimal facility with language, how do they continue to get better at using language? Obviously, something occurs within family structures, child-care situations, play groups, and other normal living environments that helps children improve their language skills. Continuing this development is a major responsibility of early education and elementary school programs.

Helping you, the teacher, meet this responsibility is the intent of this chapter. Understanding language and literacy development in young children, encouraging family support, and setting up a developmentally appropriate environment to strengthen and extend this development will be examined. (Chapter 4, Literature, is a continuation of the language arts program introduced in this chapter.)

■ EARLY LANGUAGE AND LITERACY DEVELOPMENT

Language can be defined as human speech, the written symbols for speech, or any means of communicating. **Language development** follows a predictable sequence. It is related, but not tied to, chronological age. This developmental process includes both sending and receiving information. *It is important to remember that language is learned through use.*

Literacy, the ability to read and write, gives one the command of a native language for the purpose of communicating. This involves skills in listening, speaking, reading, and writing. The excitement of learning to read and write, hopefully, will be as rewarding as a child's first words and first steps.

Long before babies can speak, they listen to sounds and words. They hear differences in voices and sounds. Infants will turn their heads in the direction of a particular sound. Friendly verbal interaction with and encouragement from nurturing adults help a baby form her first words out of randomly babbled sounds. An infant learns quickly that communicating is worthwhile because it results in action on the part of others.

Gestwicki (1999) develops this idea further when she states:

In reality it is through the same social relationships that introduce infants to the emotions of love and trust, and to the behavior of people in their environment, that babies learn language as part of the complex system of communication they will use throughout their lives.

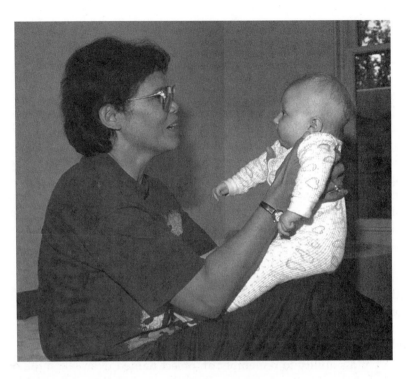

Language Development of Young Children

Children learn language through predictable stages of development. As with many other aspects of child development, individual differences are apparent in the development and use of language.

Baby's cry: This form of communication varies in pitch and intensity and relates to stimuli such as hunger, discomfort, or fear. Just as adults respond differently to a baby's cry (some touch, some talk), the baby's response varies as well. An infant can stop crying, then smile, or laugh in reaction to an adult's facial expression, to words spoken, or to being held.

Cooing: These are the sounds made when an infant's basic needs are met and she is relaxed, content, or stimulated by what is seen or heard. A baby derives a great deal of pleasure from practicing and listening to her own gurgling and cooing.

Babbling: These early random sounds made by an infant are a repetition of sequences of clear, alternating consonant and vowel sounds. This vocalization will eventually be combined into words, such as *baba* for bottle and *wawa* for water.

Association: A baby begins to get some idea of the meaning of a few words at about six to nine months. An association between the sounds an infant makes and the meanings of these sounds starts to become clear. When an adult begins to recognize and interpret these sounds, another level of communication has been reached. Playing "peek-a-boo" and "pat-a-cake" are fun to do and help the child develop an association between sounds and meanings.

Fields and Spangler (1995) explain further:

Before the first year is over, babies have narrowed their utterances from all the possible sounds to those significant in their environment. Babies in Mexico will trill the r sound, while babies in Germany will practice guttural sounds they hear, and English speaking babies will learn neither. Before long, they all begin to make the sounds of their language in combinations that mean something specific. As soon as they acquire this ability to communicate with words, they begin to string them together for even greater results.

One-word usage: Many first words are completely original, private words of the child. They may be sequences of sounds or intonations used on a consistent basis. "The physical organs need to function in a delicate unison, and the child must reach a certain level of mental maturity. At around the age of 12 months, the speech centers of the brain are poised to produce what is perhaps the most magical moment of childhood: the first word which marks the flowering of language" (Machado, 1999). In the early stages of language development, a word, such as *hot* or *no,* often stands for a whole object or an experience. The one-word stage also uses a word to get something or some action from others, such as *go, down,* or *mine.* Getting the appropriate response, approval, and smiles from adults encourages the child to make the sounds again and again. Language is a two-way process. Reaction is an important feedback to action. Although a child can speak only in "one-word sentences," he can understand more complex sentences and can react to what others are saying. From this point on, the child has progressed from receptive language, i.e., listening and understanding, to the period of expressive language, i.e., speaking.

Recall: A child's ability to remember an object named even when the object is not visible is helped by the touching, grasping, and tasting of the object. Responding to her name; identifying family members; and watching, pointing to, and naming an object usually occurs toward the end of the first year. This is sometimes called "sign-language" communication, such as when a child holds up her arms to be picked up.

Telegraphic speech: The two-word sentence is the next step in the development of language of the young child. This speech helps a child express wishes and feelings, and ask questions. "Many words are omitted because of the child's limited ability to express and remember large segments of information" (Machado, 1999). The child repeats words over and over, such as *all gone, drink milk,* or *throw ball.* It is important to talk and listen to a toddler. This is a critical language-growth period, as the young child is processing, testing, and remembering language.

Multiword speech: When a young child reaches the stage of adultlike speech with longer sentences and almost all of the words present, he asks questions and understands the answers. The child can express feelings and tell others what he wants. At the same time, the child can understand the words of other people and absorb new knowledge. The child's vocabulary increases; and the repetition of songs, stories, and poems comes more easily. Words become important tools of learning, and they help a young child grow socially. Children talk together, and friendships grow.

Allen and Schwartz (2001) remind us that our knowledge of the language acquisition and development of young children will help us understand that speech and language irregularities come and go and appear to be self-correcting unless the child is pressured. We also need to be aware of early warning signs that a child could be having some difficulty.

A number of young children have problems speaking or learning the language; some children have trouble with both. Problems may range from developmentally normal delays and dysfluencies to serious problems requiring the services of a speech and language specialist. An undiagnosed hearing loss is always a possibility and needs to be ruled out first in diagnosing a language delay or impairment in a young child. (Allen & Schwartz, 2001)

Literacy Development of Young Children

Literacy development, a lifelong process that begins at birth, includes listening, speaking, reading, and writing. Listening is a prerequisite to speaking. "Of all the language skills that human beings acquire, listening is the one they use the most throughout life, particularly during early childhood . . . and the typical child amasses extensive experience with listening long before he or she speaks, reads, or writes" (Jalongo, 1996). Learning to speak is an important step toward learning to read.

Learning to read and learning to write are inseparable. Reading exposes a child to models for writing; and writing requires reading as part of the composition process. Knowledge about one enhances understanding of the other, and both are learned simultaneously. (Fields & Spangler, 1995)

Researchers believe children learn about reading and writing through *play*. As a teacher of young children, you see this happening every day. You have observed children learning to talk, read, or write when they are playing "peek-a-boo," engaging in nonsense speech play, listening to and singing familiar jingles and rhymes, scribbling, pretending, and using objects as symbols. Because literacy is a continuous process, children are working on all aspects of oral and written language at the same time. Sometimes this constant changing is referred to as "emergent literacy." A joint position statement of the International Reading Association (IRA) and the National Association for the Education of Young Children (NAEYC), (1998) states:

Although reading and writing abilities continue to develop throughout the life span, the early childhood years—from birth through age eight—are the most important period for literacy development. . . . Children take their first critical steps toward learning to read and write very early in life. Long before they can exhibit reading and writing production skills, they begin to acquire some basic understandings of the concepts about literacy and its functions. Children learn to use symbols, combining their oral language, pictures, print, and play into a coherent mixed medium and creating and communicating meanings in a variety of ways.

Researchers and educators are also deliberating the phonics versus whole language approaches to literacy. **Phonics** emphasizes the sound-symbol relationship or "sounding out" unfamiliar syllables and words. **Whole language** introduces literacy by building on what children already know about oral language, reading, and writing while highlighting experiences and meaningful language rather than isolated skill development. NAEYC suggests a balanced view that involves teaching phonics not separately but in context, so that children make connections between letters and sounds that are meaningful to them (Bredekamp & Copple, 1997). When children sing nursery rhymes, jingles, and songs, they are playing with and exploring the sounds of language. Through shared reading experiences, writing their names, and playing games related to their letter discoveries, they are developing literacy skills at their own pace. Children learn about phonics as part of many activities based on their individual needs.

Each child who comes to you has already been busy, actively creating his own definition of what it means to interact in a literate society (Canizares, 1998). You are

building on what children already know and can do, while creating a developmentally appropriate language and literacy environment when you:

- Talk to children, even while diapering or feeding them.
- Talk to children in standard spoken language, not baby talk. Speak clearly and give simple explanations.
- Reinforce a child's native language. Understand that every child's language or dialect is worthy of respect as a valid system for communication.
- Speak in a voice that helps children listen—not too fast or too soft.
- Encourage children to talk to you.
- Enable children to use language to communicate their thoughts about ideas and problems that are real and important to them.
- Listen when children talk to you. Give children your full attention when they speak. Be on their level and make eye contact. Use nonverbal communication, such as eye-to-eye contact, smiling, and holding a child's finger or hand to reinforce that you are listening. Be patient.
- Use children's names frequently.
- Allow time and opportunity for children to listen and talk freely without interruption.
- Play music for children to listen to. Provide different types of music in the environment, such as records, tapes, or CDs of lullabies; songs from many cultures; and classical music.
- Offer toys that make noise for younger children.
- Sing songs. Make up songs with the children.
- Play finger plays, which offer a combination of stories, poems, directions, songs, and hand movements. Finger plays also offer a transition into a story or activity.
- Tell a story. Use flannelboards for extending stories.
- Read stories to children. Make a wide selection of books available to children. Be sure there are books in a variety of languages, including Braille and sign language. (Chapter 4, Literature, offers detailed information.)
- Offer shared book experiences with repeated readings of the same story, so the children themselves are encouraged to read and reread. Also, children enjoy the repetition of familiar phrases and rhythms.

■ Enhance children's concept of and exposure to print. "Some teachers use Big Books to help children distinguish many print features, including the fact that print (rather than pictures) carries the meaning of the story, that the strings of letters between spaces are words and in print correspond to the oral version, and that reading progresses from left to right and top to bottom" (IRA & NAEYC, 1998).

■ Take walks and listen to the sounds of the environment. Talk about what you see and hear. Write down what the children say and then put their words in a classroom book or on a large sheet of paper posted on an easel or a wall.

■ Play listening games to develop sound awareness, such as clapping hands in a fast or slow tempo; then have children repeat the clapping as they heard it. Audio tape the games, and then play them back to the children to see if they can associate the taped claps with the ones they did.

■ Offer pressure-free experimentation with writing, and encourage children to write often. Remember that children's first writing attempts appear as scribblings. Help them when you feel they need it. For example, "This is how I write your name. How do you write your name?"

■ Encourage children to learn written language in the same energetic and interactive ways they learn oral language. Invite children to experiment with language in any way they choose, and accept whatever the child "writes," such as lists, creative calendars, children's dictation, posters, signs, labels, songs, and "creative" spelling.

■ Encourage children to use and expand language and literacy in all learning centers.

Additional and specific examples of language and literary developmental activities are presented at the end of this chapter. As stated earlier, in a developmentally appropriate setting, speaking, listening, reading, and writing are integrated into or combined with other curriculum areas. You will find examples of this throughout the chapters of this text.

■ ENCOURAGING FAMILY SUPPORT

As previously stated, family members are a child's primary teachers of language. They are the first people a child hears speak, the first adults spoken to, and the most important people a child will communicate with throughout her life. Awareness of the importance of parents and other significant family members to a child's language and literacy development is one of the first steps in working with parents. It is also helpful to let family members know how valued their efforts are. Express to them how much you appreciate their interactions with you. Let them know what you are doing in the early childhood program. Point out ways they can contribute to or extend language and literacy development at home with their child.

Some teachers find it helpful to send notes home periodically. This chapter includes sample letters that can be sent home, once a week, as a special "language link" from you to the parents, for example:

Read to your child. Read books, stories, magazines, comic strips, and poems. Have children's books around the house for your children. Some can be purchased and some can be checked out from the library. Read them often, and add to them regularly. These are the books we are reading in class this week. (You could list several books with the author's and illustrator's names, such as *Family Pictures, Cuadros de Familia,* by Carmen Lomas Garza; *I Love My Family,* by Wade Hudson; *On Mother's Lap,* by Ann Herbert Scott, illustrated by Glo Coalson; *Friday Night Is Papa Night,* by Ruth A. Sonneborn, illustrated by Emily A. McCully; and *The Day of Ahmed's Secret,* by Florence P. Heide and Judith H. Gilliland, illustrated by Ted Lewin.)

Talk about the illustrator or photographer. Look at the pictures in the book you are sharing with your child. Can "Larry" think or guess what the story will be about? If it is a picture book, let your child tell you about the picture or photographs. You will help him use pictures or other clues for reading comprehension. (You might then tell the parent something such as: "We are looking at Tana Hoban this week. Her wonderful photographs are in these books: *Shapes, Shapes, Shapes; I Read Signs; Of Colors and Things;* and *26 Letters and 99 Cents.*")

More suggestions follow:

- Have a regular story time before or after meals or at bedtime. It will help both you and your child relax and share some private time together.
- Look at the book cover together. Use the words *front cover, back cover, title, author, illustrator, top, bottom, left, right.* This exposes your child to reading vocabulary.
- Read all kinds of signs, labels, restaurant menus, and calendars to your child. Point out print on home equipment, products, and other items of print used in your daily life. Point out signs when you are out riding together.
- Let your child see you reading newpapers, magazines, books, and letters. Reading together and sharing stories is a family affair. Enjoy it and do it often!
- Talk to your child. Listen to what your child has to say. Provide uninterrupted time for communicating.
- Do activities together, then talk about it. This includes routine shopping, worship services, the zoo, museums, movies, television viewing, and sports activities.
- Sing to, and with, your child. Music is a wonderful way to make family activities even better.
- Surround your child with opportunities to play with words. Provide a variety of things to write with: chalk, crayons, pencils, markers, and all kinds of paper.
- Encourage your child to draw. Besides clarifying thoughts and ideas, drawing tells stories and expresses feelings. It also reinforces the motor skills your child needs for writing.

- How's the "art gallery" coming along? Post your child's scribbles and drawings on the refrigerator or the wall in his room. This gives all the family members a chance to look at his efforts. It is fun to add your own drawings.
- Write to your child. Put notes in lunchboxes, in bookbags, under pillows, in pockets, on the refrigerator. Your child will look forward to "being surprised."
- Let your child see you write. When you write a letter, let her write a letter, too. When you send a birthday card, let her add some scribbles.

(Adapted from Machado, 1999; Morrow, 1989; and personal experiences and conversations with early education teachers.)

Figure 3–1 is a suggestion for a letter to be sent home with the children in your program. The younger children can add illustrations. The older children can write their own letter to explain about stories read at the center or school. It is important for the child to have "ownership" of the letter. However, some teachers prefer to send letters home that are informational and written from the teacher to the parent. Select the technique you prefer, as long as the parents receive something in writing. This, along with verbal communication, connects the parent to the teacher and the school.

If the parents speak a language other than English, get someone to help you translate your letter into the native language. Send both copies home with the child.

Respecting Language of Home and School

Many children come to early education programs from non-English-speaking families. These children are trying to master the language spoken at home as well as trying to

> Dear Mom and Dad
> (or whatever the child calls her parents using the language spoken at home),
>
>   We have been reading stories. We enjoy acting out the stories we read. One of our favorites is *The Very Hungry Caterpillar* by Eric Carle. We like to tell the story over and over in our own words. We move around as we tell the story. We can be whatever we want to be: the caterpillar, the apple, the pear, the ice cream cone, the leaf, or the butterfly. Sometimes we don't use any words. This is called pantomime. It's fun.
>   Can we act out some of the stories we read at home? You can choose what part you want to be.
>
>   Child's name

FIGURE 3–1 An example of a letter to send home with the children. Younger children can add drawings to the letter. Older children can write their own letters.

learn English in the school setting. The learning environment they are entering should be developmentally appropriate and give children opportunities to practice both native and newly established English language skills. "Children who are learning English as a second language are more likely to become readers and writers of English when they are already familiar with the vocabulary and concepts in their primary language" (IRA & NAEYC, 1998). Soto (1991) offers additional insight:

> *Young children need time to acquire, explore, and experience second language learning. Accept children's attempts to communicate, because trial and error are a part of the second language learning process. . . . Plan and incorporate opportunities for conversation such as dramatic play, storytime, puppetry, peer interactions, social experiences, field trips, cooking and other enriching activities.*

It is important to understand that accepting a child's language is part of accepting a child. The children in the classroom will model your behavior. Children can be very accepting and caring of each other. They communicate by gestures or by taking a child's hand and leading him to an activity, many times without your guidance.

Children will feel more successful if you involve their parents in activities and understand the different learning styles each child may have. The celebration of many cultural holidays at the school that include the family members of *all* the children in your class offers positive reinforcement.

Parents can help you identify some basic words used in the child's language, especially those that are important to the child. *Be sure to use the child's correct name and not an "Americanized" one. Use the name often and pronounce it correctly.* (Listen carefully to the parent's pronunciation and imitate it.)

At first and if possible, have a family member or someone who speaks the child's native language available to help the child learn the routines and expectations, as well as the new language. If another child in the class speaks the language, interaction between the two should be encouraged (Essa, 1999).

■ ORGANIZING AND PLANNING FOR INTEGRATED LANGUAGE AND LITERACY EXPERIENCES

As previously discussed, throughout a child's life listening, speaking, reading, and writing are a prominent part of a child's world. As the significant adults in a child's life, we should ensure that the environment surrounding each child be the very best it can be—developmentally, individually, and creatively. When this occurs, children use and expand their language in almost every activity and curriculum area in which they participate.

As you plan the physical space for the language and literacy activities, you should keep in mind that how you design this area will affect the choices children make in their selection of activities. This part of the environment, sometimes called the language arts center, should be arranged so children can use this area independently or in small groups.

As with everything in an early childhood environment, the organization and focus is on creating a child-centered space. For infants and toddlers, the surroundings should be sensory-rich—bright colors everywhere, the air full of soft music, words from around the world being spoken, songs being sung, books being read, drawings being scribbled, and textures within reach.

You will find the language arts center is most effective when it:

■ Is set in a part of the room that is quiet with little traffic, but is accessible from any other center

■ Invites the children to use every inch of table, floor, and wall space

■ Displays things at a child's eye level

■ Attracts them to listen, look, think, write, draw, and read

■ Includes materials, supplies, and equipment that offer explorative and developmentally appropriate hands-on experiences for young children

The language arts center should be an environment that is soft. This can be accomplished by having a carpet, rug, or carpet squares on the floor; by adding large pillows and beanbag chairs; and by adding some "creative spaces," such as enormous stuffed animals with large laps for children to sit on or an old-fashioned bathtub filled with pillows of all sizes and colors for an individual child to spend some alone time reading a book or listening to a tape.

The center also should have good lighting and easy access to child-size tables, chairs, and bookcases that are arranged for group or individual use. Include both "stand-up" (chalkboard, easels, murals, window, clipboards) and "sit-down" (tables, lap desks, floor) writing places.

■ SETTING UP A LANGUAGE AND LITERACY ENVIRONMENT

Children should have access to listening, reading, and writing materials in every learning center. Many of the items usually placed in the language arts center can be duplicated in other centers. When children want to write, copy, or draw, the "tools" should be available. "The more children write, the more knowledge they will construct about how language works" (Oken-Wright, 1998).

Materials should be available at all times for children to use for writing. They should be separated into appropriate, brightly colored containers to make it easy for children to choose what they need. The use and care of the materials should be discussed each time something new is added to the learning center.

The classroom should also be print-rich. A print-rich literacy environment includes the following:

- All types of books that are displayed attractively and within easy access of the children
- Books made and written by individual children
- Books made and written by the class of children
- Magazines and newspapers appropriate for young children
- Recorded stories
- Message boards
- Calendars
- Rebus and symbol charts
- Story props for retelling stories
- Alphabet charts
- A wide variety of pictures depicting life around the world
- Labels on materials, on supplies, on equipment, and in learning centers throughout the room and outdoors
- Lists of all kinds
- Children's names displayed
- Child dictation or writing and drawings displayed

It is important to remember that the *process* should be the emphasis of the children's activities; however, this process produces many outcomes and you will need to do something appropriate with "all that writing." Here are a few suggestions: have the children take home the items they select; take the items the children select and place them around the room; place some of the writings in a child's folder or portfolio; or mail others to family members and friends.

Guidance Techniques to Support a Developmentally Appropriate Early Childhood Environment

The establishment of trust is based on consistent daily contact and the well-being of children.

Children are comfortable and secure when they can feel, see, or hear the caregiver's closeness. To believe that adults are reliable, predictable, and accepting is essential in the development of trust.

What would you do to establish this sense of trust?

Organization of the early childhood environment is important to prevent inappropriate behavior.

The arrangement of indoor and outdoor space requires *planning* for each individual child and group of children, *understanding* of prior experiences and development of the children, and *supporting* the formation of trust, independence, and creativity in the children. If the children feel they belong and their needs are being met, appropriate behavior usually follows.

The learning environment should encourage social interaction, cooperation, sharing, and problem solving.

Provide the children with the time, opportunities, and resources to negotiate as individuals and learn to accept each other's diverse languages, knowledge levels, and thinking skills. Can you think of ways to encourage collaboration and cooperation within groups of young children?

The *daily schedule and routines* help create a framework of security for younger children. Arrival, mealtimes and snacks, diapering and toileting, rest or naptime, and departure offer opportunities to model appropriate behavior in a safe environment for young children. (For more information see Chapter 1, Starting the Process.)

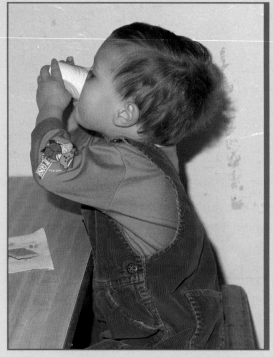

Snacks and mealtimes are opportunities for children and teachers to talk and listen to one another.

Self-help skills are further developed when children pour their own juice and milk, help themselves family-style during meals, and participate in cooking activities. Spills and accidents should be handled as a natural part of a child's day.

What would you do in advance to avoid behavior problems during snacks, mealtimes, and cooking activities?

Encourage self-help skills while planning opportunities for learning new skills — especially children's first attempt to do things for themselves.

These self-directed, open-ended activities help children feel positive about themselves in an early childhood setting.

What meaningful activities can you provide that will encourage children to achieve on their own?

A responsive, organized classroom offers a variety of well-defined learning centers where materials and supplies are combined around special groupings and common activities.

Visual clues and the arrangement of a specific learning center should suggest the desired number of children appropriate for that center.

What visual clues and arrangement would you use to set up a learning center appropriate for four children?

The *room arrangement* should offer well-defined learning centers with the noisy and quiet centers separated; areas designed for small group, large group, and alone spaces; and a place for "cool-down" time or self-directed time-out. To discourage discipline problems and encourage learning and development, a wide variety of materials and supplies should be placed on low, open shelves in each center. (For more information see Chapter 2, Creating Curriculum.)

Pictures and bulletin boards should be placed at eye level for the children.

These wall areas should be a visual extension of what is happening in the classroom. Ideas suggested by the children and their involvement in the final product should be part of the bulletin board creative process.

What could you do to develop a children-created bulletin board in your classroom?

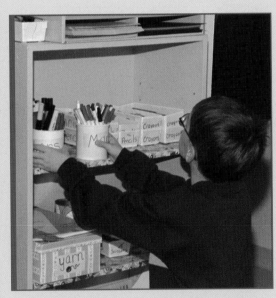

Labels, signs, and other kinds of print around the room offer additional visual guidance information for children.

Store materials in places that will make it easy for the children to use them.

How would you arrange the environment to allow children access to materials, supplies, and learning centers?

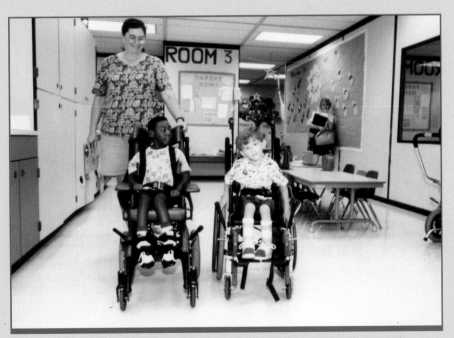

Wide pathways should be available for children with special needs.

It is crucial to provide an inclusive, educational environment in which all children can succeed. Modifications in early childhood environments should recognize, encourage, and support children's individualized development across all areas of the curriculum.

What can you do to be responsive to children with special needs?

Organization of the outdoor environment, like the indoor classroom, should set limits with reasonable, appropriate rules that are consistently reinforced to promote appropriate behavior.

The *playground* should encourage active play and exploration, offer blocks of time for uninterrupted play, provide safe equipment to develop motor skills, and have appropriate adult supervision. (For more information see Chapter 2, Creating Curriculum.)

A variety of play surfaces and a balance of sunny and shady areas help create safe outdoor surroundings for young children.

What else would you do to maintain a safe and healthy outdoor environment?

Sand play offers children a sensory activity like no other, a chance to experience their world in a different way.

Sand, water, and mud play can be an individual or small group activity. There is no right or wrong way to play with these multisensory materials.

How would you support children's exploration of sand play?

Taking inside activities outside opens the door for many creative learning activities.

These activities can also encourage independence and socialization.

What indoor activities would you take outdoors?

Teacher-child interactions can help each child change inappropriate behavior to appropriate behavior. Treat each child with respect. Take time each day to spend a few minutes with each child.

The teacher-child ratio also influences guidance. There should be an appropriate number of adults to meet the needs of each child.

Get down to the child's level when you are talking or listening to him.

What tone of voice would you use?

Help the individual child identify what he is feeling, place a limit on his behavior, and give the child an acceptable outlet for that feeling.

How can you be more attentive to a child's individual needs?

Help children develop positive feelings about being a part of a group.

These practical experiences foster a sense of positive self-esteem in young children as they live and play in a nurturing environment.

Do you pay attention to what a group of children's facial expressions and body language are telling you?

Support a positive sense of self-identity in each child.

What can you do to develop a child's sense of trust, sense of self, and feeling of control over the environment?

Playing with puppets offers a child new ways to express feelings.

Through puppets a child continues to build a positive self-image, develops independence, and learns acceptable behavior.

Can you think of appropriate ways to make puppets a part of the early childhood environment?

Provide opportunities for dramatic play that give children the opportunity to practice developing social skills.

Allow sufficient time in the schedule for children to expand dramatic play roles and themes. This type of play also handles a child's uniqueness of being little in a world of big people.

How would you plan and prepare the environment to integrate dramatic play into the learning centers and curriculum?

Teacher-family interaction creates a consistent and beneficial experience for young children. It is the teacher's responsibility to keep positive communication open to families, while respecting the individual and cultural needs of each family. If a child's behavior creates problems, open discussions between home and school are important.

Exchange positive information with families at arrival and departure time.

What would you do to establish a partnership with families?

Conduct regular parent-teacher conferences that focus on the accomplishments and needs of the individual child.

How would you plan a parent-teacher conference?

Encourage family involvement in activities.

Why is it important to know about children's family backgrounds?

Children benefit from being treated as individuals while being part of an early childhood community. Offer simple yet consistent guidelines for the group and the individual child. Be sure the expectations are in line with the children's abilities and cultural experiences.

What do you want to accomplish as a teacher of young children?

■ TIPS AND ACTIVITIES

The following is a suggested list of what to place in the language arts center, including things to write with, to write on, and to write in, Figure 3–2.

There are many techniques you can use to place items promoting language and literacy around the room. Some we have already discussed in this chapter. The following suggested activities are additional ones that teachers of young children have found to be developmentally and multiculturally appropriate, as well as lots of fun to do.

- Pencils, pens, and chalk of various sizes and colors
- Crayons of various sizes, colors, and thicknesses
- Markers of various colors, fine tipped, thick tipped, washable, permanent, and scented
- Magnetic letters and numbers
- Typewriter
- Computer
- Toy or nonworking telephone
- Toy microphone
- Paper of various sizes, colors, and textures; lined and unlined paper; drawing paper; construction paper; and scraps
- Cardboard and posterboard
- Stationery
- Note pads
- Index cards
- Envelopes
- Graph paper
- Post-its
- Order forms
- Business forms
- Large and individual chalkboards, dry erase boards, and magic slates
- Carbon paper
- Finger paints
- Pencil sharpener
- Rulers
- Tape
- Glue
- Scissors
- Stapler
- Stickers
- Date stamp and pad
- Other donated office stamps and pads
- Paper clips
- Hole punch
- Brads
- Maps and globes
- Pictionaries and dictionaries
- Message board
- Folders and notebooks
- Old newspapers and magazines

FIGURE 3–2 List of language arts center materials and supplies.

Flannelboard Activities

Often teachers hear a child say: "Tell it again." One of the ways to tell or extend a story effectively is with the use of a **flannelboard**. As children of all ages listen to the storyteller, their visual attention is focused on the characters and movement taking place on the flannelboard.

The characteristics of a good flannelboard activity are:

- It attracts attention.
- It stimulates interest.
- It is flexible in use.
- It frees a teacher's hands.
- It adds texture to the activity.
- It is a visual prop for a story, song, or poem that does not have illustrations.
- It improves communication.
- It dramatizes concepts.
- It is easily made and easily stored.

Other important aspects of this type of activity are:

- The children can help the teacher tell the story by placing the pieces on the board at the appropriate time in the story.
- After the teacher tells the story, the flannelboard and character pieces can be placed in any activity center or curriculum area.

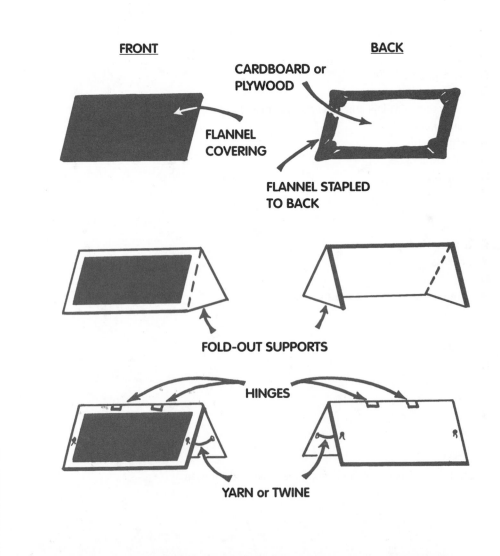

- The children or individual child can then tell the story to each other or make up another story to relate to the flannelboard pieces.
- Flannelboard figures can be touched, held, and moved, forming a bridge between the real and the abstract.

You can purchase a commercial flannelboard or you can make your own. Select plywood, masonite, or any wood-based board for durability. Styrofoam board, heavy cardboard, display board, and prestretched artist's canvas are more lightweight and easier to carry but not as durable. The board may be freestanding or placed on an easel, on a chalkboard tray, or on a chair. Smaller, individual boards can be placed in the language arts center for children to use by themselves or with a friend.

Flannel cloth is usually the best material to use for covering the base. It has excellent adhering qualities and is lightweight and colorful. Felt cloth also can be used with good results, as can most fuzzy textured material. Velour (material used for making house robes and blankets) stretches slightly to cover the board, maintains its texture, and is available in an assortment of colors.

An almost unlimited variety of materials for use with flannelboard activities can be obtained easily and inexpensively. The most commonly used items are nonwoven interfacing material from the fabric store, felt, and heavy flannel. When selecting materials to be used for flannelboards, it is important to be sure the adhesive quality of the material is great enough to support its own weight or the weight of the item to which it will be attached.

Some of the resources for finding flannelboard poems, stories, and figures are: teachers of young children, commercial activity sets, shapes and figures traced from books, magazines, photographs, illustrations, pictures, and drawings. (See Appendix A for puppet and flannelboard characters introduced in this text and Appendix B for a listing of teacher resources.) Be creative and draw some yourself.

Color can be added to the flannelboard set pieces with permanent felt markers, crayons, and paints. It is fun to accent the figures with wiggly eyes and imitation fur fabric. You will find it helpful to trace with tissue paper. For easy storage, use a folder with pockets, a large mailing envelope, a manila folder with the story stapled inside (make a pocket of tag board or construction paper to hold the pieces), or large plastic household bags.

The following are suggested books that are appropriate for early childhood flannelboard stories:

Carle, E. (1981). *The very hungry caterpillar.* New York: Philomel.

Ehlert, L. (1997). *Color farm.* (Board Book). New York: HarperCollins.

Klamath County YMCA Family Preschool. (1993). *The land of many colors.* New York: Scholastic.

Martin, B. (1967). *Brown bear, brown bear, what do you see?* Illustrated by E. Carle. New York: Henry Holt.

McQueen, L. (1995). *The little red hen/La gallinita roja.* New York: Scholastic.

Shaw, C. G. (1947). *It looked like spilt milk.* New York: HarperTrophy.

Group Time Activities

Group time presents the opportunity for listening, speaking, vocabulary development, and cognitive and social activities. Here are a few helpful hints for successful group time activities:

- Organize activities ahead of time; plan carefully; and think about what is going to happen before, during, and after.
- Have realistic expectations of the children and be flexible.

- Select a time and place where a few children can be involved or where others can join in when they finish cleaning up. Be able to accommodate the entire group.
- Select developmentally and culturally appropriate activities that relate to the children's experiences.
- Guide children in and out of group time with appropriate transitions.
- Change the pace often and include a variety of activities.
- Encourage listening and discussing skills.
- Anticipate problems and take steps to avoid them by explaining expected behaviors to the children.
- Acknowledge and reinforce *appropriate* behavior.
- Give clear, simple directions.
- Respond to each individual child as well as to the group.
- Maintain physical and emotional closeness.
- Anticipate a "good" stopping point, or stop before the children lose interest.
- Be prepared with an extra activity in case what you have planned does not work or the activity time needs to be extended.
- Evaluate and make needed changes for next time.
- Enjoy the children.

Appropriate group time activities are finger plays, poetry, songs, stories, flannelboard activities, and sensory activities. These should be developmentally appropriate and reflect multicultural/anti-bias content.

The following activity, "HOP-HOP," illustrates a musical finger play activity that toddlers and preschoolers enjoy doing.

HOP-HOP!
(finger play activity with song)

(Suitable for Ages Toddler–Three)

Teacher: Let's tell a story together. Our hands can help.
First, make a fist, like this:

(Teacher makes a fist, and continues to model for the children all the actions that follow.)

Now, hold up two fingers *(index and middle fingers).*
See, we have a bunny! These are his ears. *(Wiggle fingers.)*
Wiggle, wiggle, wiggle, it's Robby Rabbit! Can he hop? *(Make hopping motions.)*
Up and down, up and down—good!
Now, make another bunny with your other hand.
This is Reba Rabbit. Wiggle her ears—wiggle, wiggle, wiggle.
Now we have two bunnies. Can they both hop? Good!
Let them hop behind your back and hide.
Now we can begin our story.
Everyone sings softly: "Ta-dah!"

Children: Ta-dah!

Teacher: *(Bringing one hand forward with hopping motion)*
Here comes Robby Rabbit—wiggle, wiggle, wiggle!
And here comes Reba Rabbit! *(Other hand)* Wiggle, wiggle, wiggle!

(Bunnies face one another. When they speak, their ears wiggle. Reba's voice should be pitched higher than Robby's.)

Teacher: Robby Rabbit says, "Hello!"

Reba: Hello!

Robby: How are you?

Reba: I'm fine.

(Both bunnies gasp and begin to tremble.)

Teacher: Now they're both so scared that they hop behind you and hide.
Do you want to see them again? Sing, "Ta-dah!"

(Repeat the whole procedure through Reba's line, "I'm fine!" This time, only Reba begins to tremble.)

Teacher: Reba is so scared, she hops behind you to hide again. But
Robby Rabbit is not scared. He sings this song:

(Robby hops and sings:)

SONG TO ACCOMPANY HOP-HOP!*-

Hop, hop, hop! Here comes Rob- by Rab- bit! Hop, hop, hop!

Mov- in' right a- long. Hop, hop, hop! Hap- py lit- tle bun- ny!

Hop, hop, hop! Sing- in' a hap- py song!

TEACHER: Like this -- bring out Reba Rabbit --- hop, hop, hop!

Now we have two bunnies again. Let them hop and sing together:

Spring's a love- ly time of year, full of joy, full of cheer!

Spring- time flow- ers all are here, and so are al- ler- gies!

Reproduced by permission of B. Wolf - 1995
Copyright B. Wolf - 1993

The story of *The Little Red House (Una Casita Roja)* is an example of another appropriate group activity. It can be told in group time, then repeated by using flannelboard pieces (Appendix A). Follow-up activities can be: put the flannelboard pieces and the written story in the language arts center, have a special cooking center set up so children can find their own "little red house," and then make applesauce.

THE LITTLE RED HOUSE
(Una Casita Roja)

Once upon a time, there was a little girl named Maria. Maria had her favorite toys, and she had a big back yard with a garden where she liked to play. One day, she was tired of doing the things she usually did, and she wanted to do something different.

So, Maria went to her mother and asked, "Mamá, what can I do?'

Maria's mother thought for a minute, and then she said, "I know what you can do. You can try to find a little red house, *una casita roja,* with no windows and no doors, but with a star, *una estrella,* inside."

"Mamá, is there really such a thing as a little red house, *una casita roja,* with no windows and no doors, but with a star, *una estrella,* inside? How can I find something like that?" asked Maria.

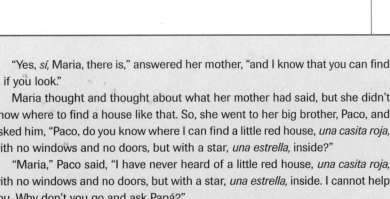

"Yes, *sí*, Maria, there is," answered her mother, "and I know that you can find it, if you look."

Maria thought and thought about what her mother had said, but she didn't know where to find a house like that. So, she went to her big brother, Paco, and asked him, "Paco, do you know where I can find a little red house, *una casita roja*, with no windows and no doors, but with a star, *una estrella*, inside?"

"Maria," Paco said, "I have never heard of a little red house, *una casita roja*, with no windows and no doors, but with a star, *una estrella*, inside. I cannot help you. Why don't you go and ask Papá?"

So, she went to the back yard, where her father was working in the garden, and asked him, "Papá, do you know where I can find a little red house, *una casita roja*, with no windows and no doors, but with a star, *una estrella*, inside?"

Papá looked at Maria, and smiled, and said, "Our house is red, *roja*, but it has doors and windows, and I don't think there is a star, *una estrella*, inside. I'm afraid I can't help you, Maria."

Maria was getting a little tired of looking by now, so she sat down in her favorite back yard spot, under the apple tree, to rest and to think. Her cat, Chica, came and sat in her lap. Maria stroked Chica's soft fur and asked, "Chica, do you know where I can find a little red house, *una casita roja*, with no windows and no doors, but with a star, *una estrella*, inside?" Chica didn't answer. She just went on purring her soft purr.

Maria thought to herself, "I'm not having much luck. I might as well ask the wind." So she did. "Señor Wind, can you help me? I am looking for a little red house, *una casita roja*, with no windows and no doors, but with a star, *una estrella*, inside." Just then, the wind began to blow gently, and down from the tree fell a bright, shiny red apple. Maria picked up the apple, and went to find her mother to tell her that she just could not find the little red house, *una casita roja*.

When Maria's mother saw her walking in the door with the apple, she said, "Maria, I see you found the little red house, *una casita roja*, with no windows and no doors, but with a star, *una estrella*, inside." Maria was puzzled, but followed her mother into the kitchen, where she took out a knife, and cut the apple in half, and . . .

THERE WAS THE STAR! (*UNA ESTRELLA!*) ★

(Cut the apple through the center perpendicular to the core.)

una—oo' na	*casita*—cas ee' ta	*roja*—ro' ha
estrella—ess tray' ya	*señor*—seen yore'	*sí*—see

Reprinted with permission.
Adapted by Janet Galantay

Putting the applesauce recipe on a **rebus chart** (Figure 3–3) is another way to integrate literacy into the curriculum. The rebus chart offers visual picture signs and directions to help children make sense of any activity, i.e., read left to right, top to bottom, and recognize letters and symbols. This helps put children in charge of their own learning. For older children, placing the rebus chart in a learning center helps them work independently without teacher direction. This chart is friendly and helpful to children whose native language is not English (Jurek & MacDonald, 1994).

Here is the recipe for applesauce:

Applesauce
6 apples
½ cup water
1 teaspoon lemon juice
sugar, to taste
⅛ teaspoon cinnamon

Peel apples. Remove core. Cut up apples. Add water, lemon juice, and sugar. Cook until tender. Add cinnamon. Press through a colander. Then eat!

APPLE SAUCE

Peel six apples.

Remove cores and cut them up.

Add ½ cup water,

Sugar to taste and

One teaspoon lemon juice.

Cook until tender.

Add ⅛ teaspoon cinnamon.

Press through a colander. THEN EAT!

FIGURE 3–3 Rebus chart of applesauce recipe.

Language Activity

The following is a language activity for toddlers that encourages self-esteem and language development while developing awareness and appreciation of differences:

At group time, after reading Bill Martin and Eric Carle's Brown Bear, Brown Bear, What Do You See? *(1967, New York: Henry Holt), sit on the floor with the children seated in a circle with you. Pull a small (unbreakable) hand mirror from your pocket. Pass the mirror from child to child.*

Teacher:	*"Janet, Janet" what do you see? (Child looks into mirror.)*
Child:	*I see "Janet" looking at me.*

Continue to pass the mirror around the circle until all the children have had a turn.

Another time you can have the children look into the mirror and say "I see a boy with brown hair *looking at me." —or— "I see a* girl with brown eyes *looking at me." —or— "I see a* boy with brown skin *looking at me."*

Additional Activities

Following are additional activities that may be used to promote language and literacy development.

- Writing with water—Take a bucket of water and several large and small paintbrushes outside. The children can "write" on or "paint" the sidewalk, the building walls, the tricycles, the wagons, and the fence. This activity helps develop large muscle control, and at the same time provides the beginnings of literacy development. It is easy and fun, too.
- Labeling—Encourage the children to label things in the classroom as well as outdoors. Start the labeling yourself and let the children help.
- Listen to the children—Let the children label what they think needs labeling. This will help them "read the room." (The children love to use Post-its to label things and they can change them whenever *they* want to.) It is also fun to make floor signs, such as traffic signs that say "enter," "exit," "stop," and "go."
- Writing to others—Have the children write thank-you letters or notes to community members who visit the class and to those visited during field trips.
- Story Starters—Have the children tell you a story about when they were babies, or what happens when the wind blows, or what sounds they hear and sights they see. Use a tape or video recorder to capture their storytelling. Older children can write and illustrate their own big book based on the story.
- Birthday Celebration—Create a birthday celebration center once a month that lasts a week. Stock it with paper to make birthday cards; markers and crayons; old birthday card fronts; and scraps of lace, yarn, fabric, stickers, and birthday words. Use happy birthday from other languages such as, *joyeux anniversaire* (French), and *feliz cumpleaños* (Spanish). Children can make cards for family members and classmates. This is a wonderful way to promote thoughtfulness, socialization, language, writing, reading, and creativity. Extend this activity by making a "Birthday Book" of the class. (If a child's family does not celebrate birthdays, the child does not have to visit this particular learning center.)

Figure 3–4 is the curriculum planning web worksheet, with language and literacy activities added. This worksheet, with appropriate additions, is included in the chapters that follow to illustrate how you could complete the lesson plan.

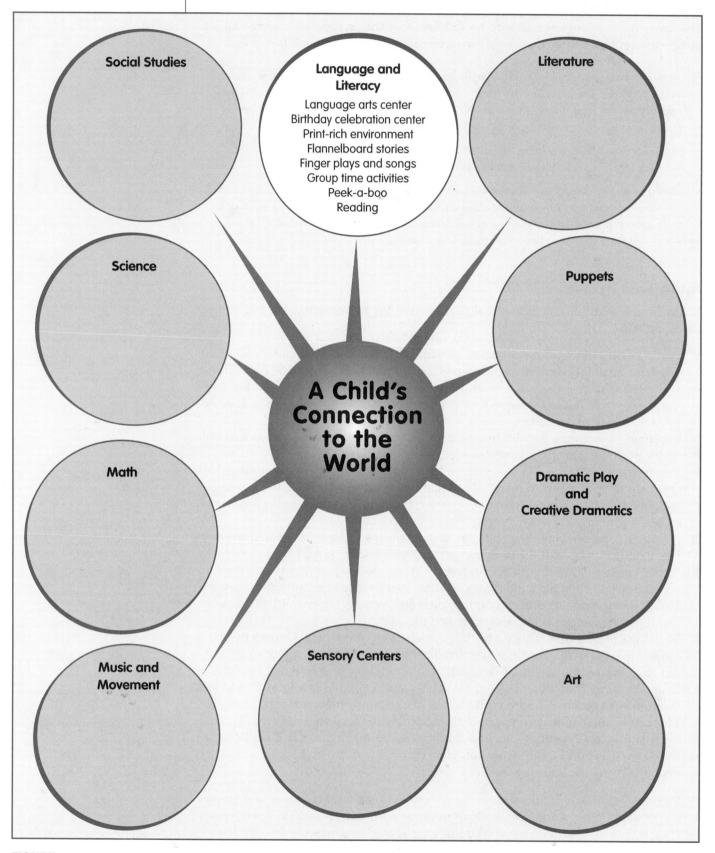

Social Studies

Language and Literacy

Language arts center
Birthday celebration center
Print-rich environment
Flannelboard stories
Finger plays and songs
Group time activities
Peek-a-boo
Reading

Literature

Science

Puppets

A Child's Connection to the World

Math

Dramatic Play and Creative Dramatics

Music and Movement

Sensory Centers

Art

FIGURE 3–4 A curriculum planning web worksheet with language and literacy activities added.

AFTERVIEW

Through language and literacy, a child

- Develops listening skills
- Develops the concept of print
- Recognizes that print is talk on paper
- Acquires verbal comprehension and association skills
- Develops letter recognition skills
- Practices scribbling, drawing, making letters, numbers, and words
- Recognizes and differentiates between shapes, sizes, signs, and sounds
- Experiments with word formation
- Learns left-to-right progression

- Strengthens visual memory
- Interprets pictures
- Recognizes sequencing of pictures and illustrations
- Practices storytelling and dictation of stories, while imagining events and situations
- Develops the ability to recall stories and experiences
- Practices writing and illustrating an original story or book
- Learns about other cultures and broadens concepts and experiences about life

KEY TERMS

flannelboard
language
language development

literacy
literacy development
phonics

rebus chart
whole language

EXPLORATIONS

1. Select an early education classroom and observe for at least one hour. Describe, in writing, six language and literacy activities the children were involved in at the time of your observation. What did you learn from this observation?

2. Select and plan a language activity for young children. Specify which age group this activity is planned for: infants, toddlers, preschoolers, or primary-age children. In writing, list objectives, materials needed, step-by-step procedures for presenting this activity, follow-up activities, and evaluation guidelines. (Use the activity plan worksheet in Chapter 2.) Prepare this activity and demonstrate it during class or with a group of children.

3. After researching agencies, schools, and individuals in your community, list and describe, in writing, at least four resources available for parents and teachers of young children with language problems. Explain why sensitive understanding of these language diffi-

culties is necessary for developing a child's self-esteem. Discuss at least three ways to create an environment that accepts language differences.

4. Select a classmate or colleague as a partner. Share ideas on games and activities to extend a child's vocabulary. Discuss ways to use or adapt these games to extend the vocabulary of children who speak other languages or dialects. Then, develop one activity that helps a child learn new words and appropriate language usage. If possible, share your activity with a group of young children. Evaluate its appropriateness and effectiveness. Did it accomplish your objectives? Explain.

5. Based on the information in this chapter and on your observations of early education environments, design a language and literacy learning center. Sketch a floor plan showing where materials, supplies, and equipment are placed.

REFERENCES

Allen, K. E., & Schwartz, I. S. (2001). *The exceptional child: Inclusion in early childhood education* (3rd ed.). Albany, NY: Delmar.

Bredekamp, S., & Copple, C. (Eds.). (1997). *Developmentally appropriate practice in early childhood programs* (Rev. ed.). Washington, DC: National Association for the Education of Young Children.

Canizares, S. (1998, October). A new look at literacy. *Early Childhood Today, 13*(2), 26–35.

Essa, E. (1999). *Introduction to early childhood education* (3rd ed.). Albany, NY: Delmar.

Fields, M. V., & Spangler, K. L. (1995). *Let's begin reading right: Developmentally appropriate literacy* (3rd ed.). Columbus, OH: Merrill.

Gestwicki, C. (1999). *Developmentally appropriate practice: Curriculum and development in early education* (2nd ed.). Albany, NY: Delmar.

International Reading Association (IRA) and the National Association for the Education of Young Children (NAEYC).

(1998, July). A joint position paper: Learning to read and write, developmentally appropriate practices for young children. *Young Children, 53*(4), 30–46. Also available at www.naeyc.org.

Jalongo, M. R. (1996, January). Teaching young children to become better listeners. *Young Children, 51*(2), 21–26.

Jurek, D., & MacDonald, S. (1994, Spring). Using rebuses with young children. *Dimensions of Early Childhood, 22*(3), 17–20.

Machado, J. M. (1999). *Early childhood experiences in language arts* (6th ed.). Albany, NY: Delmar.

Morrow, L. M. (1989). *Literacy development in the early years.* Englewood Cliffs, NJ: Prentice Hall.

Oken-Wright, P. (1998, March). Transition to writing: Drawing as a scaffold for emergent writers. *Young Children, 53*(2), 76–81.

Sawyer, W. E., & Sawyer, J. C. (1993). *Integrated language arts for emerging literacy.* Albany, NY: Delmar.

Soto, L. D. (1991, January). Understanding bilingual/bicultural young children. *Young Children, 46*(2), 30–36.

ADDITIONAL READINGS AND RESOURCES

Armington, D. (1997). *The living classroom: Writing, reading, and beyond.* Washington, DC: National Association for the Education of Young Children.

Bates, C., & Bates, R. (1999, January). Mother and daughter set out to promote literacy in a family child care home and a child care center. *Young Children, 54*(1), 12–15.

Brock, D. R., & Dodd, E. L. (1994, March). A family lending library: Promoting early literacy development. *Young Children, 49*(3), 16–21.

Brownlee, S. (1998, June 15). Baby talk: Learning language is an astonishing act of brain computation. *U.S. News and World Report,* 48–55.

Chapman, M. L. (1996, January). The development of phonemic awareness of young children: Some insights from a case study of a first-grade writer. *Young Children, 51*(2), 31–37.

Gordh, B. (1994, January). Storytelling in the classroom. *Early Childhood Today, 8*(4), 42–49.

Groves, D. H. (1993, Spring). Let's rethink children's entry points into literacy. *Dimensions of Early Childhood, 21*(3), 8–10, 39.

Kuball, Y. E. (1995, January). Goodbye dittos: A journey from skill-based teaching to developmentally appropriate language education in a bilingual kindergarten. *Young Children, 50*(2), 6–14.

Martinez, M. (1995, February). Supporting emergent writing. *Early Childhood Today, 9*(5), 30–31.

Moore, L. M. (1998, March). Learning language and some initial literacy skills through social interactions. *Young Children, 53*(2), 72–75.

Morrow, L. M. (1995, January). Literacy all around. *Early Childhood Today, 9*(4), 34–41.

Reynolds, M. R., & Milner, S. (1998, Winter). Preschoolers on camera: Using videos to explore emergent literacy. *Dimensions of Early Childhood, 26*(1), 23–24.

Schickedanz, J. A. (1999). *Much more than the ABC's: The early stages of reading and writing.* Washington, DC: National Association for the Education of Young Children.

Literature

■ OVERVIEW

Children's literature is a wondrous and exciting part of early education curriculum. Most of us can still recall favorite childhood stories that were read or told to us by a loving adult. Books have a way of connecting us to others. They put us in a different time and place and capture our imaginations and our hearts. That is the thrust of this chapter: connecting children to literature by developing ideas, and ways of making literature an integral and stimulating part of the early education curriculum.

Where you place the book center, whether it is for two children or a special privacy place for one child, indicates how much importance you place on a child's interacting with books and stories. When and how often you read a book to the group or an individual child points this out as well. Is it always at the same time each day or in the same location? Are you spontaneous? Sometimes do you just *feel* like telling a story or reading a book or developing an activity? Being flexible and creating on-the-spot activities with children's suggestions are just as important and worthwhile as the planned ones.

These interactions with children through books help us enfold literature into language and literacy development. The language of literature provides the child with vivid, imaginative, well-ordered words—words to think about, to listen to, and to try out and make her own. Oral language relates to reading and writing. It is a part of the development of both. The child who hears stories all through childhood learns language and structure, and develops attitudes and concepts about the printed word (Strickland & Morrow, 1989).

Early education emphasizes reading and writing opportunities *across the curriculum.* Sawyer (2000) explains further, "Integrating each of the content areas with literature brings a cohesiveness to the program and the classroom. It also lends stability, an important component of early childhood education. Yet, integration of content areas still allows wonderful things to happen in the classroom." (See Chapter 3, Language and Literacy, for additional information.)

Literature can reflect the joy, pleasure, sadness, and expectations that are experienced in a child's life. "Each story changes with the voice that tells it, each picture with the eyes that see it" (Thomas, 1998). Throughout a child's discovery of literature in all its forms, there should be encouragement by the significant adults the child encounters. A lifelong love of literature will be the result.

■ DEFINING CHILDREN'S LITERATURE

Literature has been defined by *Webster's New World College Dictionary, Third Edition* (1989), as "a) all writings in prose or verse of an imaginative character, b) all the writings of a people, country or period, especially those prized for beauty or force of style, c) all the writings on a particular subject."

Huck, Hepler, and Hickman (1993) define literature as:

the imaginative shaping of life and thought into the forms and structures of language. Where appropriate, we consider pictures as well as words, asking how both sets of symbols work to produce an aesthetic experience. . . . The experience of literature always involves both the book and the reader.

Finazzo (1997) extends the meaning by emphasizing the relevance of culture:

Literature as we know it encompasses the various forms of writing that reflect times, cultures, and people with special beauty and style. It includes story, song, poetry, and drama, realistic and imaginative, factual and fantastic. . . . Children's literature that is multi-cultural is written for the child's eyes, and thus it sends a simple and straight-forward message. It reflects the childhood of a culture or a group and expresses a child's viewpoint with a sense of optimism, hope, and excitement.

Hillman (1999) believes that different definitions should be applied to children's *books* and children's *literature*. "Books are concrete, tangible, objects, real and heavy. . . . Literature is an abstract concept, a composite of elements or attributes that connote excellence, such as a mesmerizing story that moves the reader to tears or laughter."

Children's literature can be defined in several other ways as well. By looking at purposes, values, types, and genres of books for early education, we can define what literature is for young children. The material comes from many sources in both language and illustrated materials. It offers a multitude of experiences to help a child define these experiences appropriately for the child's age and stage of development. Included within this explanation is the understanding that the teacher must care about and know how to make appropriate literature selections (Huck et al., 1993; Raines & Isbell, 1994; Jalongo, 1988).

■ PURPOSES AND VALUES OF CHILDREN'S BOOKS

As we explore the many purposes of including children's books in early childhood classrooms and homes, it is crucial to understand their fundamental role in the learning experience. Because learning is basically the process of associating that which is new to that which is already known, stories can be a powerful tool to accomplish this. A book introduces a child to something new which can give her greater understanding of the world and create an excitement to know more.

In addition, Sawyer (2000) and Huck et al., (1993) have suggested the following purposes and values of children's books:

■ Provide sheer enjoyment for a child
■ Help develop a child's imagination
■ Help a child find meaning in life
■ Offer a child time to reflect on experiences that relate to real life
■ Help a child reinforce discoveries about the world
■ Give a child opportunities to reread parts enjoyed or not understood
■ Introduce a child to many kinds of learning through the enjoyment of books

- Encourage a child to develop a curiosity about learning and life
- Help a child build a foundation for learning to read
- Give a child exciting experiences with books and with language
- Provide a means for a child to listen to others
- Give a child an awareness of and sensitivity to others
- Help a child appreciate the writing and illustrations in books
- Enable a child to build a foundation for the use and care of books

It is important for teachers and parents of young children to share with each other what they think the purposes are of creating an environment filled with books as part of a child's life. Open communication can offer a partnership to enrich relationships for everyone.

■ TYPES AND GENRES OF BOOKS FOR CHILDREN

Before a teacher, parent, or other significant adult selects books for children, understanding about the many *types* and *genres* of books available is essential. Raines and Isbell (1994), Machado (1999), and many other children's literature experts believe that teachers and parents should select books from a wide variety of genres and types. This is fairly easy when you are working with adult literature, which falls into familiar categories, such as fiction, nonfiction, poetry, and prose. But with children's literature in all of its many varieties, the labeling is much more difficult.

Although there are several systems used to group children's books, educators do not always agree on how a given book might be labeled or placed. Many books do not neatly fit any category or may fit more than one. Nevertheless, most books relating to children's literature fall into the categories that follow. (See Figure 4–1 for children's literature information on the Internet.) The types of literature are listed with specific characteristics that identify each kind of book. For clarity and organization, the types or categories of children's books have been arranged in alphabetical order.

Alphabet Books

Alphabet books are books based on the alphabet that

- Offer simple stories
- Present letter identification and one-object picture association
- Offer paired words and objects with matching illustrations
- Have a consistent theme
- Present opportunities to discover names and association of alphabet letters that are easily identified

Beginning-to-read Books

Beginning-to-read books may also be referred to as easy-to-read books. These books

- Present words that are simple and repetitive
- Have short sentences
- Are usually predictable
- Are designed to be read by the emergent reader

Big Books

Big books may also be called oversized, giant, or jumbo books. Big books

- Present extra-large text and illustrations
- Allow teachers to share books with a group of children easily
- Are mass published, so many popular titles are available in this format

- *American Library Association*—**www.ala.org**
- *Bookwire Index Children's Publishers and Book Awards*—
  www.bookwire.com/index/childrens-publishers.html
  www.bookwire.com/index/book-awards.html
- *Carol Hurst's Children's Literature*—**www.carolhurst.com**
- *Children's Book Council*—**www.cbcbooks.org**
- *Children's Book Links*—**www.absolute-sway.com/pfp/html/childrens.htm**
- *Children's Literature Web Guide*—**www.acs.ucalgary.ca/~dkbrown/index.html**
  (Lists children's book awards including Caldecott and Newbery)
- *Internet School Library Media Center (ISLMC) Children's Literature and Language Arts
  Page*—**http://falcon.jmu.edu/~ramseyil/childlit.htm**
- *Official Eric Carle Web site*—**www.eric-carle.com**

  Note: Internet Web sites change frequently and new links are added. This is just a suggested list to get you started.

FIGURE 4–1 Suggested children's literature Web sites on the Internet.

Board Books

Board books are usually the first books for infants and toddlers because they are made of heavy cardboard and they are laminated. Board books

- Offer ease of page-turning for children learning to handle books
- Are sometimes referred to as minibooks because they are small and can easily be picked up by a young child
- Have simple illustrations

Concept Books

Concept books have been identified as a young child's first informational book. These books

- Present themes, ideas, or concepts with specific examples
- Identify and clarify abstractions, such as color or shape
- Help with vocabulary development
- Include alphabet and counting books as favorite types of concept books

Counting Books

Counting books are books based on counting and

- Describe simple numeral and picture association
- Often tell a story
- Offer one-to-one correspondence illustrations
- Show representations of numbers in more than one format
- Vary from simple to complex
- Present illustrations that are consistent in adding to understanding for young children

Folk Literature

Folk literature may also be called folk tales, fairy tales, fables, tall tales, myths, and legends. These tales

- Come from the oral tradition of storytelling
- Appeal to the child's sense of fantasy
- Teach value systems
- Offer language that is appealing to children and create strong visual images
- Are available in picture book format
- Connect with other cultures and countries because they retell traditional stories that are shared from generation to generation. (Some specific examples: Hans Christian Andersen's original and adapted stories are modern fairy tales; fables present explicit morals with animals speaking as humans; myths describe the creation of the world and nature; and legends are based on the actions of a single hero. Story collectors, such as the Grimm brothers, wrote down stories from the oral tradition.)

Interaction Books

Interaction books are sometimes called novelty, toy, or participation books. These books

- Use some device for involving young readers, such as pop-ups, fold-outs, scratch and sniff, pasting books, puzzle pictures, humor, and riddles
- Offer books with audio cassettes
- Stimulate imagination
- Can be designed in different sizes and shapes for exploring and touching

Informational Books

Informational books offer nonfiction for emergent readers. They also

- Explore new ideas
- Answer "why" and "how"
- Stimulate and expand individual or group interest
- Give accurate facts about people (biographies) and subject matter

Mother Goose and Nursery Rhymes

Mother Goose and nursery rhyme books are often a child's first introduction to literature. These books

- Are known by children all over the world
- Are passed from generation to generation
- Offer varied illustrations of the rhymes
- Appeal to infants and toddlers

Multicultural Books

Multicultural books are also referred to as cross-cultural or culturally diverse books. These books

- Develop awareness of and sensitivity to other cultures
- Increase positive attitudes toward similarities and differences in people

■ Offer accurate portrayals and rich details of individual and group heritage
■ Can extend to seasonal and holiday books (a separate listing of *anti-bias literature* that promotes gender equity and the importance of the inclusion of children with special needs may include multicultural books as well).

Picture Books or Picture Story Books

Picture books are often referred to as the most popular type of children's literature. These books

■ Are written in a direct style that tells a simple story
■ Offer varied illustrations that complement and associate closely with the text
■ Are written especially for adults to share with children
■ Are uniquely appropriate for the young child

Poetry

Poetry is forgotten many times as part of children's literature. Poetry

■ Can be one book, one poem, or a collection of poems
■ Contributes imaginative rhyme, rhythm, and sound
■ Is another way to present culture, country, and language
■ Stimulates imagery and feelings
■ Is pleasing and can relate to life in terms that children can understand

Predictable Books

Predictable books contain familiar and repetitive sequences. These books

■ Describe events that are repeated or added to as the story continues
■ Permit successful guessing of what happens next
■ Supply opportunities for children to read along
■ Build self-confidence
■ Encourage children to read naturally

Realistic Literature

Sometimes called bibliotherapy or therapeutic literature, realistic literature deals with real-life issues. These books

■ Help children cope with common, actual experiences
■ Offer positive solutions and insights
■ Encourage talking about a child's feelings
■ Are often tied in with anti-bias literature that relates to children with special needs

Reference Books

Reference books emphasize individualized learning through special topic books, picture dictionaries, and encyclopedias. They also encourage older children to find a resource that answers questions.

Series Books

Series books are often written for primary-grade children. These books

■ Are built around a single character or group of characters
■ Can introduce the concept of books written in chapter form
■ Can be related to television characters that are familiar to children

Teacher- and Child-made Books

Teacher- and child-made books are a part of developmentally appropriate early education classrooms. These books

- Encourage self-esteem, creativity, and sharing ideas with others
- Reinforce group learning
- Develop a child's understanding of authorship by seeing her name in print
- Encourage children to articulate experiences
- Invite children to use their imagination

Wordless Picture Books

A young child develops language and reading skills with **wordless picture books**. These books

- Offer visually appealing illustrations
- Present sequential action from page to page
- Promote creativity by encouraging a child to talk about experiences
- Use imagination
- Invite older children to write a story about what is seen, with character descriptions and dialogue

■ CHILDREN'S BOOK AWARDS

An understanding of who gives awards for outstanding children's literature and the nature of each award provides a guide to choosing books.

In 1938, Frederick G. Melcher, editor of *Publisher's Weekly*, established the Caldecott Award. This medal is awarded annually to the artist of "the most distinguished picture book for children" printed in the United States and published during the preceding year. It is named in honor of the English illustrator, Randolph Caldecott (1846–1886), a nineteenth-century pioneer in the field of children's books. The selection is made by a committee, the members of which are either elected or appointed from the ranks of children's and school librarians, and who are members of the Association for Library Services to Children, a part of the American Library Association.

The Caldecott Award is presented at the same time as the Newbery Award, named for John Newbery (1713–1767), the first English publisher of children's books. Established in 1922, the Newbery Award is for "the most distinguished contribution to American literature for children" published the preceding year. It honors the quality of the author's writing and is usually a book appropriate for older children who are more mature readers. Both the Caldecott and Newbery Awards are presented at the annual conference of the American Library Association.

The Hans Christian Andersen Medal, established in 1956, is given by the International Board on Books for Young People. This award is presented every two years to a living author and an illustrator in recognition of their entire body of work.

The International Reading Association Children's Book Award is given to new authors. The Coretta Scott King Awards are presented to an African-American author and illustrator for "outstanding inspirational and educational contributions to literature for children." In addition, the National Jewish Book Awards and the Catholic Book Awards add to the list of over 100 awards made annually to recognize authors and illustrators of literature for children (Raines & Isbell, 1994; Huck et al., 1993).

Use award books as a starting point for selecting literature. Personal evaluation and knowledge of individual children, their interests, and their needs should also be criteria for selection.

■ SELECTION OF BOOKS FOR YOUNG CHILDREN

There are many appropriate books available for use in early education. The following criteria should be considered when making selections for this age group.

- Select books for enjoyment.
- Select books that encourage a child's capacity for laughter.
- Choose durable books. Books are to be handled and used by children.
- Select books with different styles of illustrations.
- Consider the length of the story. Books should be age and developmentally appropriate.
- Pick books that appeal to children and relate to their experiences.
- Choose books that have an appealing story and style. Children like sound, rhythm, and repetition in their stories.
- Avoid overly frightening, confusing stories.
- Include a wide variety of multicultural books. There are many that present the uniqueness of a present-day culture as seen through the eyes of a child.
- Select books that do not stereotype people according to gender, ethnic background, culture, age, or types of work.
- Choose books that show differently abled people in active and interactive roles. Be sure that some books have a person with special needs as the main character.
- Offer children a variety of writing styles and languages.
- Share literature from other countries to expand children's global awareness.
- Choose books that appeal to a young child's senses. Enjoyment is found in books with descriptive words that make children taste, smell, and feel, as well as see and hear.
- Pick books that help children develop positive self-esteem by emphasizing the capabilities children have.
- Share books that promote feelings of security.
- Choose books that show characters seeing themselves positively.
- Select books in which characters show emotions common to young children.
- Read several books on the same topic to provide more than one perspective.
- Introduce books that will expand vocabulary.

- Present books that reinforce concepts already being acquired.
- Select books that may help clarify misconceptions.
- Use literature as a stimulus for activities that require children to use their senses in discovery or exploration.
- Select stories that have a plot in which there is action, for example, stories that tell what people did and what they said.
- Enrich a child's experiences with literature by providing poetry selections and books of poems.

■ RECOMMENDED BOOKS

The examples of representative books have been divided into two lists: one suggests books for age and developmental appropriateness, and the other is a thematic list of children's books. Some duplications will be found in the two listings. These are books that were suggested over and over again by teachers of young children, are used as examples of quality literature by educators in the field, or have been selected as personal favorites and current discoveries. (You can add favorites of your own to these. Ask colleagues, librarians, and parents to suggest additional titles and authors.)

Age and Developmentally Appropriate Children's Books

Infants. When you hold an infant in your lap and share a special story or book, you are making a difference in that child's life. When you set up the special places in the infant room for reading or telling a story or for singing a nursery rhyme, include pillows, stuffed animals, quilts, and mats. Sawyer (2000) point out that "babies sit on laps, crawl about, and listen in various positions and in various places."

It is important for infants to interact with the books. For them, that means chewing on the pages, touching and looking at them in unique ways, and making them a part of their "personal turf." Schickendanz (1999) tells us, "Older babies will enjoy a special book nook. Crawlers and walkers can get to an area where attractively arranged books are easy to reach. . . . A book nook for babies can be made by standing some books up on the [carpeted] floor and laying others flat nearby. Because the opened and standing books can be seen from a distance, they will catch the children's attention." See Figure 4–2 for suggested books for infants.

Ahlberg, A., & Ahlberg, J. (1981). *Peek-a-boo.* New York: Viking.

Brown, M. W. (1991, First Board Book Edition). *Goodnight moon.* Illustrated by Clement Hurd. New York: HarperCollins.

Chorao, K. (1986). *The baby's good morning book.* New York: E. P. Dutton.

de Paola, T. (1985). *Tomie de Paola's Mother Goose.* New York: Putnam.

Greenfield, E. (1991). *My doll, Keshia.* Illustrated by Jan Spivey Gilchrist. New York: Black Butterfly Children's Books and Readers Publishing Inc.

Greenfield, E. (1991). *Daddy and I.* Illustrated by Jan Spivey Gilchrist. New York: Black Butterfly Children's Books and Readers Publishing Inc.

Hale, S. (1990). *Mary had a little lamb.* Illustrated by Tomie de Paola. New York: Scholastic.

Hathon, E. (1993). *Soft as a kitten.* New York: Grossett & Dunlap, Inc.

Hoban, T. (1993). *Black on white.* New York: Greenwillow.

Hoban, T. (1993). *White on black.* New York: Greenwillow.

Hoban, T. (1985). *What is it?* New York: Greenwillow.

Hudson, C. W., & Ford, B. G. (1990). *Bright eyes, brown skin.* Illustrated by George Ford. Orange, NJ: Just Us Books.

Isadora, R. (1985). *I hear.* New York: Greenwillow.

Isadora, R. (1985). *I see.* New York: Greenwillow.

Kemp, M. (1987). *Pat-a-cake.* Los Angeles: Price Stern Sloan.

Krauss, R. (1993, First Board Book Edition). *The carrot seed.* Illustrated by Crockett Johnson. New York: HarperCollins.

Kunhardt, D. (1962). *Pat the bunny.* Racine, WI: Western.

Ostarch, J., & Nex, A. (1993). *My family.* Los Angeles: Price Stern Sloan.

Oxenbury, H. (1985). *I touch.* London: Walker Books.

Sesame Street. (1998). *Baby love.* (Board Book). Photographs by John E. Barrett. New York: Children's Television Workshop, Jim Henson Company, and Random House.

Sesame Street. (1998). *Baby says.* (Board Book). Photographs by John E. Barrett. New York: Children's Television Workshop, Jim Henson Company, and Random House.

Shaw, C. G. (1993, First Board Book Edition). *It looked like spilt milk.* New York: HarperCollins.

Steptoe, J. (1988). *Baby says.* New York: Lothrop, Lee & Shepard.

Watson, C. (1983). *Catch me and kiss me and say it again.* New York: Philomel.

FIGURE 4–2 Suggested books for infants.

Toddlers. The special place for story time in the toddler room should be surrounded with colorful pillows, carpet squares, and with other comfortable spots available for these young children to listen to, participate with, and enjoy books. Small groupings offer the children a chance to turn the page, point to, and identify things, while sharing their choice of books with the teacher and each other. For those toddlers who enjoy one-on-one time with a teacher and a favorite book, sitting in a rocking chair fulfills this need in a special way.

Story time outdoors on a big quilt, under a tree, and surrounded by grass can be exciting and appropriate for toddlers, too. Bredekamp and Copple (1997) explains, "Two-year-olds are learning to produce language rapidly. They need simple books, pictures, puzzles, music, and time and space for active play such as jumping, running, and dancing." Physically enjoying the story is important for these children. See Figure 4–3 for suggested books for toddlers.

Three-, Four-, and Five-year-olds. The story center, library, or book center should be one of the most inviting and exciting learning centers or curriculum areas in a classroom for preschoolers. Huck et al., (1993) found in their research that many times the

Aldridge, J. H. (1994). *The pocket book.* Illustrated by Rene King Moreno. New York: Simon & Schuster.

Carle, E. (1996). *Have you seen my cat?* New York: Little Simon.

Carle, E. (1981). *The very hungry caterpillar.* New York: Philomel.

Crozon, A., & Lanchais, A. (1998). *What am I?* New York: Chronicle.

Dyer, J. (1998). *Animal crackers: Bedtime.* (Board Book). New York: Little Brown & Company.

Ferraro, C. (1998). *Elmo's new laugh.* (Book and Audio Tape). Illustrated by Laurent Linn. New York: Children's Television Workshop, Jim Henson Company, and Sony Wonder.

Fox, M. (1993). *Time for bed.* Illustrated by Jane Dyer. San Diego, CA: Gulliver Books.

Hoban, T. (1989). *Of colors and things.* New York: Greenwillow.

McBratney, S. (1996). *Guess how much I love you?* (Board Book). Illustrated by Anita Jeram. Cambridge, MA: Candlewick Press.

Martin, B., Jr. (1983). *Brown bear, brown bear, what do you see?* Illustrated by Eric Carle. New York: Henry Holt.

Omerod, J. (1994). *To baby with love.* New York: Lothrop, Lee & Shepard Books.

Oxenbury, H. (1992). *Mother's helper.* New York: Dial.

Rathman, P. (1996). *Good night, gorilla.* (Board Book). New York: Putnam Publishers.

Russo, M. (1994). *Time to wake up!* New York: Greenwillow.

Scott, A. H. (1992). *On mother's lap.* Illustrated by Glo Coalson. New York: Clarion.

Waddell, M. (1996). *Owl babies.* (Board Book). Illustrated by Patrick Benson. Cambridge, MA: Candlewick Press.

Winter, S. (1994). *A baby just like me.* New York: Dorling Kindersley.

Wood, A. (1984). *The napping house.* Illustrated by Don Wood. San Diego, CA: Harcourt Brace Jovanovich.

FIGURE 4–3 Suggested books for toddlers.

library corners are the least frequently chosen area and that "To fully take advantage of young children's active natures, we must reexamine the size, arrangement, and contents of the library area."

Beaty (1992) agrees and states further that in setting up the story center:

Do whatever [is] necessary to make it attractive so that children cannot wait to become involved with books. Use bright colors wherever you can: on rugs, on pillows, on furniture, on the walls, and on the shelves. . . . Have book puppets, book puzzles, and book games displayed.

For this age child, many comfortable reading spaces should be provided, such as a soft rug; a big empty "refrigerator-size" box with pillows to sit on and "windows" cut in the box to look out; and child-size tables and chairs set up with a variety of books, magazines, catalogs, newspapers, and books with audio tapes, blank paper, and writing instruments.

As teachers, you should read aloud to your three-, four-, and five-year-olds every day. Plan activities that integrate listening, speaking, reading, and writing. It is also important for you to continue to read to individual children if they ask you to, because preschool children still need this special time with a significant adult. (Review Chapter 3 for suggestions of physical space arrangement and activity plans for setting up the library, literature, or literacy center.) See Figure 4–4 for suggested books for three-, four-, and five-year-olds.

Six-, Seven-, and Eight-year-olds. Computers, movies, television shows, video games, and music videos pose a challenge to teachers, librarians, and parents trying to capture the reading attention of six-, seven-, and eight-year-olds. As a result, literature for this age reflects the addition of topics grounded in real-life issues. Illustrations are more complex and artistic, and there is a greater diversity available.

As a teacher, you should provide many opportunities for reading and writing in the primary classroom. Bredekamp and Copple (1997) point out several ways to make the environment developmentally appropriate. Set up a "tempting library area for browsing through books, reading silently, or sharing a book with a friend; a listening station; and places to practice writing stories and to play math and language games."

Aliki. (1997). *My visit to the zoo.* New York: HarperCollins.

Aliki. (1986). *Hello! Good-bye.* New York: Greenwillow.

Bunting, E. (1988). *How many days to America?* Illustrated by Beth Peck. New York: Clarion.

dePaola, T. (1983). *The legend of the bluebonnet.* New York: G.P. Putnam's Sons.

Dorros, A. (1991). *Abuela.* Illustrated by Elisa Kleven. New York: Dutton.

Ehlert, L. (1997). *Color farm.* New York: HarperCollins.

Ehlert, L. (1987). *Growing vegetable soup.* San Diego, CA: Harcourt Brace.

Fleming, D. (1993). *In the small, small pond.* New York: Henry Holt.

Gershator, P. (1998). *Greetings, sun.* Illustrated by David Gershator. New York: Dorling Kindersley.

Grohmann, S. (1994). *The dust under Mrs. Merriweather's bed.* Boston: Whispering Coyote Press, Inc.

Hoban, T. (1998). *So many circles, so many squares.* New York: Greenwillow.

Hoban, T. (1997). *Construction zone.* New York: Greenwillow.

Hoff, S. (1993). *Danny and the dinosaur.* (Reissue edition). New York: HarperTrophy.

Martin, B., Jr. (1993). *Polar bear, polar bear, what do you hear?* Illustrated by Eric Carle. New York: Henry Holt.

Martin, B., Jr. & Archambault, J. (1988). *Listen to the rain.* Illustrated by James Endicott. New York: Henry Holt.

Miller, M. (1994). *My five senses.* New York: Simon & Schuster.

Morris, A. (1990). *Loving.* Photographs by Ken Heyman. New York: Lothrop, Lee & Shepard Books.

Quattlebaum, M. (1997). *Underground train.* Illustrated by C. B. Smith. New York: Bantam.

Rehm, K., & Knike, K. (1991). *Left or right.* New York: Clarion Books.

Roth, S. L. (1998). *Cinnamon's day out: A gerbil adventure.* New York: Dial.

Showers, P. (1993). *The listening walk.* (Reprint edition.). Illustrated by Aliki. New York: HarperTrophy.

Spier, P. (1982). *Rain.* New York: Bantam Doubleday.

Wilson-Max, K. (1997). *Big red fire truck.* (Liftflap edition). New York: Cartwheel Books.

FIGURE 4–4 Suggested books for three-, four-, and five-year-olds.

The more emphasis you place on the importance of books in the lives of six-, seven-, and eight-year-olds, the more important literature will be to the children. As with all ages, *read aloud* to them as often as you can. Let them tell you and others about what they have read, and encourage open-ended questioning by everyone. Encourage parents to continue reading aloud to their children, too.

When visitors come to your classroom, have them tell a story or read to the children. Inviting parents, grandparents, community volunteers, other teachers, or staff to read provides another dimension. See Figure 4–5 for suggested books for six-, seven-, and eight-year-olds.

Aliki. (1992). *Milk: From cow to carton.* New York: HarperCollins.

Aliki. (1988). *How a book is made.* (Reprint edition.). New York: HarperTrophy.

Angelou, M. (1994). *My painted house, my friendly chicken, and me.* Photographs by Margaret Courtney-Clarke. New York: Clarkson Potter, Inc.

Brighton, C. (1990). *Mozart: Scenes from the childhood of the great composer.* New York: Doubleday.

Carle, E. (1998). *Let's paint a rainbow.* New York: Cartwheel Books.

Channin, M. (1994). *Grandfather four winds and rising moon.* Illustrated by Sally J. Smith. Tiburon, CA: H. J. Kramer, Inc.

Dorros, A. (1991). *Tonight is carnival.* Illustrated with *arpilleras* sewn by the Club de Madres Virgen del Carmen of Lima, Peru. New York: Dutton.

George, L. B. (1996). *Around the pond: Who's been here?* New York: Greenwillow.

George, L. B. (1995). *In the woods: Who's been here?* New York: Greenwillow.

Hest, A. (1997). *When Jessie came across the sea.* Illustrated by P. J. Lynch. Cambridge, MA: Candlewick Press.

Kroll, V. (1993). *A carp for Kimiko.* Illustrated by Katherine Roundtree. Watertown, MA: Charlesbridge.

Lerner, C. (1996). *Backyard birds of summer.* New York: William Morrow.

London, J. (1995). *Like butter on pancakes.* New York: Viking.

Polti, L. (1994). *Three stalks of corn.* New York: Aladdin.

Shannon, D. (1998). *A bad case of stripes.* New York: Scholastic.

Staub, F. (1998). *America's forests.* Minneapolis, MN: Carolrhoda Books.

FIGURE 4–5 Suggested books for six-, seven-, and eight-year-olds.

Thematic Selection of Children's Books

Many teachers find that using a thematic approach to literature selection gives them more individuality in curriculum development. The thematic strategy leads children to activities that suggest active exploration, problem solving, and the acquisition of specific concepts or skills. Themes can be weekly, bi-weekly, or monthly. Select the theme that relates to the children in your class according to their experiences and their age and stage of development. (Review Chapter 2 for specific explanation of themes, units, projects, and webs.) Then, select the literature that will emphasize, explain, and extend the theme. See Figure 4–6 for books about self and family and Figure 4–7 for books about friendship.

Glazer (1991) suggests that:

Books with characteristics in common can be grouped together into units that focus on a single item, describe similar content or represent literature of a particular genre or by a particular author or illustrator. . . . [C]onsider a variety of titles, but narrow the selection to those books which best fit your purposes, and include only those which you actually plan to use.

Aliki. (1990). *My feet.* New York: Crowell.

Aliki. (1990). *My hands.* New York: Crowell.

Carle, E. (1984). *The mixed-up chameleon.* New York: HarperTrophy.

Dorros, A. (1991). *Abuela.* Illustrated by Elisa Kleven. New York: Dutton Children's Books.

Friedman, I. R. (1984). *How my parents learned to eat.* Illustrated by Allen Say. Boston: Houghton Mifflin.

Garza, C. L. (1990). *Family pictures, cuadros de familia.* San Francisco: Children's Book Press.

Hazen, B. S. (1992). *Mommie's office.* Illustrated by David Soman. New York: Macmillan.

Hoban, T. (1983). *I read signs.* New York: Greenwillow.

Hoffman, M. (1991). *Amazing Grace.* New York: Dial.

Hudson, W. (1993). *I love my family.* New York: Scholastic.

Kuklin, S. (1992). *How my family lives in America.* New York: Bradbury Press.

Morris, A. (1992). *Houses and homes.* Photographs by Ken Heyman. New York: Lothrop, Lee & Shepard.

Williams, V. B. (1982). *A chair for my mother.* New York: Mulberry Books.

Weninger, B. (1998). *What's the matter, Davy?* Illustrated by Eve Tharlet. New York: North South Books.

Wood, A. (1984). *The napping house.* Illustrated by Don Wood. San Diego, CA: Harcourt Brace Jovanovich.

FIGURE 4–6 Suggested books for the theme "self and family."

■ INTEGRATING LITERATURE INTO OTHER CURRICULUM AREAS

Currently, in classrooms throughout the country, literature-based instruction is "what's happening." The connection between literature and the other curriculum areas, as Machado (1999) explains, "includes reading aloud to children, making use of informational books, and encouraging children's response to books using drama, art, and child-dictated writing."

Sawyer (2000) explains literature integrated units as being "taught around a general theme or a key idea. . . . One may wish to develop a theme around a single book. . . . The focus may also be in a content area such as science, social studies, basic concepts, or holidays."

Huck et al., (1993) continue with the philosophy of using books to extend active learning:

When children work with books in ways that are meaningful to them—through talk, making things, writing, or drama and music—many things happen. Children have greater satisfaction with and clarify personal meanings about what they have read.

Glazer (1991) presents another way of looking at integrating curriculum:

Children should be guided to perceive literature as a body of work rather than as separate and unrelated stories and poems. If you group books for presentation, you set the stage for children to see the relationships among books, to notice the recurring structural patterns of literature.

Aliki. (1995). *Best friends together again.* New York: Greenwillow.

Bunnett, R. (1992). *Friends in the park.* Photographs by Carl Sahloff. New York: Checkerboard Press.

Cheltenham Elementary School Kindergartners. (1991) *We are all alike . . . we are all different.* New York: Scholastic.

Kellogg, S. (1990). *Best friends.* New York: Dial.

Lobel, A. (1970). *Frog and toad are friends.* New York: Harper and Row.

Marxhausen, J. (1990). *Some of my best friends are trees.* St. Louis, MO: Concordia.

Morris, A. (1990). *Loving.* Photographs by Ken Heyman. New York: Lothrop, Lee & Shepard.

Palacco, P. (1992). *Mrs. Katz and Tush.* New York: Bantam Books.

Rogers, F. (1987). *Making friends.* New York: G. P. Putnam's Sons.

Russo, M. (1992). *Alex is my friend.* New York: Greenwillow.

Sunico, R. C. (1991). *Two friends, one world.* New York: Cacho Publishing House, Inc.

Wild, M. (1990). *The very best of friends.* Illustrated by Julie Vivas. New York: Harcourt Brace.

Winthrop, E. (1989). *The best friends club.* Illustrated by Martha Weston. New York: Lothrop, Lee & Shepard.

FIGURE 4–7 Suggested books for the theme "friendship."

The idea of "putting literature around the room" can be done realistically by creatively decorating containers for books with bright contact paper, wallpaper, or children's drawings and by placing books in every learning activity center. For example, books relating to houses and buildings can be put in the block center; those dealing with shapes and colors can be put in the art center; and books concerning gardening, fish, and turtles can be near the sand and water table. See Figure 4–8 for suggested books about the natural environment.

Aliki. (1988). *A weed is a flower: The life of George Washington Carver.* New York: Simon & Schuster.

Bang, M. (1997). *Common ground: Water, earth, and air.* New York: Scholastic.

Bryan, A. (1992). *Sing to the sun.* New York: HarperCollins.

Buchanan, K. (1991). *This house is made of mud.* Illustrated by Libba Tracey. New York: Northland Publishing.

Carle, E. (1990). *The very quiet cricket.* New York: Philomel.

Carle, E. (1969). *The very hungry caterpillar.* New York: Philomel.

Cassedy, S., & Kunihiro S. (1992). *Red dragonfly on my shoulder.* New York: HarperCollins.

Chief Seattle & Jeffers, S. (1991). *Brother eagle, sister sky.* New York: Penguin Books.

Cooney, B. (1985). *Miss Rumphius.* New York: Puffin Books.

Dorros, A. (1997). *A tree is growing.* Illustrated by S. D. Schindler. New York: Scholastic.

Earth Works Group. (1990). *50 simple things kids can do to save the earth.* New York: Andrews & McMell.

Ets, M. H. (1978). *Gilberto and the wind.* New York: Puffin Books.

Gibbons, G. (1984). *The seasons of Arnold's appletree.* San Diego, CA: Harcourt Brace Jovanovich.

Hirschi, R. (1990). *Winter.* Photographs by Thomas D. Mangelson. New York: Cobblehill.

Keats, E. J. (1962). *The snowy day.* New York: Viking Press.

Pfeffer, W., & Brickman, R. (1997). *A log's life.* Illustrated by Stephanie Lurie. New York: Simon & Schuster.

Rylant, C. (1982). *When I was young in the mountains.* New York: Dutton.

Wright, A. (1992). *Will we miss them? Endangered species?* Illustrated by Marshall Peck III. Watertown, MA: Charlesbridge.

FIGURE 4–8 Suggested books for the theme "natural environment."

Activities that Encourage Children to Become Authors and Illustrators

One of the most stimulating child-centered activities a teacher can use is having the children write original books or one-page stories. "In a collaborative classroom project, each child contributes a unique individual piece to the collaborative process—especially the collaborative bookmaking process—in your classroom" (Spann, 1997). You can help the youngest children put their artwork together in the form of a book, using string or rings to do so; for older children, pair them as "book buddies" or "book partners" to write and illustrate their own books. Some teacher preparation or assistance may be needed or requested. Machado (1999) presents the values of books authored by children or their teachers:

■ They promote interest in the classroom book collection.
■ They help children see connections between spoken and written words.
■ The material is based on the interests of both the children and the teacher.

- They personalize book reading.
- They prompt self-expression.
- They stimulate creativity.
- They build feelings of competence and self-worth.

Children (and teachers) as authors and illustrators can be emphasized in many ways. Having children make book covers for their books can affirm the importance of all books. In the writing or art center, provide paper, wallpaper, or contact paper that will cover a child's favorite book. The child can decorate the cover and write the title, author, and illustrator as well.

How about a "Let's Pretend Book"? In the dramatic play area have a camera (preferably a Polaroid type) ready for children to take pictures of what is going on in the grocery store, pet shop, post office, or whatever the area represents for that week. These are then placed on sheets of paper to be made into a book by the children and the teacher. The children can tell or dictate the story of who they were pretending to be. Visually and concretely, this helps children understand that their words and actions make stories and books.

As with any child-directed activity, the teacher prepares materials and space in advance and is available to offer assistance. Suggestions for putting the book together can come from the teacher as well, with the children putting the book together with yarn, staples, masking tape, metal rings, or brads. The size and shape of the cover and pages of the book can be another creative element, such as books shaped to match the current curriculum theme or children's interests. Also, books can be in the shape of a bird, butterfly, car, bus, animal, fish, vegetable, etc.

Keep in mind that however and whenever you mix and match literature with other curriculum areas, all activities should benefit the children developmentally, individually, and creatively. (There are specific examples at the end of this chapter. See Developmentally Appropriate Activities.) See Figure 4–9 for suggested authors, illustrators, and photographers of children's books to share with the children.

Teachers as Storytellers

"Throughout the world, in every culture, people have told stories," says Jimmy Neil Smith, executive director of the National Association for the Preservation and Perpetuation of Storytelling. The oral tradition was once the primary method for passing history and culture from one generation to the next. Eventually it became unpopular. "This may have been due," he continues, "to books and print media, radio, television and computerization. They fill us with images that were once the province of the oral tradition," concludes Mr. Smith (Schnedler, 1994). Sawyer and Sawyer (1993) agree. "At one time, storytelling was the dominant method for sharing a culture's heritage with the next generation."

Aliki	Lois Ehlert	Jerry Pinkney
Byron Barton	Denise Fleming	Patricia Polacco
Jan Brett	Gail Gibbons	Anne F. Rockwell
Eric Carle	Ken Heyman	Allan Say
Donald Crews	Ron Hirschi	Vera Williams
Tomie de Paola	Tana Hoban	Ken Wilson-Max
Arthur Dorros	Ann Morris	

FIGURE 4–9 Suggested list of authors, illustrators, and photographers of books for young children.

A story is one of the means by which children make sense of their world and organize events, experiences, and facts. A teacher *telling* a story without a book and using changes in pitch, tone, and dramatic flair; or using puppets, props, toys, songs, flannelboard pictures, and finger plays; or drawing a story while it is being told can captivate and entertain a small or large group of children. This unique way of presenting children's literature encourages children to tell their own stories or retell the stories back to the teachers.

It is helpful for the teacher to select stories with simple plots and small numbers of characters for the younger children. Older children like the challenge of remembering a complex plot with multiple characters.

Poetry

Teachers should read poetry to children often. Appreciation for poetry develops slowly, but the time and place for poetry is any time, any place. See Figure 4–10 for suggested poetry books for young children.

Have snack time become a "poetry break time." Start by reading a poem to the children during their snack. Then, on following days, let the children read or tell a poem to each other and the teacher after snack time. Adding a musical background, recorded or live, offers a different dimension to poetry reading.

Other activities can be to act out a poem, draw an illustration for a poem, include poetry at group time, pick a theme and make an illustrated booklet or exhibit of poems that relate to the theme, and create a "Poetry Line" (clothesline or thick yarn) stretched across the back of the room with poems attached.

The following examples of poems should be shared with young children. (You will find flannelboard characters for "Spring Showers" in Appendix A.)

Agee, J. (1993). *Flapstick: Ten ridiculous rhymes with flaps.* New York: Dutton/Penguin.

Booth, D. (1990). *Voices on the wind: Poems for all seasons.* New York: Morrow Junior Books.

Cameron, P. (1961). *I can't said the ant.* New York: Scholastic.

Carle, E. (1989). *Animals, animals.* New York: Philomel.

Ghigna, C. (1995). *Riddle rhymes.* New York: Hyperion.

Hoberman, M. A. (1993). *Fathers, mothers, sisters, brothers: A collection of family poems.* New York: Puffin Books.

Hudson, W. (1993). *Pass it on, African American poetry for children.* Illustrated by Floyd Cooper. New York: Scholastic.

Johnston, T. (1996). *Once in the country: Poems of a farm.* Illustrated by Thomas B. Allen. New York: Putnam.

Kuskin, K. (1992). *Soap soup and other verses.* New York: HarperCollins.

Prelutsky, J. (1992). *Tyrannosaurus was a beast: Dinosaur poems.* New York: Mulberry.

FIGURE 4–10 Suggested list of poetry books for young children.

ELEPHANT

The elephant is big.
The elephant is strong.
The elephant has a trunk which is very, *very*

L
   O
     N
       G!!!!

Reproduced by permission of B. Wolf—1995
Copyright B. Wolf—1993

JACK FROST

Jack Frost nips at your nose,
tingles your fingers,
tickles your toes!
Jack Frost soon will be here—
riding the breeze—
painting the trees—
That's how we know that Winter is near!

Reproduced by permission of B. Wolf—1995
Copyright B. Wolf—1993

RAINDROPS

Listen, do you hear the rain
falling on my windowpane?

Raindrops
      dropping—
           falling—
                plopping—
raindrops
      splashing—
           thumping—
                dashing—
down upon my windowpane!

Reproduced by permission of B. Wolf—1995
Copyright B. Wolf—1993

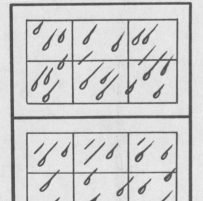

SPRING SHOWERS

The sunlight is shining down through the trees.
The flowers stir and sway in the breeze.
Then here come the clouds—crowds of clouds—
hurrying, scurrying, covering the sun.
The lightning flashes!
The thunder crashes!!
The flowers are happy, for now the rain has begun.
Listen!

Raindrops falling, Raindrops falling,

Rain falls with a lovely sound.
Rain is very fine, I think!
Rain falls on the thirsty ground, giving all the plants a drink.

Raindrops falling, Raindrops falling, down

And now the clouds all blow away—
leaving a bright, sunshiny day.
And all the flower faces glow;
and all the plants begin to grow,
s-t-r-e-t-c-h-i-n-g . . . r-e-a-c-h-i-n-g . . .

up . . . so . . . high . . .

t-r-y-i-n-g, . . . t-r-y-i-n-g . . .

to . . . touch . . . the . . . sky!

Now rainbows are sparkling over the trees.
The flowers stir and sway in the breeze.

Reproduced by permission of B. Wolf—1995
Copyright B. Wolf—1993

Family-School Connection

"One of the most important messages that can be communicated to parents during the early years is that reading to a child is essential," explains Raines and Isbell (1994). Jalongo (1988) further states, "Parents are sometimes disappointed to hear professionals say that taking the time to read to children is the best way to help children become readers. That answer seems too simple, too commonplace."

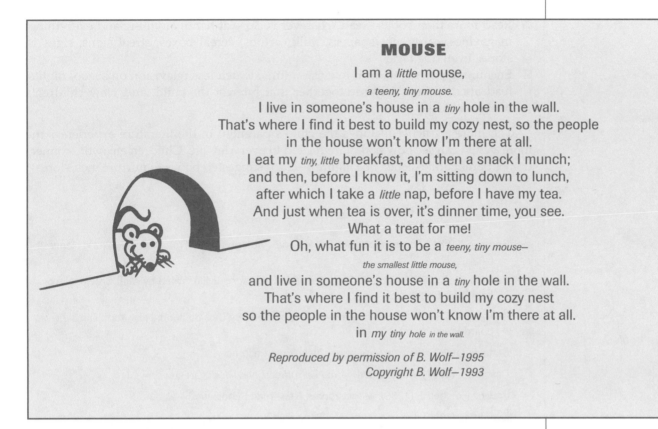

MOUSE

I am a *little* mouse,
a teeny, tiny mouse.
I live in someone's house in a *tiny* hole in the wall.
That's where I find it best to build my cozy nest, so the people
in the house won't know I'm there at all.
I eat my *tiny, little* breakfast, and then a snack I munch;
and then, before I know it, I'm sitting down to lunch,
after which I take a *little* nap, before I have my tea.
And just when tea is over, it's dinner time, you see.
What a treat for me!
Oh, what fun it is to be a *teeny, tiny mouse—*
the smallest little mouse,
and live in someone's house in a *tiny* hole in the wall.
That's where I find it best to build my cozy nest
so the people in the house won't know I'm there at all.
in *my tiny hole in the wall.*

Reproduced by permission of B. Wolf—1995
Copyright B. Wolf—1993

Part of a teacher's responsibility in early education is to effectively inform parents of this basic fact and to answer questions about ways for parents and their children to become involved with books. The following suggestions have been successful for some teachers of young children:

- Find opportunities to suggest titles and authors of books for the child and the parent.
- Give parents addresses of local libraries and list the story times.
- Suggest local bookstores that specialize in or offer a large selection of children's literature.
- Send home a list of the books that are going to be or have been read to the children. Personalize the information with a special note about a book their child especially enjoyed.
- Set up a parent-lending library at your school. Supply a bright-colored folder or large envelope in which the borrowed book can be returned.
- Encourage parents to read a story to their child at the end of the day before going home from the child-care setting. This helps both parent and child make a relaxed transition.
- For older children, ask parents to allow a block of time in the evening to have a child read to the parent and encourage parents to read aloud to the child as well.
- Ask parents to be role models by letting their children see that they read books. Talk about what they read and what the children read.
- Suggest that a special place for the children's books be provided at home.
- Encourage parents to give books as gifts to let their child know that the parents think books are important and special.

■ Read more than books. Read whatever is close at hand, anything and everything: magazines, cards, newspapers, milk cartons, cereal boxes, street signs, signs in stores, even dog tags!

■ Encourage parents to limit television time, watch less television on school nights, read about things they see together that interest the child, and view children's books on video.

The more a teacher includes the child's parent(s) in the literature experience, the more a child can see how books are related to everyday life. Children enjoy the connection of parent and teacher. See Figure 4–11 for suggested books to nurture inclusion.

Brown, T. (1984). *Someone special, just like you.* Photographs by Fran Ortiz. New York: Henry Holt.

Bunnett, R. (1997). *Amigos en la escuela/Friends at school.* Illustrated by Matt Brown. New York: Star Bright.

Bunnett, R. (1992). *Friends in the park.* Photographs by Carl Sahlhoff. New York: Checkerboard Press.

Carle, E. (1995). *The very busy spider.* New York: Philomel.

Caseley, J. (1991). *Harry and Willy and Carrothead.* New York: Greenwillow.

Cowen-Fletcher, J. (1996). *Mama zooms.* New York: Scholastic.

Dwight, L. (1998). *We can do it!* New York: Star Bright.

Fassler, J. (1987). *Howie helps himself.* Chicago: Whitman.

Latkin, P. (1994). *Dad and me in the morning.* New York: Concept Books.

Lears, L., & Ritz, K. (1998). *Ian's walk: A story about Autism.* Chicago: Whitman.

McMahon, P. (1995). *Listen for the bus: David's story.* New York: Boyds Mills Press.

Millman, I. (1996). *Moses goes to a concert.* New York: Farrar Straus & Giroux.

Moon, N. (1995). *Lucy's picture.* Illustrated by Alex Ayliffe. New York: Dial.

Powers, M. E. (1992). *Our teacher's in a wheelchair.* Chicago: Whitman.

Rankin, L. (1998). *The handmade counting book.* New York: Dutton.

FIGURE 4–11 Suggested books to nurture inclusion. Share these books with both children and parents.

■ TIPS FOR TEACHERS

When reading aloud to a group of children:

■ Start the process by selecting an appropriate piece of literature for your age group.

■ Read through the story several times before reading aloud to the children. Practice your presentation.

■ Plan the appropriate time, place, and purpose for the story time. Alternate small group and large group activities.

■ Try to maintain as much eye contact with the children as possible while you share the story.

■ Sit on the floor with the children or on a low chair.

- Hold the book so that everyone in the group will be able to see the page. The use of big books can be effective.
- Use different voices for different characters. The children will enjoy your involvement with the story, and these "voices" help children to distinguish between characters.

General Guidelines

The following guidance techniques can be helpful to use during story time.

- When a child wants to leave the group during story time, gently encourage the child to stay; but do not insist. Sometimes a reassuring arm around the child will help.
- Young children are easily distracted. Listening as part of a group is a skill that must be learned. Begin with books that have only a few pages.
- Asking a child a question about what might happen next will help direct her attention back to the story.
- While telling the story, whatever has to be said or done to handle a problem should be as brief an interruption of the story as possible. (Sometimes interruptions can be an important part of the literature experience, if they offer focused discussion of the story or book.)
- Be sure that the children have elbow and knee room. Be sure that everyone can see. For the habitual nudger or distractor, catching his attention might be achieved by inserting his name as part of the story.
- It is helpful to include the children in the process by having them retell the story using their own words, joining in to repeat lines, or letting them add the flannelboard pieces as you tell the story. Using a puppet is effective in guiding the children through the story.

ACTIVITY PLAN WORKSHEET

DEVELOPMENTALLY APPROPRIATE ACTIVITIES FOR YOUNG CHILDREN

Children's age group: Infants (3–18 months)

Name of Activity and Brief Description

Sharing nursery rhyme books with individual children
These are the books we will share:

Lincoln, Ltd., Frances. (1991). *Polly put the kettle on.* Photographs by Anthea Sieveking. Hauppauge, NY: Barron's Educational Series Inc.

Lincoln, Ltd., Frances. (1991). *Twinkle, twinkle little star and other bedtime rhymes.* Photographs by Anthea Sieveking, Hauppauge, NY: Barron's Educational Series Inc.

Lincoln, Ltd., Frances. (1991). *Mary had a little lamb.* Photographs by Anthea Sieveking. Hauppauge, NY: Barron's Educational Series Inc.

Purpose/Objectives of Activity

- To listen to a short story for the development of listening skills
- To look at books and rhymes
- To recognize and to point out objects and familiar animals
- To turn pages
- To say words and sing rhymes

Space and Materials Needed

Rocking chair, floor, pillows, and books

Procedure

The following activities are mainly inside ones, carried on next to the bookshelf while the child sits on the adult's lap, on the floor, or in a rocking chair. These activities can also be taken outside and done while you are sitting on a blanket.

1. Let the child choose a book from the low shelf.
2. Read the book to the child. Point to what is going on in the pictures. See if the child will try to say a word or part of a word with you.
3. Do the finger plays for the rhymes, such as "Twinkle, Twinkle Little Star." Have a pretend tea party for "Polly."
4. Repeat these finger plays or songs often during transition times.

Guidance

Usually this is a one-on-one activity, but other children in the group are welcomed to look at the pictures and encouraged to do the finger plays, too. If other children want a book read to them at the same time, have enough books on the shelf or nearby so they can look at them. Keep the stories short.

Evaluation and Follow-Up

These nursery rhyme books are popular with the infants, and so are the follow-up activities. Sing the nursery songs and do the rhymes often to encourage language and motor development. Play dough makes a great "Pat-a-Cake." Have a tea party for "Polly Put the Kettle On." Use cotton balls to make "Mary Had a Little Lamb." Eat muffins to relate to "Muffin Man," and do exercises (sit, stand up, and fall down) with "Humpty Dumpty."

To achieve effectiveness in this activity, keep the stories short and do not mind when a child turns the page before you finish the rhyme. However, be sure there are plenty of books available, as this age child does not share easily.

ACTIVITY PLAN WORKSHEET

DEVELOPMENTALLY APPROPRIATE ACTIVITIES FOR YOUNG CHILDREN

Children's age group: Toddlers (18 months to 3 years)

Name of Activity and Brief Description

Group time story and art activity
   This is the book we will share:

Ziefert, H., & Baruffi, A. (1992). *Where is mommy's truck?* New York: HarperCollins.

   Reading this book offers children opportunities to lift the flaps and see exactly where mommy's truck is hiding. Teacher and children can spend a few minutes together talking about the people that drive trucks, big and small. Sometimes mommy and daddy drive a truck to work. Mommies and daddies go to many different kinds of jobs. By asking open-ended, short questions, toddlers can spend time one-on-one with the teacher and the book. After reading the book, the teacher will explain the art activity: car and truck painting. This activity will be available for any child to do with minimal assistance from the teacher, if needed. The children should direct the *process.*

Purpose/Objectives of Activity

- To practice small muscle skills
- To practice hand-eye coordination
- To demonstrate cause and effect
- To practice color recognition
- To demonstrate gender equity and recognition appropriate for toddlers

Space and Materials Needed

Indoor (or outdoor) table with or without chairs, individual sheets of paper, washable paint on a tray, and small cars and trucks

Procedure

1. Place cars and trucks on a tray with paint.
2. One child at a time (wearing a painting smock) rolls the cars and trucks through the paint and then "car paints" on his sheet of paper. (If possible, have several places set up for this activity.)
3. The teacher talks to the child and asks questions throughout this activity, such as: "Can you drive the car and make some tracks?" "Show me how you can drive on the paper." "Does your car make some sounds?" "What color is your car or truck or the road you're making?"
4. At the end of the activity for each child, the teacher can say: "Your paper is full of roads and tracks." "Show me how you can wash your hands and hang your smock up." "What a great job!"

Some children will participate in this activity in their own way. That is all right. It is the process that is important, not the product.

Guidance

Anticipating what a toddler might do, the teacher can easily use her words to guide the child. This encourages the child to "use his words." Examples: "Your car drives on the tray or on the paper." "Show me how you can sit on your bottom on the chair." "Your paper is so full of roads, now it is another friend's turn." "Would you like another piece of paper?"

   It is helpful to have another teacher or teacher assistant guiding the other children into activity centers while the teacher at the art table works one-on-one with a child.

Evaluation and Follow-Up

Were all the objectives met? When an older toddler is participating in the art activity, the teacher can suggest placement of the car on the tray or paper, such as back-and-forth or up-and-down. And at this point, other paint colors on additional trays can be added. This helps a child see how one road can cross another. To further extend the activity, add puzzles of cars and trucks to the manipulative center. Sing songs such as "Little Red Wagon" or "The Wheels on the Bus."

ACTIVITY PLAN WORKSHEET

DEVELOPMENTALLY APPROPRIATE ACTIVITIES FOR YOUNG CHILDREN

Children's age group: three-, four-, and five-year-olds

Name of Activity and Brief Description

Group time story and cooking activity

These are the books we will share:

Morris, A. (1989). *Bread, bread, bread.* Photographs by Ken Heyman. New York: Lothrop, Lee, & Shepard.

Gershator, D. (1998). *Bread is for eating.* New York: Henry Holt.

After reading the book, invite the children to go to the snack table. The teacher has provided a "tasting party" of different types of bread. Blunt table knives for spreading margarine and jelly are available for the children.

The teacher (with her teacher assistant) explains how she plans to let any child who wants to help with the cooking activity.

Purpose/Objectives of Activity

- To introduce the concepts that people all over the world eat bread and that bread comes in many different shapes, sizes, and colors
- To recognize that some families serve bread for various festivities and ceremonies
- To ask open-ended questions about the type of bread each child eats at home, such as: "Which is your favorite type of bread?" "Have you ever eaten corn bread?"
- To introduce children to different ingredients
- To provide opportunities for measuring, pouring, sifting, stirring, and baking
- To practice a cooking activity and to involve children in the process of doing, thinking, talking, and asking

Space and Materials Needed

Large low table, small chairs, mixing bowls, ingredients, measuring cup, measuring spoons, large spoon for stirring, muffin pan, paper muffin cup liners, oven tray, blunt plastic knives, margarine, jams, variety of breads to taste, recipe, and book to introduce activity

Procedure

1. At group time, read the book *Bread, Bread, Bread.*
2. Ask open-ended questions about the families shown in the photographs in the book, the children's families, what kind of bread they eat at home, and which is their favorite.
3. Children go to the large table for snack time. They taste all kinds of bread, margarine, and jam.
4. The teacher explains the activity choices for the day. Making corn bread muffins is one of the activities. Three children and the teacher will make the first batch. Later the teacher will make some more corn bread with another three children. The corn bread muffins will be the afternoon snack.
5. The children and the teacher wash their hands and the table, put on smocks, put out the cooking utensils and ingredients, and read the recipe together. (The teacher has printed the recipe on a large poster with both illustrations and words.)

CORN BREAD

(1) 1 cup flour	(5) ½ teaspoon salt
(2) 1 cup cornmeal	(6) 1 egg
(3) ¼ cup sugar	(7) 1 cup milk
(4) 4 teaspoons baking powder	(8) ¼ cup cooking oil

Sift together #1, 2, 3, 4, and 5. Add #6, 7, 8. Beat until smooth. Pour into a greased pan and bake for 20 minutes at 425 degrees.

Guidance

Anticipating what could occur, the teachers prepare to help children understand why they cannot taste the ingredients that are measured to go into the corn bread. There will be time when the muffins are cooking for them to taste the ingredients. (Put some ingredients aside for small tastes. Exclude the raw egg. Then, talk about pre- and post-baking.) Remind the children of safety factors when using utensils. Supervise closely. Provide sponges and soap and water for cleanup and child-size brooms for sweeping.

ACTIVITY PLAN WORKSHEET *continued*

Evaluation and Follow-Up

After this specific activity, the children participated with open-ended questions. One child talked about Yom Kippur and that her family is Jewish. That evening they would have a "feast" and eat *challah* bread, which was also one of the breads included in the tasting activity.

Extended activities might include:

■ Read other books about bread.
■ Take a field trip to a bakery or bagel shop.
■ Relate bread to nutrition and the food groups.
■ Bake other breads, such as *tortillas*.

CORN BREAD

Sift together:

One cup flour, one cup cornmeal,

¼ cup sugar, 4 teaspoons baking powder,

and ½ teaspoon salt.

Add one egg, one cup milk and

¼ cup cooking oil. Beat until smooth.

Pour into a greased pan and bake for 20 minutes at 425 degrees.

ACTIVITY PLAN WORKSHEET *continued*

TORTILLAS

2 cups masa
1 cup water

Mix together. Roll into 1-inch balls. Press very flat, using waxed paper to keep from sticking. Cook in a greased electric skillet at 350 degrees. Turn when you can "slip" a spatula under, and cook on the other side until done.

Tortillas

Mix these ingredients in a bowl:

Two cups masa and one cup water

Roll into 1 inch balls.

Press flat using waxed paper to keep from sticking.

Fry in a greased electric skillet at 350 degrees.

Turn when you can "slip" a spatula under and cook on the other side until done.

ACTIVITY PLAN WORKSHEET *continued*

DEVELOPMENTALLLY APPROPRIATE ACTIVITIES FOR YOUNG CHILDREN

Children's age group: Kindergarten

Name of Activity and Brief Description

Group time story, writing invitations, and making no-bake cookies

This is the book we will share:

de Regniers, B. S. (1999). *May I bring a friend?* Illustrated by Beni Montresor. New York: Atheneum.

This is an introduction for the theme "Friends and Families." After reading the book, continue discussing friends, the ones in the book as well as the friends in the class.

The teacher explains how during the week each child can write an invitation to his friend in the classroom to come to the party on Friday during afternoon snack time. Another activity will be to make cookies to share with their friends at the party.

Purpose/Objectives of Activity

- To introduce concepts that friends can be people or animals, and that friends are kind to each other
- To recognize that everyone can *be* a friend and *have* a friend at the same time
- To provide opportunities for cooperation, sharing, and kindness
- To practice math skill development: counting, measuring, number value, and quantity

Space and Materials Needed

Book to introduce the activity; various colored and textured papers; markers and crayons; pencils; scissors; paste; tape; rulers; large, low table; small chairs; mixing bowls; small plastic bags; rolling pins; cookie ingredients; and recipe

Procedure

1. At group time, read the book *May I Bring a Friend?*
2. Ask open-ended questions about the animals in the book. Do the children have any pets at home? What kind of animals do they like? What animals have they seen at the zoo?
3. Explain the activity choices for the day. Making invitations for the "friend party" on Friday is one of the activities, and this center will be open for two children at a time until Thursday afternoon.
4. On Friday morning, the children give the invitations to their friends. (The teacher has asked each child to make just one invitation without a name on it.) The teacher then puts all of the invitations in a sack, and the children close their eyes and reach in to select one. Part of the fun is to see if the children get their own invitation or one that someone else made.
5. The no-bake cookies will be an activity choice for Friday morning. Two children at a time will make no-bake cookies until everyone has made some. (The teacher has printed the recipe on a large poster with both illustrations and words.)
6. The children and the teacher wash their hands and the table, put on smocks, put out the cooking utensils and ingredients, and read the recipe together.

GRAHAM CRACKER NO-BAKE COOKIES

½ cup raisins
½ cup chopped dates
2 tablespoons honey
graham crackers

Let the children pour raisins, dates, and honey into a mixing bowl. Place several graham crackers in a plastic bag. Children can crush these with a rolling pin. Add to honey-fruit mixture until dry enough to roll into balls. Eat at snack time!

Guidance

By limiting the number of children at the writing table and having fewer at a time participating in the cookie making, the teacher has anticipated many of the problems that could occur. This is a time when the teacher can talk about sharing and taking turns with friends.

As with all cooking activities, provide sponges, soap, and water for cleanup.

ACTIVITY PLAN WORKSHEET *continued*

It is helpful to have the teacher assistant moving around the room to supervise the other learning activities. This will give the teacher an opportunity to have some special one-on-one time with the other children.

Evaluation and Follow-Up

Were all the objectives met? Extended activities might include:

■ Place the recipe poster in the writing center. This gives the children an opportunity to write out the recipe to take home.
■ Make fingerprint paintings. Children can look at their own and those of their friends. Use the magnifying glass to look at the fingerprints. Are they alike? Are they different? How?

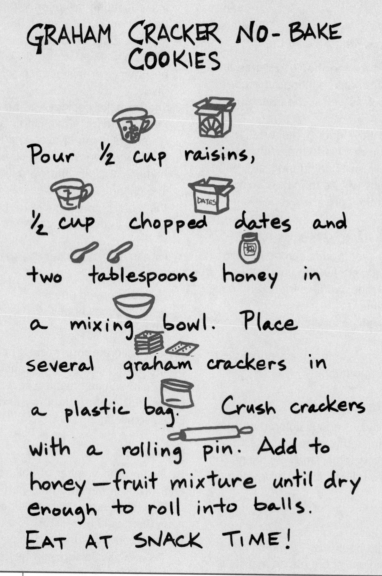

GRAHAM CRACKER NO-BAKE COOKIES

Pour ½ cup raisins, ½ cup chopped dates and two tablespoons honey in a mixing bowl. Place several graham crackers in a plastic bag. Crush crackers with a rolling pin. Add to honey—fruit mixture until dry enough to roll into balls. EAT AT SNACK TIME!

Figure 4–12 is the curriculum planning web worksheet with *literature* activities added. This worksheet with appropriate additions is included in each chapter.

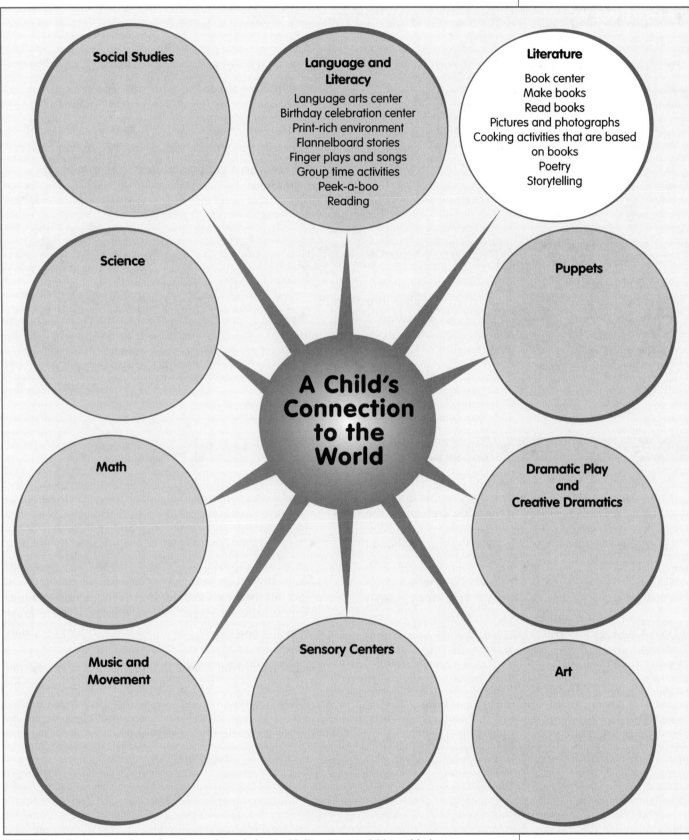

Social Studies

Language and Literacy

Language arts center
Birthday celebration center
Print-rich environment
Flannelboard stories
Finger plays and songs
Group time activities
Peek-a-boo
Reading

Literature

Book center
Make books
Read books
Pictures and photographs
Cooking activities that are based
on books
Poetry
Storytelling

Science

Puppets

A Child's Connection to the World

Math

Dramatic Play and Creative Dramatics

Music and Movement

Sensory Centers

Art

FIGURE 4–12 A curriculum planning web worksheet with literature activities added.

AFTERVIEW

Through books, a child

- Learns to listen to stories
- Develops imagination and creativity
- Gets new ideas and develops interests in many things
- Adds to previous experiences
- Learns more about the world and the people in it
- Increases attention span

- Increases vocabulary and language skills
- Develops the concept of print and the written word
- Begins to take responsibility for the care of books
- Enjoys quiet moments alone with his thoughts
- Develops a lifelong interest in literature and reading

KEY TERMS

alphabet books
beginning-to-read books
big books
board books
concept books
counting books
folk literature

interaction books
informational books
literature
Mother Goose and nursery
    rhyme books
multicultural books
picture books

poetry
predictable books
realistic literature
reference books
series books
teacher- and child-made books
wordless picture books

EXPLORATIONS

1. Read three children's books. List each book on a separate index card, and include bibliographic information and a brief summary of the book. Indicate if the book is appropriate for infants, toddlers, preschoolers, or primary-grade children, and the reasons for choosing the age you have stated. On the back of the card, list ways of extending the book for classroom use.

2. Create a book for young children. Read it to a small group of young children. Observe their responses. What age group did you select? Was your book developmentally appropriate for that age group? Explain your answer.

3. Select one of the books listed in this chapter and make a flannelboard story out of it. Share it with a child or a group of young children. What would you change? What worked well? Was it easier or more difficult than you expected?

4. Visit a library, an ethnic bookstore, or an early childhood classroom and observe during the time books or stories are being read or told to a group of children. Do the children focus visually on the storyteller? What questions do the children ask? Do they seem to understand the story? How can you tell? Does the story seem appropriate in content and vocabulary for young children? What kinds of things distract the children? What guidance techniques does the storyteller use in relating to inappropriate behavior?

5. Select a children's book that relates to a culture other than your own. Using the criteria discussed in this chapter, analyze the book for appropriateness. Would you read this book to your class of young children? Explain your reasons.

REFERENCES

Beaty, J. J. (1992). *Preschool appropriate practices.* Fort Worth, TX: Harcourt Brace Jovanovich College Publishers.

Bredekamp, S., & Copple, C. (Eds.). (1997). *Developmentally appropriate practice in early childhood programs.* Washington, DC: National Association for the Education of Young Children.

Finazzo, D. A. (1997). *All for the children: Multicultural essentials of literature.* Albany, NY: Delmar.

Glazer, J. I. (1991). *Literature for young children* (3rd ed.). New York: Merrill/Macmillan.

Hillman, J. (1999). *Discovering children's literature* (2nd. ed.). Columbus, OH: Merrill.

Huck, C. S., Hepler, S., & Hickman, J. (1993). *Children's literature in the elementary school* (5th ed.). Fort Worth, TX: Harcourt Brace Jovanovich College Publishers.

Jalongo, M. R. (1988). *Young children and picture books.* Washington, DC: National Association for the Education of Young Children.

Machado, J. (1999). *Early childhood language arts* (6th ed.). Albany, NY: Delmar.

Raines, S., & Isbell, R. (1994). *Stories—Children's literature in early education.* Albany, NY: Delmar.

Sawyer, W. E. (2000). *Growing up with literature* (3rd ed.). Albany, NY: Delmar.

Sawyer, W. E., & Sawyer, J. C. (1993). *Integrated language arts for emerging literacy.* Albany, NY: Delmar.

Schickendanz, J. A. (1999). *Much more than the ABCs: The early stages of reading and writing.* Washington, DC: National Association for the Education of Young Children.

Schnedler, M. (1994, August 14). Finding new ways to spin old yarns. *Dallas Morning News.*

Spann, M. B. (1997). *30 collaborative books for your class to make and share.* New York: Scholastic.

Strickland, D. S., & Morrow, L. M. (Eds). (1989). *Emerging literacy: Young children learn to read and write.* Newark, DE: International Reading Association.

Thomas, M. (1998). *Free to be . . . you and me.* New York: McGraw-Hill.

Webster's new world college dictionary (3rd ed.). (1989). New York: Simon & Schuster.

ADDITIONAL READINGS AND RESOURCES

Cornell, C. E. (1993, September). Language and culture monsters that lurk in our traditional rhymes and folktales. *Young Children, 48*(6), 40–46.

Davidson, J. I. (1996). *Emergent literacy and dramatic play in early education.* Albany, NY: Delmar.

Derman-Sparks, L. (1989). *Anti-bias curriculum.* Washington, DC: National Association for the Education of Young Children.

Eliason, C., & Jenkins, L. (1999). *A practical guide to early childhood curriculum* (6th ed.). New York: Merrill/Macmillan.

Fielding, L. G., & Pearson, D. P. (1994, February). Reading comprehension: What works. *Educational Leadership, 51*(5), 62–68.

Gottschall, S. M. (1995, May). Hug-a-book: A program to nurture a young child's love of books and reading. *Young Children, 50*(4), 29–35.

Gross, A. L., & Ortiz, L. W. (1994, March). Using children's literature to facilitate inclusion in kindergarten and the primary grades. *Young Children, 49*(3), 32–35.

Harris, V. J. (1991, January). Multicultural curriculum: African American children's literature. *Young Children, 46*(2), 37–44.

Hurst, C. O. (1994, August/September). Family ties in kid's books. *Teaching PreK–8, 25*(1), 134–136, 138.

Kupetz, B. N., & Green, E. J. (1997, January). Sharing books with infants and toddlers: Facing the challenges. *Young Children, 52*(2), 22–27.

Power, B. (1998, February). Author! Author! *Early Childhood Today, 12*(5), 30–37.

Raines, S. C., & Canady, R. J. (1989). *Story S-T-R-E-T-C-H-E-R-S.* Mt. Rainier, MD: Gryphon House.

Vaughn, S., & Rothlein, L. (1994). *Read it again!* Glenview, IL: GoodYear Books/Scott Foresman.

Puppets

■ OVERVIEW

Puppets can teach, entertain, and delight children and adults. Historically, puppetry has been described as a folk art, one produced by and for the people. Puppets have been around for thousands of years and are found virtually everywhere in the world, embedded in every continent and culture.

Raines and Isbell (1994) tell us:

> *Storytelling and puppetry are ancient forms of oral expression that developed historically in similar ways. The story told was passed from generation to generation and became a binding link for families and cultures. The puppeteer often augmented the storytelling by providing visualization and surprise elements to the story's presentation.*

■ HISTORICAL VIEW OF PUPPETRY

No one knows for sure when the art of **puppetry** began. Were the first puppeteers primitive people casting shadows on darkened cave walls? Were the early priests and shamans who used puppets to celebrate important life cycle events some of the first puppeteers? Did the Egyptians invent the first puppet, as some historians have suggested? According to the Center for Puppetry Arts in Atlanta, Georgia, written documentation of puppetry's beginnings can be traced back to Asia where it developed simultaneously in India and China in the ninth century B.C. In Indonesia, flat, leather shadow puppets and three-dimensional rod puppets, introduced centuries ago, are still used in performances today.

> *Vietnam is famous for its unique tradition of water puppetry which combines both rod and strings to manipulate the figures. The performance appears in a lake. The puppeteers are hidden in a structure resembling a Vietnamese communal house built in the middle of the lake. The puppets are attached to long bamboo rods and strings. When the audience views the show they see puppets acting on a watery stage with the puppeteer's house in the background. (Center for Puppetry Arts, 1994)*

Puppetry also has roots in Africa, dating back to the fifth century B.C. Puppet pageants are still performed there for the entire community to celebrate important events, such as planting and harvest time.

In Japan, *Bunraku* originated in the sixteenth century. This is a highly refined form of rod puppetry, using three puppeteers to perform a single character. One controls the head and one arm; another, the second arm; and the third, the feet. The puppeteers usually dress in black, are visible behind each puppet, and possess great skill and coordination (Center for Puppetry Arts, 1994; Henson, 1994).

Hand puppets began appearing in Europe and colonial America in the mid-1700s. The English Punch and Judy, the most popular characters, were descendants of an Italian puppet named Pulcinella. Punch and Judy appeared in marketplaces, at community fairs, on the street, in town halls, at circuses, and in schools. Similar puppets, with different names, were also performing in Germany, France, Russia, and Turkey.

The *Mamulengo* tradition in puppetry can be found in South America. These puppeteers fuse the folk traditions of native populations and black culture, as well as draw from colonial Hispanic and Portugese influences when they present street puppet theater (Center for Puppetry Arts, 1994).

As you continue through this chapter, you will find ways for you and the children to create, enjoy, and develop skills by using this ancient form of folk art. You will find that the use of puppetry can enrich all the curriculum areas in your early education program. Most importantly, a child's positive self-esteem can be enhanced by using a puppet to mirror feelings, creativity, and learning processes. A child's connection to the world can be exciting when puppets are used.

■ PLANNING FOR PUPPETS IN EARLY EDUCATION

What exactly is a puppet? Cheryl Henson (1994), daughter of the late Jim Henson (puppeteer who created the Muppets), explains, "A puppet is an object that appears to be alive when it's manipulated by a human hand. Some puppets look like dolls; others look like stuffed animals. Still others look like pieces of sculpture or even like piles of junk!"

For children in an early education program, a puppet is *whatever they say it is!* For young children, the discovery of themselves as puppeteers can be a wonderful discovery of themselves. Their excitement, enthusiasm, and imagination in creating and sharing puppets will become contagious to others, adults and children alike.

You and the children, together, should plan for and decide when and how to use puppets in your classroom. Here are some suggestions for getting started:

■ Begin by selecting a puppet for you, the teacher. Your first puppet, either one created by you or a ready-made commercial one, should become your special friend. Usually a hand puppet is the most comfortable; the more you use it, the more it fits like an old, favorite glove.

■ Identify why this particular puppet appeals to you. Does it remind you of a toy, doll, or puppet you had as a child? This discovery will help you decide on the puppet's name, personality, and voice. Remember, you do *not* have to be a ventriloquist.

■ Practice with your puppet. Watching yourself in the mirror might be useful in helping you decide how to use the puppet.

■ You do not need to use a stage or puppet theater. The personal interaction with a child or group of children is important.

■ Reinforce your own creativity and enjoyment of teaching. Let the puppet do for you what it does for a child: allow your imagination to flourish; your creative play to flow free; and your unique thoughts, feelings, and language to emerge.

■ Use puppets on a regular basis. As with any new or special materials you bring into the classroom or playground, demonstrate the appropriate use of the puppets.

■ Depending on the age of the children you teach, decide how often and how much you will use puppets. Usually, the younger the child, the more time you should take to make him feel comfortable with and trusting of the puppets. As with any toy or activity, use only safe materials.

■ For infants, having familiar stuffed toys and animals "talk to them" is a way of introducing puppets. Another way is to "walk" two of your fingers up a child's arm. Use a rhythmic, sing-song voice and say: "Here comes a little person walking up (child's name) arm. Now it's on your shoulder. Now it's on your neck. Tickle, tickle."

■ Take lots of time with toddlers. Start with finger plays and hand puppets. Leaving plenty of space between the puppet and the child usually helps this age child feel more comfortable.

■ Use puppets with your favorite finger plays, poems, songs, books, and flannelboard stories. Group time is a good opportunity to introduce puppets. When telling a familiar story, allow the children to hear the story several times. The retelling of the story allows you and the children to manipulate the puppets in a familiar setting. Children will eventually tell the story spontaneously and expand it in their own way *using puppets.*

The introduction of the puppet activities can be done in three stages:

1. Model the use of puppets during group time and in many curriculum areas. By doing this, you, as the teacher, affirm the use of puppets. By demonstrating *nonvio-*

lent behavior with puppets, you are showing the children how to enjoy them appropriately. Introduce them one at a time. As with any new activity, doing too much at one time can overstimulate the children.

2. You and the children should create and use puppets together. Allow children plenty of opportunities to practice with a variety of puppets before they begin to create their own. The guidance techniques you use will demonstrate additional and appropriate ways to enjoy puppets. Keep puppet construction, props, and stages very simple. Allow children to improvise, using their own creativity.

3. Let individual children or a group of children make and interact with puppets through activities integrated into the lesson plan and the total curriculum. The activities should be open-ended and allow children opportunities to extend the activities. Remember to make puppets accessible to children and give them time to explore with them. Provide the materials, but remember *not* to make a model for the children to copy. (The illustrations in this chapter and those in Appendix A are designed to give teachers *ideas* for making puppets, *not* to be used as models for the children to make.)

Setting Up the Environment

By introducing children to different types of puppets, you can offer alternative learning experiences. These wonderful creations can tell a story, carry on a conversation, be a good listener, and entertain. While handling materials, manipulating, and organizing them, the *process*, as always, is the major focus.

> *When adults realize the most important aspect of creativity is the process, not the product, they will support the child's desire to experiment and create in individual ways. They will understand that the thing "made" is not nearly so important as what is happening in the process. (Fortson & Reiff, 1995)*

Young children can explore and stretch their abilities in all developmental areas through the process of creating and operating their puppets. They are:

- Experiencing the sheer joy of playing and fantasizing
- Developing positive self-images and independence
- Using a safe and acceptable outlet for expressing themselves
- Expanding vocabulary and communication skills
- Improving social skills by sharing and cooperating and communicating ideas
- Learning problem-solving skills and abstract thinking
- Using fine motor skills
- Practicing hand-eye coordination, hand-hand coordination, and muscle control

■ EASY-TO-MAKE PUPPETS

There are three basic categories of puppets: hand puppets, marionettes, and rod puppets.

Hand Puppets

Hand puppets come in many types and varieties, and are easy for young children to make and manipulate. Starting with finger puppets, the child gains ownership right away. It is fun to put two eyes, a nose, and a mouth on the child's thumb and fingers with a felt-tip pen. You will find some children do not want to wash their fingers after this activity. They like their puppets and want to keep them (see Figure 5–1).

FIGURE 5–1 Examples of finger puppets that are appropriate for young children.

Another kind of simple finger puppet can be made out of felt. Glue the two pieces together (as shown in the three-step illustration of Figure 5–2). Place eyes, a nose, and a mouth on the puppet. These can be easily manipulated by younger children and offer an unusual small muscle activity.

Other finger puppets can be made easily to illustrate shapes, numbers, nursery rhymes, or other concepts. You can first introduce them at group time, then put them in the manipulative center for the children to play with. By placing two fingers in one of these, the child can add "legs" to make the puppet walk and dance. (See the three-step illustration in Figure 5–3.)

Basic hand, glove, and mitt puppets provide a close link between the puppet and the puppeteer. Toddlers, especially, enjoy this type of puppet. There are many commerically made examples, but the ones the teacher and children make are the most fun.

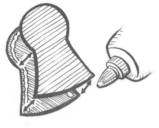

STEP 1: Cut 2 finger puppet shapes out of felt (see Appendix A).

STEP 2: Glue the 2 shapes together along outside edges. Be sure to leave bottom open for finger.

STEP 3: Decorate with marker, glitter, cut shapes of felt, etc.

FIGURE 5–2 Example of how to make finger puppets out of felt fabric.

STEP 1: Cut puppet figure out of cardboard or paper (see Appendix A).

STEP 2: Decorate with markers, paints, crayons, glitter, buttons, cut shapes of fabric, etc,

STEP 3: Play!

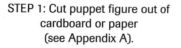

FIGURE 5–3 Example of how to make finger puppets out of cardboard.

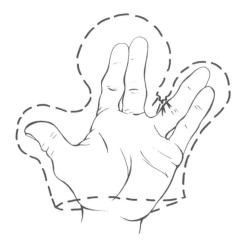

FIGURE 5–4 Placement of the hand in a hand puppet.

FIGURE 5–5 Example of a completed hand puppet.

Figures 5–4 and 5–5 illustrate the easy-to-make basic design. The hand can be the whole body, with two fingers as the arms and one finger operating the head. This hand puppet can be made easily from two pieces of felt or other fabric glued or sewn together and cut to fit a child's or an adult's hand. Eyes, nose, mouth, ears, hands, and hair can be attached with Velcro, glued, or sewn to the fabric. Felt squares of tan, beige, cream, brown, peach, and black can be used so a child can make a puppet that has his or her skin tone. (See Appendix A for basic patterns.)

Rubber household gloves, which have a smooth surface, and garden gloves, which are available in many colors and designs, can be used to make another kind of hand puppet. This variety allows you to move all five fingers, independently as separate characters or together to make a creature, such as a "creepy crawler." Use double-stick tape on the rubber glove or sew small pieces of Velcro to the fingertips of the garden glove. Place the same kind of material on matching story pieces. This gives you and the children flexibility in creating hand puppets (see Figures 5–6 and 5–7).

FIGURE 5–6 Example of a rubber glove puppet with finger characters.

FIGURE 5–7 Example of a "Creepy Crawler" puppet made from a glove.

Ready-made mittens or household hot pad mitts can also be used to create another variety of hand puppets. Commercially crocheted puppets, usually representing animals, and sets of puppets are also available. Evaluate these carefully to be sure they are safe and appropriate for use with young children.

Think of all the finger plays, poems, songs, and stories you and the children can share with each other using sock puppets. These are probably the easiest puppets to make and use. Ask parents to donate unneeded children's socks in all sizes and colors. Once a child puts the sock on his hand, the puppet will "come to life." Add eyes made from buttons, commercial wiggly eyes, or anything you wish. Hair, made from yarn, string, steel wool, or cotton balls, and ears give extra personality to the character (see Figures 5–8 and 5–9).

Paper plate and paper bag puppets are some of the most fun to make and use. They are inexpensive, children can create more than one, and they are easily remade if they get torn. You and the children will design many kinds of paper puppets, but to get you started, a few examples follow.

Staple two paper plates together, leaving the bottom portion open for the puppeteer's hand. (You will find thin plates are easy for the children to handle.) Decorate this puppet, and it is ready to use!

A more complex type of puppet can be made by folding one paper plate in half and cutting another in half. Staple one of the cut halves to the back of the folded plate, leaving the bottom part open. Repeat this with the other half. The puppeteer's hand fits into the open part—fingers in the top, thumb in the bottom (Figure 5–10). This puppet can become any character. Add a construction paper body to give it a more complete look.

For a paper bag, floppy-mouth puppet, use a small- or medium-sized bag. Draw a puppet face on the bag or cut and glue one from a magazine. Use crayons, markers, paints, glue, yarn, cotton balls, or other material to finish the puppet. It is easy to work by placing your fingers inside the flap of the bag and moving them up and down.

Other paper puppets can be made from products such as paper cups or pudding, oatmeal, or small cereal boxes. Add these to the other creative materials in your puppet center for the children's exploration and experimentation.

FIGURE 5–8 The hand position for a sock puppet.

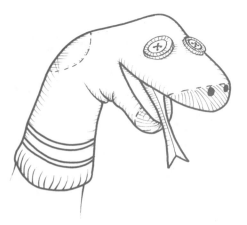

FIGURE 5–9 Example of a sock puppet.

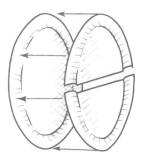

STEP 1: Staple two halves of a paper plate to a whole one.

STEP 2: Fold uncut plate in half and decorate face and mouth.

STEP 3: Add hair, ears, body, etc.

FIGURE 5–10 Making a paper plate puppet.

Stick or Rod Puppets

Stick or rod puppets are controlled by a single stick, such as a tongue depressor, dowel rod, paper towel roll, craft stick, or ice cream stick. An even smaller character might be placed on a paper straw. The figure itself can be cut from magazines, catalogs, and wrapping paper; traced from a pattern; or drawn by hand. Then it is glued to the stick or straw. Many card shops or toy stores have paper plates in the shape of animals. These make wonderful puppets when stapled to a dowel rod. These can be reinforced with tagboard and covered with contact paper or laminated.

A wooden spoon makes another delightful puppet. The bowl of the spoon makes a perfect head, and the handle becomes the body. Use felt-tip markers, crayons, or paint to make the face.

The "people puppet" (Figure 5–11) is made out of cardboard or tagboard and then attached to a stick or dowel rod. Encourage children to add eyes, a nose, a mouth, hair, clothes, and shoes. Multicultural or skin-toned paints, crayons, and construction paper should be available for the children to use. This promotes self-awareness and positive self-esteem. Another variation of the people puppet is one depicting a face

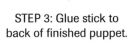

STEP 1: Cut out people puppet shape from cardboard (See Appendix A).

STEP 2: Decorate with paint markers, crayons, cut shapes of paper, fabric, etc.

STEP 3: Glue stick to back of finished puppet.

FIGURE 5–11 Making a stick people puppet.

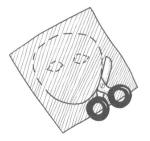

STEP 1: Cut face shapes from cardboard or paper (see Appendix A).

STEP 2: Decorate with paint markers, crayons, cut shapes of paper, fabric, etc.

STEP 3: Glue stick to back of decorated face shape.

STEP 4: Let it dry and then play!

FIGURE 5–12 Making a people mask puppet.

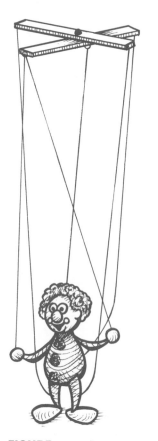

FIGURE 5–13 Example of a marionette.

(Figure 5–12). The children can cut out the eyes, then add a nose, a mouth, and hair. Attach a straw or craft stick to create a stick puppet or a mask.

Make a paper plate and stick puppet combination. Staple or glue a paper plate—any size—onto a stick, such as a tongue depressor, craft stick, or dowel rod. Put a happy, tearful, angry, or other emotional face on the puppet. You could make enough of these to create a family of paper plate puppets, human or animal; the children will know what to do.

Marionettes

Marionettes, controlled by strings, offer an extra range of expression and full body movement. As teachers, we should appreciate the sophisticated skills needed to make and operate a marionette. In encouraging a school-ager who wants to make this type of puppet, the first question asked should be, "What do you want it to do?" It is important to think through and plan each step in the creation of a marionette. The "airplane control" is the simplest design to manipulate, usually with one string to the head and a string to each of the hands (Figure 5–13). Children need time to experiment and to experience the frustration of the puppet not working the first time it is tried. It is important to support them through the frustration. The failure and success of making and manipulating a marionette is part of their *process*. Maintenance and care of the marionette is also part of the experience. To avoid tangling the strings, it should be hung after it is used. Hanging marionettes make a distinctive classroom decoration.

Other Types of Puppets

Shadow puppets offer a visual dimension to puppetry that other types do not. Shown in a darkened room, they are held from below by rods against a translucent screen lit from behind. Puppeteers manipulate flat, cut-out silhouettes that the audience can see on the other side of the screen as moving figures. One of the simplest shadow animal puppets, a flying bird, is described by Cheryl Henson (1994):

All you need is a single light source—a standing lamp with the shade removed or a desk lamp tilted to the side. Interlock your thumbs and slowly flap your hands. When you pass them between the light source and a blank wall, the shadow they cast will look like a bird in flight.

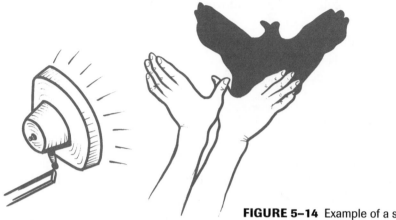

FIGURE 5–14 Example of a shadow hand puppet.

Progression from this simple example to more complex shadow puppets will occur as older children discover creative ways to investigate and make these puppets (Figure 5–14).

Papier mâché-headed puppets are made with strips of newspaper soaked in a thick flour-and-water paste placed over a balloon, molded piece of clay, or Nerf ball. After drying, the "head" is cut in half to remove the clay or ball. Then the halves are glued back together. Paint facial features to create the puppet character. Make the neck long enough to hold fabric, which becomes the body of the puppet (Figure 5–15).

STEP 1: Cover ball in paper strips soaked in flour paste.

STEP 2: When dry, cut in half to remove ball. Then glue halves together.

STEP 3: Cut a hole for finger, decorate, make a body and attach to head.

FIGURE 5–15 Making a papier mâché puppet.

■ MATERIALS NEEDED

All of the various types of puppets can be made from a wide variety of materials. (Puppet patterns for teachers can be found in Appendix A.) An easy way to collect these is to place a box in the classroom simply labeled, "Materials for Puppet Making." This keeps it visible for parents and children while reminding them that all kinds of things are needed. The following is a list of what needs to be gathered:

Boxes—especially small cereal and salt boxes

Buttons and wiggly eyes—especially the larger ones

Clothespins

Cloth scraps—felt, lace, cotton, towels, and washcloths in tan, beige, cream, brown, peach, and black

Cotton balls, steel wool, sponges, pipe cleaners, corks, hair curlers

Crayons, markers, pencils, pens, paints

Egg cartons

Feathers

Gloves—cloth, garden-type, and rubber

Leather scraps

Magazines, catalogs, and newspapers

Office supplies—scissors, envelopes, paper clips, glue, brads, rubber bands, gummed labels and stickers, stapler and staples, and rulers

Paper products—cardboard; sandpaper; all sizes of paper bags, plates, and cups; towel and toilet paper rolls; crepe paper; wrapping paper; tissue paper; wall paper; wax paper; foil; straws; and construction paper in all colors representing skin tones, including tan, beige, cream, brown, black, and peach

Socks—especially those that will fit a child's hand and soccer socks for making adult-size puppets

Spools

Sticks—tongue depressors, ice cream sticks, craft sticks, yardsticks, toothpicks, and dowel rods

Styrofoam balls and scraps

Tape—clear, masking, and double-stick types

Wood scraps—preferably already sanded smooth

Wooden spoons

Yarn, string, ribbons, and shoelaces

■ SUGGESTIONS FOR PLACEMENT AND STORAGE OF PUPPETS

Whether you offer a puppet center or puppets in every center, make it possible for the children to select and interact with any puppet they want to make or play with. The children should feel the freedom to move the puppets to another location to best meet their needs. Children are more likely to use puppets if the guidelines for use are clearly explained and if the puppets and puppet materials are organized and displayed attractively and accessibly.

At first, some children prefer just to examine the puppets and try them on to see how they feel. Others enjoy making puppets, and still others just like to play with ready-made puppets. Allow for individual and developmental preferences.

For the creative and spontaneous use of puppets, a stage is not necessary. As mentioned earlier, you, as a teacher, do not need to use a stage, and neither do the children. If you feel you need a creative boost, Hunt and Renfro (1982) suggest a story apron.

This is an ideal costume for you to wear as a puppeteller. It signals that Puppetime is about to begin, it provides a background for your story, poem, or song and it hides puppets and props until you are ready to use them. . . . A general all-purpose story apron can be made by adding pockets to a storebought apron or by creating your own custom apron from selected fabric.

If the children insist on needing a stage for their puppets, here are some easy ways to provide one:

■ Construct a puppet stage from a large packing carton. Cut the center out of the box to form a "stage opening."
■ Drape a cloth over a piece of rope.
■ Turn a small, sturdy table on its side so the children can "hide" behind it and show only the puppets, or use a table top draped in front with a sheet.
■ Using a shower curtain rod, hang a piece of fabric low across an open doorway.
■ Place two adult-sized chairs back to back at a short distance. Drop a curtain or cloth over a yardstick placed between the chairs.
■ Use a "gutted TV" (a television set from which the insides have been removed). This offers another dimension to a child's puppet play.

The following suggestions for the storage of puppets are utilized by many teachers and suggested by Hunt and Renfro (1982), Raines and Isbell (1994), and the author's personal preference:

■ Hang a clothesline along a wall at child's eye and arm level, and use clothespins to clip the puppets to the line.
■ Place the puppets on an accordion clothes rack.
■ Clip the puppets to a multiple-skirt hanger.
■ Store finger puppets and stick puppets in egg cartons or plastic bags.
■ Store puppets in tiered hanging baskets.
■ Use a shoe bag or shoe rack to organize puppets.
■ Place shoe boxes or clear plastic boxes on low shelves.
■ Store puppets in a toybox or chest.

A child might like to make a home for his or her very special puppet. Select a box into which the puppet will fit. Have the child decorate the box any way she chooses, including adding windows and a door. A scrap of soft material inside the box makes a bed for the puppet friend. The box can be placed in or near the child's cubbie.

■ CONNECTING PUPPETS TO CURRICULUM AREAS

It is helpful to brainstorm ideas with colleagues and classmates, but here are a few suggestions to stimulate your creativity:

- Puppets can speak in any language. This shows that all languages are valued. For example, Mister Number is a puppet that can count from one to twenty in many languages. Another puppet only says "yes and no" or "hello and goodbye," but does so in ten different languages. The puppet may speak only the language of the child talking or the child being spoken to. Multicultural puppets can also be used to introduce cultural celebrations.

- Expand the language arts center by adding puppets and props. A puppet with a microphone can encourage creative play. Puppets can even interview other puppets. Because the characters can be human, animal, or "Mr. and Ms. Anything," the questions asked can be about families, feelings, favorite foods, where you come from, or where you live. For older children, the questions can also concern current events, nutrition, math, science, or ecology.

- Encourage storytelling with sock puppets representing *The Billy Goats Gruff, The Little Red Hen*, or characters from *Winnie the Pooh* and *The Velveteen Rabbit*. Use finger puppets or hand puppets to read the story books *Corduroy, Leo the Late Bloomer*, or *Horton Hatches the Egg*. Relating puppets to familiar stories can extend the retelling.

- Add a puppet holding a toy telephone to the dramatic play center. This presents an additional dimension to telephone talk.

- A puppet "helper of the day" can offer you a unique way to reinforce cooperation, cleanup rules, and problem solving. The puppet can ask the children questions, leading *them* to solve the existing problem instead of the teacher. This puppet character can help defuse many disputes and difficulties that occur in an early childhood setting.

- Introducing a "listening puppet," one with big ears, can help you emphasize the importance of listening. One puppet might only talk to or answer children in song or verse. Perhaps another only dances. A very shy puppet who will not talk can learn to do so with help from the children.

- Create some puppets for outdoor play. Have all types of clothing available for these puppet personalities. The children can select the appropriate clothes for the weather that day.

■ PUPPETS AND TELEVISION

Since the beginning of television, puppets have been a part of the daily viewing schedule. Local television stations usually began their day of live broadcasting with programs that featured puppets.

In the United States, six great puppeteers introduced their creations to children who had never before seen puppets. They are:

- Edgar Bergen (1903–1978)—a ventriloquist, who entertained children and their parents with his wooden partners, Charlie McCarthy and Mortimer Snerd, on radio, stage, and television.

- Bil Baird (1904–1987)—puppeteered marionettes for over sixty years and created more than 3,000 puppets seen on stage, television, and film.

- "Buffalo Bob" Smith (1917–1998)—"Hey kids, what time is it?" "It's *Howdy Doody* time!" Hundreds of children, in the studio and at home, answered the question from 1947–1960 when "Buffalo Bob" and his marionette Howdy Doody, real-life but nontalking clown, Clarabell, and their friends entertained children during the early days of live television.

(text continues on p. 137)

© 1997 Jim Henson/Sesame Street Productions

For thirty-one years, and counting, *Sesame Street* has entertained and educated young children and their families. One of the most delightful and favorite puppet characters on television is Big Bird. Caroll Spinney is the talented and thoughtful puppeteer who, along with Jim Henson, gave birth to Big Bird and Oscar the Grouch. Spinney continues to give life to these two very special puppet individuals. The following is a conversation between the author (HJ), Caroll Spinney (CS), and Big Bird (BB).

HJ Why do you think puppets have become so successful for children's television?

CS There has been a change in the way puppets have been perceived. Jim Henson and his approach to puppets on television—this really isn't biased when I say it—was such a change. It just seems natural now. How else would you do it? Up to 1969 you couldn't sell puppets on television. It was cartoons and cartoons. TV saw puppets as "silly little things." Jim's approach was something that was more alive and more exciting. It succeeded in overwhelming cartooning. Cartoons are now enjoying the best age they've ever had. Every time you see puppets on TV now, they all look like something Jim made.

HJ Why do you think children respond so well to puppets, especially on TV? What is it about puppets that is better than cartoons?

CS My experience with "The Bird" is that he seems to live, talk, and include in his life those who are watching. Cartoons are celluloid. They don't relate to you. They have their own life and you just observe.
    The Muppets on *Sesame Street* "stroke the camera" all the time. The children all feel they're involved. It's something you can't do with cartoons, and if they do it, it's not spontaneous. We have the advantage with television and its immediacy. The puppets communicate more directly. Children identify with us. After thirty-one years, I still admire *Sesame Street.*

HJ Why do you think Oscar the Grouch has been so successful? Why do you think showing his kind of personality through a puppet instead of through a person makes it more appealing to you?

CS That's a good question, because I've always said I wouldn't walk across the street to talk to a "creep" like Oscar the Grouch. I'm amazed that I can play a character like that, because I'm appalled at things he says. I've even talked to the producers of *Sesame Street* and told them that he's rude. I asked what is he teaching? I've decided he's not evil, he does have a heart. Oscar is really a grouch, but he's moral. We are trying to teach. I sometimes act like a censor or critic. I edit Oscar myself, it's instinctual. Perhaps it's a lot like teaching.

HJ What makes Big Bird different? Why is he so loved and respected?

CS He doesn't change. He's constant. It's his longevity. Big Bird is like a "teddy bear." He's a compassionate kid, as human as anyone on the show.

With *Sesame Street* there are elements of entertainment and teaching at the same time. We show the children that there's something worth looking at. We're not annoying. *Sesame Street* is a counterforce until the children are about seven years old. We're together until then.

HJ Why do you think puppets are important in early childhood education? What can teachers do to introduce children to puppets?

CS Introduce children to a good group of "live" puppeteers. Have them visit the classroom. It becomes more personal. Puppeteers of America [is] a good resource. [There are regional and community groups in most areas.]

Teachers should try puppets themselves. Give life to each puppet. There is a power of puppets to teach, to explore, and [to] learn. Have fun with puppets! Use puppets to get the children's attention. Have lots of puppets available. If I had been a teacher I would have had to use them all the time. Puppets give adults another way to relate to children. You can teach real humanity.

HJ Now, I'd like for Big Bird to talk to the teachers. This is a question for you. You went to bird preschool, didn't you?

BB Yes, I was with a bunch of sparrows.

HJ What were some of your favorite things when you were in preschool?

BB I built towers with blocks. Teacher had a big, yellow and white box full of wooden musical instruments like clackers and we asked the teacher when we could play with them. She always said "by-and-by," and we never did. I never did trust "by-and-by" as an answer anymore. The afternoon children she liked much better. They got to play with the instruments. It wasn't easy being only 3½ years old and 5 feet 11 inches. Now I'm 6 years old and 8 feet 2 inches tall.

HJ If you could talk to the teachers, what would you tell them to teach the children?

BB I remember asking Gordon, on *Sesame Street,* because he is very wise. He's a teacher. I asked him why did he do that. He said, "It's important to raise the children in the way they should go." Wouldn't it be smart to teach 'em about the good, nice stuff, not just about the bad stuff?

HJ Why do you think it's important to go to school and meet friends?

BB Because friends are important. They're the ones who make up the rest of the world besides me.

HJ Anything else you'd like to say?

BB Yes. When I grow up, I'm going to be a Professor-Bird.

HJ Thank you both so much. I've enjoyed being on *Sesame Street* and visiting with you.

© 1994 Richard Termine/Children's Television Workshop

Sesame Street has been broadcast in more than 140 countries around the world. Some countries air the original American show, while others create new versions in their own languages (Borgenicht, 1998). For example, in 1998 the Israeli/Palestinian co-production Rechov Sumsum/Shara's Simsim began and China introduced Hu Hu Zhu. The children in Mexico enjoy Plaza Sesamo.

The charming Carmen Osbahr, who previously performed on Plaza Sesamo, is the puppeteer who gives voice and personality to Rosita on Sesame Street. Rosita, a delightful turquoise Muppet, speaks both English and Spanish, her native language. She's the first bilingual Muppet to ever appear on Sesame Street. The following is a conversation between the author (HJ), Carmen Osbahr (CO), and Rosita (R) when we met on Sesame Street.

HJ   Carmen, why do you think puppets are so successful for children's television?

CO   I grew up with puppets and television, Sesame Street–Plaza Sesamo. I think puppets have always been fun for children and grown-ups. With the introduction of puppets on television you are able to reach more people. Speaking as a puppeteer, you can be everything you want to be, go everywhere, and take the children watching along with you.

HJ   You mentioned that you were always interested in puppets. What were the puppets in Mexico?

CO   My parents used to take me to live shows. In kindergarten I remember my teachers, on Fridays at lunch, used to have these little theaters with puppets and little sets to go with the stories they told. I remember Capervsita Roja (Little Red Riding Hood) and La Bella Durmiente (Sleeping Beauty). They were very simple, little "guignol" hand puppets. I think simple is best. I remember they changed the costumes with a little color and added different backgrounds. The teachers had fun too. I was just fascinated. Puppets were always around my life. I was 10 or 11 years old when Plaza Sesamo began. I was amazed.

HJ   Did you make puppets? When did you get started?

CO   I probably started in kindergarten. I remember doing the sock with the eyes glued on and making the puppet with the little ball head where we created our own little face. I'd go home and try to do more by myself.

HJ Well, here's Rosita. Hi, Rosita.

R HI! (Rosita uses a very big voice.)

HJ Do you mind if I ask you some questions?

R OKAY!

HJ How old are you?

R One, two, like this (holds up fingers). One, two, three, four, five, SIX! I just turned SIX! Uno, dos, tres, quatro, cinco, seis. I'm a 6-year-old little monster. My whole name is Rosita, La Monstrua de las Cuevas—Rosita, the monster of the caves. See my wings? I can't fly, I don't know why I have them. I have my mommy, my daddy, my uncle Tito, my aunt Lola, and my cousin. I asked why do we all have wings and they don't know why because none of us can fly.

HJ It's part of who you are.

R YEAH! YEAH! (in a very big voice)

HJ Do you go to school?

R Yes, I do. I play. I have my friends. I run around, I sing a lot, and I learn my ABCs. I know how to count and I know all the colors, and I love my teacher, and that's it.

HJ Do you help teach the other children about all those things in Spanish?

R Yes, the ones that are curious, you know, but yeah, they like Mexican food, so I have to explain that that's an enchilada, and that's the mole, and of course to count in Spanish. Everybody knows how to count in Spanish.

HJ Do you think you'll be a teacher when you grow up?

R I never thought about it. Yeah, I will teach Spanish.

HJ I think you'll be very good and you love to hug children . . .

R Everybody, I love to hug everybody. I like to hug you.

HJ Muchos gracias. How do you say my name Hilda in Spanish?

R "Ilda" (whispering). In Spanish the H is silent. "Ilda." I want to sing to you. My song is *Sing to the Sun.*
    Solecito que temprano,
    Siempre me llenas de alegria y calor mi vida.
In English, I said:
    The sun that comes out really early in the morning
    Always brings me happiness and warms my life.
There's about 200 verses, but I only know one. Well, I'm going to go play with my dolly, so I'll be around. 'Bye.

HJ	Good-bye, Rosita. I really enjoyed talking to you. Thank you again for the hug.
R	Mucho gracias. That means thank you!
HJ	Mucho gracias. Thank you.
R	No, thank you.
HJ	Let me know if you ever fly.
R	OKAY! I'll have my mommy send you an e-mail.
HJ	And mucho gracias to you too, Carmen.

- Burr Tillstrom (1917–1985)—best known during the 1950s on television for his hand puppets Kukla and Ollie, along with Fran, a real human being who stood in front of the stage and interacted with the puppets.
- Jim Henson (1937–1989)—created the Muppets and to this day inspires children and families all over the world to laugh and learn together while enjoying *Sesame Street* and the Muppet movies and home videos.
- Shari Lewis (1934–1998)—innovative ventriloquist-puppeteer shared her endearing sock puppets Lamb Chop, Charlie Horse, and Hush Puppy with children and their parents for four decades in person and on television, the latest being *Lamb Chops Play-Along* and *The Charlie Horse Music Pizza*.

■ TAKING PUPPETS HOME

Getting parents involved with and enthusiastic about puppetry will take time and patience on your part. You might find the following suggestions helpful:

- Send information home to parents about puppet presentations available in your community. It is important that children have opportunities to see live performances.
- Figure 5–16 shows a letter to be sent home with the children in your program. The younger children can add illustrations to the letter. The older children can write their own letter to invite their parents to a special evening at the center. If the parents speak a language other than English, ask someone to help you translate the letter into their native language. Send both copies home with the child.
- Have an informal parents meeting. After a light supper, including foods the children have made, the parents and children go to different learning centers in the room. This is a good time to introduce new or favorite activities. Set up the centers with materials and supplies for the families to make things together. One of the activities should be making puppets. Whatever the family group makes, they take home.

Dear Mom and/or Dad
(or whatever the child calls her
parent using the language spoken
at home),

Please come visit my school on
(date and time). We are cooking for
you. We have planned some special
things for you to do. One thing is
to make puppets with me. We have
been doing this and it's lots of fun.
It will be lots of fun for you too.
You can see my teacher and all my
friends.

(Child's name)

FIGURE 5–16 An example of a letter to send home with the children.

■ Offer a puppet lending library to the children and parents. Display durable, commercially made puppets available for the families to sign out. Encourage parents to enjoy the puppets with their children. Supply a bright-colored sack or large envelope in which the borrowed puppet can be returned.

■ TIPS FOR TEACHERS

Throughout this chapter, I have suggested guidance techniques and tips for introducing and using puppets. Puppet creations will become a valuable teaching tool for you. They can help you encourage appropriate behavior and speech. Once you feel comfortable in creating and using puppets yourself, you will discover that these wonderful characters can help you throughout the day. The more you use puppets, the more you will see for yourself how much children relate to and love puppets.

It is important for you to establish the following guidelines with the children in your classroom. These will affirm their creativity and promote puppetry:

■ Take all the time you need to make your puppet.
■ Make the puppet your own way.
■ Be creative and imaginative.
■ Wait until *you* are ready.
■ Please explore, experiment, and create.

ACTIVITY PLAN WORKSHEET

DEVELOPMENTALLY APPROPRIATE ACTIVITIES

Children's age group: appropriate for toddlers if the activity is simplified; otherwise, the activity is appropriate for preschoolers and kindergarten children

Name of Activity and Brief Description

"Sound game with puppets and props"

Purpose/Objectives of Activity

- To listen to different sounds that promote auditory discrimination
- To recognize sounds in the environment
- To classify sounds
- To develop mental images of what is heard
- To recognize loud and soft sounds
- To recognize high and low sounds
- To listen to instructions

Space and Materials Needed

Depending on the number of children playing the game at one time, the area of floor space needed may be large or small. A puppet with attachable puppet ears is needed along with a cloth bag filled with objects having distinctive sounds, such as an eggbeater, a timer, a box of rice, some maracas, and a musical triangle.

Procedure

1. Have the children sit on the floor in a circle.
2. Attach large ears to "Ms. I Listen" puppet. (You can use the basic hand puppet suggested in Figure 5–4. The pattern can be found in Appendix A. Ears can be attached easily with Velcro.)
3. Use the puppet to introduce the activity by singing "Put Your Finger in the Air." End with "Put your finger on your ear and tell me what you hear."
4. Use the puppet to lead a discussion on why we have ears.
5. After discussion, use "Ms. I Listen" puppet to introduce the sound bag. Have her choose one child to be "it."
6. Give "it" the sound bag.

7. Have children stand, join hands, and circle clockwise, while the child who is "it" remains stationary outside the circle holding the sound bag.
8. The children continue circling until they hear "it" call "Stop!"
9. The child who is "it" chooses something from the sound bag and makes a sound with it. The child who has stopped directly in front of "it" must guess what is making the sound.
10. If she guesses correctly, she becomes "it" and changes places.
11. If the guess is incorrect, the teacher using the puppet guides the child into making the correct choice, and then she changes places with "it."
12. Continue until all items in the sound bag have been identified.
13. Use the puppet to direct children into the next activity.

Guidance

If possible, a small group of children should do this activity the first time it is presented. Once they know how the activity is played, then they can help the puppet, "Ms. I Listen," explain the game to the other children.

It is important to establish limits for behavior and boundaries of the activity.

It is helpful to anticipate problems that may develop during this activity and consider ways in which they may be handled. You know your group of children best. Therefore, use the guidance that will work best for your situation.

Evaluation and Follow-Up

Evaluate this activity to see if the children were able to achieve the skills or understand the concepts presented. Consider how this activity could be changed to be more effective.

Follow-up activities could include attaching a large nose to the same puppet or big eyes or large hands with fingers. Put appropriate items in the cloth bag to correspond with the added body parts.

ACTIVITY PLAN WORKSHEET *continued*

Another activity could utilize sound cans filled with rice, beans, sand, large nails, paper clips, and metal washers. For the children to match sounds, use two cans for each item (small film cans or Band-Aid cans). Children first match sounds, then identify sounds.

Develop your own list of activities, using the puppet, that can extend or give practice to the skills or concepts of this activity.

Figure 5–17 is the curriculum planning web worksheet with puppet activities added. This worksheet with appropriate additions is included in each chapter.

AFTERVIEW

Through puppets, a child

- Builds self-esteem
- Develops independence
- Learns acceptable behavior
- Improves listening skills
- Learns new ways to express feelings
- Learns to share with others and to take turns
- Learns to make choices

- Develops large and small muscle skills
- Practices language skills
- Uses creative thinking and imagination
- Strengthens problem-solving skills and abstract thinking
- Reveals thoughts and attitudes through conversation

KEY TERMS

hand puppets
marionettes
puppetry

stick or rod puppets
shadow puppets

EXPLORATIONS

1. Select a classmate or colleague as a partner. Share ideas on how a teacher can encourage social, emotional, and language development with puppets.

2. Review the types of puppets discussed in this chapter. Then create a puppet.

3. Using the puppet from Exploration 2, plan how you would introduce your puppet to a group of children. Select a specific age group: infants, toddlers, preschoolers, or school-agers. This plan should include objectives, materials needed, step-by-step procedures for presenting this activity, follow-up activities, and evaluation guidelines. (Use the activity plan worksheet in Chapter 2.)

4. Present your puppet and planned activity to your classmates, then present it and the activity to a group of children. Using the evaluation portion of the activity plan worksheet, evaluate how effective your puppet was. What were the children's reactions and interactions? What would you change? What would you keep the same?

5. Either through research or personal interviews, find out which community resources or agencies present puppet activities or puppet plays and which early education programs offer puppets as part of their learning environment. Share your findings with your classmates or colleagues.

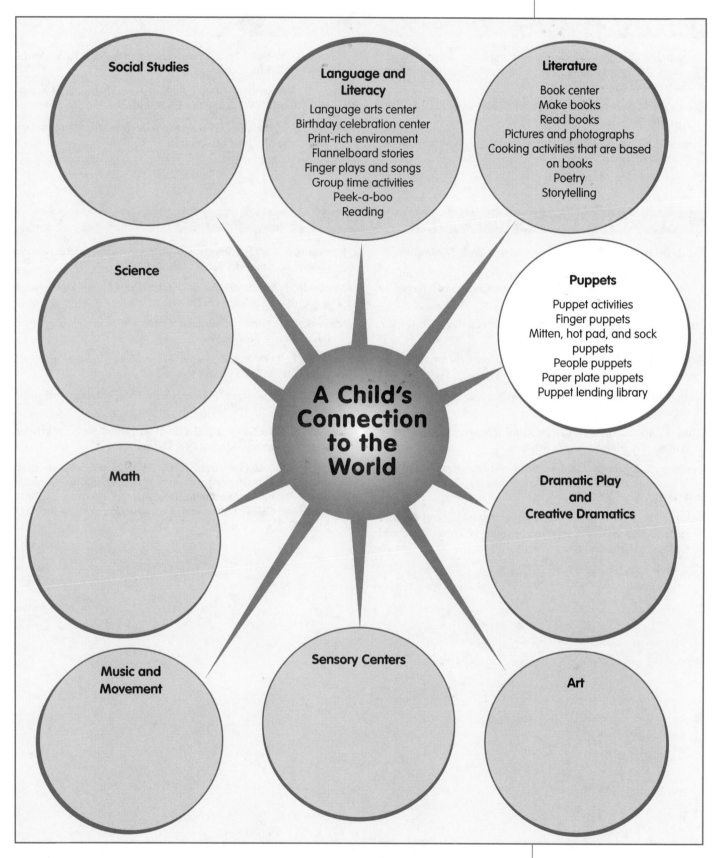

FIGURE 5–17 A curriculum planning web worksheet with puppet activities added.

REFERENCES

Borgenicht, D. (1998). *Sesame Street unpaved: Scripts, stories, secrets, and songs.* New York: Children's Television Workshop and Hyperion.

Center for Puppetry Arts. (1994). *Museum guide.* Atlanta, GA: Author.

Fortson, L. R., & Reiff, J. C. (1995). *Early childhood curriculum.* Boston: Allyn and Bacon.

Henson, C. (1994). *The Muppets make puppets.* New York: Workman Publishing.

Hunt, T., & Renfro, N. (1982). *Puppetry in early childhood education.* Austin, TX: Nancy Renfro Studios.

Raines, S., & Isbell, R. (1994). *Stories: Children's literature in early education.* Albany, NY: Delmar.

ADDITIONAL READINGS AND RESOURCES

Baird, B. (1965). *The art of the puppet.* New York: Macmillan.

Dolci, M. (1994, July/August). When the wolf both is and is not a wolf—The language of puppets. *Child Care Information Exchange, 98,* 43–46.

Entz, S. (1995, January/February). A puppet a day. *First Teacher, 16*(1), 26.

Finch, C. (Ed.). (1993). *Jim Henson: The works—the art, the magic, the imagination.* New York: Random House.

Forte, I. (1992). *Puppet parade.* Nashville, TN: Incentive Publications Inc.

Hunt, T., & Renfro, N. (1982). *Pocketful of puppets: Mother Goose.* Austin, TX: Nancy Renfro Studios.

Isenberg, J., & Jalongo, M. J. (1997). *Creative expression and play in the early childhood curriculum* (2nd ed.). Columbus, OH: Merrill.

Jackman, H. L. (1999). *Sing me a story! Tell me a song! Creative curriculum activities for teachers of young children.* Thousand Oaks, CA: Corwin Press.

Jamieson, R. (1993). *Puppets with purpose: Instant puppets for the classroom.* Newport Beach, CA: Author.

Machedo, J. M. (1999). *Early childhood experiences in language arts* (6th ed.). Albany, NY: Delmar.

Mayesky, M. (1998). *Creative activities for young children* (6th ed.). Albany, NY: Delmar.

Roberts, L. (1985). *Mitt magic: Fingerplays for finger puppets.* Beltsville, MD: Gryphon House.

Root, S. (1995, January/February). Problem solving with puppetry. *First Teacher, 16*(1), 27.

Sawyer, W. E., & Sawyer, J. C. (1993). *Integrated language arts for emerging literacy.* Albany, NY: Delmar.

Skelton, S. C., & Hamilton, A. C. (1990). *Using puppets with young children* (Paper presented at the Annual Conference of the Alabama Association for Young Children). Mobile, Alabama. (ERIC Document Reproduction Service No. ED 317275)

Dramatic Play and Creative Dramatics

■ OVERVIEW

Play is the natural language of the child. It helps a child observe and respond to the world in which he lives. "The impulse to play, if encouraged, can become a continuing way of learning, a medium of expression, and eventually a creative art" (McCaslin, 1980).

From pat-a-cake to peek-a-boo, a baby watches others and then copies them. The more you can play such pretend games with an infant, the more the infant learns. As the baby coos and babbles, your smiles and hugs give encouragement. When you say a word over and over, the baby will try to say it too. An infant's awareness of human expression, gestures, and sounds is the beginning of creative thinking.

Toddlers love the world of pretend. They will use dishes and pretend to eat and drink. They enjoy pretend hellos and goodbyes. As you talk and enter such play, you are helping them learn about the real world. Children learn by repetition. Your willingness to do the same thing over and over is the key that opens the door to their learning. Although toddlers may pretend for short periods of time alone, they need other children and adults to give words and some direction to their play.

Dramatic play is one of the most valuable forms of play in children. Preschool children love to have stories read to them. They will retell the stories as they play. A few props will get them going on the story. They may give their own twist to the story each time they "play the role." They're trying out new ways to solve problems as well as "trying on" being adults.

Children are fond of imitating people they have seen at the grocery store, the doctor's office, the service station, and the restaurant. Preschoolers like to emulate family members as well as define their own relationships with them. Home relationships are intense, and in dramatic play children graphically show their varying relationships to different family members. This creative play reveals children's pressing needs at the moment. They may seek in play the warmth and affection they fail to get at home. If they are consistently urged toward mature behavior at home, they may seek infantile roles in their role-playing.

Play also handles a child's uniqueness of being little in a world of big people. Through dramatic play, a young child can indicate confusion or misinterpretation of facts, as well as possible fears and attempts to master these fears.

School-age children enjoy creating their own activities. They may make them up as they go along. You will see familiar stories in most of their dramatic play. Children's group play usually has "the bestest good guys" and "the baddest bad guys." The good guys will win and often invite the bad ones to be good and win with them.

Children will play out their ideas of death, marriage, parenting, daredevil escapades, superheroes, and everyday life. Although the plots may be complicated, the theme remains the same. That theme of "everything turns out right" adds to a child's feeling of security. With this in mind, it is crucial that we provide an environment that is healing to children in our violent society. "Because very young children are affected by violence, awareness of how to address violence in young children's lives is critical for early childhood professionals" (Jackson, 1997). The dramatic play area offers a safe haven for children to act out their fears and anger, knowing that the teacher will be there to respond to their individual needs.

As we continue through this chapter, we will explore how theorists, researchers, and educators explain the developmental stages of dramatic play and creative dramatics. We will also appropriately plan and prepare the early childhood environment to integrate this fantasy play into the learning centers and curriculum, as we increase children's cooperative interaction skills. David Elkind (1994) explains, "When children are engaged in dramatic play, one of the things they are learning is how to transfer what they learned in one setting and apply it in another. One could hardly wish for a better learning activity than that!"

■ DRAMATIC PLAY AND CREATIVE DRAMATICS DEFINED

Nellie McCaslin (1980) helps us define *dramatic play, creative dramatics,* and *pantomime* in relationship to the play of young children. She describes **dramatic play** as "the *free play* of the very young child in which he explores his universe, imitating the actions and character traits of those around him." Dramatic play is spontaneous and can be expanded or repeated over and over again just for the fun of it.

Creative dramatics refers to the *improvised* drama of children, age five or six and older. This process of improvisation is an extension of dramatic play as interpreted by older children. It involves more elaborate situations and imaginative characters. It is child-centered drama used in a "nonperformance" way. You may introduce an idea or theme and set limits for the activity, but then you should "back off" and let the children create.

McCaslin defines **pantomime** as the art of conveying ideas without words. Children enjoy pantomime, and for the young child this is an excellent way to begin creative dramatics. Because many of his thoughts are spoken entirely through the body, the five- or six-year-old finds pantomime a natural means of expression. Simple group pantomimes challenge the imagination and sharpen awareness.

Researchers believe the *fantasy* element of dramatic play is quite useful. It enables the child to discharge or accomplish through imagination what he or she is unable to do in reality. Fantasizing relieves tensions and offers a way to interpret and put together the pieces of the complex puzzle that is a child's world. For example, animal play releases aggression, but this is not the only function of this type of dramatic play. A child will often impersonate animals because he is shy or feels insecure when verbalizing.

> *Michael, a three-year-old, was such a child. He came into the classroom growling like an animal. His hands were in the position of paws. Michael entered freely into dramatic play with other children as a dragon, tiger, or wolf. Many times he got the attention of several children when he played the big bad wolf. Morning after morning,* The Three Little Pigs *was played out. The other children, laughing and chattering happily, hid under the tables to escape the wolf. Michael was capable of expressing himself verbally, but he didn't. Instead, he found peer acceptance in dramatic play. Later, when he was ready to talk and enter into other dramatic play activities, he did so.*

■ DEVELOPMENTAL STAGES OF DRAMATIC PLAY

Theorists, researchers, and educators emphasize the importance of *developmental stages* of dramatic play in varying ways. As discussed in Chapter 1, Mildred Parten (1932) categorizes six stages of social play: unoccupied behavior, onlooker behavior, solitary play (infants), parallel play (toddlers), associative play (young preschoolers), and cooperative play (older preschoolers, kindergartners, and primary-age children).

Jean Piaget's research (1962) has helped us understand play in terms of cognitive development by presenting play in three stages:

■ **Practice play,** during the sensorimotor stage of development (infancy to two years), in which infants explore the sensory qualities of objects and practice motor skills. This is observable through a child's physical movements and interactions with objects in the environment.

■ **Symbolic play,** during the preoperational stage of development (two to seven years), when we see children transfer objects into symbols, things that represent something else. Symbolic thinking is observable during dramatic play when realistic objects such as pots and pans are used for "cooking soup"; a block becomes a "real" telephone and the child "talks" into it; and older children, using gestures and actions, pantomime props when there are none.

■ **Games with rules,** during the concrete operations stage of development (seven years and older), in which children's spontaneous play develops into games involved with perfecting physical skills and organizing games with rules that are both physical and cognitive. This type of play is observable when it demonstrates children making up their own rules for the games they play; their ability to accept and relate to another person's point of view; and their ability to understand rules to a game that cannot be changed.

Sara Smilansky (1968) divides play into four types of sociodramatic play:

■ **Functional play** (infancy through early years) occurs when a child takes on a role and pretends to be someone else. This type of play embodies sensory and motor exploration of the environment and the people in the environment. This is observable when children play in "dress-up clothes," or use props to identify the person they are portraying.

■ **Constructive play** (toddlers and preschoolers) helps children understand their experiences. This type of play can occur alone or with others as the child plans the manipulation of objects or people to create a specific experience. This is observable when a child puts keys in a pretend car, starts the motor, adds the sound effects ("Vroooom"), and lets others ride in the car with her.

■ **Dramatic play** (toddlers through primary-age children) involves pretending and make-believe. This represents a higher level of play behavior and is observable when two or more children take on related roles and interact with one another. (This is demonstrated later in the chapter when specific dramatic play learning centers are discussed.)

■ **Games with rules** (older preschoolers and primary-age children) require children to behave according to pre-existing rules. This is observable when children play board games and many outdoor sports.

Erik Erikson (1963) emphasizes how social-emotional stages of development help us understand the importance of allowing children to play out their feelings in an environment of acceptance. These psychosocial stages are:

■ *Basic Trust vs. Mistrust* (first year of life). This developmental stage is important to an infant's learning that people can be depended upon and that the child can

depend upon himself. Love and acceptance are important for the child to learn that the world is a safe place in which to live. This foundation of trust will be developed if the infant's needs are met. This is observable when the infant babbles, coos, laughs, crawls, pulls up, and is comfortable with the environment.

- *Autonomy vs. Shame and Doubt* (second year of life). This stage helps a child develop a basic sense of self-control and independence. The child is growing rapidly. It is significant during this stage that the toddler has opportunities to do things for himself. This is observable when a toddler feeds and dresses himself, and generally has an "I can do it myself" attitude that is accepted and reinforced by the adults in his life. Putting on and taking off "dress-up" clothes also demonstrates this.

- *Initiative vs. Guilt* (preschool years). During this stage of life, children are becoming interested in exploring and are ready to learn. Children need to express their natural curiosity and creativity through opportunities in the environment. This stage of development is observable by watching how children demonstrate body control and motor skills while riding a tricycle and running. Initiative is reinforced when children are given freedom to engage in fantasy and other dramatic play activities. Social roles in dramatic play continue to show children identifying with adult roles. They enjoy making adult situations conform to their notion of the ways things are. Roles can be reversed and new roles can be tried out.

- *Industry vs. Inferiority* (school-age years). At this stage of life, the child is ready for challenges of new and exciting ideas. The child needs opportunities for accomplishment in physical, intellectual, and social development. This is observable by watching older children during creative dramatics activities. They improvise their own dialogue, play the scenes, and evaluate the results. This is informal and demonstrates individual and group imagination, problem solving, critical thinking, and cooperation with others.

George Maxim (1997) divides play into two major categories or dimensions. The *social dimension* deals with the ways children progress from solitary pursuits to an interest and skill in collaborating and cooperating with others. The *content dimension* refers to the composition of play—what children play with, such as sand and blocks, or what the children play at, such as serving tea. The key point to remember about the two dimensions is that each is developmental.

Fantasy and Reality Understanding in Young Children

Dramatic play experiences help young children sort out what is make-believe and what is real. "In addition to its general utility in relieving tensions and externalizing inner experiences it helps the child set the boundaries between reality and unreality" (Hartley, Frank, & Goldenson, 1964). "Children need ample supplies of fantasy and reality. Gradually children learn to separate fantasy and reality, identify which is which, and travel between them purposefully" (Vail, 1999).

It is both appropriate and developmental that young children try out ways to differentiate fantasy from reality. The younger the child, the more dramatic play is rooted in fantasy. Children confuse fantasy with reality, because they believe what they think is true, whether or not it is true in reality. Read, Gardner, and Mahler (1993) explain further: "Children need help and time to make the distinction between reality and fantasy without having to reject their fantasies. They have a right to imagine and to create fantasies as well as a need to learn to identify reality."

At age five or older, children understand when they are pretending and when they are in the real world. Their understanding is sometimes very sophisticated. "Rather than try to force understanding, which is usually in place by the end of kindergarten, encourage children to use language as a tool to ask questions and explore their thinking. . . . 'Do you think that could really happen?'" (Vail, 1999).

■ PLANNING AND PREPARING THE ENVIRONMENT

Dramatic play offers many opportunities for supporting a young child's growth and development. Dramatic play produces sheer joy and delight. A child's total being is involved in the activity. His body, face, language, and emotions mirror enthusiasm for life. To support all of this, you should provide unstructured time, adequate space, flexible materials, and uninterrupted opportunity for the children to enjoy dramatic play. Most importantly, *let the children have input!* The environment should say "pretending is welcome here!"

If you see that a child is not ready to enter freely into dramatic play, your understanding is vitally important. This child needs sufficient time to watch and learn and proceed at her own pace. Perhaps if you pretend with the child at first and then gradually pull away, this will be all that is needed. "Subtle, unobtrusive guidance from the teacher can make dramatic play an instrument of growth, not only for the timid, hesitant child, but for the scattered, aggressive youngster as well" (Hartley et al., 1964).

The Teacher's Role in Children's Dramatic Play

The following guidelines should help to define the teacher's role in children's dramatic play. Here, as in other curriculum areas, the teacher's role is primarily that of facilitator.

- Keep in mind the children's developmental capabilities.
- Value this type of play.
- Allow children opportunities to "try on" adult roles, both male and female.
- Provide stimulating props, unstructured time, and adequate space for dramatic play.
- Limit the number of children in the area at one time.
- Introduce props to small groups of children.
- Select props that are authentic and can be used naturally and safely.
- Change props frequently and include ones that reflect different cultures.
- Avoid props and activities that are sexist and racist.

- Serve as a facilitator rather than teacher so dramatic play remains a child-initiated activity.
- Monitor the dramatic play area so all children have the opportunity to participate.
- Assist children in learning acceptable kinds of social interaction.
- Allow children to solve their own problems as often as possible.
- Encourage creativity in language and play.

Some teachers keep the home living (housekeeping) area intact as a permanent center and set up a second dramatic play area that expands the theme of the lesson plan. Others, who are limited in classroom space, may choose to have a dramatic play center that changes periodically and sometimes will include the kitchen area or another room in the home. Still others take the dramatic play center outdoors to take advantage of the additional space available.

The basic equipment for the home living/dramatic play center should be: child-sized furniture made of wood or sturdy plastic including tables; chairs; rocking chair; shelves; a "play" sink, stove, and refrigerator; and a full-length mirror. Dolls of both sexes representing differing features and skin coloring; a doll bed or cradle; and a sturdy, nonworking telephone should also be included.

Sometimes, the most creative and appropriate dramatic play area is one that has very little in it and does not have a specific theme. When a special "soft area" is created by adding some pillows, beanbag chairs, and a soft area rug, it becomes a totally child-directed dramatic play area. The children feel relaxed and safe, free to be creative and imaginative. The pillows become props, as needed, or the children can bring in props from around the room. The children in one class I observed used a "soft area" dramatic play setting to discuss and act out their fears and anxieties after the 1995 bombing in Oklahoma City.

■ MAKING PROP BOXES

A vital part of the planning and preparing process for dramatic play activities is the creation of prop boxes. A **prop box** is a collection of actual items related to the development and enrichment of dramatic play activities focused on a specific theme or lesson plan. These items should be collected for easy accessibility and placed in sturdy boxes that can be stacked for storage (empty paper boxes with lids make great prop boxes).

Label each prop box clearly for identification. A picture or drawing on the outside can suggest what is inside. Cover the boxes with colored contact paper to give them an uncluttered and uniform appearance.

The props selected for the dramatic play areas should stimulate interest, encourage creative expression, create opportunities for problem solving, relate to and expand the experiences of the children, and represent many cultures. These props can be found anywhere and everywhere: in the parents' and staff's closets and garages, at surplus stores, thrift stores, garage sales, and at local businesses and offices that have used and throwaway items. Invite the children to bring appropriate props from home that represent their interests, hobbies, lifestyles, or current theme.

Maxim (1990) suggests that teachers fix some special prop boxes for the children to take home for specific periods of time. "Children and parents can sign-out for them. Encourage children to talk about their play when they return the boxes. This will stimulate others to want to take them home."

Clothes for the Dramatic Play Center

Clothing that helps children "dress-up" in various roles is an important part of dramatic play. The clothes should be easy for children to put on and take off, as well as

attractive, durable, and washable. Wash and dry donated clothing before sharing them with the children. Hem the garments to make sure the children can wear them comfortably and safely. Remove long rope belts, or stitch them into place so they cannot be used around children's necks. Replace back zippers with Velcro hook-and-loop fasteners (Parks, 1992). Teenager-size clothes are useful for young children, or (if you do not sew) perhaps there is a parent who will be willing to make some new "dress-up" clothes for the class.

There should be a special place where clothing is displayed or stored. A cardboard box "closet" with a rod placed across at the children's height can hold clothes on hangers. Clothing hooks or a shortened clothes or hat rack is also appropriate. Whatever you select will help the children understand that, after they have used the article of clothing, it should be placed back where they found it.

A variety of cultures should be represented by using clothing fabric that is tie-dyed, batik, madras prints, and kente cloth. The clothing styles should offer saris, kimonos, serapes, ponchos, grass skirts, and dashikis (Allen, McNeill, & Schmidt, 1992). You should research many cultures and consult with parents as you develop your dramatic play center.

Easy-to-make Clothes

An easy way to create dramatic play clothes is by selecting large pieces of square, rectangular, and triangular fabric. For example, here are two suggestions for using a square yard of fabric (adapted from Parks, 1992).

To Make a Skirt. Wrap the square of fabric around the child's waist. Adjust the length to the height of the child, and tie a knot at the waist.

FIGURE 6–1 Examples of easy-to-make clothes for the dramatic play center.

To Make a Robe. Wrap the square of fabric around the child's chest and under one arm. Tie a knot over the opposite shoulder (Figure 6–1). Adjust the length to the height of the child.

■ INTEGRATING DRAMATIC PLAY INTO THE CURRICULUM

The following examples of dramatic play centers, and the prop boxes to accompany each, have proven to be successful in early education curriculum. They represent developmentally appropriate play areas and offer creative opportunities for individual or small groups of children.

In setting up areas for infants and toddlers, change very little from what they are used to. Add props or change room arrangement very slowly. The children will guide you by what they will or will not play with. Older children will help you decide when to change, when to add additional props and materials, and what areas of the room need to be expanded for more dramatic play.

Dramatic Play for Infants

- *A doll corner.* Select sock or soft dolls (depicting many cultures) that are easy to launder and simple cardboard beds for the dolls. The clothing on the dolls should be washable and easy to take off and put on.
- *A home living area.* Choose washable household items that the infant can grasp, such as pots, pans, lids, boxes, plastic cups, bowls, and baskets. These will encourage the child to bang, stack, squeeze, and put the objects together.
- *An area* (indoor and/or outdoor) *for push and pull toys.* This should include doll buggies, wagons, wheelbarrows, and trucks.
- *An area for crawling and climbing.* Provide a rocking boat, short tunnel, climbing steps, and slide.

Dramatic Play for Toddlers

- *Home living area.* In addition to all types of dolls and child-sized furniture, add empty food boxes of all sizes and shapes that represent what the children eat at home. This should include empty food boxes with print in different languages on them to represent foods from diverse cultures.
- *Dress-up clothes.* Include items that relate to community helpers. Toddlers love sunglasses with plastic lenses, gloves, purses, and clothing that fits them.
- *Prop box.* Fill it with shopping bags, lunch boxes, toy telephones, keys, pots, pans, small cars, and trucks. (Miniature animals and people can be added to the block center prop box as well. This is discussed fully in Chapter 8.)
- *A corner for puppet and mask play.* This should offer glove puppets, finger puppets, and people puppets; animal masks with eyes, mouth, and nose cut out and a handle under the chin for easy manipulation, as described in Chapter 5.
- *A beauty/barber shop.* Provide washable black, brown, blond, and red wigs, both male and female styles; curlers; empty, plastic shampoo bottles; old hair dryers with the plugs and cords cut off. (Note: Wash or spray wigs and hats often with bleach water—½ teaspoon bleach to a quart of water.)

Dramatic Play for Preschoolers

The dramatic play center in the three-, four-, and five-year-old classroom can start with one specific theme. The concept can be expanded to include adjacent space as more children become involved.

- *Travel agency.* Set up a ticket counter and chairs. The prop box for this activity can include tickets, maps, brochures, posters, pens, pencils, flight schedules, boat schedules, and car and hotel information. The tickets, maps, schedules, and information sheets can also be made by the children.
- *Ship.* All it takes is a balance beam becoming the gangplank, cardboard boxes becoming the outer part of the ship, and "water" (painted by the children) surrounding the ship. Let the children help you add to this adventure by deciding where the ship will land. This is a wonderful opportunity to expand the dramatic

play into various ports and countries, such as Hawaii, Africa, Mexico, Alaska, and the Caribbean. Set up prop boxes for each country. Selecting what goes in each is both creative and educational and helps children develop problem-solving skills. Packing small suitcases or briefcases with clothing for warm climates (straw hats, thongs, beach toys, suntan lotion, sunglasses, and short-sleeved shirts) and clothing for colder areas (gloves, earmuffs, muffler, stocking caps, and sweaters) helps start this dramatic play.

■ *Train station and train, or airport and airplane.* This can expand the travel agency dramatic play or add to the lesson plan relating to transportation. As with the ship theme, develop a prop box for each, including appropriate clothing. Plan the destination with maps and brochures.

■ *Supermarket/grocery store/farmer's market/mercado.* Fill the prop box with a toy cash register, calculator, play money (or money the children make), price tags, sales slip pad, empty food containers (some with print in different languages on them to represent foods from diverse cultures), artificial fruit and vegetables, grocery boxes, shopping bags, small shopping carts, brown paper bags, telephone, coupons, and shopping lists. Make signs in several languages and with pictures to explain what is for sale.

■ *Picnic.* This is fun for indoor or outdoor and is an excellent dramatic play activity to plan for snack or lunch time. The children decide what to take on the picnic and place the items in a picnic basket. They decide if they are themselves or someone else. They can wear "dress-up" clothes and use props from the prop box, such as plastic or paper cups, plates, tableware, tablecloth, napkins, eating utensils, aprons, and blankets.

■ *Ants at a picnic.* Put several large picnic baskets in the dramatic play area. Add play food. Then, make a tunnel by taking the ends out of boxes. Line the boxes up, and tape them together to form a tunnel. You can use a cloth tunnel, if you already have one, to have more than one tunnel for the "ants." The children can pretend to be ants taking the "food" from the picnic basket to their home through the tunnels. Continue to add items that the children want to use (Jackman, 1999).

Other suggestions for dramatic play centers are restaurant, florist shop, pet shop, post office, library, book store, music shop, musical instrument store, recording studio, health center, doctor or dentist office, gymnasium, campsite, shoe store, fix-it shop, and apartments in the loft and lower level of the dramatic play area.

Dramatic Play for Primary-Grade Children

Any of the dramatic play suggestions listed for the preschoolers can be expanded or adapted for older children. Give them the list of acceptable themes and allow them the freedom to make choices and select their own activities. For example, if they choose to visit another country as they play, the children may "discover the rain forest" or "go on a safari in Africa." This child-initiated form of dramatic play encourages the older child to take an interest in the wider world, and it is exciting to watch as it unfolds. Some children get involved with one aspect and tackle it as an independent project. Others make the theme a special event or a cooperative venture.

Creative dramatics is a more mature form of the spontaneous dramatic play of young children. Group activities such as story improvisations, body movement, and pantomime give older children a chance to articulate their thoughts and feelings and to socialize and work together toward a goal (Blau, Brady, Bucher, Hiteshew, & Zavitkovsky, 1985).

The following are a few examples of creative dramatics exercises and activities that are appropriate for school-age children:

■ Rag doll–tin man–marionette. Have the children perform simple warm-up exercises as limp as a rag doll; they can bend from the waist and bob up and down and swing their shoulders. As stiffened tin men, let them discover how their movements change. Expand this activity and have the children choose a partner. One becomes a marionette and the other becomes the puppeteer. The puppeteer stands in front of the marionette and moves the strings attached to the various parts of the marionette's body. The marionette responds with the proper movement.

■ Paper exploration. Give each child a piece of 9 × 12 construction paper. Have them balance the paper on different parts of the body. Run with the paper on the palm of their hand. Try putting paper on their feet and raising and lowering the legs.

■ The imaginary machine. First, one child will form a "machine-part shape" with his body and add a made-up sound to fit that shape. Each successive child connects to the shape last made with his own unique shape and sound until all of the children are involved in the imaginary machine. Slow the machine down and speed it up. To demonstrate the importance of the parts on the whole, "break" one of the parts. What happens to the machine?

■ Mirror images. Each child chooses a partner. They face each other, always keeping each other in full view. One child becomes a mirror that reflects what she sees her partner doing. Perhaps the child puts on clown makeup, exercises, or puts on a tie. After a while, the partners change places; the other partner becoming the mirror.

Dramatic Play and Other Learning Centers

Dramatic play and creative dramatics lend themselves to every aspect of the curriculum. Language and literacy development, socialization, exploration of feelings and fears, and problem solving are ongoing components of these activities. Music and rhythmic movement become dramatic and creative when a child makes use of them to become someone or something other than himself.

Math and science concepts can be applied. Charlesworth and Lind (1999) offer some examples:

■ One-to-one correspondence can be practiced by exchanging play money for goods or services.

■ Sets and classifying are involved in organizing each dramatic play center in an orderly manner.

- Counting can be applied to figuring out how many items have been purchased and how much money must be exchanged.
- Comparing and measuring can be used to decide if clothing fits, or to determine the weight of fruits and vegetables purchased.
- Spatial relations and volume concepts are applied as items purchased are placed in bags, boxes, and/or baskets; and as children discover how many passengers will fit in the space shuttle or can ride on the bus.
- Number symbols can be found throughout dramatic play props, for example, on price tags, play money, telephones, cash registers, and scales.

As you select the theme, brainstorm using the curriculum planning web worksheet in Chapter 2. Develop your lesson plan, integrate the learning centers, and gather supplies and materials to discover how to meet your goals and objectives through the use of dramatic play.

■ TIPS FOR TEACHERS

The appearance of television or movie heroes may change children's dramatic play. When you hear these heroes' names, you will want to observe the children's play more closely. Sometimes the stunts on television and in movies are dangerous when children try to do them. Violence may become too much a part of the play as they pretend to be superheroes. Your observation will give you an opportunity to teach better ways to solve problems without violence.

Beaty (1992) suggests there are both positive and negative aspects of children's imitation of superheroes.

> *The superhero is a good character who is good-looking, strong, loyal, helpful, unselfish, ready to fight against evil, and always the winner. The bad character is evil-looking, strong, selfish, disloyal, underhanded, sneaky, always challenging the good character, and always the loser. . . . Children are going to attempt superhero play whether or not it is allowed. . . . [S]uperheroes are powerful symbols, indeed, to young children. When you understand that such symbols can represent positive values in our society, then you may want to consider allowing superhero dramatic play in the classroom if it can be controlled and directed into prosocial channels.*

Let's think about how we can deal effectively with the superhero characters in an early education setting. One of the first things to do is to become familiar with *what* is available for the children to watch on television, video, and the movies. Secondly, think about *why* the children are imitating these characters. Ask questions of the children and talk to them about other, more appropriate, choices for play. *It's important to establish limits ahead of time.*

Slaby, Roedell, Arezzo, and Hendrix (1995) explain further:

> *Because young children have relatively little real-world experience by which to evaluate the relation of media violence to real life, they stand to benefit greatly from discussing these connections with adults. . . . A teacher might say, "He wants to stop that man from doing bad things, but the only way he knows how to do that is to fight him. I'll bet you can think of other ways that he could stop him without fighting."*

According to Levin (1995), children will need help working through the content they are seeing. Besides open discussions with the children, teach conflict resolution skills, and invite real, healthier role models (such as community helpers and parents) to visit the classroom. Help children regain control of their play by changing it from imitative play to creative, imaginative play. And importantly, work with parents, other teachers, and the early childhood community to understand and support each other's efforts to deal with the marketing of violence to children.

■ DEVELOPMENTALLY APPROPRIATE AND MULTICULTURAL/ANTI-BIAS ACTIVITIES

The following song and activities ("Humpty Dumpty" by Bea Wolf) show how a finger play activity that is developmentally appropriate for toddlers and three-year-olds can be expanded to a dramatic play activity that is appropriate for four- and five-year-olds. The "Humpty Dumpty Song" is provided in Figure 6–2.

HUMPTY DUMPTY
(finger play activity with song)

(Suitable for Toddlers and Three-Year-Olds)

Before attempting this activity, read or recite the rhyme to the children on several occasions so they become thoroughly familiar with it. If possible, find a colorful illustration to stimulate their interest. Teacher asks children questions while pointing to various features of the illustration:

Teacher: Who is this?

Children: Humpty Dumpty!

Teacher: What is Humpty Dumpty sitting on?

Children: The wall!

   (If children are too young to answer, Teacher supplies the answers.)

   Teacher guides the children in identifying articles of clothing worn by Humpty Dumpty, points out the horses and soldiers and anything else of visual interest. If children are old enough to understand, some discussion may take place about the fact that Humpty Dumpty is an egg and eggs can break. Children are prepared for the activity when they appear well acquainted with the rhyme.

Teacher: Now we're going to tell the story of Humpty Dumpty with our hands. First, make a wall, like this:

   (Teacher holds forearm as though looking at a wristwatch.)
   Now, make a fist with your other hand. This is Humpty Dumpty! Set him down on the wall. Is he happy there? Let him sway back and forth.
   (Sway fist as though rocking back and forth on forearm.)

Teacher: Now everyone sing (or say):
   Humpty Dumpty sat on a wall.
   Humpty Dumpty had a great fall—Boom!

   (Bend wrist down so that Humpty Dumpty drops off wall. Establish a rhythm by beating hands on thighs to simulate horses galloping. Sing or chant the next lines to this rhythm:)

   All the king's horses and all the king's men
   Couldn't put Humpty together again—
   Couldn't put Humpty together again!
   Why? (Extend hands outward in a large shrug.)

continued

Figure 6–2 "Humpty Dumpty Song" and activity for young children.

(During the next phrase extended hands slowly rise to meet over head, simulating an egg shape. Fingers meet on the word egg.*)*

Because he was an egg!

(This activity provides a good opportunity to point out that an egg is oval shaped, and to practice shaping ovals using fingers, hands, and arms.)

Review the nursery rhyme. Conduct a group discussion based on the fact that, once broken, an egg can never be put together again. Many children will have their own experiences to relate regarding this subject.

Announce that we are about to dramatize Humpty Dumpty. Explain that the word *dramatize* means to act out.

Guide the children in "falling" safely from a seated position to a lying down position on the floor. For this practice, children should already be seated on the floor so there is very little distance to fall. Explain that this is a fake fall, that we are acting, and that everyone must fall softly so as not to be hurt. Allow a very short time for fake fall practice (two or three falls should do it). Then guide children in pretending to be soldiers, or king's men, on horseback. Let them pretend to hold reins and gallop about for a short time; then announce that everyone seems ready to dramatize the story.

Divide the class into two groups. Group 1 consists of Humpty Dumptys, and group 2 of king's men. Instruct the king's men to wait quietly in a designated area until they hear their cue, which is the galloping rhythm the teacher will clap at the appropriate time. Instruct the Humpty Dumptys to sit on their wall, which can be a line on the floor. When everyone is ready, start the Humpty Dumptys swaying back and forth as all sing or say the first two lines of the rhyme. On "had a great fall," all Humpty Dumptys fake-fall on the floor and lie still. The teacher then claps the gallop rhythm. All the king's men then gallop over to the fallen Humpty Dumptys, dismount, and pat them gently, trying to put them together. On "Why?", the Humpty Dumptys sit up and all the children shrug with hands out. On "Because he was an egg," all slowly form an oval shape with arms above heads, fingers meeting on the word *egg*.

Repeat the dramatization, group 1 switching roles with group 2.

continued

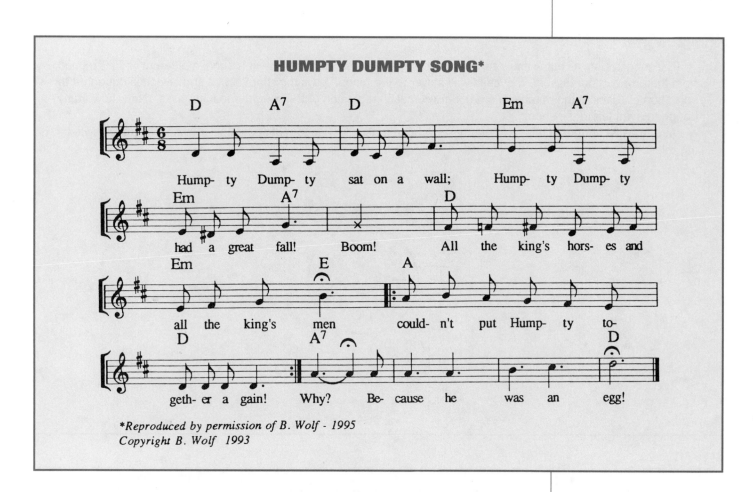

HUMPTY DUMPTY SONG*

*Reproduced by permission of B. Wolf - 1995
Copyright B. Wolf 1993*

This song and dramatic play activity ("The Doughnut Shop" by Bea Wolf) is appropriate for four- and five-year-olds. Think about how you could expand it for other age groups. "The Doughnut Song" is provided in Figure 6–3.

THE DOUGHNUT SHOP
(dramatic play for four- and five- year olds)*

(Entertainingly illustrates the concept of subtraction)

This activity requires the following cast:

1. A group of children who act as doughnuts.
2. A group of children who each purchase a doughnut.
3. A cashier or shopkeeper.

Begin by selecting the shopkeeper. The teacher can either fill that role herself, delegate it to a child who has earned a special privilege, or select the shopkeeper in some impartial way.

The children who act as doughnuts are seated in a row, on chairs, or on the floor in a designated area. The purchasers, each equipped with an imaginary or simulated coin, sit or stand in a different area. The shopkeeper sits near the doughnuts and operates an imaginary cash register.

continued

FIGURE 6–3 "The Doughnut Song" and activity for young children.

The song is sung as many times as there are doughnuts lined up. Each time it is sung, a different child is named from the group of purchasers. That child walks over to the "shop," pays the shopkeeper, and selects a doughnut to take "home" (back to the purchaser area). Between each repetition of the song the teacher asks, "Now, how many doughnuts are left in the shop?"

After the last doughnut has been purchased, children usually wish to repeat the activity, with the groups switching roles.

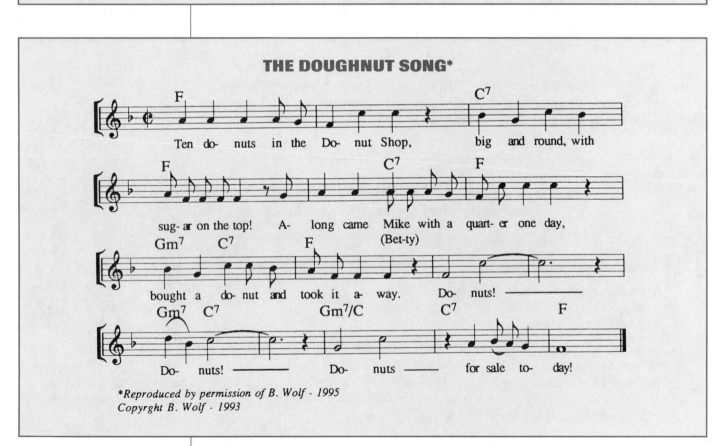

THE DOUGHNUT SONG*

Ten do-nuts in the Do- nut Shop, big and round, with
sug- ar on the top! A- long came Mike with a quart- er one day, (Bet-ty)
bought a do- nut and took it a- way. Do- nuts!
Do- nuts! Do- nuts for sale to- day!

*Reproduced by permission of B. Wolf - 1995
Copyrght B. Wolf - 1993

Books and stories can be used to integrate all areas of the curriculum, including dramatic play. The selection of a familiar story such as *Three Billy Goats Gruff* or *The Three Little Pigs* can be the first tale to be acted out. Then add a new book, such as *Brown Bear, Brown Bear, What Do You See?* by Bill Martin, Jr. (1983) or *Gilberto and the Wind* by Marie Hall Ets (1978). Put the book away once you and the children are familiar and comfortable with the story. This gives more freedom to add to or change the basic story as you go along. Simple props and settings can add to the dramatic play. Once the children experience the enjoyment of this kind of activity, then you can expand the activity.

Figure 6–4 is the curriculum planning web worksheet with dramatic play activities added. This worksheet with appropriate additions is included in each chapter.

AFTERVIEW

Through dramatic play, a child

- Improves socialization skills
- Practices social skills through role negotiation and conflict resolution
- Develops external expressions of emotions
- Chooses safe outlets for aggression and creates a climate for nonviolence
- Identifies and empathizes with feelings of others
- Develops self-confidence through role-playing
- Acts out familiar situations, "tries on" family roles, works out problems and concerns, and experiments with solutions
- Distinguishes fantasy from reality
- Stimulates imagination and creativity
- Improves problem-solving skills
- Enhances sensorimotor skills
- Develops muscular coordination, listening and oral language skills, and math readiness
- Learns to make choices

KEY TERMS

constructive play	functional play	practice play
creative dramatics	games with rules	prop box
dramatic play	pantomime	symbolic play

EXPLORATIONS

1. Select an early education classroom and observe for at least one hour. Describe, in writing, how the teacher sets up the environment and curriculum to encourage dramatic play. Give specific examples.

2. Select an early education classroom (the same or different from Exploration 1) and observe for at least one hour. Describe, in writing, several dramatic play activities the children were involved with at the time of your observation. Describe the activities, which learning centers were part of the activities, how props were used, who initiated the play, and how many joined it.

3. Visit a child life center in a local hospital or health facility. Observe how children's dramatic play is the same or different from classroom play. Describe objectively (factually) what you saw. (For example, were the children giving shots to stuffed animals and placing bandages on the hurt places? Were dolls getting casts put on their arms or legs?) Discuss subjectively (opinion) what you felt and learned from this observation.

4. Select and plan a dramatic play or creative dramatics activity for young children. Specify which age group this activity is planned for: infants, toddlers, pre-

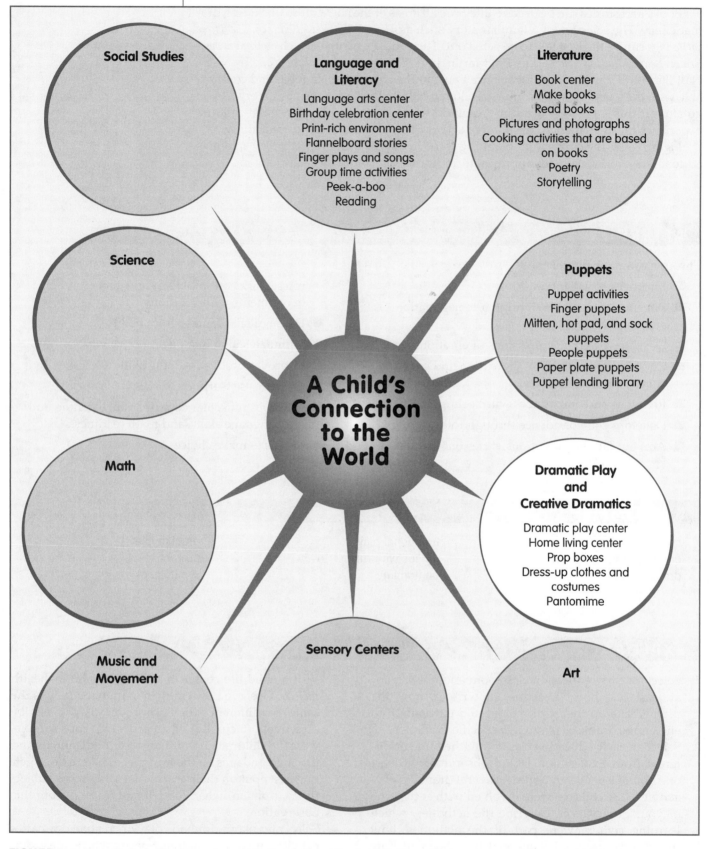

Social Studies

Language and Literacy

Language arts center
Birthday celebration center
Print-rich environment
Flannelboard stories
Finger plays and songs
Group time activities
Peek-a-boo
Reading

Literature

Book center
Make books
Read books
Pictures and photographs
Cooking activities that are based
on books
Poetry
Storytelling

Science

Puppets

Puppet activities
Finger puppets
Mitten, hot pad, and sock
puppets
People puppets
Paper plate puppets
Puppet lending library

A Child's Connection to the World

Math

Dramatic Play and Creative Dramatics

Dramatic play center
Home living center
Prop boxes
Dress-up clothes and
costumes
Pantomime

Music and Movement

Sensory Centers

Art

FIGURE 6–4 A curriculum planning web worksheet with dramatic play activities added.

EXPLORATIONS continued

schoolers, or primary-age children. In writing, list objectives, materials needed, step-by-step procedures for presenting this activity, follow-up activities, and evaluation guidelines. (Use the activity plan worksheet in Chapter 2.) Prepare this activity and demonstrate it during class or with a group of children.

5. Based on the information in this chapter and on your observations of early education environments, select a partner and develop a dramatic play prop box appropriate for a group of young children. Describe the theme of the lesson plan and discuss how the prop box will be used within the context of the curriculum. Present this activity and demonstrate it during class or with a group of children.

REFERENCES

Allen, J., McNeill, E., & Schmidt, V. (1992). *Cultural awareness for children.* Menlo Park, CA: Addison-Wesley Publishing Company.

Beaty, J. J. (1992). *Preschool appropriate practices.* Fort Worth, TX: Harcourt Brace Jovanovich.

Blau, R., Brady, E. H., Bucher, I., Hiteshew, B., & Zavitkovsky, D. (1985). *Activities for school-age care.* Washington, DC: National Association for the Education of Young Children.

Charlesworth, R., & Lind, K. K. (1999). *Math and science for young children* (3rd ed.). Albany, NY: Delmar.

Elkind, D. (1994). *A sympathetic understanding of the child, birth to sixteen* (3rd ed.). Boston: Allyn and Bacon.

Erikson, E. (1963). *Childhood and society* (2nd ed.). New York: W. W. Norton and Co., Inc.

Hartley, R., Frank, L. K., & Goldenson, R. M. (1964). *Understanding children's play.* New York: Columbia University Press.

Jackman, H. L. (1999). *Sing me a story! Tell me a song! Creative curriculum activities for teachers of young children.* Thousand Oaks, CA: Corwin Press.

Jackson, B. R. (1997, November). Creating a climate for healing in a violent society. *Young Children, 52*(7), 68–70.

Levin, D. E. (1995, March/April). Power Rangers: An explosive topic. *Child Care Information Exchange, 102,* 50–51.

Maxim, G. W. (1997). *The very young* (5th ed.). Columbus, OH: Merrill.

Maxim, G. W. (1990). *The sourcebook: Activities for infants and young children* (2nd ed.). Columbus, OH: Merrill.

McCaslin, N. (1980). *Creative dramatics in the classroom* (3rd ed.). New York: S. G. Phillips.

Parks, L. (Ed.) (1992, Fall). Easy-to-make clothes for dramatic play. *Texas Child Care, 16*(2), 30–38.

Parten, M. B. (1932). Social participation among preschool children. *Journal of Abnormal and Social Psychology, 27,* 243–269.

Piaget, J. (1962). *Play, dreams and imitation in childhood.* New York: W. W. Norton.

Read, K., Gardner, P., & Mahler, B. (1993). *Early childhood programs: Human relationships and learning* (9th ed.). Fort Worth, TX: Harcourt Brace Jovanovich.

Slaby, R. G., Roedell, W. C., Arezzo, D., & Hendrix, K. (1995). *Early violence prevention.* Washington, DC: National Association for the Education of Young Children.

Smilansky, S. (1968). *The effects of sociodramatic play on disadvantaged pre-school children.* New York: John Wiley & Sons.

Vail, P. L. (1999, January). Observing learning styles in the classroom. *Early Childhood Today, 13*(4), 20–27.

ADDITIONAL READINGS AND RESOURCES

Boyatzis, C. J. (1997, November). Of power rangers and V-chips. *Young Children, 52*(7), 74–79.

Berk, L. E. (1994, November). Vygotsky's theory: The importance of make-believe play. *Young Children, 50*(1), 30–39.

Cohen, S. (1993/94, Winter). Television in the lives of children and their families. *Childhood Education, 70*(2), 103–104.

David, J. (1994, February). Let's play good guys and bad guys. *Early Childhood Today, 8*(5), 51.

Davidson, J. I. (1996). *Emergent literacy and dramatic play.* Albany, NY: Delmar.

Gowen, J. W. (1995, March). The early development of symbolic play. *Young Children, 50*(3), 75–84.

Grollman, S. (1994, September/October). Fantasy and exploration: Two approaches to playing. *Child Care Information Exchange, 99,* 48–50.

Howell, J., & Corbey-Scullen, L. (1997, September). Out of the housekeeping corner and onto the stage—Extending dramatic play. *Young Children, 52*(6), 82–88.

Ishee N., & Goldhaber, J. (1990, March). Story re-enactment: Let the play begin! *Young Children, 45*(3), 70–75.

Kosoff, S., & Doane, A. (1996, January). Creative dramatics. *Early Childhood Today, 10*(4), 18–29.

Levin, P. E. (1994, November/December). Speaking of super-heroes. *Early Childhood Today, 9*(3), 53–57.

Marian, M. (1997, November). Guiding young children's understanding and management of anger. *Young Children, 52*(7), 62–67.

McCaslin, N. (1987). *Creative drama in the primary grades: A handbook for teachers.* New York: Longman.

McCune, L. (1994, September/October). Infants don't pretend, do they? *Child Care Information Exchange, 99,* 55–59.

Myhre, S. M. (1993, July). Enhancing your dramatic play area through the use of prop boxes. *Young Children, 48*(5), 6–11.

Perlmutter, J. C., & Laminack, J. L. (1993, Summer). Sociodramatic play, a stage for practicing literacy. *Dimensions of Early Childhood, 21*(4), 13–16, 31.

Scarlett, W. G. (1994, September/October). Problems in make-believe: Real and pretend. *Child Care Information Exchange, 99,* 60–62.

Williamson, P. A. (1993, Summer). Encouraging social competence and story comprehension through thematic fantasy play. *Dimensions of Early Childhood, 21*(4), 17–20.

Wolf, D. P. (1994, September/October). Make-believe play: Why bother? *Child Care Information Exchange, 99,* 44–47.

Art

CHAPTER

7

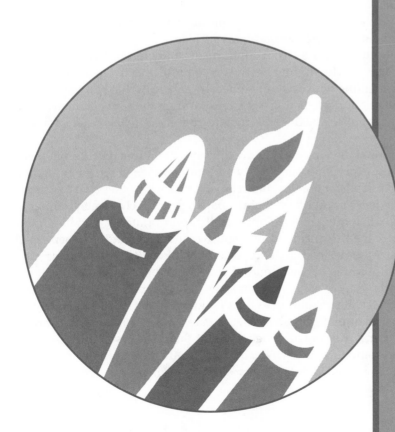

KEY CONCEPTS

- Children's developmental stages in art
- Infants and toddlers
- Preschoolers and kindergartners
- Five- to eight-year-old children
- Teacher as facilitator and observer
- Establishing an environment for creative expression and experimentation
- General guidelines
- Guidance guidelines
- Use of food in art projects
- Outdoor environment
- Aesthetic environment
- Involving children in all forms of art
  - Tearing, cutting, and gluing
  - Painting
  - Crayons, markers, and chalk
  - Three-dimensional materials
  - Art as a stimulus for other curriculum areas
  - Sharing a child's art with the family
- Tips for displaying children's art
- Developmentally appropriate and multicultural/anti-bias activities

■ OVERVIEW

As we begin this chapter, it is important to understand that a child's art—or artwork, as some educators call it—belongs to the child. No adult interpretations or descriptions can or should describe what a child has created. This is part of the child's own process of communication and creativity.

Fortson and Reiff (1995) explain further:

When a young child brings to you, a teacher or parent, something made through desire, effort, and originality (a scribbled drawing, a bulky shape squeezed out of clay, or a splash of bold colors), this child is intuitively attempting to bring into being a type of relationship that lies at the very core of living. When bringing to you a "creation," however simple or strange, this child is unconsciously saying, "Here is a part of myself I am giving you."

The first time a child makes a mark with a crayon, dips a brush into paint, or glues colored circles onto paper, it is the birth of a *creative process*. A child's blank sheet of paper soon becomes a creation that never existed before. This sensory event with paints, crayons, and glue enables the child to freely experience the sheer pleasure of getting to know herself in a new way—through self-expression, "the shaping of inner worlds through outer forms" (Dyson, 1990).

Art is *fundamental* to the growth of a child and is an integration of many skills and basic experiences that begin at home and are continued and expanded in early childhood programs. Art is *visual* communicating through the elements of color, line, shape, and texture instead of words. Smith, Fucigna, Kennedy, and Lord (1993) call it "graphic language." Art is *developmental* and its contributions can be seen in physical, cognitive, social, and emotional development.

Physical development involves children using large muscles (gross motor) in activities such as easel painting or clay pounding; manipulating small muscles (fine motor) in actions such as finger painting or cutting; developing eye-hand coordination (using eyes and hands at the same time) through involvement with all types of materials; and acquiring self-help skills (gaining control over what the body can do) by freely manipulating materials to create expressions in art.

Cognitive development relates to children making art forms that represent and clarify how they see the world; finding new ways to problem solve with art materials and supplies; experimenting with cause and effect by asking "What happens if?"; comparing sizes and shapes; and predicting outcomes through their involvement with art activities. All of these projects actively stimulate cognitive development for young children.

Social and emotional development in art consists of children developing positive images of themselves; expressing personality and individualism; representing imagination and fantasy; establishing enjoyable relationships with others; and expressing feelings by using as their "vocabulary" paints, paper, pencils, chalk, clay, fabrics, and other media while participating in developmentally appropriate art activities.

Language development is included in cognitive and social development as children clarify color, size, shape, texture, and patterns while talking about their art and the art of others. For example, when a toddler picks out a piece of velvet from the art materials box and asks you to "sof' it," in her stage of telegraphic speech she is saying to you, "Touch it and feel how soft it is!" Older children are introduced to new words when they pound the clay, make brush strokes, create a design, and make an arrangement of lines and patterns. Koster (2001) believes that "art is the first written language."

Perceptual development occurs when children use their senses to learn about the nature of objects, actions, and events. Koster (2001) explains, "Teachers need to provide experiences that are sensually rich and varied, and which require children to use their perceptual abilities in many different ways. Observational and visual perception skills are heightened as children use their senses to study the patterns, colors, textures, and shapes found in nature and in the artwork of others."

As we continue through this chapter, we will look at how the developmental stages relate to specific art activities for infants, toddlers, preschoolers, and school-age children. Creating an environment that values artistic expression and encourages children's creativity and experimentation is the focus of your role as teacher, facilitator, and observer. So, here we go to do what one child has suggested, "Let's do some arting today!"

■ CHILDREN'S DEVELOPMENTAL STAGES IN ART

Looking at developmental stages in children's art reminds us that growth in this area is part of the continuing development of the total child. This wholeness includes not only the physical, cognitive, social, emotional, perceptual, and language development of each child; it also accounts for "social, cultural, religious, individual and environmental factors in tracing the development of child art" (Schirrmacher, 1998).

A teacher can recognize characteristics that are identifiable to help in understanding the needs and interests of the children in an early childhood program. Children proceed from one stage to the next in a predictable sequence relating to developmental stages, *not* ages. What happens at a given *age* is not as sure as the stage of development of children's art (Upton, 1991). Understanding what has come before helps in knowing what to look for as the child matures.

> *Infants pat their hands against the textures of blanket, water, oatmeal—mother's nose. Toddlers pile or drag everything that can be piled or dragged: cooking utensils, rocks, books, dolls, and blankets. Nursery school children select and arrange blocks, scraps, chairs, buttons, and lines of paint on paper. Patting and touching evolves to piling and dragging which in its turn evolves to sorting and arranging. (Smith, Fucigna, Kennedy, & Lord, 1993)*

Infants and Toddlers

Art is a sensory experience for infants and toddlers. The child uses his entire body when interacting with the art materials. The enjoyment for the child comes from this exploration.

Think about safety and appropriateness when selecting supplies and materials for this age. Younger children may be overwhelmed or overstimulated at first by too many choices, so start slowly and add items a few at a time. Crayons, finger paints, paints, paper, play dough, and water play should be available. The child needs opportunities to poke, pat, pound, shake, taste, smell, and scribble.

Transitions into and out of art activities are very important. The younger the child, the more verbal and visual clues are needed to help her move from one activity to another.

Flexibility, both inside and on the playground, is needed. This age child loves to water paint on the floor, table, brick wall, and sidewalk. Opportunities for experiencing color (add food coloring to the water or play dough), texture (art materials box or texture board), and temperature (warm water, cold play dough) can encourage a child to participate.

Scribbling begins around age two, but as with all developmental stages, it can begin earlier or later. The important thing is to supply the opportunity. "*Scribbles* are

FIGURE 7–1 Drawing made by a 14-month-old child.

FIGURE 7–2 Drawing made by an 18-month-old-child.

FIGURE 7–3 Drawing made by a child 2 years 6 months old.

FIGURE 7–4 Drawing made by a child 2 years 6 months old.

the building blocks of children's art. From the moment the child discovers what it looks like and feels like to put these lines down on paper, he has found something he will never lose, he has found art" (Kellogg & O'Dell, 1967).

Expect an older infant and toddler to explore and manipulate art materials, but do not expect them to produce a finished art product (Bredekamp & Copple, 1997). See Figures 7–1, 7–2, 7–3, and 7–4 for infant and toddler drawings.

Preschoolers and Kindergartners

Kellogg's "20 Basic Scribbles" (vertical, horizontal, diagonal, circular, curving, waving, zig-zag lines, and dots) continue to be discovered by preschoolers. Their art also shows them passing through the Placement Stage (definite patterns of scribbles placed in the left half, right half, center, or all over the page), then into the Shape and Design Stages (combinations of scribbles forming definite shapes and designs), and then into the Pictorial Stage (structured designs that begin to look like something adults have seen before) around ages four and five (Kellogg & O'Dell, 1967).

The child enjoys exploration and manipulation of materials. Watch for a younger preschool child to paint her hands, for example. An older child still enjoys sensory experiences but will demonstrate this by experimenting with the materials in new and unusual ways. It is important for the child to develop control over the process. A child may tear up her work during the process.

At this stage the child enjoys doing the same thing over and over again. Art represents feelings and perceptions of a child's world. The child creates what is important to him. A child uses colors that please her, and these colors may bear little relation to the actual colors of the objects created. An older preschooler creates forms and shapes,

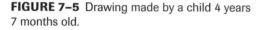

FIGURE 7–5 Drawing made by a child 4 years 7 months old.

FIGURE 7–6 Drawing made by a child 4 years 8 months old.

FIGURE 7–7 Drawing made by a child 7 years 5 months old.

FIGURE 7–8 Drawing made by a child 8 years 10 months old.

chooses materials carefully, and looks at the materials in new ways. Using different materials of different textures and consistencies enriches the child's sensitivity in using his sense of touch (Lowenfeld, 1972). See Figures 7–5 and 7–6 for children's drawings.

A child enjoys using her imagination. Copying a model changes the whole experience for her. A child who has had coloring books or dittos tends to lose the capacity to create naturally and individualistically. (This is discussed more fully later in this chapter.)

Five- to Eight-Year-Old Children

The child at this stage becomes more serious and focused in the art process. The child's early concrete experimenting and learning-by-doing art activities become a bridge to complex thinking and an understanding of the abstract. Realistic color and proportion is evident in the child's finished art. Careful planning is also becoming more apparent as part of the process.

The opinion of the adult observer becomes important. The child feels her art must be recognizable in both content and subject matter to the viewer. Often the child offers critical evaluation about his own work.

Individual, creative, and cultural differences begin to emerge. Look for all types of art, such as realistic, impressionistic, expressionistic, and abstract styles (Schirrmacher, 1998). See Figures 7–7 and 7–8 for drawings. Young children have many thoughts and ideas. They will express these ideas if they have a chance to experiment with a variety of art media and if they work in a physical and social environment that accepts their art (Schmidt, 1976).

■ TEACHER AS FACILITATOR AND OBSERVER

When you were young you probably had experiences, some of which were positive but some that were negative, concerning what teachers thought about *your* art. You should strive to be the kind of teacher the children in your care will remember as a positive and supportive influence in their lives.

In this chapter, as in all chapters of this book, you are asked to view what a child has created with different eyes than perhaps you have used before. Do not focus on the outcome or product: look at the *process*. Is the child participating, interacting, experimenting, exploring, and getting involved "up to the elbows"? This is what you should be observing as you plan, initiate, and evaluate the art center and the art activities.

Your role as teacher is one of facilitator and observer. You set up the developmentally appropriate environment; furnish a variety of safe materials and supplies; provide opportunities for child-directed art experiences; and offer support and encouragement to the children as you observe their unique creations.

Approaching children's art from the perspective of facilitator can take any real or imagined pressures off of you *and* the children. For example, let the *children* decide whether to talk about their art or not talk about it. If they freely describe it and want you to write down a description, do so—otherwise *don't*.

Many times we try to get some response from the children and ask them to "Tell me about your picture" or "Tell me a story about what you're painting." This puts stress on the child to say what he or she thinks *you* want to hear. I overheard one child emphatically tell a teacher, "This is not a story! This is a picture to look at!" (That answer certainly made the teacher reflect on what she had asked the child.)

Some suggestions of what you could say are: "I see you used different colors in your picture." "You're feeling the finger paint, aren't you?" "You have a lot of dots on your paper today." "I see you covered the whole page." These statements and others like them do not ask for the child to "come up with an answer." This type of response from you offers affirmation and encouragement.

Another part of your responsibility as a facilitator is to make materials available where children can create in an undisturbed environment. As you decide which activities and materials are appropriate, try them out yourself before you put them out for the children. This will enable you to introduce new supplies or materials comfortably and show the children how to use them appropriately. Once this is accomplished, step back and allow the children to investigate, explore, and try out the materials for themselves.

■ ESTABLISHING AN ENVIRONMENT FOR CREATIVE EXPRESSION AND EXPERIMENTATION

"Creativity requires practice to flourish" (Schmirrmacher, 1998). *There is no right or wrong way to create!* We should value what the child is creating or attempting to create and provide many opportunities for him to do so. We should facilitate the development of creative thinkers and problem solvers. Setting up an appropriate art center is the first step in establishing this priority. "The simplest choices for teachers become major decisionmaking opportunities for children. What color paper to choose, what color crayons or paint, what shape and size of paper, which way to hold the paper are all options the child should have" (Szyba, 1999).

Young children learn by active involvement with people and by manipulating objects. It becomes clear that such activities as workbooks, worksheets, patterns, coloring books, stereotyped cutouts, and teacher-made models of art are not appropriate for young children (Bredekamp & Copple, 1997).

Lowenfeld (1972) explains further:

In filling the outline drawings, children are regimented into the same type of activity, with no provision for their differences as individuals. . . . A child once conditioned to coloring books will have difficulties in enjoying the freedom of creating. The dependency which the coloring book creates is devastating.

For you as a teacher, you will find that making models and examples actually take more time and energy on your part than planning for developmentally appropriate art. The children will become more dependent on you to create patterns because they feel their creative expressions are not valued by you and therefore are unacceptable.

Mayesky (1998) offers an additional thought:

If you do use an occasional model or example, it can function positively as a springboard to unlocking each child's own creative approach to a shared, common theme (or object). Many times, a brief look at one or two examples (which should not then be displayed for "copying" during the activity) can help motivate children to get started on making one of their own.

General Guidelines

As you plan or redesign your art center, provide *time, space,* and *materials* that allow children to work at their own pace without interference. The area should be large enough to accommodate the easels and art table. The art center should be a free-choice center, like the other centers in the classroom.

- ■ The art area should be close to a sink for easy cleanup. If this is not possible, place a bucket or plastic tub with warm soapy water nearby. Change the water often.
- ■ Encourage the children to participate in all phases of an art activity, including preparation and cleanup. Have sponges and paper towels handy for the children to use. Protect the environment and the children so they do not have to be concerned about making a mess. Have smocks or aprons available for the children to wear during art activities.
- ■ Continue to keep safety in mind as you select supplies and materials for the children to use in the art center. Select only nontoxic materials. Think carefully about using balloons in any project. They are fun, but can be dangerous for young children, sometimes causing choking.
- ■ It is important to think about using recycled materials, but a word of caution: *Do not reuse Styrofoam trays that have had meat or poultry on them.* Even after washing they may contain bacteria from the raw meat or poultry. Use clean, unused Styrofoam trays, which many grocery stores will give you at very little or no cost.

- Add several drops of liquid dishwashing soap to tempera paint. It washes out of clothes more easily and it also prevents paint from chipping off the children's art when dry.
- A place for finished art should be provided. If they need to dry, plan ahead of time for a special drying place or a hanging rack.
- Place the art center near a window, if possible, so the children can see outside while they are creating. Extend freedom of movement and free expression by allowing children to stand or sit at the art table as well as use the floor to spread out large sheets of paper for art activities.
- Balance the activities: new with familiar, messy with clean, indoor with outdoor, large muscle and small muscle.
- Children are fascinated by color, texture, shape, and design. You can attract the children to the art center by including activities that promote each of these. For example, invite the children to make a collage (pasting objects together onto a surface) of varying yellow colors found in magazines. This activity encourages preschoolers to cut, glue, look for, and discover that any color can have many shades.

Guidance Guidelines

"Good guidance begins with planning" (Hildebrand & Hearron, 1999). Clarify your goals and objectives for the art center and each art activity. Relate them to the theme and lesson plan when appropriate. (Review Chapter 2 for detailed information.)

Establish rules with the children concerning the care and use of art materials and limits within the art center. Guide them toward assuming responsibility for the use, care, and cleaning of materials and tools. Give visual and verbal clues as to the number of children allowed in the center at any given time. For example, put up a sign that shows three children with the numeral 3 written next to the figures of children (Figure 7–9).

Help children and their parents deal with being messy. Messy is okay! Supply smocks or aprons on hooks near the art center. The children can be responsible for getting a smock, putting it on during an art activity, and putting it back when they have finished. Continue to repeat rules of the art center when necessary.

FIGURE 7–9 Visual clues help children understand rules and limits in the classroom.

The type and number of materials supplied at one time should depend on the development and ages of the children involved in the activity as well as the number of children participating.

As you introduce each new activity or group of materials or supplies, explain the appropriate ways to use them. "[T]oo little structure can inhibit children's expression just as too-directed experience can. Children must clearly understand your expectations for the organized routines of working with art materials. Feeling *safe and stimulated* allows them to learn and grow" (Levinger & Mott, 1992).

For younger children, you will have to say, "Treat the paint (or the crayons, or the markers) gently," and probably repeat it many times. It is important to begin early to explain how art materials are to be used, and that they are not to be used to touch or hit others.

Help all children learn to respect their own art and the art of others. Many times a cooperative art activity, such as painting a mural with each child having her own space on the paper, will demonstrate to a child how to focus on her own creation and not to interfere with others.

Give verbal or sound cues to let the children know when it will be time to clean up. Set a timer for five minutes and tell the children what you are doing. When it goes off, let them know it is time to clean up.

Use of Food in Art Projects

Using food in art activities with children is a continuing topic of discussion. Teachers and administrators are divided on this issue. I have found that not using food works better for the following reasons:

- It is difficult to justify using food when many parents are working long hours to put food on the table for their families. Food is expensive. Also, the casual use of food in art when many are homeless and hungry can be upsetting to some adults.
- The use of food in an art activity may offend some cultural groups who use that food item for religious or ethnic celebration (Schirrmacher, 1998).
- It is important *not* to use foods for art because toddlers are developing self-regulatory skills and must learn to distinguish between food and other objects that are not to be eaten (Bredekamp & Copple, 1997).
- Using cornstarch, flour, salt, and food coloring is acceptable because these are used in small amounts as additives to make play dough and other recipes for art.
- There are other alternatives for art projects. For example, instead of using macaroni, string together paper shapes with a hole punched in the middle or paper straws cut in various lengths. Sand, glitter, or buttons can be glued instead of rice. Use cotton balls, Styrofoam, or toothpicks instead of beans for collages and textured art. It is fun to come up with other creative choices.

You will need to decide for yourself whether you want to use food in art projects or not. Consider your own values, economic factors, and the policies of your center or school.

Outdoor Environment

Take it all outdoors! Children enjoy the space and freedom offered by outdoor art activities. Take the easels, a table, long sheets of butcher paper, paints, and cleanup buckets outdoors. Let the children use chalk on the sidewalk; explore rocks, shells, flowers, trees, birds, and butterflies; go for walks and look for colors, textures, and shapes; and gather leaves for making rubbings or prints or for using as materials on paintings and collages.

If your playground has a chain link fence, it can be used as a drying area. Clothespins easily attach the paintings or murals to the fence. A safe drying area can also be arranged inside a large cardboard box. Plan for cleanup with buckets, hoses, and lots of paper towels. "Easy 'mess management' makes outdoor art inviting and enjoyable for everyone" (Jurek & MacDonald, 1990).

Chapter 8 offers additional ideas for outdoor activities with sand, water, and woodworking.

Aesthetic Environment

Jim Greenman (1987) captures the essence of environmental aesthetics in the following description:

> *Imagine a room where there are bright splashes of color, often attached to moving bodies, and warm muted hues on carpet and walls. Sunshine catches the light of a prism in one corner, and there is a small patch of sunlight so bright you have to squint. There are soft indirect lights, shadows, and cool dark corners.*
>
> *There are hanging baskets of trailing green plants, flowers, pussy willows and cattails, angel hair and dried grasses. The beauty of life is captured by Monet and Wyeth and assorted four-year-olds.*

We can actively create such an **aesthetic environment** for children, one that cultivates an appreciation for beauty and a feeling of wonder and excitement of the world in which we live. We can do this by:

- Designing indoor and outdoor environments to emphasize beauty, attention to detail, color, shape, textures, lines, and patterns in carefully thought-out space and arrangements
- Allowing time for looking at and talking about all kinds of art
- Providing beautiful books with all types of illustrations
- Introducing children to fine art by displaying prints of paintings and sculptures in the classroom (the water gardens of Monet, the mothers and children of Cassatt, the ballerinas of Degas, and the splashed action paintings of Pollock) and by visiting local galleries and museums

- Including art, wall hangings, weavings, and tapestry from diverse cultures as part of the aesthetic room environment
- Exposing children to nature by allowing time to watch a spider spin a web or to look closely at a wildflower
- Supporting children's self-expression and creativity as they reflect the world around them

A SPECIAL STORY

One weekend in May 1991, Operation Solomon occurred: 14,600 Ethiopian Jews were brought safely to Israel. The confused newcomers thronged the lobbies of Jerusalem hotels and were offered assistance from Jewish agencies and volunteers. TV and newspaper reporters were eager to record the astonishing event.

Nurit Shilo-Cohen, Chief Curator of the Ruth Youth Wing, The Israel Museum, Jerusalem, continues the story:

Ruth Youth Wing teachers were there bearing drawing paper, pencils, crayons and plasticene. Amidst the excitement, the teachers quietly made a clearing in a corner of the lobby, spread out their "wares," and waited. Hesitantly, one by one, adults and children approached. Tentatively, hand was put to paper as the Ethiopians silently set to work drawing the first lines. And they drew, and drew for days, with growing enthusiasm, their art offering a medium for expressing their overwhelming feelings beyond verbal language.

(Excerpt from *Stork, Stork, How Is Our Land?* Works by newly arrived Ethiopian Immigrant Children, 1991)

This book is filled with the art of children. It covers a period of some two months. The children and their art reflect a special time and a unique event.

■ INVOLVING CHILDREN IN ALL FORMS OF ART

Children involved with art develop sensory awareness, aesthetic appreciation, self-expression, and improve visual and motor coordination. The process of experimenting with and creating two- and three-dimensional projects from a variety of media connects children to another facet of their world.

Davidson (1996) tells us:

When children are introduced to a new medium, they explore what can be done with it. The first time children use finger paints they will swish it, squish it, pile it in the middle, run it through their fingers, makes lines in it and experiment in other ways to see what they can do with this thick wet stuff. It is not until after this exploration that children will begin to use the materials imaginatively. . . . It is important to know what one can make a material do, to be in control of a material, before putting it to use as a tool to create something.

We see, time and again, a young preschooler put one color of paint on the easel paper and then place another color exactly on top of the first, and then continue this process until the result is a mass of "indescribable" color. The color is beautiful to the child, and she has created it. This newfound ability to change color is important and exemplifies learning for the child. The older child paints masses of color next to each other and may surround the color with dots and shapes. Both exemplify the process of making art.

The emphasis throughout this chapter is on allowing appropriate time, space, and flexibility for creating; to give permission and responsibility to the children; and to nurture and value their creativity. This will provide children with many opportunities to move beyond investigation to using these materials in unique, imaginative, and individually creative ways.

Tearing, Cutting, and Gluing

Tearing, cutting, and gluing offer individual activities to young children and provide small muscle development and tactile experiences; offer opportunities for controlling scissors and direction of cutting for creative purposes; provide discovery of form, shapes, colors, sizes, and textures; develop eye-hand coordination; and encourage verbal communication and sharing.

Let the children do the tearing, cutting, and gluing. Use white glue, school paste, flour and water paste, glue stick, masking tape, and clear tape. Pour white glue into small plastic squeeze bottles or pour small, individual amounts of glue into jar lids, small bowls, or other containers. Children can use cotton swabs or their fingers to manipulate and spread the glue. Supply a wet paper towel for each child to have at his place, or moisten a sponge that several children can share to wipe their fingers.

Children can tear and cut tissue paper, construction paper, fabric scraps, old greeting cards, wallpaper samples, newspapers, and catalogs. Glue these materials to construction paper, corrugated paper, all sizes of paper plates, index cards, box lids, brown wrapping paper, foil, or gift wrapping paper.

Painting

Painting, in all its forms, provides sensory experiences, allows for coordinated use of many body muscles, encourages language development, helps with the judgment of spatial relationships, provides an opportunity for manipulation and experimentation, develops form perception, is often a two-handed experience, and develops skill in handling a brush and other art materials and tools.

Painting develops skills that are used in reading and writing. The curves, patterns, and lines that children make are similar to letters and words. The awareness of spatial relationship and configurations on the page relates to reading skills. Distinguishing painted forms, lines, and patterns from the background requires the same discrimination as reading. When you read, you separate or "pull out" letters from the background.

Organizing the art environment for painting will help make the activities successful for children. When finger painting, children can use the paint directly on the table top, on a table that is covered with butcher paper, or on individual pieces of paper. For younger children, place a spoonful or two of finger paint into plastic bags. Close the bags carefully and seal with tape to prevent leaks. Each process offers a different experience for children. They have direct sensory contact with the material. They create changeable patterns, designs, and shapes in a short amount of time while maintaining their interest for a long time. To preserve a table-top painting, blot the finger painting with a piece of butcher paper to get the reverse design that the child can keep.

Finger paints in many colors are commercially available. Selecting skin-tone colors offer young children another way to develop self-esteem. Other items to use as finger paints are toothpaste, cold cream, hand lotion, or wet sand.

Easel painting is popular with young children. Easels can be placed indoors and/or outdoors. If several are set up, place them close together. This encourages interaction and conversation between the painters. Easels should be the correct height for young children, washable, and sturdy, and should have a tray for holding containers of paint. You could also tape the easel paper to a wall indoors or a fence outdoors.

Furnish large sheets of easel paper or paper cut into different shapes, brushes (one for each color being used) in a wide variety of sizes, and a choice of colors. For younger children, it is helpful to start with one color at a time. Have them use the primary colors of red, blue, and yellow; the secondary colors of orange, purple, and green (the colors obtained by blending pairs of primary colors); and black, brown, and white. Mixing black or white with primary colors teaches pastel tints and grayed tones. Children quickly discover for themselves what happens when colors are mixed together.

To thicken paint, add liquid starch or cornstarch (children will need large brushes to paint with thick paint). A teaspoon of alcohol added to each pint of paint or a drop or two of oil of wintergreen will prevent the paint from souring. Adding sand or talcum powder to the tempera paint gives other consistencies.

Before children start to paint, you may have to remind them to put on a smock or apron. After the children are through, let them wash the brushes with soap and water, shape them, and place them brush-end up in a container to dry. Additional things that can be used as brushes are paint rollers, pot scrubbers, sponges, feathers, toothbrushes, and fly swatters.

String painting is another art activity that young children enjoy doing. If they want to move the string around the paper to make a design, you might first attach a button to one end of the string so that the children can hold the button to manipulate the string more easily.

They can also dip short lengths of string or yarn into bowls of paint mixed with a small amount of white glue (holding the string with a clothespin can help those children who do not want to get their fingers in the paint). They then lay the yarn or string onto a piece of construction paper to form a design. Children can vary the lengths of yarn, string, or twine to add texture to the painting. An extension of this activity for older children is to guide them into mixing four different shades of blue (or any color) and then make a string painting with the various shades of color.

FIGURE 7–10 The feet painting process.

Children can fold a sheet of paper in half, then open it and place the paint-wet string on one side of the paper. Fold the other side of the paper over and hold it with one hand. Then gently pull the string through while holding the folded paper in place with the other hand. To complete this activity, younger children may need assistance from you or another child.

Children enjoy experimenting with object *or* gadget painting. Provide items such as kitchen utensils, forks, corks, sponges, pieces of wood, combs, and cookie cutters for dipping into paint or a paint pad (made by pouring thick tempera paint onto several layers of paper towels or a thin sponge). The children press the object down onto a piece of manila or colored construction paper. A unique print is the result.

Painting with feet offers another sensory experience for children. (This is an extension of hand painting.) Begin by covering the floor or outdoor sidewalk with newspaper, and then place long pieces of butcher paper or brown wrapping paper over the newspaper. Tape the corners so that the paper will stay in place. The children remove their shoes and socks and then stand at one end of the paper. Help them step into containers or tubs you have prepared with tempera paint. Paint is slippery, so you may need to assist some children as they walk on the paper. At the other end of the paper place a tub of warm, soapy water and some towels. After the children make their "feet design," they will end up by stepping into the tub of water (Figure 7–10). It makes a wonderful mural. This is a fun activity to do with parents as well. (I still remember the first time I did feet painting when my oldest child was in preschool. It was a parent-child activity during an open house. I have used it many times since with children, parents, and teachers.)

Other types of painting for young children are fingerprint painting (walking fingers dipped in paint across paper), sand mixed with paint (gritty paint), salt and paint (sparkle paint), flour and paint (lumpy paint), ball or marble painting (dipped items rolled over paper placed in a box), painting on rocks, and painting with watercolors.

Crayons, Markers, and Chalk

Crayons and markers are familiar to most young children. They have used them at home and other places, such as at restaurants that welcome children to color on the paper table covering or on the children's menu. A word of caution: Young children should use only water-based markers. Permanent markers may contain toxic solvents. Chalk provides another type of drawing experience. All these materials are ready-to-use, easy to store, and require very little cleanup.

When using crayons, markers, and chalk, children utilize different types of muscular coordination than those they use to control a paintbrush or a finger. They also encourage exploration of what colors can do, provide an excellent prewriting experience, develop hand-eye coordination, and stimulate the imagination.

Scribbling, as discussed earlier in this chapter, is important to young children. Crayon scribbling is usually one of the first activities children enjoy doing over and over again. A sitting position makes it easier to control a crayon. Children often use pressure to make marks on the paper, so having large crayons available for younger children works well. Older children prefer the small crayons.

By starting with large sheets of paper, then moving on to all sizes, shapes, and textures of paper, you can extend the crayon scribbling and drawing activities. Using crayons on colored paper teaches children what happens when one color is applied to another.

Crayon rubbings can be introduced early in the year, then continued as the variety of objects to be rubbed changes throughout the year. To make a crayon rubbing of a texture, children place an object under newsprint or other type paper and rub with a crayon. (You might need to tape objects down on the table at first.) Rubbing the side of the crayon across the paper sometimes works best. Suggestions of objects to be rubbed: cardboard squares, circles, rectangles, triangles, and ovals; coins and leaves of various sizes and shapes; different textures of wallpaper; bricks, tree barks, and sandpaper. (Let the children discover these and others.)

A favorite art activity of toddlers and preschoolers is to "draw a child." For the young ones, you can draw around each child lying on a large piece of paper. The older child chooses a partner, and they can draw around each other. Then each child colors herself. Face, hair, clothes, and shoes can be added with additional materials from the art materials scrap box (see Figure 7–11).

FIGURE 7–11 An example of the "drawing a child" process.

Crayon resist is an interesting art activity for older children. They draw a picture on paper with light-colored crayons, then cover the picture with watercolors or thin tempera paint. The paint will cover all but the crayon markings. A variation of this project is for the children to place waxed paper over a sheet of white paper and draw on it with a pencil, pressing wax lines and design into the bottom paper. They then remove the waxed paper and brush thin paint over the wax lines on the paper. A design of white lines will appear on the painted surface.

Younger children can develop their small muscle ability, which is necessary to hold and control a writing implement on their own, by using chalk. Offer them the opportunity to write with colored chalk on the sidewalk, on a large chalkboard placed inside or outside, or on small individual chalkboards.

For a wet chalk project (wet chalk provides an interesting texture different from dry chalk), have the children dip the chalk in a cup of water before writing on paper. Another way to do this is for the children to wet the paper, including paper plates, instead of the chalk. For big pictures and designs, sweep the sides of the chalk across the paper. The children can then mix the colors together by blending them with their fingers or with a tissue.

An additional way of using crayons, markers, and chalk is to attach these to an easel with yarn or string. The children can use these independently or can mix and match for self-discovery. Children can also copy printed words from books, rebus charts, and other printed material around the room. This will help with learning the left-to-right progression of words for reading.

Three-Dimensional Materials

The sensory experience of working with a variety of textures encourages young children to experiment, explore, and discover original ways to create art. These activities can help children release emotional tensions and frustrations; work with their hands; develop small muscles; and provide opportunities to manipulate, construct, and learn about spatial relationships.

Three-dimensional art (having three sides) is demonstrated through the use of play dough, clay, and "goop." These materials should be used on a surface that is easily cleaned and is large enough for children to have plenty of "elbow room." These materials should be soft enough for the children to manipulate easily, neither too wet nor too dry. Placing individual amounts of these materials on a tray, linoleum square, or manila folder for each child helps the children identify limits and gives them personal space. It is helpful to provide a bucket of water for the children to wash their hands when they are finished with the activity. This will keep the residue of the materials out of the sinks.

Play dough, clay, and goop are extremely valuable because the children are able to use the materials with their hands without having to learn how to manage a tool, such as a paintbrush. (Younger children do better with play dough because it is softer and easier to manipulate.) The children are concerned with managing the material and learning what they can do with it. You can add rolling pins, cookie cutters, or other accessories after the children have had a lot of time to handle and experience the feel of the clay or dough. Many classrooms have both commercial clay and play dough. In others, the teachers prefer to make these materials themselves. You might wish to supply both to the children.

The following is the recipe for cooked play dough (do not eat). You can make this first and then give it to the younger children. You and the older children can make it together so they can see the process.

COOKED PLAY DOUGH

1 cup flour	1 tablespoon cooking oil
½ cup salt	2 teaspoons cream of tartar
1 cup water	

Mix the above ingredients. Heat and stir over low heat until the mixture forms a ball. Remove from heat and wrap in waxed paper to cool. Knead it well. Store in an airtight container. The dough will last much longer if kept in the refrigerator. Add food coloring, if desired. (Some teachers put the food coloring in before cooking; others add color after cooking so the children can see the change from white, to marbled, to the final color.)

The following is the recipe for uncooked play dough (do not eat). For younger children, give it to them already made. Let the older children make it with your guidance.

UNCOOKED PLAY DOUGH

1 cup flour	food coloring (optional)
1 cup salt	water
1 tablespoon salad oil	

Mix flour and salt. Add oil. Slowly add water until the mixture sticks together but does not feel sticky. Knead it well. Store in airtight container.

The recipe for goop follows.

GOOP

½ box to 1 box of cornstarch
water

Add water slowly to cornstarch until it is semifirm. Mix it with your hands (or let the children help you). You can feel and see the changes in the texture. Store covered in the refrigerator. As it becomes dry from storage and handling, simply add more water.

Other three-dimensional works of art can be made into the form of sculptures by adding the following materials: toothpicks, Styrofoam, boxes, pieces of wood, egg cartons, paper towels, and toilet paper rolls.

ART AS A STIMULUS FOR OTHER CURRICULUM AREAS

Try connecting art to everything you do. For example, children can listen to music and draw or paint in rhythm to the music. They can express in their creations how the music makes them feel. Verbal and nonverbal language is expressed through art. As pointed out earlier in this chapter, children learn to include an art vocabulary into their everyday conversations with other children and adults. They express and represent what they know through their art. The art activities discussed in this chapter also give children an understanding of themselves and others. Their study of artists and their visits to art galleries and museums help them relate to their community and to the world.

Williams (1995) suggests that math and art content can be combined on a regular basis. For example: the math concepts of problem solving, inventing patterns, measurement, sorting, and classifying relate to the art concepts of awareness of line and shape, decoration of line and pattern, and awareness of texture and changing shape.

Schirrmacher (1998) points out that children quantify art materials, equipment, and supplies by counting the number of brushes and jars of paint that are in use and by deciding which brushes have longer handles, which crayons are fatter, and which geometric shapes are being used in their art creations.

Many scientific principles that have already been discussed in this chapter are:

- Discovering what a specific material can do and what the child can do to control it
- Observing what happens when colors are mixed together
- Noticing what happens when flour and water are combined
- Experimenting with thick paint and thin paint
- Discovering what happens when you press down hard or lightly with a brush or crayon on paper
- Observing what happens when paint is brushed over a crayon picture
- Determining what occurs when different ingredients are mixed together

SHARING A CHILD'S ART WITH THE FAMILY

Another part of the teacher's role is to help parents understand that the many pages or examples of art the children bring home are the results of creative and imaginative processes—all of them from the children. If the family understands *why* art is valued in the early childhood setting, they can more easily offer support to their child at home.

You can also guide the parents into setting up a special place at home for their child to continue experimenting and creating with art. Send home suggestions and lists of what materials and supplies are appropriate as well as explanations of what he or she has been doing in the classroom. *Interpret the child's developmental progress to the parents, not what the child's art is or is not.*

It's important to explain to the families of a child with special needs how their child participates in art activities.

Because of the open-ended nature of well-designed art activities, children with special needs can participate fully in most art programs, often without many modifications. If necessary, changes can be made in the tools and environment to allow active participation. The other children also need to be encouraged to accept and support those with special needs. (Koster, 2001)

For example, Koster suggests the following:

- Put trays across wheelchairs.
- Provide wheelchair-height tables.
- Wrap art tools such as crayons, markers, pencils, and brushes in foam haircurlers to improve grip.
- Use scented crayons and markers.
- Provide many tactile materials.
- Tape papers to the table to keep them from wrinkling or moving when the children are using them.

■ TIPS FOR DISPLAYING CHILDREN'S ART

As you send the children's art home, remember to save some of the creations to place around the classroom, with the child's permission, of course. The early education environment should reflect the children, and a wonderful way to do this is to display their art. (This also actively creates an aesthetic environment, as previously discussed in this chapter.)

> *Your goal is not to display children's "best" work, but to represent all the styles and levels created in your room, from scribble shapes to detailed portraits. When you do this, you send a clear message that you truly respect children's individual artistic expressions. (Feinburg, 1993)*

Displays show the parents what is happening in their child's classroom. Provide a place with wall and table displays outside the classroom in a hall or lobby for parents' enjoyment.

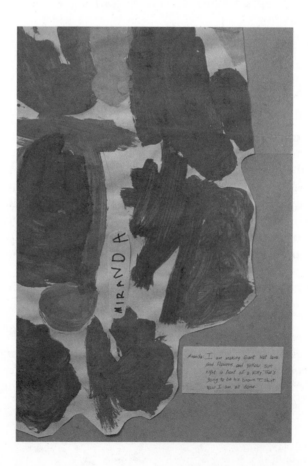

Art should be displayed at the child's eye level. Frame children's art attractively in a variety of ways using colored paper, wallpaper, or gift wrap as a background; rick-rack, fabric, or yarn to outline pictures; and a large group finger painting to serve as a mounting for individual art. Taking the time and effort to mat and frame the children's art is another way to show that you value what they have done.

Display all kinds of children's creations (clay models, Styrofoam structures, mobiles, wood sculpture, and collages). These kinds of art can be displayed on tables or shelves and arranged attractively on brightly colored paper. With permission, place the child's name in the upper left-hand corner to encourage left to right eye movement and to encourage the children to sign their art work. Change the art displays frequently. Let the children help decide when to change the selections and what to put up next. Arrange art in different kinds of groupings, such as several art items belonging to an individual child, several pictures that share the same colors, pictures with the same theme created from different media, and art connected to the theme or lesson plan of the week (see Figure 7–12).

FIGURE 7–12 A kiosk is a self-standing display with three or more sides.

An art kiosk is a workable solution to limited wall space. A kiosk is a self-standing display with three or more sides. It can be constructed of panels of sturdy cardboard, wood, or stacked cartons. It is space-efficient in that many pictures can be simultaneously displayed on a number of sides in a few feet of floor space. (Schirrmacher, 1998)

Feinburg (1993) sums it all up for us. "Just as photographs of children tell us much about what children look like on the outside, their art work tells us—boldly!—what they look like on the inside."

■ DEVELOPMENTALLY APPROPRIATE AND MULTICULTURAL/ ANTI-BIAS ACTIVITIES

A book, first introduced in 1955, that is one of the most popular ones for both children and teachers is Crockett Johnson's *Harold and the Purple Crayon.* You can use this imaginative story as a springboard for many art activities in an early childhood program. For example:

■ Read the book to the children at group time. Ask the children to think of other things Harold can do with his purple crayon. At the next group time introduce a flannelboard story that has Harold as the main character doing some of the things the children suggested.

■ In the art center place only purple items, such as crayons, markers, and construction paper. This is a creative way to introduce children to all the different shades of purple. Let the children experiment with paints and problem solve which ones to mix together to make purple. Also have purple play dough available for creative play.

■ For their snack you can serve purple grapes, or introduce the children to eggplant or other purple foods.

■ The children will also suggest other purple things to do.

For older children, a self-awareness and self-expression activity called "The Me Bag" is suggested by Aronson (1995). Give the children a plain brown grocery bag to decorate any way they choose. They take the bag home and fill it with things that are important to them, things they value and are proudest of. The next day they bring the bag back and share what is in it.

Aronson explains further:

Although each bag looks different, they all contain precious items. Children learn that the things that make them unique are as valuable as the things they have in common. They learn to appreciate differences rather than fear them. And they learn to see themselves as others might see them: as individuals with their own enthusiasms and cultural traditions, neither better nor worse than others.

The following activities offer opportunities for sharing other cultures with the children in an early education program:

- Each March 3, Japanese girls celebrate *Hina Matsuri* (HEE-nah maht-SOO-ree) or the Doll Festival. On this day the family's collection of ceremonial dolls, many of which are handed down from generation to generation, are placed on display. The girls themselves are also honored on this day (Milord, 1992).
- Each May in Japan, the skies are filled with flying fish, carp-shaped windsocks hung high from bamboo poles in honor of young boys. This special occasion is called *Tango no sekku* (tahn-goh noh SEH-koo). It is celebrated on the fifth day of the fifth month (Milord, 1992).

Both of these special celebration days suggest exciting art projects in an early education classroom. The younger children can bring in their dolls or stuffed animals to share. Simple commercial kites or windsocks can be hung around the room to brighten the environment. Japanese music can be played in the background.

- For preschoolers you can read the book *A Carp for Kimiko* (1993) by Virginia Kroll. Older children can read the book by themselves. This is a delightful story that deals with sharing and gender identity as well as traditional Japanese celebrations. This book discusses Children's Day, which is celebrated in May.

You can follow up with a cooperative group art activity of making kites. This incorporates problem solving, experimentation, creativity, planning, and sharing of responsibilities. You can start the process by asking the children to think about what makes a kite fly. What kind of a kite do they want to make? What materials will they need? Have a selection of books on kites and some suggestions for designs as well.

This activity can be the theme or lesson plan of the week. You will probably have to rearrange the room to accommodate the many aspects of the project going on at once. Figure 7–13 suggests a four-step process to make a paper cup windsock.

STEP 1: Cut out the bottom of a paper cup (use the type that is not waxed on the outside).

STEP 2: Decorate with paint, markers, etc.

STEP 3: Glue long pieces of ribbon around bottom edge.

STEP 4: Hang with string and let it blow in the wind!

FIGURE 7–13 Making a paper cup windsock. The children will think of many different ways to make windsocks if you provide all kinds of materials for them.

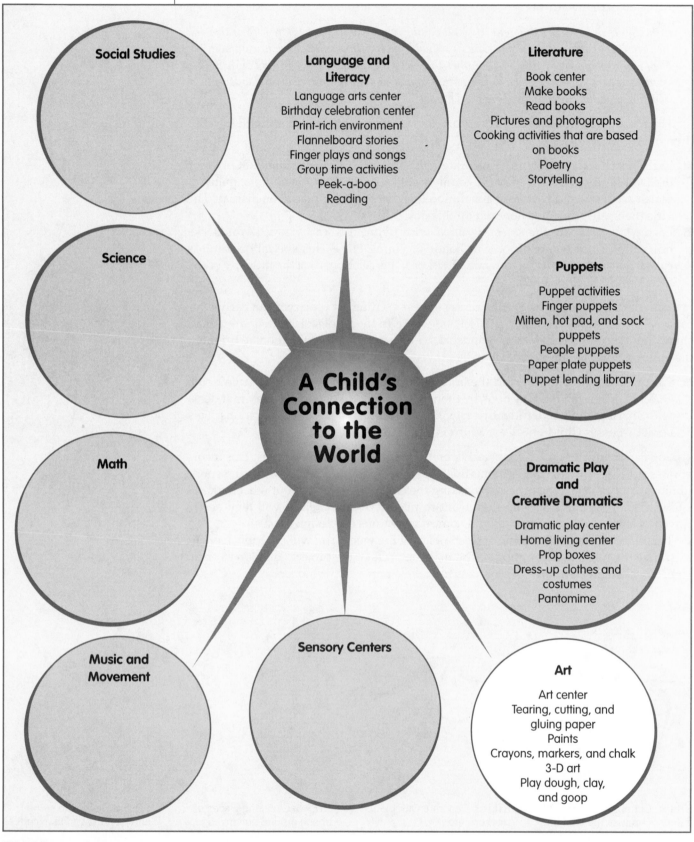

Social Studies

Language and Literacy
Language arts center
Birthday celebration center
Print-rich environment
Flannelboard stories
Finger plays and songs
Group time activities
Peek-a-boo
Reading

Literature
Book center
Make books
Read books
Pictures and photographs
Cooking activities that are based
on books
Poetry
Storytelling

Science

Puppets
Puppet activities
Finger puppets
Mitten, hot pad, and sock
puppets
People puppets
Paper plate puppets
Puppet lending library

A Child's Connection to the World

Math

Dramatic Play and Creative Dramatics
Dramatic play center
Home living center
Prop boxes
Dress-up clothes and
costumes
Pantomime

Music and Movement

Sensory Centers

Art
Art center
Tearing, cutting, and
gluing paper
Paints
Crayons, markers, and chalk
3-D art
Play dough, clay,
and goop

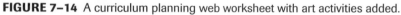

FIGURE 7–14 A curriculum planning web worksheet with art activities added.

■ Other countries include dolls and kites in their cultures, for example, Russian *matrioshka* (mah-TROYSH-kah) nesting dolls. Koreans have many traditions involving kites. One is used in celebration of the new year. A bird-shaped kite is used to fly messages away. (Parents can be a great resource to help you learn about celebrations in their families.)

■ Remember to include skin-tone colors of crayons, markers, and construction paper; different colors of yarn to represent hair; and multicolors of play dough among the materials and supplies in the art center.

Figure 7–14 is the curriculum planning web worksheet with art activities added. This worksheet with appropriate additions is included in each chapter.

AFTERVIEW

Through art, a child

■ Heightens an awareness of and appreciation for an aesthetic environment

■ Strengthens his or her self-expression, self-understanding, patience, and self-control

■ Acquires visual, spatial, and tactile awareness

■ Develops small and large muscles

■ Develops eye-hand coordination and hand-hand coordination

■ Experiments with color, line, form, shape, texture, size, balance, and configurations

■ Increases creative problem solving, decision making, and abstract thinking abilities

■ Experiments with different art media and recycled materials

■ Communicates ideas nonverbally

■ Releases emotional tensions and frustrations

■ Grows in social relationships

■ Increases vocabulary and language skills

■ Develops respect for artistic expressions of others

KEY TERMS

aesthetic environment
art
cognitive development
crayon resist

crayon rubbings
physical development
language development
perceptual development

social and emotional
    development
string painting
three-dimensional art

EXPLORATIONS

1. Based on information in this chapter and on your observations of early childhood environments, develop a list of appropriate materials and supplies to have available in the art center for young children.

2. Make a list of recyclable materials that are appropriate for use by young children in art activities. Identify how you determined that these would be safe for children to use.

3. Choose a partner or colleague and together complete the following "Art Brainstorming" activity:
   a. List five ways to use tempera paint.
   b. List five ways to use crayons.
   c. List five ways to use scissors.
   d. List five uses for glue.

   e. List five ways to make collages.
   f. List five uses for string.
   Discuss whether or not the activities are developmentally appropriate. If not, what could you do to make them appropriate? Review this chapter for assistance.

4. Select and plan an art activity for young children. Specify which age group this activity is planned for: infants, toddlers, preschoolers, or primary-age children. Write a list of objectives, materials needed, step-by-step procedures for presenting this activity, follow-up activities, and evaluation guidelines. (Use the activity plan worksheet in Chapter 2.) Prepare this activity and demonstrate it during class or with a group of children.

5. Select two early childhood classrooms and observe for at least one hour in each. Describe, in writing, six art activities you observed. Were these new to you? How did the teacher present the activities to the children? Which ones were child-directed? Were any of these teacher-directed? What transitions did the teacher use before and after the activities? Will you use or have you used any of the six activities with children? Explain.

REFERENCES

Aronson, D. (1995, Spring). The inside story. *Teaching Tolerance, 4*(1), 23–29.

Bredekamp, S., & Copple, C. (Eds.). (1997). *Developmentally appropriate practice in early childhood programs* (Rev. ed.). Washington, DC: National Association for the Education of Young Children.

Davidson, J. I. (1996). *Emergent literacy and dramatic play in early education*. Albany, NY: Delmar.

Dyson, A. H. (1990, January). Symbol makers, symbol weavers: How children link play, pictures, and print. *Young Children, 45*(2), 50–57.

Ethiopian Immigrant Children. (1991). *Stork, stork, how is our land?* Jerusalem: The Israel Museum.

Feinburg, S. G. (1993, October). Learning through art. *Early Childhood Today, 8*(2), 58–66, 72–73.

Fortson, L. R., & Reiff, J. C. (1995). *Early childhood curriculum*. Boston: Allyn and Bacon.

Greenman, J. (1987, November). Thinking about the aesthetics of children's environments. *Child Care Information Exchange, 58*, 9–12.

Hildebrand, V., & Hearron, P. F. (1999). *Guiding young children* (6th ed.). Columbus, OH: Merrill.

Jurek, D., & MacDonald, S. (1990, May/June). Outdoor art: The sky's the limit. *Pre-K Today, 4*(8), 30–37.

Kellogg, R., & O'Dell, S. (1967). *The psychology of children's art.* New York: Random House.

Koster, J. (2001). *Growing artists: Teaching art to young children* (2nd ed.). Albany, NY: Delmar.

Levinger, L., & Mott, A. M. (1992). Art in early childhood. In A. Mitchell and J. David (Eds.), *Explorations with young children: A curriculum guide from the Bank Street College of Education.* Mt. Rainier, MD: Gryphon House.

Lowenfeld, V. (1972). *Your child and his art: A guide for parents.* New York: Macmillan.

Mayesky, M. (1998). *Creative activities for young children* (6th ed.). Albany, NY: Delmar.

Milord, S. (1992). *Hands around the world.* Charlotte, VT: Williamson Publishing.

Schmidt, V. E. (1976). *Early childhood development.* Dallas, TX: Hendrick-Long Publishing Company.

Schirrmacher, R. (1998). *Art and creative development for young children* (2nd ed.). Albany, NY: Delmar.

Smith, N. R., Fucigna, C., Kennedy, M., & Lord, L. (1993). *Experience and art* (2nd ed.). New York: Teachers College Press.

Szyba, C. M. (1999, January). Why do some teachers resist offering appropriate, open-ended art activities for young children? *Young Children, 54*(1), 16–20.

Williams, D. (1995). *Teaching mathematics through children's art.* Portsmouth, NH: Heinemann.

Upton, D. B. (1991). *I can do it!* (3rd ed.). Dallas, TX: Author.

ADDITIONAL READINGS AND RESOURCES

Alter-Muri, S. (1994, Fall). Art eases the process of attachment and separation. *Day Care and Early Education, 22*(1), 4–6.

Burn, B. (1984). *Metropolitan children.* New York: The Metropolitan Museum of Art.

Cole, E., & Schaefer, C. (1990, January). Can young children be art critics? *Young Children, 45*(2), 33–38.

DeBoer, K. (1994). *Multicultural activities.* Waterloo, Ontario Canada: Roylco Limited.

Dever, M. T., & Jared, E. J. (1996, March). Remember to include arts and crafts in your integrated curriculum. *Young Children, 51*(3), 69–73.

Edwards, L. C., & Nabors, M. L. (1993, March). The creative arts process: What it is and what it is not. *Young Children, 48*(3), 77–81.

Engle, B. S. (1996, March). Learning to look: Appreciating child art. *Young Children, 51*(3), 74–79.

Goldhaber, J. (1992, November). Sticky to dry; red to purple: Exploring transformation with play dough. *Young Children, 48*(1), 26–28.

Hall, N. S. (1999). *Creative resources for the anti-bias classroom.* Albany, NY: Delmar.

Jones, E., & Villarino, G. (1994, January). What goes up on the classroom walls—and why? *Young Children, 49*(2), 38–40.

Lowenfeld, V., & Brittain, W. L. (1987). *Creative and mental growth.* New York: Macmillan.

Manolson, I. (1993, November/December). Homemade wrapping paper—Papel de envolver hecho a mano. *Early Childhood Today, 8*(3), 29–30.

Oken-Wright, P. (1998, March). Transition to writing: Drawing as a scaffold for emergent writers. *Young Children, 53*(2), 76–81.

Rankin, B. (1994, November/December). Making your classroom beautiful. *Early Childhood Today, 9*(3), 42–43.

Readdick, C. A., & Bartlett, P. M. (1994/95, Winter). Vertical learning environments. *Childhood Education, 71*(2), 86–90.

Schiller, M. (1995, March). An emergent art curriculum that fosters understanding. *Young Children, 50*(3), 33–38.

Seefeldt, C. (1995, March). Art—A serious work. *Young Children, 50*(3), 39–45.

Terzian, A. M. (1993). *The kids' multicultural art book.* Charlotte, VT: Williamson Publishing.

Voss, G. (1993). *Museum shapes.* Boston: Museum of Fine Arts.

Warash, B. G., & Saab, J. F. (1999, Winter). Exploring the visual arts with young children. *Dimensions of Early Childhood, 27*(1), 11–15.

Wolf, A. D. (1990, January) Art postcards—another aspect of your aesthetics program? *Young Children, 45*(2), 39–43.

Sensory Centers

■ OVERVIEW

Young children learn through **sensory experiences** that offer them opportunities for free exploration in a variety of curriculum areas. Children learn best through repeated explorations, and the sensory area gives them multiple possibilities to do this. As you read this chapter, focus on how children see, hear, feel, touch, and taste the world around them. Observe carefully how the children in an early education setting make choices and react to the environment. Ask yourself if the classroom is "their room." Is it set up so that they can claim ownership? Is it giving them hands-on knowledge about their world?

Young children learn through their five senses. They have the ability to take in and make sense of information obtained from their senses. We have discussed this previously, and this chapter uses that information as a foundation on which to build additional developmentally appropriate experiences. The six *sensory centers* in the early childhood curriculum—water-sand-mud play, blocks, woodworking, cooking experiences, manipulatives, and computer-enhanced learning—can be indoors or outdoors, separate, or a part of other learning centers. They can be changed easily as the children's developmental needs change, and they give children sensory involvement with their environment.

> *Children and adults inhabit different sensory worlds. Imagine a young infant's world of touch and taste—a world where you see and hear more than you look and listen—where you, in effect, think with your body and actions, and your whole body is your only means of reacting. (Gestwicki, 1999)*

The *quality* of the environment also contributes to the sensory development of children. Soft materials in the environment offer tactile sensory stimuli experiences. Softness creates the warmth and comfort young children need. Prescott (1994) helps us to understand this even more:

> *A common characteristic of these soft materials is that they provide experiences where the environment responds to the child. You can use your body the way you want to on a rug. You push sand around or pound on clay, and each does what you want it to do.*

Miller (1996) extends our awareness by pointing out that "Sensory experiences are very accessible to all children. Very often children with special needs gravitate to sensory activities because of the ease with which they are able to be involved, because they might contain familiar elements and because they are able to exercise some control over the activity without becoming frustrated." As you continue through this chapter, sharpen *your* sensory awareness. Observe how the sensory centers interact and interconnect with the total curriculum.

■ WATER, SAND, AND MUD PLAY

Water, sand, and mud play can be an individual or a small group activity. Projects can be done indoors and outdoors. There is no right or wrong way to play with these multisensory materials. They are used in many different ways by the children using them. Even very young children enjoy splashing, pouring, squishing, and mixing.

"The unstructured nature of sand and water encourages children of all ages to play with imagination and confidence" (Miller, 1994). Water, sand, and mud can relate to any theme, lesson plan, or curriculum web.

Water play can be lively and at the same time relaxing. Young children enjoy running through a sprinkler, playing at the water table, bathing dolls in a plastic tub, filling and emptying containers with water, and watering plants. It is fun, and children are naturally drawn to water play.

Sand play is irresistible to young children. Starting with dry sand, in the sandpile or sand table, children can spoon, pour, measure, dig, and shovel. They add props as they construct cities, farms, and airports, and they love to drive trucks through and over sandy roads.

Adding water to sand creates opportunities for additional sensory learning to take place. Combining props such as sunglasses, hats, towels, and an umbrella can turn the outdoor sand area into a beach. Have you tried adding live small crabs in a sand bucket to the "beach"? The children will be fascinated as the crabs crawl in and out of their shells.

Mud play is a sensory activity like no other. After a rain, the playground takes on an added dimension. It is special. "The water has transformed the everyday playground into a wonderland with endless possibilities. . . . Mix water and dirt and you get mud—ooey, gooey mud" (Betz, 1992). What you and the children do with the mud offers many possiblities. Try experimenting with a bucketful of mud. Make mud pies or "pizza," for example. Mix the mud to make paint. Brush the mud on different textures of paper. Dirt taken from different areas of the playground shows different pigmentations, which the children themselves will point out to you.

This child-centered activity of mud play offers children another way to experience their world. "When so much of our good earth is being covered with wall to wall concrete, it is imperative to save more than a spot of earth for growing children" (Hill, 1977).

Purposes and Objectives

When you plan opportunities for children to develop and practice skills in the water, sand, and mud learning centers, you will encourage children to do the following:

Perform Simple Experiments. Predict if objects will sink or float in plain water—such as rocks, marbles, Styrofoam, ping-pong balls, coins, corks, and sponges. Add salt to the water to see if the objects will sink or float. Explore various types of sand with magnets by running the magnet through the sand to see if any grains stick to the magnet, or search for hidden metal objects buried in the sand. Discover how long it takes for water to evaporate outside on a hot or a cold day. Examine dirt using magnifying glasses and sifters.

Measure, Compare, and Problem Solve. Provide empty cardboard milk cartons, such as half-pint, pint, quart, half-gallon, and gallon containers, for children to pour from one carton to another to discover how much water each one holds. Measure equal amounts of wet and dry sand and put them on opposite sides of a balance scale to determine which is heavier. Use the mud puddle after a rain for the children to problem solve how to get the water out of the mud puddle.

Play Creatively. Provide soapy water, sponges, and washable toys for the children to clean. Experiment with sand molds and determine whether dry sand or wet sand works best. Have boat races with children problem solving how to get their boats across the water-filled tub. (Hint: Children can either blow on the boats to make them move or pull them across with a string.) Make designs in the sand with sand combs made from pliable plastic containers such as bleach or detergent bottles. Put out buckets and sponges to scrub the playground equipment. Set up a "truck wash" for sand box construction toys.

Develop New Vocabulary. Introduce words, such as pour, fill, flow, spray, squirt, splatter, empty, full, shallow, deep, measure, absorb, droplets, sift, sink, float, evaporate, melt, and dissolve.

Demonstrate New Concepts. Demonstrate how gravity causes water to flow downhill through tubes and funnels, how water takes the shape of its container, and how the liquid form of water can change into a solid by freezing in ice trays, paper cups, or milk cartons.

The Teacher's Role

The following suggestions should be helpful to you in defining the teacher's role in water, sand, and mud play:

- Observe, ask open-ended questions, and make comments to show support and interest.
- Encourage children to talk about what they are doing and what is happening.
- Support children's exploration by providing space for messy activities and materials that can be fully explored without concern about waste (Feeney, Christensen, & Moravcik, 1996).
- Structure the centers so children have interesting and challenging materials to stimulate their water and sand play.
- Depending on the type and size of the area used for the water and sand activities, decide when and if you should limit the number of children playing at one time.
- Take your cues from the children on what to change and when to change it.
- Have smocks, aprons, and changes of clothes available for the children.
- Remember the safety and health rules of water, sand, and mud play: (1) never leave children unattended around any type of water; (2) empty the water tub or table daily; and (3) sanitize the water and wet sand toys and the tub each day with a fresh bleach solution of one tablespoon bleach to one quart of water in a spray bottle, then rinse with running water (Miller, 1994).
- Discuss with older children the importance of water and the shortages that will arise if we do not work to preserve this resource. Get the children's families involved, too.

Props and Materials

The following is a suggested list of props and materials to include in water, sand, and mud play. It is best to use dry, finely textured sand available at toy stores and lumber or building supply stores. Use plastic props and containers, if possible, because metal will rust.

Suggested Props

Basters	Rotary eggbeaters
Eyedroppers	Spray bottles
Funnels	Cookie cutters
Measuring cups and spoons	Gelatin molds
Scoops	Salt shakers
Sieves	Scale
Colander	Sand timer
Straws	Sand combs
Slotted spoon	Spoons and shovels
Buckets, pails, and tubs	Bowls and pitchers
Magnifying glass	Paintbrushes
Plastic tubing	Sponges
Child-size brooms and dust pan	

Suggested Containers

Sand and water table	Outdoor sandpile
Wading pool	Wash tubs
Dishpan	Boxes
Bathtub	Infant tub

Suggested Substitutes for Sand

Seashells	Styrofoam pieces
Washed gravel	Birdseed

■ BLOCKS

When you are setting up an early childhood environment, one of the first items you should purchase is blocks. Many teachers consider blocks to be the most used and the most useful materials in a program for young children. "They are the most versatile and open-ended of the nonconsumable materials in the early childhood setting, and well worth the investment of their price" (Petersen, 1996). Along with selecting blocks, you should plan carefully what type and quantity you choose, the way in which the blocks will be organized, and how you will arrange the physical environment to ensure developmentally appropriate activities with blocks.

Unit blocks are the most popular variety used in early education environments. These sturdy hardwood blocks were designed by Carolyn Pratt in the early 1890s. The individual unit block is $1\frac{3}{8}$ inches by $2\frac{3}{4}$ inches by $5\frac{1}{2}$ inches, and all other blocks are multiples or divisions of this basic size. The cylinders and curved blocks are of similar width and thickness. Pratt's blocks were of "smooth, natural-finish hardwood—free from details or color. In addition, she designed unpainted wooden people, 6 inches tall, in the form of family members and community workers, to be used with the unit blocks. She omitted painted details on any of her toys because she wanted children to apply their own imagination in their use of the materials" (Beaty, 1992). See Figure 8–1 for a description of unit blocks.

Hollow blocks are also made of wood and are larger than unit blocks. "The basic square is $5\frac{1}{2}$ inches by 11 inches by 11 inches. There are five other pieces in a set: a half-square, a double square, two lengths of flat board, and a ramp. Hollow blocks are open on the sides so they can be carried more easily" (Dodge & Colker, 1992). Hollow blocks

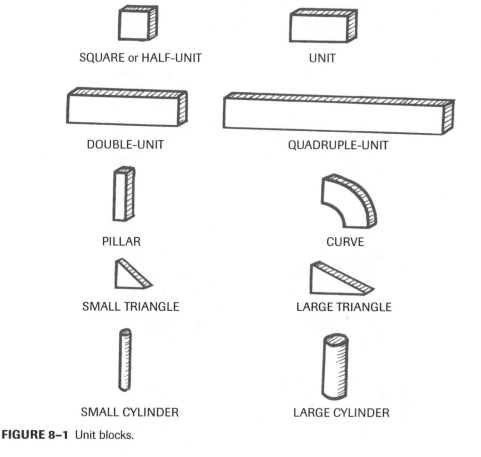

SQUARE or HALF-UNIT   UNIT

DOUBLE-UNIT   QUADRUPLE-UNIT

PILLAR   CURVE

SMALL TRIANGLE   LARGE TRIANGLE

SMALL CYLINDER   LARGE CYLINDER

FIGURE 8–1 Unit blocks.

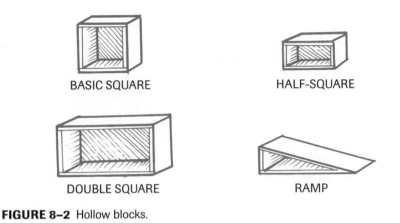

BASIC SQUARE   HALF-SQUARE

DOUBLE SQUARE   RAMP

FIGURE 8–2 Hollow blocks.

require additional space both indoors and outdoors for optimal use by the children (see Figure 8–2).

Other types of blocks appropriate for young children's play are: shoe-box size cardboard blocks, some of which are designed to look like bricks; small, wooden, colored ones that can be used as table blocks; log-type building blocks; interlocking blocks, such as Legos or Bristle Blocks; and foam blocks and large brightly colored lightweight blocks for infants' and toddlers' first experiences with block play.

The unit blocks should be placed on low shelves according to shape and size for organization and storage. Label the shelves with the outlines of the shapes and sizes of the different types of blocks. This assists children with cleanup and emphasizes classification. Place blocks other than the unit or hollow blocks in plastic containers or boxes clearly labeled for identification (see Figure 8–3).

Block play is noisy, so the center should be placed next to other active areas, such as dramatic play. The block area should be clearly defined on three sides. This offers protection and security for the children's activities. An area rug or carpeting should be on the floor to absorb some of the noise as well as to offer comfort to the children playing (Dodge & Colker, 1992).

> *If children are taught to build slightly away from the shelves, fighting and stress will be reduced as other youngsters also try to reach in for blocks. The construction area needs to be shielded from traffic to discourage children from delivering a kick at some treasured structure as they pass by. (Hendrick, 1998)*

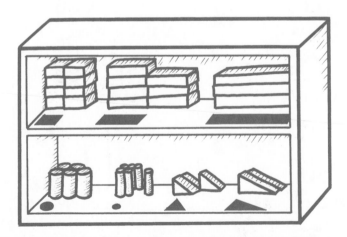

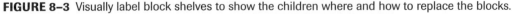

FIGURE 8–3 Visually label block shelves to show the children where and how to replace the blocks.

Developmental Stages of Block Building

Harriet M. Johnson (1982) helps us understand that there are developmental stages in the way children use and play with blocks:

First, children carry blocks from place to place. They are learning about how the blocks feel, how heavy they are, and how many they can carry at once (under two years of age).

Next, the children pile blocks one on top of another. In the beginning there is an irregular pattern to the stacking, then the blocks begin to form a tower, which often falls when additional blocks are added. Repetition of this activity will help children know how many blocks they can add before the tower will fall (toddlers).

At the same time children are making block towers, they are also trying to make block rows. They lay blocks close together, side by side or edge to edge (flat rows suggest roads, so adding small trucks and cars will be appropriate). The children may also space the blocks, alternating the sizes as they place them in rows (toddlers and three-year-olds).

Each of these steps in developmental block building includes repetition (see Figure 8–4). Practicing their accomplishments over and over is important to young children as they get more comfortable with using blocks. The next stage for children is bridging. This is observable by watching children set up two blocks, leaving space between them, and roofing that space with another block. Through repetition, the structures increase in elaboration and difficulty (three- and four-year-olds).

Enclosures made by children, sometimes simultaneously with bridging, put blocks together to enclose a space. Placing four blocks together so that a space is completely enclosed is not a simple task (two-, three-, and four-year-olds). Patterns and designs begin to appear when children feel comfortable enough with blocks to build balanced

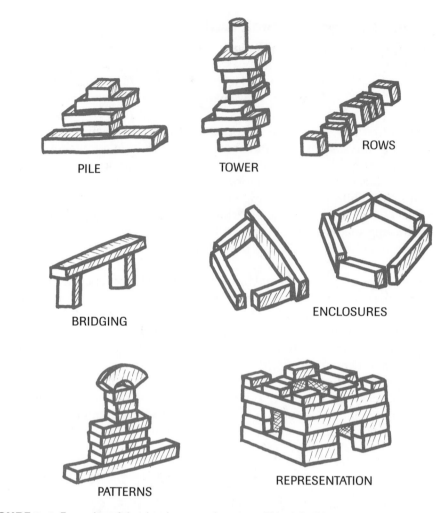

PILE   TOWER   ROWS

BRIDGING   ENCLOSURES

PATTERNS   REPRESENTATION

FIGURE 8–4 Examples of the developmental stages of block building.

and decorative patterns (four-year-olds). Finally, representation occurs with the naming of block constructions and the combination of all elements of block building. Children (four-year-olds and older) demonstrate that they are aware of their world and their place in it with these structures (Hirsch, 1993).

The addition of miniature people representing various cultures, doll furniture, small animals, cars, trucks, boats, barges, canoes, sleds, airplanes, trains, and buses extends children's block play. For self-selection by the children, put each group of small items in clearly labeled (with pictures and words) plastic tubs or boxes near the unit blocks. This will also help with cleanup.

Books and pictures of different buildings from all around the world can stimulate children to build all kinds of structures. Older children create elaborate highways, bridges, and ramps. They add traffic signs, "Do Not Touch!" signs, and other kinds of labels.

Purposes and Objectives

When you provide time, space, materials, and freedom for children to gain sensory and creative experiences with blocks, you will encourage children to:

■ Strengthen such perceptions of space as under, below, in front of, behind, above, inside, and outside

- Develop concepts of big/little, more than/less than, equal to, and taller/shorter
- Become aware of whole-part relationships
- Practice balancing, stabilizing, and matching skills
- Classify according to shapes, sizes, colors, textures, and types
- Develop symbolic representations as the blocks become whatever the children want them to be
- Create architectural forms by bridging, making tunnels, ramps, and grids
- Make use of imagery and recall by reproducing and recreating forms from past experiences
- Strengthen large and small muscle skills, and eye-hand coordination
- Develop oral language skills
- Participate in cooperative block play with peers while combining ideas and solving problems
- Release emotions in an acceptable way

The Teacher's Role

- Let the parents know what the children are accomplishing through their block play. Invite the parents to participate in the block center when they drop off or pick up their children. Provide opportunities for a family member who is in construction or architectural work to share her time and talent with the children.
- Observe developmental levels of the children. This knowledge will enable you to know when to introduce hollow blocks, other blocks, or accessories to the block center.
- Keep in mind the natural stages of block building as you support the children's efforts to gain confidence and to feel comfortable with blocks.
- Take instant photographs, often, of the block constructions. This offers an alternative to leaving the structures up for extra long periods of time if you do not have the space to do so. The children can have the photo to remember their special buildings. This will also help the children understand that you value their efforts. The photos can lead to children dictating stories about their creations. Perhaps they will recreate them in the art center as well.
- Set limits on the number of children in the block center at one time, and clearly label the rule (as discussed in Chapter 7). Define a few other basic rules, such as blocks are not for throwing or hitting. If the building project continues to grow, expand the space to another center so more children can be involved. This will eliminate some difficulties before they start.
- Help children plan cooperatively and recognize the problems they have encountered and solved. This will contribute to postive self-esteem development.

■ WOODWORKING

The woodworking center in an early childhood environment is not new. It has been a part of a traditional early education classroom for a number of years. This activity center provides young children with many different sensory experiences.

There is physical pleasure in the rhythmical movement of using saw and hammer as muscles and nerves are coordinated to achieve control and movement. Sensory pleasure is obtained from the feeling of the bite of the saw against the grain of the wood and the feeling of smoothness that comes from sanding it. Even the sound of these tools is satisfying. (Moffitt, 1974)

Unfortunately, in some settings the woodworking center is often nonexistent or underused. Think about how and when you can successfully incorporate carpentry into your curriculum. Boys *and* girls develop physical, cognitive, social, and language skills through woodworking activities (see Figure 8–5).

The Teacher's Role

The following guidelines can assist you through planning, setting up, and evaluating a woodworking center for young children.

■ Before beginning carpentry with real tools, plan for the children to have many spontaneous play experiences with bits of wood used as building blocks (Pitcher, Feinburg, & Alexander, 1990).

■ If you have not worked with tools or wood before, practice *before* you supervise the children. Ask a colleague or a parent to share their knowledge with you and the children. Practice using all the tools yourself until you are comfortable with them. If you are a female teacher competently using tools, you become a role model, especially for girls.

■ When starting, be sure you (or another teacher) are available the entire time to closely supervise the children. Limit the center to one child at a time. Add a second child later, when all children are comfortable with the tools.

■ Place this center away from quiet centers. Many teachers like to take woodworking outdoors or into the hallway right outside the classroom door.

■ Allow enough time for the children to explore the materials at their own pace.

■ The woodworking center requires specific rules that are consistently reinforced:

Goggles must be worn at all times.

Tools must be kept at the workbench, and they are to be used for the purpose for which they are designed. (Help the children learn to use tools properly.) Return the tools to the tool kit or rack when finished.

When two children are working at the workbench, let one stand on each side with plenty of space between them. Safety is always the first consideration when children are using tools. They must learn where to put their hands when hammering and sawing.

■ Remember, it is the *process* that is important.

■ To ensure success for children from the beginning, start with white glue and wood. Then gradually add hammers, roofing nails, soft wood, and a saw.

■ If a child is using a hammer for the first time, you can pound several nails halfway into the wood to get her started. Roofing nails with large heads are the easiest for young children to use.

■ Children may want to paint the projects they have made. Allow time for completion of this activity, too.

■ Evaluate throughout each step of the process. Planning, initiating, and evaluating will help you and the children be successful in the woodworking center.

Essa (1999) suggests additional guidelines:

For very young children, wood can be replaced by thick styrofoam packing material, which is much softer and easier to saw. . . . Older preschoolers who have gained proficiency in using the tools and purposefully made objects in wood, will be interested in adding props. These should include round objects that suggest wheels, such as wooden spools, slices of large dowels, bottle caps, the metal ends from 6-ounce frozen juice containers, and a variety of other items.

FIGURE 8–5 The woodworking center provides sensory experiences for young children.

Purposes and Objectives

When you include woodworking experiences in early education, you will encourage children to:

- Develop and coordinate large and small muscles
- Improve eye-hand coordination
- Use wood as a medium of creative expression
- Communicate, plan, and work cooperatively with others
- Use woodworking as an emotional release and means of nonverbal expression
- Focus on the process while mastering the skills of sanding, gluing, hammering, nailing, sawing, and drilling to gain a sense of self-esteem
- Sharpen their senses through the smells, textures, and sounds of woodworking
- Learn to sustain interest and overcome frustration successfully
- Extend concepts of experimenting, creating, investigating, and problem solving into other areas of the curriculum

Figure 8–6 illustrates how woodworking equipment can be stored.

Equipment and Materials

Use *real* tools. They are much safer than toy ones. You may have to remind children to put on *safety goggles* before they start working with wood.

Workbench—sturdy in construction, with vise or C-clamps attached, approximately 24 inches high or as high as the children's waists; a sturdy table can also be used

Hammers—small claw hammers weighing 8 to 12 ounces

Nails—roofing nails and assorted other sizes

Soft wood—white pine, cedar, spruce, and redwood are light in weight and take nails easily. Lumber companies and construction sites are sources for soft wood scraps

Glue

Cross-cut saw—approximately 18 inches long

Clamps

Braces and bits

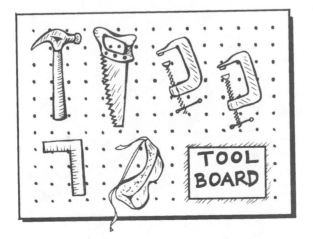

FIGURE 8–6 Children should properly replace woodworking tools after using them.

Sandpaper or sanding sponges

Ruler or square

Pencils and paper

Tool box

Pegboard tool rack or tool cabinet to store items

Markers, crayons, and thinned tempera paint

Screws and screwdrivers are difficult for young children to use. Perhaps you can add these to activities for older children.

■ COOKING AND CREATIVE FOOD EXPERIENCES

Cooking activities give children firsthand experiences that involve them in the process from planning to cleanup. A sense of accomplishment; the thrills of experimentation; and an awareness of taste, touch, and smell are all rewards of cooking experiences. Early positive encounters with food also help children gain the knowledge they will use to form lifelong eating habits. Cooking is fun! Just watch what infants and toddlers can do with a banana.

By including opportunities for children to cook, you offer additional times for them to practice math (comparing sizes, shapes, and measurements, one-to-one correspondence, fractions, and temperature), science (vegetables that are stems or roots, fruit that grows on trees, what happens to sugar on hot cereal), reading and writing (making lists and using recipes and rebus charts), social studies (learning more about their world, and community resources), following directions, putting things in sequence, and learning to communicate and cooperate with each other.

Introduce the USDA's *Food Guide Pyramid for Young Children* (1999). (See Appendix B, Chapter 8, for ordering information.) This is an adaptation of the original pyramid (1992) designed especially for 2- to 6-year-olds. Place photos or posters of nutritious

foods in the cooking activity area and where children eat meals and snacks. Include the colorful Food Guide Pyramid. "See if children can tell you when they are eating a food that is pictured on the posters. Talk about where the food fits into the food group sections of the Food Guide Pyramid" (Cryer, Harms, & Ray, 1996).

It is important that the cooking projects are appropriate for the children's age, interest, and understanding, and that these experiences value cultural diversity. Foods from other cultures offer opportunities for children to taste the different ingredients and flavors. This also helps to develop their understanding that many of the foods they eat are both different *and* similar to those eaten in other countries. On an even deeper level of understanding, children can relate to the fact that many of the foods eaten in the United States are greatly influenced by all the cultures represented in America today.

Principles of developmentally appropriate practice can link cooking-related activities at home to school activities. You could meet with parents to discuss relationships between family and classroom goals of working together. "Think of ways that children can become actively involved in planning dinner for the family. Children will benefit from learning to make choices and deciding which steps to take to complete the task" (Newman, 1995). Family members play a major role in teaching their children how to develop healthful eating habits that will last a lifetime.

Purposes and Objectives

When you include cooking activities in an early childhood environment, you will encourge children to:

- Feel responsible, independent, and successful
- Learn about nutrition and the food groups
- Work independently or cooperatively in small groups (the younger the children, the smaller the group should be)
- Complete tasks from preparation to cleanup
- Learn about new foods and become aware of recipes from cultures other than their own
- Learn about different careers that involve foods and cooking (farmers, truckers, grocers, bakers, and chefs, for example)
- Introduce new vocabulary and concepts, such as measure, melt, knead, shake, sift, spread, baste, peel, hull, grind, grate, chop, slice, and boil
- Develop beginning reading skills with rebus charts and simple recipe cards
- Learn math and science concepts
- Develop small and large muscle control and eye-hand coordination
- Extend cooking into dramatic play, puppetry, art, and other centers

The Teacher's Role

- Plan cooking on days when you have another adult helping you, such as an assistant, a parent, or a volunteer. Supervision is critical to ensure safety for the children.
- Review the food allergies of the children. Provide alternative activities for those children who are allergic to certain foods.
- Be sensitive to the beliefs of the families in your program concerning foods. Some families may have restrictions on what foods they can or cannot eat.
- Integrate cooking opportunities into the theme and lesson plan. Cooking is a creative sensory activity and not necessarily a separate center. Plan appropriate transition activities into and out of each experience.
- Explain the limits and the rules to the children, such as: their hands should be washed with soap and water before and after they prepare foods, smocks or aprons should be worn while cooking (not those used for art projects), and fingers and

utensils should be kept out of their mouths while they are cooking. Let the children help you establish other rules.

■ At first, and with younger children, attempt food activities that require no cooking. The children can mix ingredients together and feel successful when they taste the snack. Washing fruits and vegetables before they cut and eat them provides additional opportunities for beginning cooks. Remember, all cooks need practice and support to succeed.

■ When interacting with the children, use correct terms for foods, measurements, equipment, and processes. Repeating and explaining terms will help extend language skills.

■ Take the time to discuss foods with the children. Allow them to smell the food and ingredients, taste small portions at various stages of preparation, and experience the feel of textures.

■ Ample time should be available for children to complete the recipe, permitting them to learn from the process as well as the product. Even while the food is cooking, baking, or freezing, children can benefit by observing the changes taking place and by noting the length of time the process takes (Wanamaker, Hearn, & Richarz, 1979).

■ With older children, take time to explain the sequence of how things are grown, harvested, packaged, transported, placed in stores and markets, sold, transported to homes, cooked, and served. Allow time for you to answer the children's questions. Repeat this information in different ways, such as lotto games, matching games, reading books, making books, and field trips.

Equipment and Supplies

Use real kitchen utensils and equipment. A list of suggested supplies follows:

Unbreakable nesting bowls for mixing

Individual bowls for children

Measuring cups and spoons

Wooden stirring spoons

Slotted spoons

Unbreakable pitchers

Rubber spatula

Vegetable peelers

Plastic grater

Pastry brushes

Wire whisks

Funnel

Tongs

Rolling pins

Hand eggbeater

Potato masher

Colander

Sifter

Hand squeezing orange juicer

Plastic serrated knives (for younger children)

Serrated steel knives and kitchen shears (for older children)

Plastic cutting boards or trays

Cookie cutters and cookie sheets

Muffin tins

Bread loaf pans and cake pans

Airtight containers with lids

Hot plate or electric skillet

Toaster oven

Electric wok

Electric blender and/or mixer

Can opener

Timer

Smocks or aprons (not the ones used in art center)

Hot pads and mitts or holders

Sponges used just for cooking activities

Paper towels and paper napkins

Waxed paper, foil, plastic wrap, and plastic bags

Basic ingredients to keep on hand include:

Flour	Salt	Oil
Milk	Baking soda and powder	Vinegar
Sugar	Peanut butter	Bread
Cornstarch	Cornmeal	Honey

Sensory Snacks

- Dried fruits: apples, raisins, apricots, pitted prunes (Let children spoon out portions.)
- Bananas sliced in orange juice (Let children slice bananas and drop them in their own bowls of orange juice.)
- Melon chunks (Let the children feel, hold, and cut the fruit and then remove and plant the seeds.)
- Finger foods (that children can help prepare): cinnamon toast, cheese toast, popcorn, raw or cooked vegetables, hard cooked eggs (whole, quarters, half, slices), apple slices dipped in honey, tangerine wedges, pear sections, or plum pieces

Snacks with Peanut Butter

Make peanut butter with the children. (Note: Be aware of children with peanut allergies and provide substitutions.)

PEANUT BUTTER

1½ tablespoons vegetable oil
1 cup roasted peanuts
½ teaspoon salt

Put ingredients into an electric blender. Blend to desired smoothness. If needed, add a little more oil.

After washing hands, children can spread the peanut butter, and this shows them how to stay within the lines much better than any coloring book or worksheet. Think of this when you observe the children doing the following:

- Spreading peanut butter on celery sticks
- Spreading peanut butter on apple wedges or slices
- Spreading peanut butter on different kinds of bread and toast

More peanut butter recipes follow:

BANANAS AND PEANUT BUTTER

bananas	rolling pin
graham crackers	plastic knives
peanut butter	waxed or foil paper
	clear bags or paper

Wash hands. Crush graham crackers in bag with rolling pin. Cut bananas into halves or quarters. Spread one side with peanut butter and roll bananas with crumbs. Yum!

Additional Snacks

Make the following recipes with the children.

APPLESAUCE

6 apples	1 teaspoon lemon juice
½ cup water	sugar to taste
⅛ teaspoon cinnamon	

Wash hands, then peel apples. Remove core from each apple. Cut up the apples and add water, sugar, and lemon juice. Put apple mixture in a pan, cover, and cook until tender on medium heat, approximately 15 to 20 minutes. Add cinnamon. Mash apples with a fork or potato masher, or press through a colander. Serve and eat!

SHAPE SANDWICHES

wheat or white sandwich bread
pimento cheese spread
small jar of pimentos
black olives

After washing hands, you and the children make sandwiches using the pimento cheese spread. With a star-shaped cookie cutter (or choose another shape), press out a sandwich. Decorate the individual shape sandwiches with pimento eyes and olive mouths. Enjoy!

FROSTED GRAHAM CRACKERS

1 cup powdered sugar	1 box graham crackers
¼ cup margarine	nuts or shredded coconut
food coloring	1 tablespoon milk
1 teaspoon vanilla extract	

Wash hands. Make this recipe several times with different small groups of children. Mix sugar, margarine, and two to three drops of food coloring. Mix vanilla and milk. Slowly add the vanilla-milk mixture, a drop or two at a time, until you have a spreading consistency. Spread over graham crackers. Decorate with chopped nuts or shredded coconut. Yum!

■ MANIPULATIVES

Using **manipulative toys and materials** enables young children to gain the fine motor control they need to accomplish tasks important to their growth and development. Essa (1999) explains, "Manipulatives are sensory materials, involving visual and tactile discrimination; they require skill in coordinating the eyes with what the hands can do." "Children benefit from hands-on exploration of materials and activities of their choice. Whether the child has special needs or not, all children have the potential to benefit from these experiences" (Miller, 1996).

The manipulative center should be a quiet place for an individual child or several children at a time to practice using their small muscles with materials especially designed for them, such as puzzles, pegboards with pegs, and board games. Within this area, children experience the freedom to explore materials, become problem solvers, and develop their own thoughts.

Purposes and Objectives

When you plan opportunities to develop small muscle skills, you will encourage children to:

- Make choices
- Develop self-discipline and self-esteem by working independently and successfully completing a task
- Participate cooperatively with others in completing a task
- Use open-ended materials that develop creativity
- Develop skills in patterning, sequencing, matching, pairing, comparing, classifying, and differentiating by color, size, and shape
- Strengthen small muscle control, hand-hand coordination, and hand-eye coordination
- Develop readiness skills and explore basic concepts in a variety of curriculum areas
- Develop concentration skills

The Teacher's Role

Careful selection of materials and planning to meet the developmental needs of the children are the most important responsibilities for you as a teacher. A variety of materials that give the children choices should be considered for the manipulative center.

In setting up the center, choose child-size tables and chairs, accessible shelves, and enough room for the children to play with the manipulatives on the floor, if they choose. It is also important to teach children how the manipulatives should be used, shared, and put away. Make sure the puzzles have all the pieces, the games are complete, and the table blocks are kept in clearly labeled containers. There should be enough toys and materials available for the number of children who choose to be in the manipulative center. As you have done before, give visual cues with pictures and numbers that let the children know how many can be in the center at one time.

Ask yourself these questions when you select manipulatives for young children:

- Are they safe?
- Are the ones with small parts used by older children only?
- Are they durable and long-lasting? Manipulatives are meant to be handled.
- Are these toys, games, and materials adaptable to many uses, or are they limited to one?
- Are they culturally diverse and nonsexist?

Manipulative Toys, Games, and Materials

A list of self-correcting, structured toys follows.

Puzzles—wooden, wooden pieces with handles, rubber inset, sturdy cardboard—ones with larger and fewer pieces are for younger children

Stacking, nesting, and sorting boxes/blocks

Self-help skill forms (buttoning, zipping, and tying)

Open-ended or construction toys have no right or wrong way to put them together or play with them. They include:

Sewing cards with yarn

Snap blocks

Magnetic blocks, numbers, and letters

Small, wooden table blocks

Parquetry blocks

Legos

Pegs and pegboards—for younger children, use those that have large holes and pegs—for older children, use those that have smaller holes and pegs

Wooden beads—larger ones for younger children; yarn or sturdy string for stringing (Older children often string the beads in intricate patterns.)

Table games and materials are used for classifying, sorting, and matching. They include:

Board games

Lotto

Bingo

Dominos with pictures for younger children

Checkers and Chinese checkers with marbles for older children

Coins from many countries

Ethnic fabric squares

Buttons

Shells

Styrofoam pieces

Texture board with matching pieces

Plastic containers and jars with lids

Flannelboard with flannelboard pieces

Multicultural puppets and small dolls to dress

■ COMPUTERS

Many early education programs are past the issue of determining whether or not to put a computer or computers in their classrooms. The questions now focus on whether or not the budget can support the decision to do so or how to set up a developmentally appropriate computer center for young children.

The role of computers in the early childhood curriculum should be that of uniquely adding to children's experiences (SECA, 1989). Buckleitner (1995) additionally cautions:

> *Computers are no substitute for running, jumping, playing with blocks, digging in the sand, and enjoying storybooks—all of which help foster intellectual development. However, if the right software is used the computer can be an excellent supplement to these traditional activities.*

If you offer the computer as another learning center for the children to choose, they will accomplish many of the same objectives that they do in other areas. The emphasis should be to encourage children to develop positive self-esteem while playing

FIGURE 8–7 Placement of the computer center is important.

cooperatively with others (Figure 8–7). Placing two computers side by side can accomplish this.

The children's response to computers will be within their developmental range. You should continue to offer children developmentally appropriate explorations of concepts through hands-on activities with concrete materials, then offer computer experiences that build on these explorations.

> *Children gain confidence in themselves as learners when, for example, they confirm at the computer their earlier discoveries at the easel about mixing colors. . . . Display children's computer creations the same way that you display their productions using other media. (Thouvenelle, 1994)*

Purposes and Objectives ADD TO LECTURE NOTES

The selection of software (a set of instructions used to direct a computer to perform some activity) will determine whether or not you are offering developmentally appropriate experiences to young children. Consider the following when you are making decisions:

- Select programs that present age-appropriate concepts, such as problem solving; making choices; predicting outcomes; creativity development; asking open-ended questions; and reading, writing, and language skill development.
- Give preference to the software that includes both printed instructions and graphic choices that make options clear to children. If you have a CD-ROM drive, the children can receive these instructions verbally. Touch pads and touch screens also offer opportunities to support the children.
- Make choices that allow one child to work independently or work as a partner with another child.
- The children should be able to use the software as a process. As we have stated previously, it is the process, not the product, that's important.
- Look closely at which programs offer opportunities for the children to develop patience while completing a software task and incorporate an exploratory mode—one where a child can *stop* any activity and move on to the next at any time, thereby setting her own pace.
- Select programs that respond positively (such as "good try") rather than negatively ("wrong").

■ Look closely at software packages to be sure that you have the equipment, computer memory, and materials to use the program.

Select only those programs that you have screened, tested, and personally used prior to purchase. New ones are being produced every day. For example, storyboard software is called the "flannelboard in the computer age."

Shade (1995) describes this software:

Storyboard software is any software that allows a reading or nonreading child to 'build' a story by picking one of several backgrounds for the computer screen, such as a beautiful meadow with tall mountains and trees in the background. Next the child can add animated icons or graphic characters like bunnies, butterflies, or frogs to the background and build a story based on those characters.

The Teacher's Role   ADD TO LECTURE NOTES ·

■ Evaluate your own comfort level in the use of computers. Are you "computer literate"? Do you use and value what a computer can do? Do you take advantage of or seek out training opportunities? You should know about and use computers and the accompanying software before you set up a center for young children.

■ Follow the same guidelines for setting up a computer center as you do in creating any developmentally appropriate learning center.

■ Place the center near another quiet one, such as the book center. Clearly define the center. Avoid lighting that will place a glare on the screen. Put the computer center against a wall with electric outlets so children will not trip over cables and cords.

■ Work with other teachers in finding local resources, both individuals and businesses, who can offer expertise and assistance to help you get started. Oftentimes parents will be able to give you guidance.

■ Make back-up copies of the program disks for the children to use, and keep the original software in a protected cabinet.

■ Considering the budget and the appropriateness for the children, start with one computer for two children and then add another one later.

■ Place the hardware (physical components of the computer system: monitor, keyboard, printer, disk drive, peripherals, electronic circuitry, mouse, etc.) on a child-size table. Have child-size chairs available so that two children at a time can share the computer.

■ Guide children through the stages of becoming comfortable with a computer (clean hands and learning how to take care of the hardware and the software). Limit the amount of time the children can spend at the computer center. You will be able to decide how much time is appropriate (15 to 30 minutes depending on the children's developmental level).

■ Establish a "help me" signal, such as a paper cup or a small stuffed animal you name Help-Me-Harry or What's-Up-Wanda to be placed on top of the monitor (Stiles, 1999).

■ Talk to the children often so you will know what they are thinking. It is important to reflect on what they are doing and whether they feel successful or frustrated. Encourage vocabulary development by using correct terminology, such as monitor, disk, disk drive, mouse, keyboard, hardware, software, and cursor.

■ Provide extensions of classroom computer activities in other learning centers. Computer software should be interrelated in content to the theme, lesson plan, and other center activities.

■ Help parents understand that the computer is set up like all the curriculum centers in the classroom. The software programs are developmentally appropriate, the rules and limits are necessary, and that the emphasis is on playing and learning both independently and cooperatively with others. Evaluate, evaluate, evaluate as you go along!

■ Read the current early education professional journals and magazines to see what is new in computers and software. Technology changes daily.

Bredekamp and Rosegrant (1994) give us their perspective on technology:

Technology—including video and audiotapes and, especially, computers—should not be abandoned because it has at times been misused or because mismatches have occurred in the past. The potentials of technology are far-reaching and ever-changing. The risk is for adults to become complacent, assuming that their current knowledge or experience is adequate. Technology is an area of the curriculum, as well as a tool for learning, in which teachers must demonstrate their own capacity for learning. If teachers themselves become models of exploration and inquiry, children are likely to follow.

■ DEVELOPMENTALLY APPROPRIATE AND MULTICULTURAL/ANTI-BIAS ACTIVITIES

Differing types of activities for the sensory centers are suggested here. Figure 8–8 is a curriculum web using the children's book *My Five Senses* by Aliki as the theme. This web offers books, activities, and a special recipe.

Books Used in the Curriculum Web

Ahlberg, A., & Ahlberg, J. (1981). *Peek-a-boo*. New York: Viking.

Aliki. (1989). *My five senses*. New York: HarperTrophy.

Brown, M. (1947). *Stone soup*. New York: Aladdin Books.

Carle, E. (1990). *Pancakes! Pancakes!* New York: Scholastic.

de Paola, T. (1978). *Pancakes for breakfast*. New York: Harcourt Brace.

Dr. Seuss. (1960). *Green eggs and ham*. New York: Beginner Books.

Friedman, I. R. (1984). *How my parents learned to eat*. Illustrated by A. Say. Boston: Houghton Mifflin.

Haley, G. E. (1970). *A story, a story*. New York: Aladdin Books.

Hathon, E. (1993). *Soft as a kitten*. New York: Grossett & Dunlap.

Hoban, T. (1971). *Look again!* New York: Macmillan.

Hughes, S. (1985). *Noisy*. New York: Lothrop, Lee & Shepard Books.

Isadora, R. (1985). *I hear*. New York: Greenwillow.

Isadora, R. (1985). *I see*. New York: Greenwillow.

Kunhardt, D. (1962). *Pat the bunny*. Racine, WI: Western.

Martin, B. (1967). *Brown bear, brown bear, what do you see?* Illustrated by E. Carle. New York: Henry Holt.

Martin, B., & Archambault, J. (1988). *Listen to the rain*. Illustrated by J. Endicott. New York: Henry Holt.

Martin, B., & Archambault, J. (1987). *Knots on a counting rope*. Illustrated by T. Rand. New York: Henry Holt.

Morris, A. (1989). *Bread, bread, bread*. Photographs by K. Heyman. New York: Lothrop, Lee & Shepard Books.

Oxenbury, H. (1985). *I touch*. London: Walker Books.

Sendak, M. (1962). *Chicken soup with rice*. New York: Harper & Row.

Shaw, C. G. (1988). *It looked like spilt milk*. New York: Harper & Row.

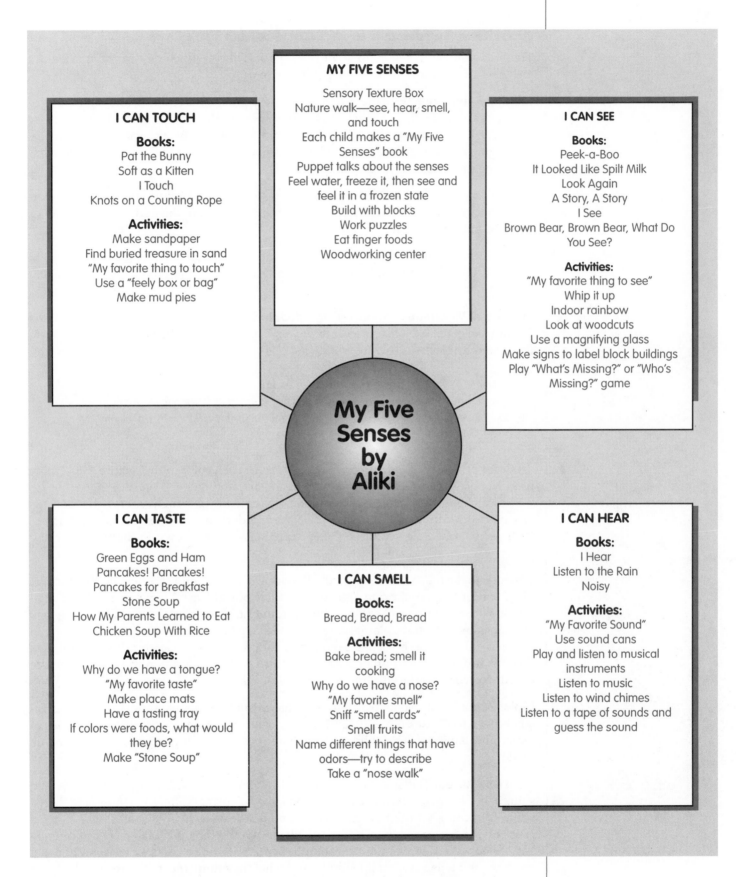

MY FIVE SENSES

Sensory Texture Box
Nature walk—see, hear, smell,
and touch
Each child makes a "My Five
Senses" book
Puppet talks about the senses
Feel water, freeze it, then see and
feel it in a frozen state
Build with blocks
Work puzzles
Eat finger foods
Woodworking center

I CAN TOUCH

Books:
Pat the Bunny
Soft as a Kitten
I Touch
Knots on a Counting Rope

Activities:
Make sandpaper
Find buried treasure in sand
"My favorite thing to touch"
Use a "feely box or bag"
Make mud pies

I CAN SEE

Books:
Peek-a-Boo
It Looked Like Spilt Milk
Look Again
A Story, A Story
I See
Brown Bear, Brown Bear, What Do
You See?

Activities:
"My favorite thing to see"
Whip it up
Indoor rainbow
Look at woodcuts
Use a magnifying glass
Make signs to label block buildings
Play "What's Missing?" or "Who's
Missing?" game

**My Five
Senses
by
Aliki**

I CAN TASTE

Books:
Green Eggs and Ham
Pancakes! Pancakes!
Pancakes for Breakfast
Stone Soup
How My Parents Learned to Eat
Chicken Soup With Rice

Activities:
Why do we have a tongue?
"My favorite taste"
Make place mats
Have a tasting tray
If colors were foods, what would
they be?
Make "Stone Soup"

I CAN SMELL

Books:
Bread, Bread, Bread

Activities:
Bake bread; smell it
cooking
Why do we have a nose?
"My favorite smell"
Sniff "smell cards"
Smell fruits
Name different things that have
odors—try to describe
Take a "nose walk"

I CAN HEAR

Books:
I Hear
Listen to the Rain
Noisy

Activities:
"My Favorite Sound"
Use sound cans
Play and listen to musical
instruments
Listen to music
Listen to wind chimes
Listen to a tape of sounds and
guess the sound

FIGURE 8–8 A curriculum planning web using the children's book *My Five Senses* by Aliki.

Activities Suggested in the Curriculum Web

The following activities involve all the senses. They are included in the curriculum web and are appropriate for young children to do.

Making Sandpaper. Provide cardstock, watery glue, paintbrushes, and containers of sand of various grades. Children first paint on one side of the cardstock with watery glue. Then they choose a grade of sand and sprinkle it on the card. Allow to dry overnight. When dry, the cards can be examined and touched by the children to compare how the different types of sand feel.

Whip It Up. Using a hand rotary eggbeater, dish pan, and liquid dishwashing detergent, children can turn the beaters and whip up bubbles in the individual dishpan or the sand and water table.

Indoor Rainbow. Fill a clear glass jar with water and set on a window sill in the bright sunlight. Place white paper on the floor to "capture the rainbow." The children can paint rainbows with watercolors.

Looking at Woodcuts. Woodcuts or woodblocks are among the oldest artistic media in both Western and Eastern cultures. Some of the earliest books for children were illustrated by black-and-white woodcuts.

> *To create a woodcut, an artist draws an image on a block of wood and cuts away the areas around the design. After rolling ink onto this raised surface, the artist presses the woodblock against paper, transferring the image from the block to the paper. (Norton, 1999)*

Color prints require a different woodblock for each color in the picture. Gail Haley used woodcuts to illustrate her version of an African folktale, *A Story, A Story.*

Research local artists in your community to see if any of them have created woodcuts or woodblocks. Invite them to visit the class and demonstrate their art to the children. Perhaps the school-age children could make some of their own in the woodworking center.

Sensory Texture Box. You can make this for the infants and toddlers *or* you and the older children can make one. Use an appliance box at least 3 feet square. Put several pounds of sand or gravel sacks in the bottom of the box to stabilize it. Close the box and tape down the flaps. Paint or decorate the box. Glue textured materials securely to the four sides of the box. Use sandpaper, cotton balls, egg cartons, kente cloth, silk flowers, foil, twigs, and other textured materials. This is a different kind of "texture board" for you and the children to enjoy in the classroom (adapted from Parks, 1994).

Make Place Mats. Make place mats for use at snack and meal time. Cut out colorful labels from food packaging, magazines, or constuction paper. Glue these on a piece of paper and laminate. The children can share these, or each child can use the one he made.

Let's Use All Our Senses. Set up a special "tasting tray" with foods that taste sweet, sour, salty, spicy, or bitter. Create "smell cards" using different spices and herbs secured to cards with white glue. (The glue does not have any odor.) Make "sound cans" by placing paper clips, beans, etc., in empty film cans. Make a "feely box or feely bag" filled with different items that emphasize shape and softness. Let the children feel an object and tell you what it feels like and what they think the items are without looking. Then they get to see if they guessed it or not.

Recipe Suggested in the Curriculum Web

STONE SOUP

(Read the story first. Have 3 clean rocks ready!)

3 stalks of celery
2 large carrots
2 medium onions
2 medium potatoes
3 medium tomatoes
½ teaspoon each: basil, thyme, marjoram
1 bayleaf
½ cup snipped parsley
1½ tablespoons salt
½ teaspoon pepper

Everyone can chop or measure something. Put into a big pan on the stove. (An electric crock pot will work, too.) Add water to cover. Cook using low heat 2 to 3 hours. You can add rice (½ cup) to thicken.

The following songs can also be part of the sensory activities.

I HAVE TWO EARS
Words and Music by Jo Eklof

I have two ears to hear, hear, hear. I have a brain to think. I have two eyes to look, look, look. I have two lids to blink. I have a nose to sniff, sniff, sniff. I have some hands to touch. I have a mouth to give a smile and say, "I love you so much!"

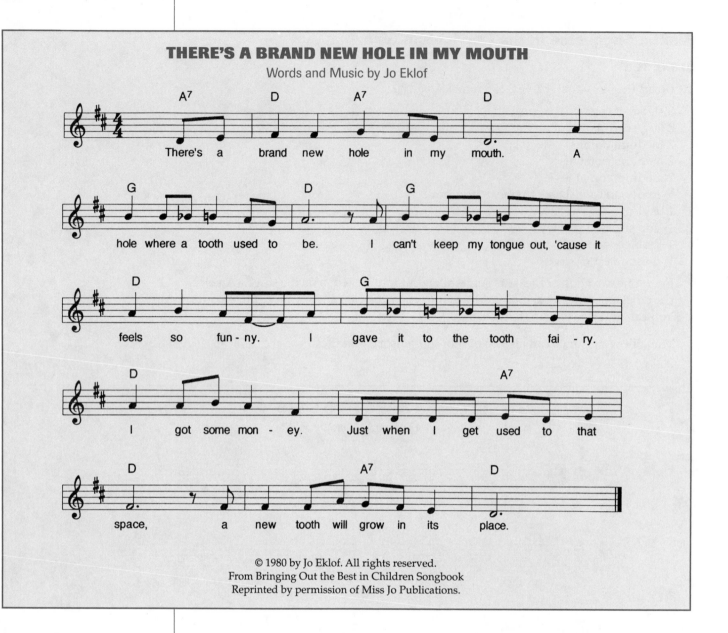

THERE'S A BRAND NEW HOLE IN MY MOUTH

Words and Music by Jo Eklof

Figure 8–9 is the curriculum planning web worksheet with sensory activities added. This worksheet with appropriate additions is included in each chapter.

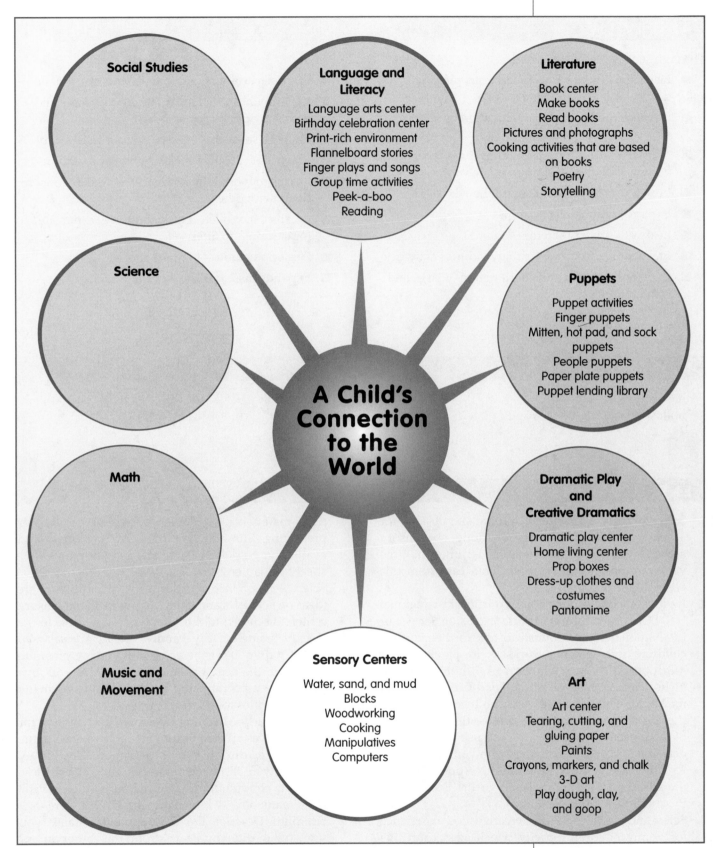

Social Studies

Language and Literacy
Language arts center
Birthday celebration center
Print-rich environment
Flannelboard stories
Finger plays and songs
Group time activities
Peek-a-boo
Reading

Literature
Book center
Make books
Read books
Pictures and photographs
Cooking activities that are based on books
Poetry
Storytelling

Science

Puppets
Puppet activities
Finger puppets
Mitten, hot pad, and sock puppets
People puppets
Paper plate puppets
Puppet lending library

A Child's Connection to the World

Math

Dramatic Play and Creative Dramatics
Dramatic play center
Home living center
Prop boxes
Dress-up clothes and costumes
Pantomime

Music and Movement

Sensory Centers
Water, sand, and mud
Blocks
Woodworking
Cooking
Manipulatives
Computers

Art
Art center
Tearing, cutting, and gluing paper
Paints
Crayons, markers, and chalk
3-D art
Play dough, clay, and goop

FIGURE 8–9 A curriculum planning web worksheet with sensory activities added.

AFTERVIEW

Through sensory activities, a child

- Has opportunities to develop taste, olfactory, tactile, auditory, and visual skills
- Develops perceptual discrimination by shape, size, color, detail, and design
- Experiments with concepts of balance, leverage, volume, weights, and measurements
- Learns that the parts make up the whole
- Explores spatial relationships
- Learns to solve problems
- Practices reading and writing readiness activities
- Develops strength and coordination of large and small muscles

- Practices eye-hand and hand-hand coordination
- Experiments with new materials and tools and learns to apply rules of safety
- Enjoys a sense of achievement and self-control
- Practices oral language by interaction with peers
- Learns to work independently as well as cooperatively with others
- Learns to complete a task and to be responsible for cleaning up after self
- Has opportunities to make choices
- Expands his knowledge of the world

KEY TERMS

hardware
hollow blocks

manipulative toys and materials
sensory experiences

software
unit blocks

EXPLORATIONS

1. Select an early education classroom and observe for at least one hour. Describe, in writing, six sensory activities the children were involved in at the time you were observing. What did you learn from this observation? Explain.

2. Invite someone representing your local or regional U.S. Department of Agriculture Extension Service or the National Dairy Council to talk to the class (or children) or to present a workshop for parents about nutrition and young children. Ask him or her to include an explanation of the Food Guide Pyramid for Young Children that was introduced in 1999 by the USDA. In writing, briefly discuss the main points of the presentation. How will you use this information in your cooking activities with young children? Explain. (See Teacher Resources in Appendix B for the address to write for a copy of the Food Guide Pyramid poster and booklet.)

3. Select and plan a cooking or creative food experience for young children. Specify which age group this activity is planned for: infants, toddlers, preschoolers, or primary-age children. In writing, list objec-

tives, materials needed, step-by-step procedures for presenting this activity, follow-up activities, and evaluation guidelines. (Use the activity plan worksheet in Chapter 2.)

4. Select a classmate or colleague as a partner. Share ideas on activities and games to put in all the sensory centers discussed in this chapter. Relate these to the weekly theme of "My Family." Select a *lesson plan form* (Chapter 2) for the age group you are planning for. Fill in the activities and games. (This will give you a start on completing a lesson plan using many of the activities found in this text.)

5. Select an early education classroom and observe for one hour. Describe, in writing, what happened in the block center during your observation. How many children were in the center at one time? Were these the same children for the entire hour you observed? How many boys? How many girls? What were they building? Describe the developmental stages you saw. What did you learn from this observation? Explain.

REFERENCES

Beaty, J. J. (1992). *Preschool appropriate practices*. Fort Worth, TX: Harcourt Brace.

Betz, C. (1992, March). The happy medium. *Young Children, 47*(3), 34–35.

Bredekamp, S., & Rosegrant, T. (1994). Learning and teaching with technology. In J. L. Wright and D. Shade (Eds.), *Young children: Active learners in a technological age*. Washington, DC: National Association for the Education of Young Children.

Buckleitner, W. (1995, Summer). Moving beyond the myths—computers and children. *Scholastic Parent and Child*, 24–25.

Cryer, D., Harms, T., & Ray, A. R. (1996). *Nutrition activities for preschoolers*. Menlo Park, CA: Addison-Wesley.

Dodge, D. T., & Colker, L. J. (1992). *The creative curriculum for early childhood* (3rd ed.). Washington, DC: Teaching Strategies, Inc.

Essa, E. (1999). *Introduction to early childhood education* (3rd ed.). Albany, NY: Delmar.

Feeney, S., Christensen, D., & Moravcik, E. (1996). *Who am I in the lives of children?* (5th ed.). Columbus, OH: Merrill.

Gestwicki, C. (1999). *Developmentally appropriate practice—curriculum and development in early education* (2nd ed.). Albany, NY: Delmar.

Hendrick, J. (1998). *Total learning—developmental curriculum for the young child* (5th ed.). Columbus, OH: Merrill.

Hill, D. M. (1977). *Mud, sand, and water*. Washington, DC: National Association for the Education of Young Children.

Hirsch, E. S. (Ed.). (1993). *The block book* (Rev. ed.). Washington, DC: National Association for the Education of Young Children.

Johnson, H. M. (1982). *The act of block building*. New York: Bank Street.

Miller, R. (1996). *The developmentally appropriate inclusive classroom in early education*. Albany, NY: Delmar.

Miller, S. A. (1994, March). Sand and water around the room. *Early Childhood Today, 8*(6), 37–45.

Moffitt, M. W. (1974). *Woodworking for children*. New York: Early Childhood Education Council of New York.

Newman, R. (1995, Winter). Bringing the classroom into the kitchen: Lessons learned at home. *Childhood Education, 71*(2), 107–108.

Norton, D. E. (1999). *Through the eyes of a child—an introduction to children's literature* (5th ed.). Columbus, OH: Merrill.

Parks, L. (Ed.). (1994, Fall). Make it with a box. *Texas Child Care, 18*(2), 22–28.

Petersen, E. A. (1996). *Early childhood planning, methods, and materials*. Boston: Allyn and Bacon.

Pitcher, E., Feinburg, S. G., & Alexander, D. A. (1990). *Helping young children learn* (5th ed.). Columbus, OH: Merrill.

Prescott, E. (November/December, 1994). The physical environment—A powerful regulator of experience. *Child Care Information Exchange, 100*, 9–12, 14–15.

Shade, D. D. (1995, Spring). Storyboard software: Flannel boards in the computer age. *Day Care and Early Education, 22*(3), 45–46.

Southern Early Childhood Association (SECA). (1989). *Appropriate uses of computers in the early childhood curriculum* [Brochure]. Little Rock, AR: Author.

Stiles, G. (1999, March). Logging on! *Early Childhood Today, 13*(6), 8.

Thouvenelle, S. (1994, February). Do computers belong in early childhood? *Early Childhood Today, 8*(5), 48–49.

Wanamaker, N., Hearn, K., & Richarz, S. (1979). *More than graham crackers*. Washington, DC: National Association for the Education of Young Children.

ADDITIONAL READINGS AND RESOURCES

Birch, L. L., Johnson, S. L., & Fisher, J. A. (1995, January). Children's eating: The development of food acceptance patterns. *Young Children, 50*(2), 71–78.

Boals, B. (1992, Winter). Cooking in the classroom. *Dimensions of Early Childhood, 20*(2), 19–24.

Brett, A. (1995, Spring). Technology in inclusive early childhood settings. *Day Care and Early Education, 22*(3), 8–11.

Brett, A. (1994, Fall). Computers and social development of young children. *Dimensions of Early Childhod, 23*(1), 10–13, 48.

Buckleitner, W. (1995, January/February). Getting started with computers and children. *Child Care Exchange, 101*, 21–22.

Caulfield, R. (1994, Summer). Infants' sensory abilities: Caregiving implications and recommendations. *Day Care and Early Education, 21*(2), 31–35.

Clements, D. H., Nastasi, B. K., & Swaminathan, S. (1993, January). Young children and computers: Crossroads and directions from research. *Young Children, 48*(2), 56–64.

Crosser, S. (1994, July). Making the most of water play. *Young Children, 49*(5), 28–32.

Dahl, K. (1998, January). Why cooking in the classroom? *Young Children, 53*(1), 81–83.

Ewing, J., & Eddowes, E. A. (1994, Summer). Sand play in the primary classroom. *Dimensions of Early Childhood, 22*(4), 24–25.

Fuhr, J. E., & Barclay, K. H. (1998, January). The importance of appropriate nutrition and nutrition education. *Young Children, 53*(1), 74–80.

Haugland, S. (1995, Winter). Computers and young children. *Early Childhood Education Journal, 23*(2), 99–100.

Hawkins, J. A. (1995, Spring). Technology for tolerance. *Teaching Tolerance, 4*(1), 16–21.

Heath, P. (1994, Winter). Developing tactile learning experiences. *Day Care and Early Education, 22*(2), 12–13.

Huber, L. K. (1998, March/April). Woodworking in my classroom? You bet! *Early Childhood News, 10*(2), 72–74.

Johnston, C. B. (1998, Spring). Four easels, five sand tables, and a billion blocks: Setting up an early childhood classroom. *Dimensions of Early Childhood, 26*(2), 24–27.

Karges-Bone, L. (1991, Fall). Blocks are *not* (circle all): Messy, expensive, difficult. *Dimensions of Early Childhood, 20*(1), 5–7, 37.

McKenney, D. (1998, March/April). Trees, trees everywhere, but know a bit of woodworking. *Early Childhood News, 10*(2), 64–71.

Miller, S. A. (1994). *Learning through play: Sand, water, clay, and wood*. New York: Scholastic.

Mogard, S. M., & McDonnell, G. (1994). *Gobble up math*. Santa Barbara, CA: The Learning Works Inc.

Patnaude, C. A., & Costantino, C. (1995, Winter). Owning a piece of the forest: Woodworking in the early childhood curriculum. *Early Childhood Education Journal, 23*(2) 115–118.

Planje, A. (1997, January). Playing with water in primary ways. *Young Children, 52*(2), 33.

Skeen, P., Garner, A. P., & Cartwright, S. (1984). *Woodworking for young children*. Washington, DC: National Association for the Education of Young Children.

Strohl, M., & Schenck, S. (1993). *The big book of animal manipulatives: Grades K–3*. New York: Scholastic Professional Books.

Wright, J. L., & Shade, D. D. (Eds.). (1994). *Young children: Active learners in a technological age*. Washington, DC: National Association for the Education of Young Children.

Music and Movement

■ OVERVIEW

"'Music' and 'the young child' are almost synonymous terms. They both invoke a sense of wonderment, enjoyment, laughter, movement, freedom, creativity, and expression" (Greenberg, 1979). A developmentally appropriate and creative classroom for young children has music and movement experiences woven into the daily curriculum. In fact, if you stop and listen to an active early childhood classroom, you will discover that it has a rhythmic pattern and beat all its own.

Unplanned, spontaneous moments occur daily in an early education environment. Young children hum, sing, clap hands, and move their bodies as they play and complete activities. Music, sound, and movement continuously contribute to the learning processes of young children. Human bodies function to rhythms (e.g., heartbeat, breathing), and children respond by moving. Music comes out of rhythm. "Music is one of our greatest inheritances as human beings. So global is the human experience of music that it has often been called the universal language of humankind" (Moomaw, 1984).

Music is a language, a means of communication. It is communicated through tone, rhythm, volume, range, tempo, and movement (Greenberg, 1979). Music can communicate feelings to children even when its cultural origin and language is foreign to them. Children are acquainted with music from birth. The tone of a mother's voice, the rhythm of a rocking chair, and the chanting of nonsense syllables are basic to a child's life. Before she knows words, an infant experiments with vocal sounds and understands tones and rhythms.

A child's involvement with music includes listening; creative activities related to singing, body movement, playing, and making instruments; and aesthetic examination. "Perhaps most important, music exploration fosters children's aesthetic growth, giving them the experiences and skills to appreciate and create the beauty of music throughout their lives" (Day, 1994).

Music and movement are intertwined. They reinforce and strengthen each other. A child hears music and he moves. A child's physical maturation process motivates him to move naturally in response to internal and external stimuli. Griss (1994) emphasizes that "children exposed to creative movement as a language for learning are becoming more aware of their own natural resources. They are expanding their concepts of creativity and of how they can use their own bodies."

In this chapter, we explore the ways music and movement can introduce concepts, foster growth in motor skills, reinforce and develop language skills, nourish positive self-esteem, encourage self-expression, and connect to other curriculum areas and chapters of this text.

■ MUSIC AND CREATIVE MOVEMENT EDUCATION FOR YOUNG CHILDREN

Music makes children want to clap hands, tap toes, beat drums, and dance. *Children learn best through acting upon what they experience.* Moving can be fun for its own sake and a way to enjoy music even more. Children express the music's aesthetic qualities through the movement of their bodies as they listen to, perform, and create music. "By using the body the child expresses what he *perceives* in the music, how he *feels* about the music, and what he *understands* in it" (Greenberg, 1979).

For young children in early education settings, including infants and toddlers, music and movement activities nurture the development of minds, bodies, emotions, and language. As you plan developmentally appropriate goals and objectives to encourage music and movement experiences, consider the following:

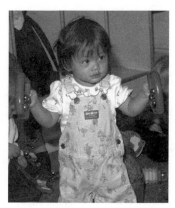

Include *physical development* activities that can help children gain increasing control over their large and small muscles, experiment with the movement of their bodies, and experience success in movement. Pica (2000) believes that "if a child's early encounters with movement are successful, confidence-building, and fun, that child is much more likely to want to keep moving throughout his or her life. So the early childhood professional's most vital role in creating physically fit adults may simply be ensuring that her children do not lose their love for movement."

Incorporate *intellectual growth* activities that can stimulate children to experiment with how sound is created through their voices or musical instruments, to recognize songs, and explore melodies by varying tempo, rhythm, tone, and volume.

Include *listening* activities that make music a part of the daily environment by asking for a response, remembering a song or parts of a song, recognizing musical instruments, focusing on sound, and developing auditory discrimination. Every time a child engages in a music experience, she is listening.

Provide children with *social* and *emotional* responsive activities that energize, soothe, and enhance children's expression of feelings and sharpen their awareness of feelings for others. Music and movement experiences can also help children know and appreciate themselves and promote cultural identity and pride in themselves and others.

Include musical *language development* activities that encourage the acquisition and use of language to extend vocabulary, to learn word and sound patterns through singing and listening, and to describe musical happenings that can help children develop an appreciation for the music and language of diverse cultures. "The songs and music of childhood are a part of our cultural heritage. The folk songs and ballads that have survived to the present day and the regional tunes parents and teachers offer are part of each child's cultural literacy" (Machado, 1999).

Take advantage of music and movement opportunities that stimulate children's *creativity* and *uniqueness*. Give children musically creative group time by offering each child the opportunity to add to songs and finger plays and to create new movements for action songs. Each musical creation adds to the creativity of the whole group. Haines and Gerber (1996) suggest that children create through active listening to the sounds of their environment and through moving, singing, and playing percussion instruments. All these are integral to early childhood musical education.

■ LARGE AND SMALL MUSCLE DEVELOPMENT AND PHYSICAL FITNESS

Early education curriculum should include well-defined opportunities, both indoor and outdoor, for young children to develop motor skills. As discussed in previous chapters, setting up the environment and planning appropriate activities depends on the developmental skills, interests, and needs of the children.

Large muscle (gross motor) development usually precedes small muscle (fine motor) development. For this chapter, we will focus on motor development that includes locomotor skills, large muscle activities, and physical fitness. Underlying all of this is the understanding that possibilities for exploration, creativity, and self-expression are included as part of the motor skill planning process.

Small muscle development is discussed in other chapters and includes such activities as turning pages of a book, finger plays, scribbling, drawing, writing, tearing, cutting, pouring, stringing beads, inserting pegs, pounding nails, and building with blocks. Involvement with music and movement projects can be very effective in furthering the development of small muscles.

Basic types of movement in young children, identified by Greenberg (1979) and expanded by Ingico (1994) and Pica (2000), are locomotor, nonlocomotor, combination,

and manipulative. All these actions need practice, encouragement, and an adult's understanding of individual growth patterns.

Locomotor (fundamental) **movement** is the ability to move the whole body from one place to another. This is demonstrated by crawling, creeping, walking, running, jumping, hopping, skipping, and climbing.

Nonlocomotor (axial or body) **movement** occurs when the feet remain stationary (as in standing, kneeling, sitting, or lying) while other parts of the body move. Examples would be stretching, reaching, bending, twisting, bouncing, shaking, and clapping.

A combination of the previous two types of movement involves various motions that enhance coordination while giving children movement and rhythm combinations that occur simultaneously. This is demonstrated by walking and clapping at the same time or hopping and shaking (Greenberg, 1979).

Manipulative movement skills in the physical education field are described by Pica (2000) as "gross motor movements involving force imparted to or received from objects . . . [or] any gross motor skill in which an object is usually involved (manipulated)." This is demonstrated by pulling, pushing, lifting, striking, throwing, kicking, and ball catching.

Physical fitness, according to Poest, Williams, Witt, and Atwood (1990), refers to "the level of health development and functional capacity of the body." For teachers of young children this means planning physical activities that provide daily developmentally appropriate movement experiences that will produce acceptable levels of fitness for the children in their care.

Physical education for young children should be a well-planned regular exercise program. This means allowing time for movement exploration. Start with slow stretches to get their bodies "warmed up." For example, the children touch their toes, then make circles with their arms, and finally stretch them way above their heads.

The National Association for Sport and Physical Education (1992) defines the physically educated person as someone who demonstrates competence in a variety of manipulative, locomotor, and nonlocomotor skills and who participates regularly in physical activity. With this definition in mind, preschool educators can plan developmentally appropriate learning activities that will promote motor skill acquisition, fitness development, and a lifetime of physical activity. (Ingico, 1994)

Locomotor, large muscle, and fitness activities can easily be combined with creative movement and music activities. There are no limits on how to accomplish this. You and the children together can discover wonderful things through movement and music!

■ TYPES OF MUSIC

A music curriculum for young children should include many opportunities to explore sound through singing, moving, listening, and playing instruments, as well as introductory experiences with verbalization and visualization of musical ideas. The music literature included in the curriculum should be of high quality and lasting value, including traditional children's songs, folk songs, classical music, and music from a variety of cultures, styles, and time periods (Music Educators National Conference Position Statement, 1994).

The basic sources of music are the human voice, instruments, environmental sounds, and music from radio, television, audio cassettes, records, and CDs. As you use these sources to plan music experiences for young children, remember to connect them to their life experiences. See Figure 9–1 for basic terms.

Beat—An accent of sound or a continuing series of accents.

Melody—A sequence of tones of varying pitches organized in a rhythmically meaningful way.

Pitch—The highness or lowness of a tone on a musical scale.

Rhythm—A sense of movement and patterns in music created by beats, the duration and volume of sounds, and the silences between sounds.

Tempo—A sense of slowness or rapidity in music.

Timbre (TAM'-bur)—The unique tone quality of a voice or musical instrument.

Tone—An individual musical sound.

Volume—The softness or loudness of sound.

FIGURE 9–1 Basic musical terms.

Songs and Singing

Young children love to sing. Beginning in infancy and continuing on throughout their childhood, they are experimenting with their voices and the sounds that they can make.

- Singing can be experienced alone or shared with others.
- Songs encourage the children to make up new words and to move with the music.
- Young children usually sing in the middle and upper registers so teachers need to be careful not to start a song too low for them.

There are many delightful and fun-filled songs to sing, such as the ones included in the developmentally appropriate activities at the end of this chapter and the following ones:

- Songs that offer repetition and chorus, such as "Polly Put the Kettle On," "Mary Had A Little Lamb," and "Here We Go Round the Mulberry Bush."
- Songs with repeated words or phrases that can be treated like an echo, such as "Miss Mary Mack" and "She'll Be Comin' 'round the Mountain."
- Songs that ask children to supply sound effects or animal noises, such as "If You're Happy and You Know It" and "Old MacDonald Had A Farm."
- Ballads or songs that tell a story, such as "Hush Little Baby," "Humpty Dumpty," and "Little Bo Peep."
- Question-and-answer songs or name games that help children make the transition from speaking to singing, such as "Do You Know the Muffin Man?"

Using the Voice

When young children experiment with their voices and tongues, they can sound like musical instruments, animals, and the wind. Encourage the children to make some of these sounds:

Whisper very quietly	Cluck
Talk very softly, then loudly	Buz-z-z
Whistle	Growl
Sneeze	Bark
Purr	Snore
Hum	Cry

Choosing Classical Selections

Research tells us that classical music stimulates musical responses from young children. Whether they are "conducting," relaxing, listening, or moving creatively to these recorded musical works, children enjoy and can get caught up in them. "Because children's tastes are so variable, it is best if the teacher introduces a wide variety of orchestral and instrumental pieces and lets the children select those they particularly like" (Moomaw, 1984). Records, tapes, and CDs are available in libraries or stores under many different labels and performing artists. Here are a few children's favorites:

- Britten/"A Young Person's Guide to the Orchestra"
- Copeland/"Rodeo"
- Dukas/"The Sorcerer's Apprentice"
- Grofé/"Grand Canyon Suite"
- Mozart/"Concerto for Flute, Harp, and String (K.299)"
- Prokofiev/"Peter and the Wolf"
- Rimski-Korsakov/"Flight of the Bumble Bee"
- Rossini/"William Tell Overture"
- Saint-Saëns/"Carnival of the Animals"
- Strauss, R./"Till Eulenspiegel's Merry Pranks"
- Stravinsky/"The Firebird"
- Tchaikovsky/"The Nutcracker Suite"
- Tchaikovsky/"The Sleeping Beauty"

Other Musical Experiences

"As with language, children should not be deprived of the whole musical picture because they are too young to understand it. Children learn and understand a great deal more than they can speak about during their first years, but we would never think of not speaking to infants and toddlers just because they cannot speak. . . . Music deserves the same natural assimilation" (Andress & Walker, 1992).

When selecting songs, records, and tapes, include those you remember and enjoyed from your childhood. This will add a personal touch for you and the children. Also, select other music from chants; nursery tunes; American folk music; folk music from around the world; popular music; show tunes; country music; patriotic music; religious, holiday, and seasonal music; electronic experimental music; music for dancing and marching; rock music; and jazz.

For infants and toddlers, heavily orchestrated musical selections typically offer too much too soon. Gradually introduce this type of music into the environment. As you plan your music curriculum for all the developmental stages, remember that children are bombarded with sound (sound pollution) today. Background music in early childhood settings should be selective. Think about when and why you want to have music playing, and then choose it carefully.

■ MUSICAL INSTRUMENTS

Instruments of all kinds have value in the musical environment of young children. They should be encouraged to listen to the instrument, touch it, and experiment with making sounds and music on it. Have instruments of good quality that are well-cared-for, such as tambourines, wooden maracas, woodblocks, rhythm sticks, drums, finger cymbals, bells, triangles, and rain sticks. Teacher- and child-made instruments should always be included, as well as wind chimes, gongs, and music boxes.

"Invite a musician to play an instrument for the children, tell about it, and pass it around to be touched most respectfully. The children should have many listening experiences and exposures to many kinds of music and musical instruments" (Andress & Walker, 1992).

Types of Instruments

Usually the first instrument sounds a child hears and experiments with are those created in the home, such as banging on pots and pans (drums), jingling two spoons together (castanets), shaking a ring of metal measuring spoons (tambourine), banging two wooden spoons together (rhythm sticks), and crashing two lids or metal pie pans together (cymbals).

It is important for early education programs to encourage young children to continue this exploration of sounds and to broaden their understanding of musical instruments and the sounds they make. Percussion instruments are the ones most widely used in an early childhood setting. See Figure 9.2 for a list of musical instruments

Dee Lillegard (1988), in her *Introduction to Musical Instruments Series,* tells us:

Percussion means hitting.
Bang on a can. Bang on a pan.
That's percussion.
Pound on a drum. Tap with your thumb.
That's percussion.

"Musical instruments have many uses, actually. Everybody knows that music can be entertaining. But instruments can do more than please an audience. Around the world, they play a big role in religion, celebration, communication, and even politics and war. In fact, you can travel anywhere on earth and you'll find musical instruments in almost every culture along the way" (Corbett, 1995).

Drums are used in the music and dances of many cultures, including African, Native American, Korean, and Thai (hand drums, tom-toms, and long ones carried on one shoulder with a strap). Maracas and claves sticks (short, polished hardwood sticks) are part of the Mexican and Caribbean musical heritage.

Other instruments also have been a part of ethnic music for centuries, such as the flute from Native American and African cultures and the bamboo flute from Chinese, Japanese, and Korean cultures. Stringed instruments, such as the Chinese *samisen,* the

Percussion Instruments

Drums
Triangle
Cymbals
Tambourine
Xylophone
Chimes and bells
Castanets
Maracas
Claves
Glockenspiel
Piano

Wind Instruments

Flute
Piccolo
Oboe
Clarinet
Bassoon
Saxophones (soprano,
    tenor, and baritone)

String Instruments

(bowed)

Viola
Cello
Bass
Violin

(plucked)

Guitar
Mandolin
Ukulele
Harp
Banjo

Brass Instruments

Trumpet
Cornet
Bugle
Trombone
French horn
Tuba

FIGURE 9–2 List of musical instruments.

Japanese *koto* (a type of harp), and Thailand's *so sam sai*, add beautiful sounds to music selections (Allen, McNeill, & Schmidt, 1992).

Ask parents and community musicians to visit your class and share their music and musical instruments with the children. The combination of personal experiences and hands-on involvement with percussion, string, woodwind, and brass instruments will enrich the children *now* during their formative years.

Introducing Musical Sounds and Instruments

We know that music is a spontaneous and joyous part of young children's lives. They hear it in the world around them and they respond by cooing, babbling, singing, dancing, and interpreting it in their individual ways from infancy onward. How we gather and keep the energy and interest of the children is dependent on how we include music in our daily curriculum.

Bea Wolf, composer and performer of children's music, suggests the following activities for sharing musical experiences with young children:

■ Introduce musical recordings that children can sway to. Have the children close their eyes and move their arms to the music. Ask them "What do you hear?" Listen to their response. Suggest that they sway their bodies with the music. (A waltz tempo is one you can begin with, swaying on the beat of 1— 1–2–3, 1–2–3, 1–2–3, etc.)

■ Select a favorite song and have the children clap to the rhythm of the music. They can clap their hands together, clap hands on knees, and clap hands on the floor.

Often they will continue this activity on their own by humming, singing, and clapping to themselves throughout the day.

■ Wind chimes offer a delightful way to have the children focus on soft sounds. Group time can be a special time for children to listen closely as you share the sounds of several different kinds of wind chimes. Have each child listen closely to what these sound like. Then let them play the chimes gently by themselves.

■ Music boxes offer other unique sounds for children to listen to. Bring in several different sizes and types for the children to explore. Ask them to bring ones from home, too.

■ It is helpful to introduce musical instruments one at a time before combining all the instruments in conjunction with musical recordings. The *triangle* extends listening skills and shapes awareness. Shaking the *maracas* (use only one at first) invites children to shake their own rhythm, as does shaking the *jingle bells,* tap-tap-tapping and then rub-rub-rubbing with wooden sticks, shake-shake-shaking the tambourine, and beat-beat-beating the drums. Try having the children play the instruments to this beat:

sshhh-sshhh/ssh-ssh-ssh/sshhh-sshhh/ssh-ssh-ssh or 1–2/1–2–3/1–2/1–2–3, etc.

■ With preschoolers and older children it is fun to divide them into two groups facing each other with each child having an individual instrument. For example, one group has jingle bells, the other group has one maraca each. Play a recording of an instrumental musical selection. Explain to the children that you (or one of the children) will be the conductor and direct each group when to play individually or together. It is helpful to have the children sitting in groups at first. When the bells play, the maracas are placed gently on the floor; then when the maracas play, the bells are placed gently on the floor, so that the children can listen to their friends play. Then both groups can play together when the conductor directs them to do so.

■ Jingle bell instruments are fun to play along with the song "Jingle Bells," even in the month of June. Other songs are Stephen Foster's "Oh, Susanna" and lively folk songs such as "This Ole' Man" and "She'll Be Comin' 'round the Mountain."

■ Children five years and older enjoy discriminating between sounds and listening to the vibrations of various instruments. Introduce gongs and give the children time to experiment with them. Wooden sticks offer vibrations that sound differently. Place the serrated stick flat against the floor and rub it with the other stick. The floor becomes the amplifier. Different sounds are heard when sticks are placed on a carpeted floor and then on a noncarpeted floor.

Making Musical Instruments

Young children enjoy making their own musical instruments with materials collected from home, including:

■ Rolls from bathroom tissue and paper towels
■ Aluminum pie plates
■ Paper plates
■ Salt, cereal, and oatmeal boxes
■ Large, round ice-cream cartons
■ Bottle caps
■ Spools
■ Embroidery hoops
■ Wooden blocks

FIGURE 9–3 Drum.

FIGURE 9–4 Tambourine.

FIGURE 9–5 Wood-block tambourine.

FIGURE 9–6 Sandpaper blocks.

FIGURE 9–7 Examples of two types of musical shakers.

The process of making musical instruments further extends the children's self-expression, their knowledge of how sounds can be made from their environment, and possibilities for hands-on experiences. This activity also combines language, art, science, math, social studies, and sensory learning opportunities (younger children will need guidance and supervision from the teacher). Some easy-to-make instruments include:

Drums. Children can make drums from salt or cereal boxes or from large ice-cream cartons. Glue the lid to the box or carton and decorate with markers and paint. Drums can be played by hitting or tapping with the fingers or with soft drum sticks made from pencils covered at one end with felt. See Figure 9–3.

Tambourine. Take an aluminum pie plate or a heavy paper plate, punch several holes on the rim, and tie small bells or bottle caps with thin wire, string, or pipe cleaners to the plate in such a way that the bells hang freely. Then, shake to the musical beat. See Figure 9–4.

Wood-Block Tambourine. The materials needed to make a wood-block tambourine are one block of wood (approximately ¾ inch by 1½ inches by 6 inches), six or more bottle caps, and nails with wide heads. Hammer a nail through the bottle caps partway into the wood block (Figure 9–5). Be sure the hole in the bottle cap is wide enough so the cap will slide freely along the nail. Any number of nails and bottle caps can be used.

Sandpaper Blocks. Glue, staple, or thumbtack sandpaper to two wooden blocks (approximately 3 inches by 2 inches by 1 inch) on one 3-inch side of each block. On the opposite side, glue a spool or a small drawer handle. Try experimenting with sandpaper squares of different coarseness. Rub the sandpaper blocks together to make interesting sounds (when the squares wear out, replace them with fresh sandpaper). See Figure 9–6.

Shakers. Young children can make shakers from small boxes or clean plastic milk cartons of various sizes. (The handle is easy to hold onto.) Place clothespins, small pieces of wood, pebbles, dried beans, or birdseed in the container. Another type of shaker is made with paper plates. Take two paper plates and decorate them with crayons, markers, or paint. Place pebbles, dried beans, or birdseed between the two paper plates. Staple the plates together or sew them together with brightly colored yarn. Then, shake and shake to the rhythm of the music! See Figure 9–7.

Wind Chimes. Wind chimes can be made from many different materials, such as various sizes of nails, scraps of metal, pieces of bamboo, or old silverware. Tie various lengths of string, evenly spaced, to a coat hanger or embroidery hoop. Tie nails to the strings, and adjust string lengths so that the nails strike each other when blown by the wind or gently swayed. For a variety of sounds, use pieces of several different sizes, and substitute silverware, pieces of bamboo, or scraps of metal for the nails. See Figure 9–8.

Nail Scraper. Materials needed to make the nail scraper are a block of wood about 2 inches by 2 inches by 8 inches and nails of different sizes. Hammer a few nails of the same size into a block of wood so that they are all the same height. Leave a large space, then hammer some other size nails into the wood making these all the same height. Continue placing nails in the wood until there is no more room. To play this instrument, take a large nail and run it quickly along the row of nails. The different lengths of the nails will make different sounds. See Figure 9–9.

Shoe Box Guitar. This instrument is made by taking a shoe box and cutting a 2-inch oval hole on the top of the box. Stretch strong rubber bands lengthwise around the box.

Place a pencil at one end of the top of the box under the rubber bands. Move the pencil to get different tones as the shoe box guitar is strummed or plucked with the fingers. See Figure 9–10.

Flute. The children can make their flutes from bathroom tissue, paper towel, or wrapping paper cardboard tubes. Cut a circle of tissue paper or waxed paper and place over one end of the tube. Attach with a rubber band. Cut several small holes on the side of the tube. The children can hum into their flutes while they place their fingers on the holes to change the sound. See Figure 9–11.

Storing and Caring for Instruments

All instruments, including those made by the children, should be treated with care. Guide the children into understanding that each instrument is to be cared for, handled carefully, and valued. *Musical instruments are not to be used as toys or weapons.*

Each type of instrument should be stored in a special storage place. According to Haines and Gerber (1996):

> *Instruments should never be dumped indiscriminately into a cardboard carton or piled in a basket or on a shelf. This is not good for the instrument or for the attitudes of children toward them. Attractive, accessible storage that the children can use independently should be provided. Damaged instruments should be discarded.*

■ MUSIC AND MOVEMENT ENVIRONMENTS AND ACTIVITIES

"Play is the primary vehicle for young children's growth, and developmentally appropriate early music experiences should occur in child-initiated, child-directed, teacher-supported play environments" (MENC, 1994). We should provide numerous music and movement activities that invite and encourage children to move around, especially because many children live in confined spaces. Integral to the success of these activities is well-planned space that is adaptable to a number of uses. Consider sound levels that will not interfere with the simultaneous activities of other groups or individuals. These spaces should not be confined to the outdoors or a large muscle room. Classrooms should be arranged (or rearranged) to accommodate music and movement activities. See Figure 9–12 for music and movement books for children.

"Simon Says Move Fingers, Hands, and Arms" Activity

Start this activity by explaining to the children that they will play a game by moving a part of the body without music, such as their fingers, hands, or arms. Later add music. This can be played as a "Simon Says" type of game. Introduce the movements first, a few at a time, suggesting only the movement exercises that are applicable to the age and stage of development of the children in your classroom. Remind the children to stay in their "own space." Let one of the children take your place, inserting the child's name to replace "Simon" or "Teacher Says." Accept whatever movement each individual child makes, unless it is inappropriate. The following are some examples:

■ Moving fingers and hands: bending, separating, stretching, curling, making fists
■ Moving arms: pushing, pulling, stretching, swinging
■ Moving feet and legs: stomping, kicking, crossing, and uncrossing
■ Moving elbows: touching, making circles
■ Moving head: bending, shaking, rolling, nodding
■ Moving eyes: opening; shutting; looking up, down, side to side, around
■ Nose: wiggling, breathing in and out
■ Mouth: opening wide, making shapes, shutting tight

FIGURE 9–8 Wind chimes.

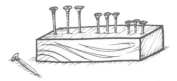

FIGURE 9–9 Nail scraper.

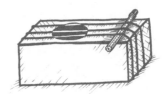

FIGURE 9–10 Shoebox guitar.

FIGURE 9–11 Flute.

Ackerman, K. (1988). *Song and dance man.* New York: Alfred Knopf.

Carle, E. (1992). *Today is Monday.* New York: Scholastic.

Carle, E. (1973). *I see a song.* New York: Scholastic.

Cole, J. (1987). *Norma Jean jumping bean.* New York: Random House.

Drew, H. (1993). *My first music book.* New York: Dorling-Kindersley.

Haseley, D. (1983). *The old banjo.* New York: Macmillan.

Hayes, A. (1991). *Meet the orchestra.* Orlando, FL: Harcourt Brace.

Kuskin, K. (1982). *The philharmonic gets dressed.* New York: Harper & Row.

Lillegard, D. (1988). *An introduction to musical instruments:* (Series) *Brass, percussion, strings, woodwinds.* Chicago: Children's Press.

McMillan, B. (1987). *Step-by-step.* New York: Lothrop, Lee & Shepard Books.

Ormerod, J. (1987). *Bend and stretch.* New York: Lothrop, Lee & Shepard Books.

Pica, R. (2000). *Experiences in movement with music, activities, and theory* (2nd ed.). Albany, NY: Delmar.

Pica, R. (2000). *Moving & learning series: Early elementary children.* Albany, NY: Delmar.

Pica, R. (2000). *Moving & learning series: Toddlers.* Albany, NY: Delmar.

Pica, R. (2000). *Moving & learning series: Preschoolers and kindergartners.* Albany, NY: Delmar.

Platz, H. (1988). *A week of lullabies.* New York: Greenwillow Books.

Rae, M. M. (1989). *The farmer in the dell.* New York: Scholastic.

Raffi. (1987). *Shake my sillies out.* New York: Crown.

Raschka, C. (1992). *Charlie Parker played be bop.* New York: Orchard Books.

Rounds, G. (1989). *Old MacDonald had a farm.* New York: Holiday House.

Rubin, M., & Daniel, A. (1992) *The orchestra.* Buffalo, NY: Firefly Books.

Seeger, P. (1986). *Abiyoyo.* New York: Macmillan.

Sharma, E. (1993). *Live music!* (Series): *The voice, percussion, brass, woodwinds, strings.* New York: Thomson Learning.

Williams, V. B. (1984). *Music, music for everyone.* New York: Greenwillow Books.

FIGURE 9–12 Selected books about music and movement for children.

Move the Body Activity

The following are exercises that require the children to move their whole bodies (with or without music or with a drum beat):

■ Walk in the following ways: with arms swinging, without arms swinging, fast, slowly, with feet spread apart, heel to toe, on tip-toe, on heels, and with big steps.
■ March in place with knees raised high.

Poem, Music, and Movement Activity

The following are several verses of a poem a kindergarten class of children helped me create. We tried to move like many animals and fly like a lot of birds before we decided on the ones included in the poem. The next day we tried to put the poem to music.

Each child selected a part of the poem to sing and made up his or her own tune. This activity continued for several days as the children proceeded to think up new words and melodies. I recorded their wonderful songs and put the tape in the music center for them to listen to whenever they chose to do so. We also made a book of the poem, with the children drawing the illustrations. This went into the book center.

Here is the poem:

> I can hop like a bunny.
> I can spin like a top.
> Hop, spin,
> Hop, hop, hop!
> I can gallop like a horse.
> I can jump like a clown.
> Gallop, jump,
> Up and down!

Here is another verse the children created later:

> I can bark like a dog. Arf! Arf!
> I can moo like a cow. Moo! Moo!
> I can sound like a cat. Mee-ow!
> I can hoot like an owl. Whoo! Whoo!

Obstacle Course Activity

Design an obstacle course for older children by setting up a path that leads around chairs and boxes, over piles of pillows, and through tunnels made of tables covered with blankets (or commercially made tunnels of varying lengths). For the younger children, set up an obstacle course with fewer parts.

Beanbag Activity

Use beanbags for many lively activities. They are easier for some children to catch than a ball. Ask the older children to experiment with how many different ways they can catch a beanbag, such as with one hand, two hands, their feet, or their head.

Set up several baskets into which children can practice throwing beanbags. Mark a tossing line on the floor with masking tape (or a wide chalk line, if the activity is played outdoors). The children can take turns tossing beanbags into the basket. A variation of this game can be two teams tossing beanbags at the same time or moving the toss line up closer or further back to make the activity easier or more difficult.

Make beanbags from colorful fabric or felt. The children can help you by deciding if they want them to be circles, squares, rectangles, triangles, or ovals. Fill the beanbags with bird seed, Styrofoam "squiggles," or dried beans.

Move with Scarves Activity

Moving with scarves (or any lightweight material) is another way for children to practice their creativity by moving and swaying to music. These scarves can encourage them to create stories through movement and act out stories using the scarves and other props.

■ CONNECTING MUSIC AND MOVEMENT WITH OTHER AREAS OF THE CURRICULUM

Many activities already mentioned in this chapter offer ways to connect music and movement experiences with other areas of the curriculum. It is important to think specifically about this when you select your theme and organize your lesson plan. Mayesky (1998) suggests,

> When making lesson plans for the week, include music in at least two other curricular areas. For example, plan to play music during art activities, and note which selections you will use and on which day. Be sure to make a note to have the tape ready and the tape player set up for the days required. Then, plan to read a book at group time that relates to the new song(s) introduced that week.

Music and movement are vital components of an early education environment. They contribute to language curriculum by introducing vocabulary, sound patterns, and literacy skills. Simple songs, such as question-and-answer songs or name games, can help children make the transition from speaking to singing. (Examples of this are included in the songs in this chapter.) They support social studies by bringing into the classroom music, musical instruments, and dances from around the world and creating a vibrant early childhood setting. Use the suggestions discussed in this chapter to stimulate your curriculum.

Children of the World. (1991). *Multicultural rhythmic activities for preschool.* Long Branch, NJ: Kimbo.

Eklof, J. (2000). *My favorite animal—Mi Animal Favorito; So many ways to say, "good morning."* (Cassette tapes with picture song books.) Dallas, TX: Miss Jo Publications.

Fiedler and the Boston Pops. (1986). *Favorites for children.* NY: RCA.

Grunsky, J. (1990). *Imaginary window.* Cypress, CA: Youngheart Music.

Henson, J. (1992). *A sesame street celebration.* NY: Children's Television Workshop and Henson Productions.

Jenkins, E. (1997). *Multicultural children's songs; Counting games and rhythms for little ones; You'll sing a song and I'll sing a song.* NY: Folkway Records.

Moore, T. (1990). *The family; Celebrate children; I am special.* Charlotte, NC: Thomas Moore Records.

Ott, P. (2000). *Dancing 'round the world; Happy tunes and more!* Thousand Oaks, CA: Corwin Press.

Palmer, H. (2000). *Early childhood classics—Old favorites with a new twist.* Freeport, NY: Educational Activities.

Raffi. (1998). *Rise and shine.* Willowdale, Ontario, Canada: Troubadour Records Ltd.

Scelsa, G., & Millang, S. (1998). *Kids in motion.* Cypress, CA: Youngheart Music.

Seeger, P. (2000). *American folk, game, and activity songs.* NY: Folkway Records.

Valeri, M. (1986). *Mi casa es su casa: My house is your house.* NY: Caedmon/Harper Audio.

FIGURE 9–13 Selected musical records and tapes for children.

■ TIPS FOR TEACHERS

"Of all the beautiful things in this world, there are few that surpass the images of music in childhood" (Campbell & Scott-Kassner, 1995). Use music as a transition from home to school and from school to home. Play recorded music of different types each day. Include this in your lesson plan and have information relating to the selection, the artist performing the music, or the instrument or orchestra featured. Share these musical moments with parents. The following are more suggestions:

■ Tape the children singing their favorite songs or playing musical instruments. Share with their parents. You might also make copies of the tape for parents who want to learn the songs.

■ Invite parents to participate in your music experiences. Ask them to think about songs that hold special cultural and family memories—songs they learned from their parents and grandparents when they were younger. Encourage them to bring musical instruments and music that are a part of their cultural heritage and share them with the children.

■ Use instruments as cues for transitions from one activity to another, such as cleanup time. Rotate which instruments you choose for this purpose for more variety.

■ Use a "singing hand puppet" as another transition activity. Sing songs the children are familiar with, ones that are included in the lesson plan.

■ Marching music is a wonderful way to move children from one activity to the next. Try it!

■ Observe and listen to the children. They will let you know what is working and what is not.

■ Use a variety of approaches in introducing songs. Use flannelboard characters, puppets, books, or simple props. Know the songs well yourself and sing them to the children several times while they listen. New songs should be sung to the children in their entirety, not phrase by phrase. Children pick up the tune and words naturally without having to be taught them. Incorporate simple actions into the songs. This offers visual clues to help children remember the words.

■ Rules (limits) should be developed and explained when you introduce musical instruments to the children. For example, "treat the instruments gently," "be careful not to touch anyone else with the instrument, stretch both arms out until you don't touch anyone else—this is your personal space," and "be careful not to hit instruments on the floor or anything else."

Enjoy singing songs, playing musical instruments, and movement activities. *Be involved! Be part of the activity!* The children pick up on your enthusiasm (or lack of it). Do not be concerned about your singing voice. Young children are not critical!

■ DEVELOPMENTALLY APPROPRIATE AND MULTICULTURAL/ ANTI-BIAS ACTIVITIES

Hildebrandt (1998) reminds us, "Just as children need to spend many hours listening to the language of their culture before they can talk, they need to listen to the music of their culture before they can sing and play. We need to continue to expose children to the music of their own culture as well as other cultures." As stated earlier in this chapter, music is a universal language. "If as a caregiver you have a first language different from that of the infants and toddlers you care for, be sure to use the folk songs and lullaby songs of your people at naptimes" (Honig, 1995). Feel free to sing your songs to the children no matter what age you have in your class. They will be learning about you, and that is important.

Griss (1994) offers insight into the importance of dance as a multicultural activity for young children:

> *Dance provides a wonderful way to explore both the universality and particularity of human cultures. By learning ethnic dances and physically interpreting the poetry, literature, and folklores of diverse cultures, children develop deeper insights into the aesthetics and value systems of those cultures. Including multi-cultural dance in the curriculum also offers an excellent opportunity to invite professional artists to share their expertise with children.*

The following two groups of songs by Bea Wolf and Jo Eklof are some of the favorites requested by young children in early childhood settings. Once they and their teachers know these songs, they sing them often. These songs and stories offer a multitude of opportunities for stimulating creativity and enjoyment of music and movement activities. (Wolf and Eklof songs are included in many other chapters throughout this text. They are also listed in Appendix B, Teacher Resources.)

NAME SONG*

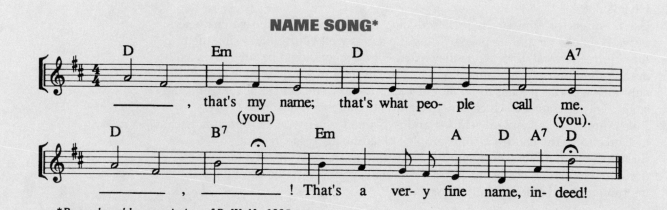

Reproduced by permission of B. Wolf - 1995
Copyright B. Wolf - 1993

PUPPY DOG STORY

Once there was a puppy dog, as nice as he could be.
He thought he'd like a little playmate, just for company.
One day he saw a kitty who was playing in a tree.
He called to her, "Sweet kitty cat! Won't you come play with me?"

And the puppy dog said, "Bow-wow!"
And the kitty cat said, "Meow!"
Then the puppy dog said, "Let's play!"
But the kitty cat said, "Go 'way!"

Then the puppy saw the kitty was afraid of him.
She thought that he would bite her,
so she climbed out on a limb!
But then the puppy told her he was gentle, good, and kind;
he'd be the nicest playmate anyone could ever find.
And the puppy dog said, "Bow-wow!"
And the kitty cat said, "Meow!"
Then the puppy dog said, "Let's play!"
And the kitty cat said, "Okay!"

The pup was very gentle, and the kitty wasn't rough,
and all the time they played
they never got into a huff!
Now the puppy and the kitty are the best of friends.
They play together every day,
and so our story ends,
with the puppy who says, "Bow-wow!",
and the kitty who says, "Meow!"
When the puppy dog says, "Let's play!",
then the kitty cat says, "Okay!"

Reproduced by permission of B. Wolf—1995

Copyright B. Wolf—1993

SONG TO ACCOMPANY
PUPPY DOG STORY*

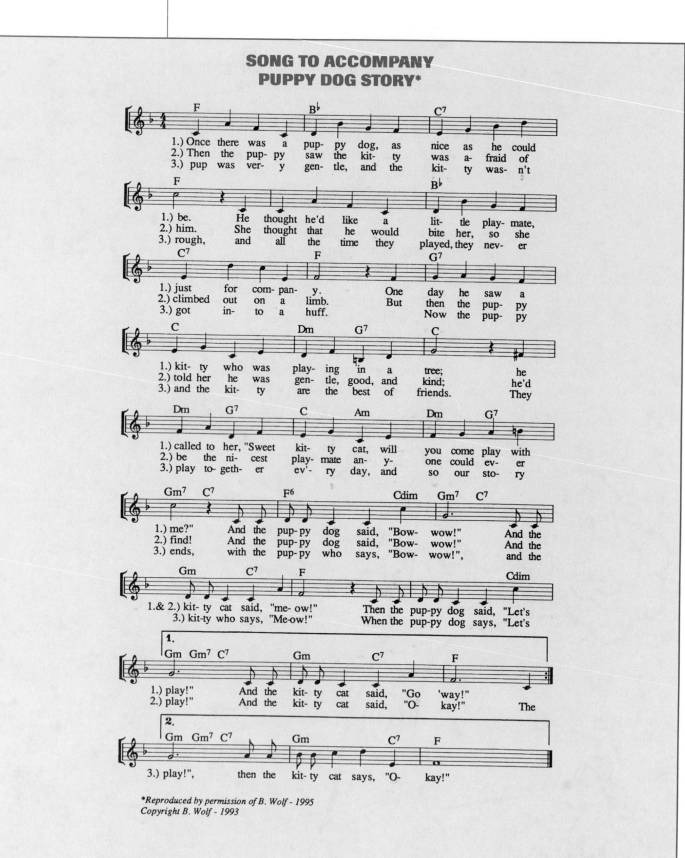

WINDSHIELD WIPERS
(activity song)

(Suitable for Two- to Five-Year-Olds—Entertainingly
Presents Concepts of Big/Little, Loud/Soft)

If children are old enough to understand, lead a short discussion about windshield wipers—when they are used and why. Then introduce the song, and proceed to the following three activities:

Part 1: With children seated, explain that first we are going to be the windshield wipers on a very small car; therefore, we will use our small, soft voices to sing. As the song is sung, children use upraised index fingers and move hands in rhythm to simulate small windshield wipers.

Part 2: Explain that next we will be windshield wipers on a larger vehicle, such as a big car, or perhaps even a pickup truck. We will use medium voices for this, and we will make the windshield wipers by extending arms in front of us, bent at the elbows, with hands and fingers stretching up. Fore-arms, hands, and fingers then act as a unit to imitate wiper motions as song is sung. Children may perform this part of the activity either seated or standing.

Part 3: Now we are going to be windshield wipers on a *really big* vehicle, such as a bus. Children may wish to contribute their own examples of huge vehicles—fire trucks, eighteen wheelers, etc. We will become the largest windshield wipers we can be by standing, extending arms up as high as we can, and using our bodies from the waist up to simulate the wipers in motion. We will sing the song with our *very loud voices!*

SONG TO ACCOMPANY
WINDSHIELD WIPERS*

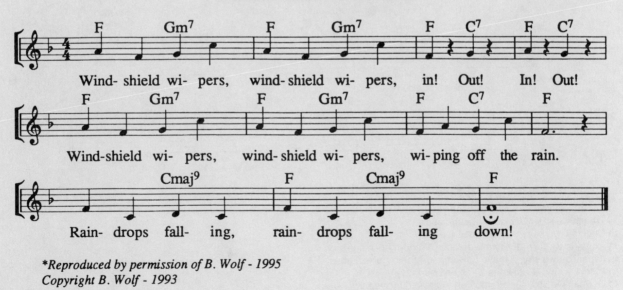

Wind-shield wi-pers, wind-shield wi-pers, in! Out! In! Out!

Wind-shield wi-pers, wind-shield wi-pers, wi-ping off the rain.

Rain-drops fall-ing, rain-drops fall-ing down!

Reproduced by permission of B. Wolf - 1995
Copyright B. Wolf - 1993

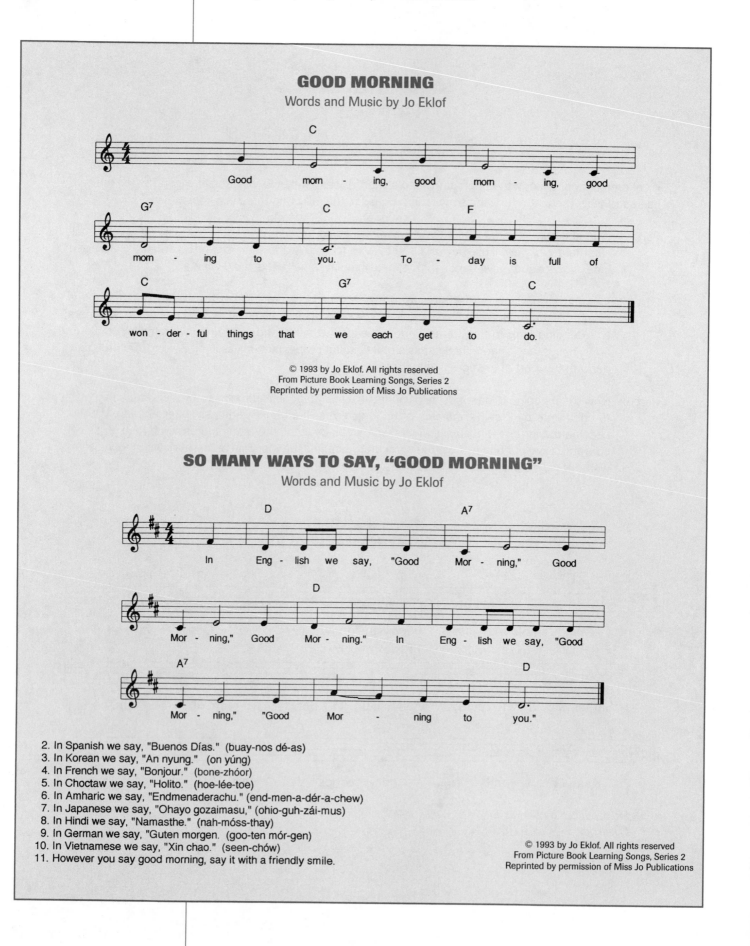

GOOD MORNING
Words and Music by Jo Eklof

Good morn-ing, good morn-ing, good morn-ing to you. To-day is full of won-der-ful things that we each get to do.

SO MANY WAYS TO SAY, "GOOD MORNING"
Words and Music by Jo Eklof

In Eng-lish we say, "Good Mor-ning," Good Mor-ning," Good Mor-ning." In Eng-lish we say, "Good Mor-ning," "Good Mor-ning to you."

2. In Spanish we say, "Buenos Días." (buay-nos dé-as)
3. In Korean we say, "An nyung." (on yúng)
4. In French we say, "Bonjour." (bone-zhóor)
5. In Choctaw we say, "Holito." (hoe-lée-toe)
6. In Amharic we say, "Endmenaderachu." (end-men-a-dér-a-chew)
7. In Japanese we say, "Ohayo gozaimasu," (ohio-guh-zái-mus)
8. In Hindi we say, "Namasthe." (nah-móss-thay)
9. In German we say, "Guten morgen. (goo-ten mór-gen)
10. In Vietnamese we say, "Xin chao." (seen-chów)
11. However you say good morning, say it with a friendly smile.

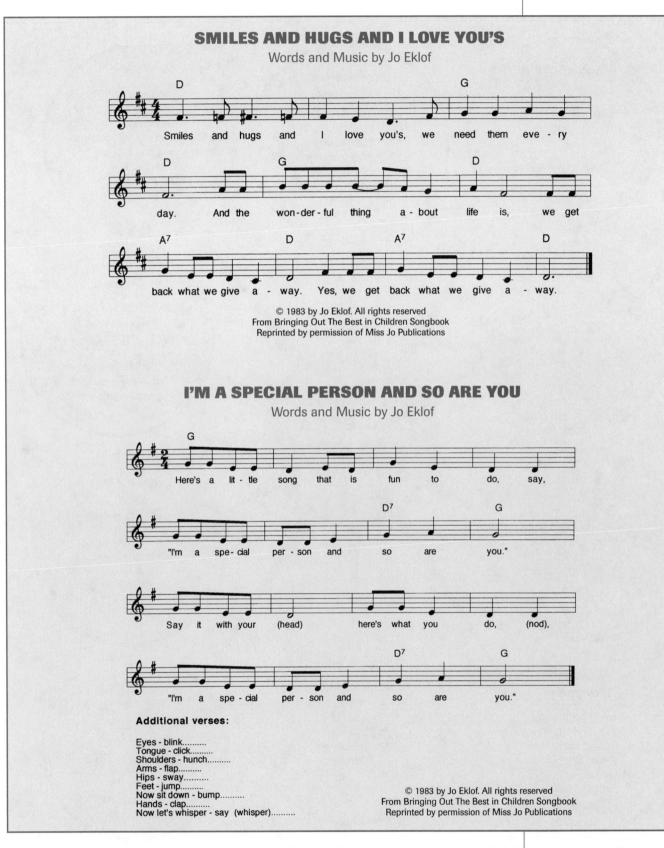

SMILES AND HUGS AND I LOVE YOU'S
Words and Music by Jo Eklof

Smiles and hugs and I love you's, we need them eve - ry

day. And the won - der - ful thing a - bout life is, we get

back what we give a - way. Yes, we get back what we give a - way.

I'M A SPECIAL PERSON AND SO ARE YOU
Words and Music by Jo Eklof

Here's a lit - tle song that is fun to do, say,

"I'm a spe - cial per - son and so are you."

Say it with your (head) here's what you do, (nod),

"I'm a spe - cial per - son and so are you."

Additional verses:

Eyes - blink..........
Tongue - click..........
Shoulders - hunch..........
Arms - flap..........
Hips - sway..........
Feet - jump..........
Now sit down - bump..........
Hands - clap..........
Now let's whisper - say (whisper)..........

Figure 9–14 is the curriculum planning web with music and movement activities added. This worksheet, with appropriate additions, is included in each chapter.

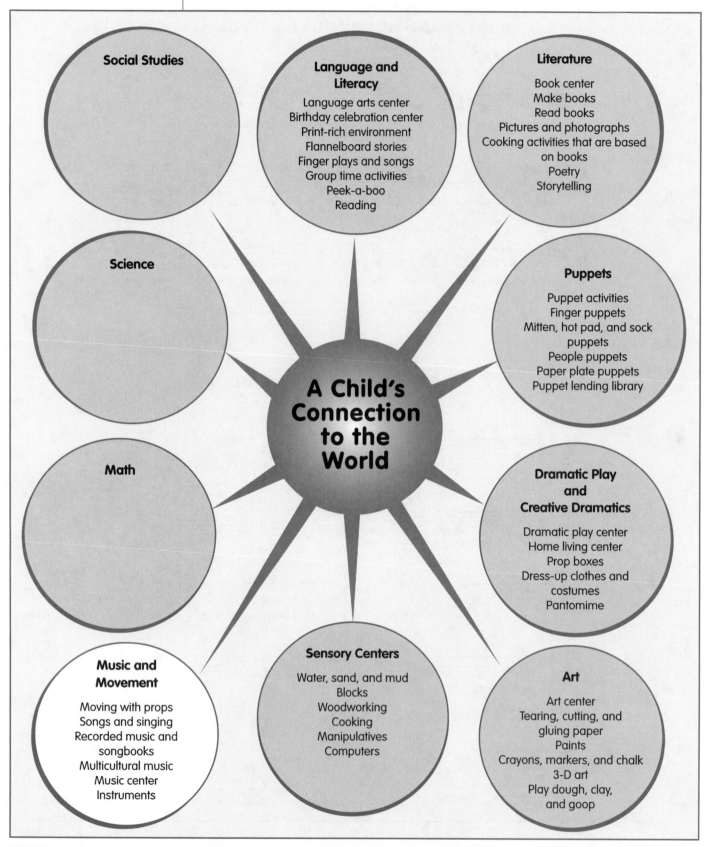

Social Studies

Language and Literacy

Language arts center
Birthday celebration center
Print-rich environment
Flannelboard stories
Finger plays and songs
Group time activities
Peek-a-boo
Reading

Literature

Book center
Make books
Read books
Pictures and photographs
Cooking activities that are based
on books
Poetry
Storytelling

Science

Puppets

Puppet activities
Finger puppets
Mitten, hot pad, and sock
puppets
People puppets
Paper plate puppets
Puppet lending library

A Child's Connection to the World

Math

Dramatic Play and Creative Dramatics

Dramatic play center
Home living center
Prop boxes
Dress-up clothes and
costumes
Pantomime

Music and Movement

Moving with props
Songs and singing
Recorded music and
songbooks
Multicultural music
Music center
Instruments

Sensory Centers

Water, sand, and mud
Blocks
Woodworking
Cooking
Manipulatives
Computers

Art

Art center
Tearing, cutting, and
gluing paper
Paints
Crayons, markers, and chalk
3-D art
Play dough, clay,
and goop

FIGURE 9–14 A curriculum planning web worksheet with music and movement activities added.

AFTERVIEW

Through music and movement activities, a child

- Becomes sensitive to beauty and harmony
- Validates creativity, individuality, and self-expression
- Reinforces auditory, visual, and comprehension skills
- Explores and differentiates sounds
- Practices listening skills
- Expands vocabulary and language development
- Explores large and small muscle movement
- Develops awareness of the body and how it works and moves
- Has an opportunity to release energy and express emotions

- Practices moving through space
- Expresses herself freely through creative movement, playing musical instruments, and singing
- Experiences a wide variety of music
- Experiments with creating and performing music
- Derives pleasure from musical experiences
- Develops positive feelings about being part of a group and participates both as a leader and follower
- Expresses pride in his ethnic heritage by using songs, dances, musical instruments, and recordings from his culture

KEY TERMS

beat	nonlocomotor movement	timbre
locomotor movement	pitch	tone
manipulative movement	rhythm	volume
melody	tempo	

EXPLORATIONS

1. Select an early childhood classroom. Observe for at least one hour. In writing, describe any music and movement activities you observed. Did the children or the teacher initiate these activities? Describe some examples of how the children spontaneously approached these activities.

2. Choose five selections of music from your favorite recordings. Experiment with basic rhythmic movement activities, such as clapping, swaying, stretching, walking, and skipping to accompany each piece of music. Then, list in writing the name of each selection, the composer, the name of the album or tape, and the artists or orchestra performing the selection. Describe the movement activity or activities you do for each musical piece.

   Select an early childhood setting. Play the same five selections for a group of young children. Encourage them to move to the music. Which rhythmic movements did they do? Were they the same or similar to what you did? Explain. What did you learn from completing this activity?

3. In writing, discuss the ways musical instruments can be used in music activities with young children. Make one of the musical instruments suggested in this chapter. Introduce the use of the instrument to a group of children. Discuss why you chose this instrument. Did you achieve your objectives? What were the children's reactions? Were they stimulated to make this and other instruments? What would you do differently if you presented this activity again? Explain.

4. With a classmate or colleague, develop music and movement activities and transitions to be included in a weekly lesson plan or curriculum web for a group of young children. Specify which age group these activities are planned for: infants, toddlers, preschoolers, or primary-aged children. Include names of the songs, a list of the recordings you plan to use, and the titles and authors of any books included.

5. Select one of the activities from your lesson plan or web completed in Exploration 4. Write a list of objectives, materials needed, step-by-step procedures for presenting the activity, follow-up activities, and evaluation guidelines. (Use the activity plan worksheet in Chapter 2.)

REFERENCES

Allen, J., McNeill, E., & Schmidt, V. (1992). *Cultural awareness for children*. Menlo Park, CA: Addison-Wesley Publishing Co.

Andress, B. L., & Walker, L. M. (Eds.). (1992). *Readings in early childhood music education*. Reston, VA: Music Educators National Conference.

Campbell, P. S., & Scott-Kassner, C. (1995). *Music in childhood*. New York: Schirmer Books.

Corbett, S. (1995). *A world of difference: Shake, rattle, and strum*. Chicago: Children's Press.

Day, B. (1994). *Early childhood education* (4th ed.). Columbus, OH: Merrill.

Greenberg, M. (1979). *Your children need music*. Englewood Cliffs, NJ: Prentice Hall.

Griss, S. (1994, February). Creative movement: A language for learning. *Educational Leadership, 51*(5), 78–80.

Haines, B. J. E., & Gerber, L. L. (1996). *Leading young children to music* (5th ed.). Columbus, OH: Merrill.

Hildebrandt, C. (1998, November). Creativity in music and early childhood. *Young Children, 53*(6), 68–74.

Honig, A. S. (1995, July). Singing with infants and toddlers. *Young Children, 50*(5), 72–78.

Ingico, A. (1994, August). Early childhood physical education: Providing the foundation. *Journal of Physical Education, Recreation and Dance*, 28–30.

Lillegard, D. (1988). *Percussion*. Chicago: Children's Press.

Machado, J. (1999). *Early childhood experiences in language arts* (6th ed.). Albany, NY: Delmar.

Mayesky, M. (1998). *Creative activities for young children* (6th ed.). Albany, NY: Delmar.

Moomaw, S. (1984). *Discovering music in early childhood*. Boston: Allyn and Bacon.

Music Educators National Conference (MENC). (1994). *The school music program: A new vision*. Reston, VA: Author.

Pica, R. (2000). *Experiences in movement with music, activities, and theory* (2nd ed.). Albany, NY: Delmar.

Poest, C. A., Williams, J. R., Witt, D. D., & Atwood, M. E. (1990, July). Challenge me to move: Large muscle development in young children. *Young Children, 45*(5), 4–10.

ADDITIONAL READINGS AND RESOURCES

Achilles, E. (1999, January). Creating music environments in early childhood programs. *Young Children, 54*(1), 21–26.

Buchoff, R. (1995, Spring). Jump rope rhymes . . . in the classroom? *Childhood Education, 71*(3), 149–151.

Buchoff, R. (1994, May). Joyful voices: Facilitating language growth through the rhythmic response to chants. *Young Children, 49*(4), 26–30.

Carter, M. (1994, May/June). Moving teachers to move children. *Child Care Exchange, 97,* 46–50.

Church, E. B. (1995, April). Rhythm is a part of me! *Early Childhood Today, 9*(7), 26–27.

Feierabend, J. M. (1995). *First steps in music for infants and toddlers*. Simsbury, CT: First Steps in Music, Inc.

Foltz-Gray, D. (1995, Spring). World rhythms. *Teaching Tolerance, 4*(1), 58–61.

Fox, D. B. (1991, January) Music, development, and the young child. *Music Educators Journal, 77*(5), 42–46.

Gober, B. E. (1998, April). Moving outdoors: All the right moves. *Early Childhood Today, 12*(7), 31–38.

Guilmartin, K. K. (1995, September). A new understanding of music in early childhood. *Principal, 75*(1), 40–42.

Hart, A., & Mantell, P. (1993). *Kids make music: Clapping and tapping from Bach to rock*. Charlotte, VT: Williamson Publishing.

Jackman, H. L. (1999). *Sing me a story! Tell me a song! Creative curriculum activities for teachers of young children*. Thousand Oaks, CA: Corwin Press.

Jalongo, M. R. (1996, July). Using recorded music with young children. *Young Children, 51*(5), 6–13.

Jenkins, E. (1995, April). Music is culture. *Early Childhood Today, 9*(7), 40.

Kranowitz, C. S. (1994, May/June). Kids gotta move: Adapting movement experiences for children with differing abilities. *Child Care Exchange, 97,* 37–43.

Moomaw, S. (1997). *More than singing: Discovering music in preschool and kindergarten.* St. Paul, MN: Redleaf Press.

Pica, R. (1999). *Moving and learning across the curriculum: 315 activities and games.* Albany, NY: Delmar.

Pica, R. (1997, September). Beyond physical development: Why young children need to move. *Young Children, 52*(6), 4–11.

Rodger, L. (1996, March). Adding movement throughout the day. *Young Children, 51*(3), 4–6.

Tythacott, L. (1995). *Traditions around the world: Musical instruments.* New York: Thomson Learning.

Weikart, P. (1990). *Movement in steady beat.* Ypsilanti, MI: High/Scope Press.

Wolf, J. (1992). Let's sing it again: Creating music with young children. *Young Children, 47*(2), 56–61.

Math

CHAPTER

10

■ OVERVIEW

Math is everywhere! We are involved with math concepts from infancy onward. Much of what we do as part of our everyday lives relates to mathematics: telling time with clocks and watches, cooking and eating, getting dressed, planning our lives by the calendar (electronic or otherwise). Daily activities involve problem solving, one-to-one correspondence, classifying, measuring, and sequencing. This is true for children, too.

As you progress through this chapter, the approach to setting up the developmentally appropriate math center will parallel the approach to, and interconnect with, all the content areas in this text. The math-rich environment is built on basic math concepts, the children's developmental level (individually and collectively), and their interests.

"Active, hands-on math experiences in a safe and trusting environment help children become learners who take risks, think independently, and see math learning as enjoyable" (Mitchell & David, 1992). This way of developing math awareness and understanding is very different from the rote learning, rigid rules, workbooks, and flash cards many of us grew up with. The goal for children today is to focus on conceptual math, not pencil-and-paper figuring. The new view of math is relaxed and comfortable for the teacher and the children. Children need to acquire basic skills and concepts *first* to live in our world that is exploding with information and continuously changing.

> *What does this mean for you as an early childhood teacher? It means that when you provide hands-on, child-directed experiences related to math skills and concepts such as classification, seriation, patterning, measurement, and numbers, you are helping your children to "think" math. (Waite-Stupiansky, 1995)*

It is also important to understand that the *acquisition of math skills and concepts comes in stages over time,* as with all growth and development in young children. "[F]or young children, mathematics is a way of viewing the world and their experiences in it. It is a way of solving real problems. . . . As children grow and develop, their mathematical activities change" (Brewer, 1998). Repetition is meaningful during this process. Children need to rethink and practice what they know as they continue to add new skills and concepts. Making the environment, both indoors and outside, available for young children to experience the world and their place in it will encourage children to understand that math is everywhere!

■ CONCEPT DEVELOPMENT IN YOUNG CHILDREN

> *Early childhood is a period when children actively engage in acquiring basic concepts. Concepts are the building blocks of knowledge; they allow people to organize and categorize information. . . . Concepts are acquired through children's active involvement with the environment. (Charlesworth & Lind, 1999)*

Interaction with their surroundings through play and firsthand experiences with concrete objects helps children discover basic math concepts.

Jean Piaget pioneered the study of children's thinking (cognitive growth and development) and described how each child creates his own mental image or knowledge of the world, based on his encounters with the environment. Piaget called this *physical knowledge* or learning about objects in the environment and their characteristics, such as color, weight, and size. Piaget's *logico-mathematical knowledge* is the type that includes relationships each individual constructs in order to make sense out of the

world and to organize information, such as classification, counting, and comparing (Charlesworth & Lind, 1999).

Howard Gardner also includes logical/mathematical thinking in his research relating to multiple intelligences, sometimes referred to as "different ways of knowing." Children strong in this form of intelligence think conceptually.

> *Logical/mathematical intelligence is the ability to understand the basic properties of numbers, adding or taking away; appreciate principles of cause and effect; one-to-one correspondence; ability to predict, as in which objects will float, sink, etc. (Gardner, 1995)*

Charlesworth and Lind (1999) explain, "The major objective for mathematics instruction is *teaching for understanding.* Understanding occurs when a mathematical concept or procedure becomes a real part of the mental structure. Understanding is not present to any great degree when mathematics is learned as isolated skills and procedures."

When you observe children, you become aware of how they think (problem solve) and talk (communicate) about what they are discovering. Concept development is fostered by *solving problems* or figuring things out. Constructing knowledge by making mistakes is part of this process as well.

A curriculum that accommodates a variety of developmental levels as well as individual differences in young children sets the stage for problem-solving opportunities (Bredekamp & Copple, 1997). This too is a process. Beginning with the needs and interests of the children; the development of themes, lesson plans, and webs; and providing time, space, and materials, encourages problem solving. "Children must have problems to solve, opportunities to work at solving them, and then experience the results of their decisions" (Eliason & Jenkins, 1999).

■ MATH LANGUAGE OF EARLY CHILDHOOD

Young children understand math in relationship to how it affects them. The infant discovers the shape of the object by putting it in her mouth and holding on to it. The

1. Learning to value mathematics

2. Becoming confident of one's own ability

3. Becoming a mathematical problem solver

4. Learning to communicate mathematically

5. Learning to reason mathematically

(Charlesworth & Lind, 1999)

FIGURE 10–1 National Council of Teachers of Mathematics (NCTM) Curriculum Standards Goals for students.

toddler can let you know he is two years old by trying to show you two fingers. The three-year-old likes to sing a number song, while the four-year-old counts "onetwothreefourfivesix." The five-year-old shows you how tall her block building is, and the school-age child wants to win at the board game he is playing. All these children are using *math language*.

In the beginning, children can say the names of numbers in order. They remember the *words*, but they do not understand the *meaning* of what they are saying. "To understand the meaning of numbers the child must be able to associate quantities with symbols" (Eliason & Jenkins, 1999). This number sense evolves during the first eight years of a child's life. How you set up the early education environment will determine how often the child has opportunities to develop number sense and logical ways of thinking about time, space, and other mathematical ideas.

For young children, infants and toddlers especially, the schedules and routines of the day become a consistent sequence of events. This regular predictable pattern helps put order to things, which is part of the process of math learning. When you sing number songs and finger plays, read number books, share number flannelboard stories, and repeat numerals often, you are placing math in the environment and making it part of the day's routine. See Figure 10–1 for NCTM's Curriculum Standards Goals.

One-to-One Correspondence

One-to-one correspondence is based on the premise that each object has the value of one. One-to-one correspondence is established when one object is paired with one other object or a group of objects is paired with another group of equal number. The assigning of a number name (one, two, three, etc.) to each object helps children place the objects in a one-to-one correspondence. Children show an awareness of this relationship daily.

One-to-one correspondence activities develop from the infant's early sensorimotor activity. He finds out that he can hold one thing in each hand, but he can put only one object at a time in his mouth. (Charlesworth & Lind, 1999)

The following are examples of this awareness:

- Language is important to toddlers, so a teacher touching and counting aloud (one child, one book, one block, one doll) is expressing one-to-one correspondence. A child is learning self-help skills and one-to-one correspondence when he puts one arm into a coat sleeve.

- For preschoolers and older children, "counting objects they can get their hands on makes one-to-one correspondence meaningful" (Burns, 1998). Putting one peg in one hole, setting the table with one napkin for each child, or putting one sock on one foot is one-to-one correspondence. Giving a child four pennies and asking him to put one penny in each of four cups also demonstrates one-to-one correspondence.

Classifying and Sorting

Children grouping objects by a common characteristic, such as size, shape, or color, are **classifying and sorting**. These children are interacting with the environment, using visual discrimination, and manipulating real objects.

Dawes (1977) gives us an example. "Children are surrounded by shapes of all types: they sit on shapes, sleep on shapes, eat off and drink out of shapes, climb over and through shapes, they build with shapes, etc." Teachers name and talk about shapes as part of the daily conversation in the classroom. Other examples follow:

- Infants learn about shapes through using their hands, mouth, and eyes. They are discovering that some toys are easier to hold, while others roll better.

- During late infancy, babies grasp an important developmental concept—object permanence. "This realization is key for learning and is especially important for developing thinking and number skills. Once toddlers grasp object constancy, sorting by size and color is within reach" (Poole, 1998).

- Toddlers begin noticing alike and different when they sort colored blocks into blues and reds or big and little ones. It is important to remember to keep concepts simple and consistent for toddlers. For example, have all the blue and red blocks they are sorting be the same size and shape so the children are only dealing with the concept of color. Simple puzzles also help toddlers begin to develop classification skills.

- Preschool children begin by sorting objects with one characteristic or quality. They enjoy sorting buttons, plastic animals, wooden beads, and shells. Provide a muffin tin (see Figure 10–2), plastic cups, or an empty, clean egg carton for the sorted objects. For older preschoolers, classifying becomes more involved by isolating a set from a collection, such as counting children and sorting them into boys and girls, and then observing which children are wearing stripes and which are not.

- Primary-grade children use more complex concepts by sorting sets into sub-sets and looking at what materials objects are made of (wood, plastic, metal) or what function they have (forks, knives, spoons). Older children can explain to you their rule for making the sorting decision.

FIGURE 10–2 Classifying and sorting objects by a common characteristic.

Patterns

Patterning is another way for children to see order in their world. A **pattern** is a sequence of colors, objects, sounds, stories, or movements that repeat, in the same order, over and over again. Some examples follow:

- For infants, patterning is recognizing the human face with eyes, nose, and mouth in a specific place. For older infants, looking in a mirror helps them place their face in the same pattern.

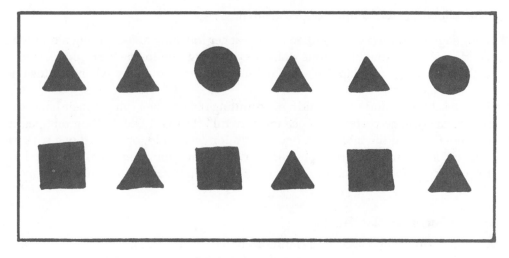

VISUAL PATTERNING

TACTILE PATTERNING

FIGURE 10–3 Examples of visual and tactile patterning.

■ Toddlers asking for the same book to be read again and again soon begin to "read" the story along with the teacher. They are placing the events of the story in a sequencing pattern.

■ For preschoolers and older children, stringing beads or putting pegs in a pegboard in a specific pattern, such as blue, red, green, and yellow, is visual patterning. The younger children can duplicate the pattern and the older children can duplicate and extend it. Auditory patterning is repeating sounds (such as soft, loud, soft, loud, soft) over and over again and then having the children repeat the sequence. You can do this with tactile patterning by creating a texture board with articles that are smooth, rough, smooth, rough, smooth (see Figure 10–3).

Spatial Relationships

Spatial relationships are comparisons that relate children to space and time. Howard Gardner's research has helped us understand spatial intelligence as one of his eight multiple intelligences. "Spatial intelligence is the ability to be able to form a mental image of large (a home) and local (a block building) spatial layouts [and to] find one's way around a new building" (Gardner, 1995).

Games and movement activities can be the keys to spatial relationship awareness, such as position (on/off, over/under), direction (up/down, forward/backward), and distance (near/far, close to/far from).

"Imagine, for example, the wealth of concepts relating to *space, position, time, sound, rhythm, body parts, and body control* a child might grasp through a group activity involving music and rhythmic movement" (Fortson & Reiff, 1995). Toddlers and young preschoolers enjoy moving streamers in time with the music. You can help increase spatial awareness by saying "move your streamer over your head or in front of you." You are encouraging them to change the arrangement of space they are in.

Play the "hide an object" game with preschoolers. For example, hide a block or a beanbag somewhere in the room. Let the children guess if you have hidden it over, under, on top of, etc. The child who guesses where the object is hidden becomes "it" and hides the object for the other children to guess where it is. The children are thinking in images and pictures. They are finding the object that has been placed in space and out of sight. Older children extend spatial relationships to board games where they count squares and move forward or backward on the game board. They are exploring a new spatial layout and varying the arrangement of the game pieces in space.

Appropriate software is available for children to learn more about spatial relationships using the computer. But first, it is critical that they understand the basic math concepts used in the relationships (Figure 10–4). Math language of early childhood overlaps, interconnects, and involves all the senses. No matter what terminology is used, children are counting, classifying, thinking, reasoning, comparing, measuring, problem solving, and learning about math naturally as they play.

FIGURE 10–4 Helping children understand spatial relationships.

■ MATH EXPERIENCES IN AN EARLY CHILDHOOD ENVIRONMENT

Math awareness continues outdoors too.

- Toddlers enjoy play structures that are lower and wider and allow them opportunities to climb up and down. The wheels on the tricycles are round and the sandpile is a square.
- Preschool children can look for rough and smooth objects to compare, light/heavy or small/large rocks to pick up, and many leaves to count.
- Older children can take chalk and make a giant hopscotch area with numerals from 0 to 20.
- You can help the children collect boxes, small to large, and set up an outdoor obstacle course for them to crawl through, around, over, and under. This will also help the children order their movements to reach a particular goal.
- Line up two rows of smooth stones with each row having six stones. Space the stones farther apart in one row. Ask the children if one row has more or less than the other. Most preschoolers will answer that the longer row has more rocks than the other. When children reach the developmental stage of knowing that both rows have the same amount of stones, no matter how they are spaced, they are also practicing the concept of conservation.

Ask open-ended questions to learn more about children's thinking, such as, "Which of the cups do you think will hold the most sand?" or "How many circles can you find in our room?" or "How many steps do you think it will take to go from the tricycle to the sandbox?" or "What can we use to measure the length of the art table?" You will get a lot of wonderful answers. Expect and accept whatever the children say. This will guide you as you evaluate where you and the children go next.

Folder and Lotto Games

Folder games and lotto games are additional ways of including math in the classroom. Older children can match numerals, identify sets, and recognize objects that are alike and different.

The following folder game can be available when children celebrate their birthdays. This will give them something concrete to help identify how old they are. You can also weigh and measure the children on their birthdays.

FIGURE 10–5 Example of a folder game.

FIGURE 10–6 Example of a lotto game.

Take an ordinary folder, open it, and place ten figures of birthday cakes in two rows of four and one row of two. The cakes are all alike, except for the number of candles and large dots on each cake. On separate square pieces of construction paper or tagboard, make individual cakes with the same number of candles that correspond to those in the folder. You may want to add the written numeral to match the number of candles and dots. This will give the children an opportunity to match "how many candles each cake has" with several visual clues. Laminate or cover all the items of the folder game with clear contact paper. To keep materials organized, make a pocket on the back of the folder to hold the pieces of the game. This can be a plastic bag or a paper pocket that is glued or taped onto the folder. To extend this activity, make flannelboard characters that represent the birthday cakes and candles. The children can place the correct number of candles to match the number of dots on each cake, Figure 10–5. (The flannelboard characters are included in Appendix A.)

To make a lotto game (bingo or matching), take two identical pieces of cardboard or tagboard and line both pieces in the same way to make as many squares as you want. Leave one piece of cardboard whole. (This is the game board.) Cut the other piece up into equal squares (the game pieces). Draw or paste pairs of identical pictures or stickers, one to each cut-up square and one to each square of the large card. Laminate or cover all the lotto game pieces with clear contact paper. Make a pocket on the back of the whole lotto card, as you did with the folder game. This will help to keep all the game pieces organized and together, Figure 10–6.

Other general math activities can include talking to the children about their addresses and phone numbers; asking children to bring you supplies, such as five sheets of red construction paper, three paintbrushes, and two small bottles of glue; and letting the children count the number of children present in the classroom, figuring out how many are missing, then naming those who are absent.

■ INTEGRATING MATH WITH OTHER CURRICULUM AREAS

Math concepts are better understood when they are a part of the daily activities. Other curriculum areas can include math easily and successfully.

Math and Science

Math and science are like a two-piece puzzle. They fit together to make a whole, but each piece is important by itself. That is why these two curriculum areas are separate chapters in this text. Chapter 11, the next chapter, covers the science curriculum in early childhood. Here are several suggestions on how to use math concepts and relate them to the science center and theme.

- Sort collections of shells, magnets, leaves, seeds, rocks. Classify them according to size.
- Use a thermometer and ask open-ended questions, such as: "What happens when you put the thermometer into hot water?" or "What happens when you put it in cold water?"
- Older children can graph the daily temperature. This can extend the daily calendar activity of marking the day of the week and month of the year.
- Have children count the number of legs on insects. Use both pictures and real insects, if possible.
- Plants offer opportunities for children to keep a chart or graph of the days or times plants should be watered and how much they have grown.
- Children's literature can create strategies to integrate math and science concepts in the curriculum. "Nearly any topic of interest can be developed using books, real-life artifacts, and related hands-on learning experiences" (Benson & Downing, 1999).
- *Planting A Rainbow* (1988) and *Growing Vegetable Soup* (1987), both by Lois Ehlert, are two books that integrate math and science in an exciting way. "Gardens in all their colors, shapes, and sizes offer linkages with many books that support a wide variety of activities, and of course more thinking, problem solving, and questioning" (Hinnant, 1999).

Cooking

One of the most delightful ways to invite children into the world of math is through cooking. Ask a young child playing in the dramatic play area to explain the ingredients of the imaginary cake he is baking, and the answer will probably be something like this: "I put in 20 cups of sugar, a bunch of flour, two eggs (one for each hand), and mix 'em all up and put it in the stove for ten minutes." Even though their numbers may be inaccurate, it shows that they are aware of quantities in recipes.

Extend both the dramatic play and math. Let the children bake an actual cake. Just think about the ways you can help children clarify math concepts through experiences with cooking. You are involving children with counting, one-to-one correspondence, fractions, time, temperature, weight, shapes, sizes, amounts, measurements, reading a recipe, and following a sequence.

Here's an easy cake recipe, and all you do is "dump" everything together.

Put 1 can of fruit, including juice, into a buttered cake pan. Dump 1 box of cake mix over the fruit. Chop up 1 stick of butter or margarine. Dump these pieces on the top of the cake mix. Bake at 350 degrees for 30 to 40 minutes. Then divide into servings, one for each child, and eat!

Incorporating math concepts into snacktime is another way to make math more mean-ingful. Developmentally appropriate math lessons occur every day in my prekinder-garten classroom since I converted our former teacher-directed group snacktime to a self-serve center open through the middle of the morning. Enthusiastic children eagerly count and measure their own portions and construct useful early math concepts with immediate personal relevance. (Meriwether, 1997)

Art

Children need to relate math to themselves, and adding art projects to the math activ-ities will help them do this. For example, make an "All About Me" book, poster, or chart. Include the child's weight, height, and shoe size or foot outline at the beginning of the year, during the year, and at the end of the year. This offers a child a concrete way to compare his stages of growth.

Another art and math activity is to draw an outline around a child's body on a large piece of white butcher paper or brown wrapping paper. The younger child will need you to do it, but the older child can select a partner to do it. Each child can then weigh himself on a scale in the classroom, measure different parts of her body, and record the results on the drawing. Next, the child can add finishing art to the drawing by adding facial features, hair, clothing, and shoes.

Language, Literacy, and Literature

For language, literacy, and literature development, select math books of all types and genres to read to the children, or have the children read and discuss during group time. Here are a few to get you started:

Brown, M. W. (1991). *Afro-Bets book of shapes.* Illustrated by C. Blair. Orange, NJ: Just Us Books, Inc.

Carle, E. (1974). *My very first book of numbers.* New York: Thomas Y. Crowell.

Feelings, M. (1972). *Moja means one.* Illustrated by T. Feelings. New York: Dial Books.

Haskins, J. (1987). *Count your way through the Arab world.* Illustrated by D. Gustafson. Minneapolis, MN: Carolrhoda Books Inc.

Haskins, J. (1987). *Count your way through China.* Illustrated by D. Hockerman. Min-neapolis, MN: Carolrhoda Books Inc.

Haskins, J. (1987). *Count your way through Japan.* Illustrated by M. Skoro. Min-neapolis, MN: Carolrhoda Books Inc.

Hoban, T. (1998). *So many circles, so many squares.* New York: Greenwillow Books.

Hoban, T. (1986). *Shapes, shapes, shapes.* New York: Greenwillow Books.

McMillan, B. (1991). *Eating fractions.* New York: Scholastic.

Politi, L. (1994). *Three stalks of corn.* New York: Aladdin Books.

Xiong, B. (1989). *Nine-in-one Grr! Grr!* Adapted by C. Spagnoli. Illustrated by N. Hom. San Francisco: Children's Book Press.

Ziefert, H. (1991). *City shapes.* Illustrated by S. Baum. New York: HarperCollins.

Rhythm and Rhyme

Young children enjoy number rhythm and rhymes. The following are two traditional ones that are still popular.

ONE POTATO

One potato	Four potato	Six potato	Eight potato
Two potato	Five potato	Seven potato	Nine potato
Three potato	Six potato	Eight potato	Ten potato
FOUR	MORE	SHOUT	OUT

ONE, TWO, BUCKLE MY SHOE

1,2,
Buckle my shoe;
3,4,
Shut the door;
5,6,
Pick up sticks;
7,8,
Lay them straight;
9,10,
Let's say it again.

■ MATERIALS FOR DEVELOPING MATH CONCEPTS

The following materials offer children many ways to develop their understanding of math concepts:

- Bingo cards
- Calendar
- Cans or egg cartons, with numbers on them to put a matching number of objects into
- Children's socks, shoes, mittens, and gloves, to match in pairs
- Clocks with numbers (*not* digital)
- Geometric boards (geoboards): to manipulate rubber bands or elastic loopers to form shapes or designs
- Magnetic board with plastic numerals
- Measuring cups, spoons, and pitchers
- Milk cartons to demonstrate liquid measures and relationships between half-pints, pints, quarts, and gallons
- Number strips and counting boards
- Objects to count, sort, and classify, such as buttons, paper clips, pennies, colored cubes, bottle caps, aluminum washers, colored plastic clothespins, empty spools, shells, popsicle or craft sticks, keys, bread tags, and nuts and bolts
- Rulers, yardsticks, and measuring tapes
- Sandpaper numerals
- Shape puzzles and flannelboard characters, such as circle, square, rectangle, triangle, cone, sphere, cube, cylinder, oval, diamond, star, and heart
- Table games, such as parquetry blocks, pattern blocks, card games, and dominos

- Telephones, both dial and touchtone
- Timer
- Unit, hollow, shape, and table blocks, which offer opportunities to learn about balance, measurement and estimation, width, height, length and dimensionality, size relationships, and how shapes fit into space
- Wooden pegboard and pegs

■ TIPS FOR TEACHERS

As you plan, facilitate, observe, and evaluate the math activities in your early education classroom, think about the following:

- Let the children know it is acceptable not to have an immediate answer to the math activity on which they are working. Let them know that there may be more than one way to solve a problem or complete a task.
- Let the children make mistakes and correct them themselves.
- Encourage collective or cooperative problem solving, which builds positive self-esteem.
- Allow time for trying out new ideas and taking risks.
- Guide the children to develop math skills needed for the new changing information age of sophisticated machines, technology, computers, and calculators.
- Allow math materials to be moved to other curriculum centers. Spontaneity and creativity are exciting and important!

■ ENCOURAGING FAMILY SUPPORT

Young children enjoy assisting Mom or Dad in the kitchen or helping to sort the laundry. You can help the parents understand that these experiences offer their children math activities.

Following are a few ways to explain this to the family members. Hopefully, this will get parents started in asking you questions about what else they can do at home. They may even start observing the schedule, routines, and activities that are occurring daily in their child's classroom.

ACTIVITY PLAN WORKSHEET

DEVELOPMENTALLY APPROPRIATE AND MULTICULTURAL/ANTI-BIAS ACTIVITIES

Children's age group: appropriate for older preschool, kindergarten, and school-age children

Name of Activity and Brief Description

Name Game is designed for the children to find opportunities to measure, count, and have fun with their names.

Purpose/Objectives of Activity

■ To develop an awareness that math is everywhere
■ To develop math concepts, such as one-to-one correspondence, counting, and measuring
■ To encourage cooperative problem solving
■ To become aware of similarities and differences in names
■ To recognize the importance of names and to learn names from other cultures
■ To increase listening skills and encourage language development

Space and Materials Needed

This activity can be done in the math center, the art center, on the floor, or anywhere that the children can use rulers, measuring tape, pencils, crayons, markers, and paper.

Procedure

1. At group time introduce the activity. Briefly talk about names. Ask the children if they have ever thought about the number of letters in their names. Have they ever counted the letters? Have they ever measured their names?
2. Using your name as an example, you can demonstrate what you want them to do. Show your name printed on a piece of paper. Have the children count the number of letters in your name. Then place a ruler along the bottom of your name and measure how many inches long your name is.
3. Explain that this is what you would like for them to do with their names. They can do it now or they can do it another time. They get to choose. Count how many want to do it now and how many want to do it later. Add the two numbers together to figure out how many children are in class today.
4. Use a transitional activity, such as: the child whose first name begins with A goes to a center of his choice or begins the name activity. Continue through the alphabet until all the children have selected what they want to do.
5. You can then observe who needs assistance in getting started and who does not need any help.

Guidance

In anticipating what the children might do, remember to guide them through this activity. Let them work together to problem solve. The children will probably discover for themselves that some names are shorter than others and compare the shortest name with the longest one. You may need to facilitate, especially with the younger children.

Some children may not want to participate in this activity. That is acceptable. Guide them into another activity center.

Evaluation and Follow-Up

Were all the objectives met? Did the younger children participate for a short or long period of time? How much did the children discover? Did they share and problem solve together? What would you leave the same and what would you change the next time you did this activity with the children?

Extend this activity by having children assign a color to each letter. When they use crayons and markers to "decorate" their names, they are adding another dimension to the activity. The next day at group time have the children rhyme their name with another word. Then go around the circle and have the children try to say all the rhymes together.

MATH AT HOME

Your child will learn to sort and classify objects by helping you with the clean laundry. She could start with sorting clothes by color. She could help put all the white clothes in one pile and the dark clothes in another pile. She can learn to sort and classify items by types, putting the shirts in one pile, the sheets in another pile, and the towels in another pile. Start simply and then go to the complex sorting. For example, sorting socks gives practice in pairing by color, size, and design. Putting rough jeans in one pile and soft bedclothes in another pile offers sorting and classifying of items by texture.

Your child can learn math concepts in the kitchen, too. He can learn number concepts when helping you to set the table. How many people will be at breakfast or dinner? How many knives will you need? How many forks? How many spoons?

Your child also learns spatial concepts by setting the table. The fork goes next to the plate on the left. The knife goes next to the plate on the right. He learns about the sequence of your meal time. First, you set the table. Next, you eat your dinner. Last, you wash the dishes. Keep the steps to three at first, and gradually add more steps. This sequencing helps your child recognize the pattern or sequence of events in the world around him.

Children learning these basic concepts in early childhood will be able to understand and adjust to the growing technology that is and will be a part of their lives. They will likely be the ones who will one day help us set the VCR correctly and to understand the complexity of computers and the Internet.

Number Songs

The following songs offer additional appropriate activities for you to do with the children. Both of these offer opportunities to add puppets, flannelboard characters, finger plays, or whatever else the children suggest. "Birds on the Rooftop" can also be used as a transitional song for the children to "fly" from one activity to another.

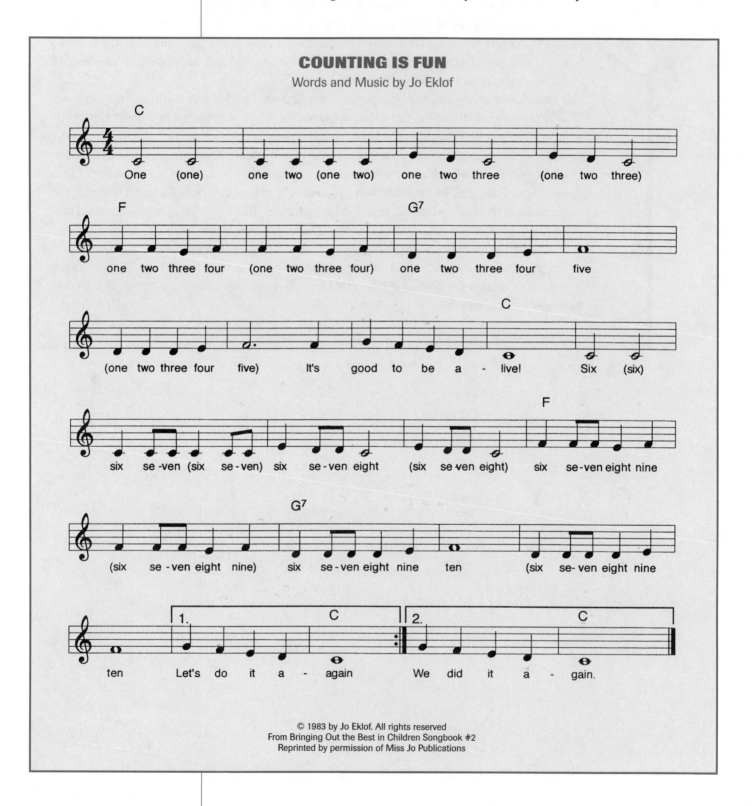

COUNTING IS FUN
Words and Music by Jo Eklof

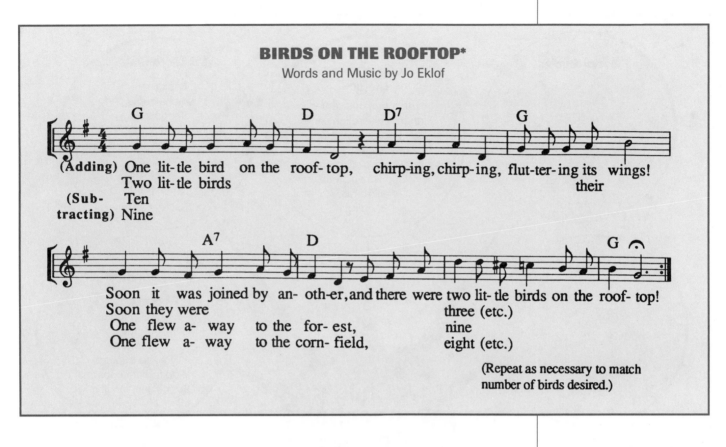

BIRDS ON THE ROOFTOP*

Words and Music by Jo Eklof

(Adding) One lit-tle bird on the roof-top, chirp-ing, chirp-ing, flut-ter-ing its wings!
Two lit-tle birds their
(Sub- Ten
tracting) Nine

Soon it was joined by an-oth-er, and there were two lit-tle birds on the roof-top!
Soon they were three (etc.)
One flew a-way to the for-est, nine
One flew a-way to the corn-field, eight (etc.)

(Repeat as necessary to match number of birds desired.)

Figure 10–7 is the curriculum planning web worksheet with math activities added. This worksheet, with appropriate additions, is included in each chapter.

AFTERVIEW

Through math activities, a child

- Relates life experiences to math
- Develops number concepts through concrete experiences
- Learns one-to-one correspondence
- Sorts and classifies objects by size, shape, color, and texture
- Identifies shapes and numerals
- Explores spatial relationships and develops math language
- Experiments with concepts of volume, weight, and measurement
- Learns how to interpret the calendar and the clock
- Has opportunities to make comparisons and to see relationships of concrete objects
- Develops problem-solving skills through experimentation
- Learns to cooperate with others
- Continues with language development by incorporating math vocabulary, such as less than, greater than, and equal

KEY TERMS

concept development

classifying and sorting

one-to-one correspondence

pattern

spatial relationships

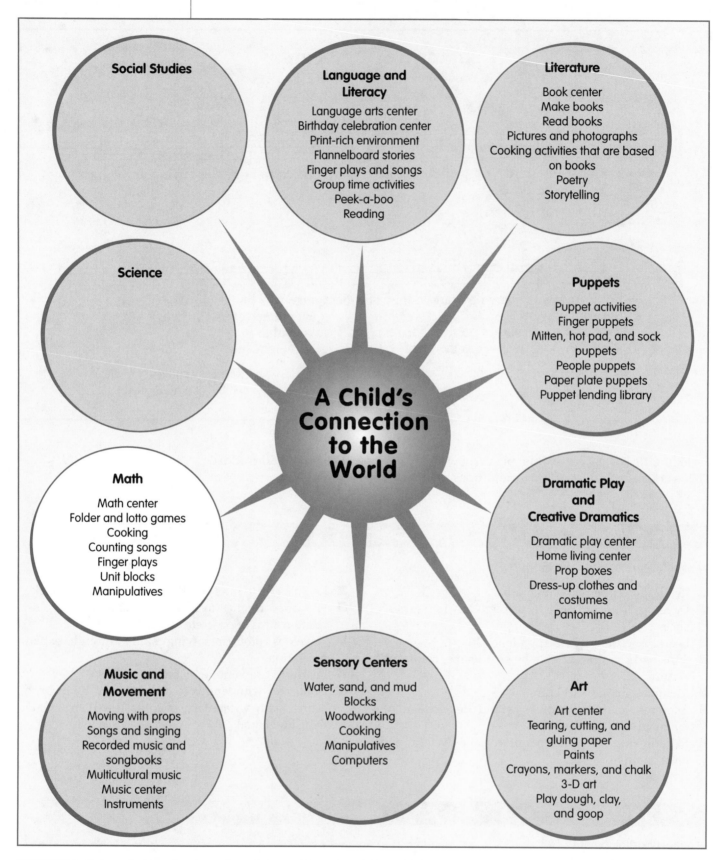

Social Studies

Language and Literacy

Language arts center
Birthday celebration center
Print-rich environment
Flannelboard stories
Finger plays and songs
Group time activities
Peek-a-boo
Reading

Literature

Book center
Make books
Read books
Pictures and photographs
Cooking activities that are based
on books
Poetry
Storytelling

Science

Puppets

Puppet activities
Finger puppets
Mitten, hot pad, and sock
puppets
People puppets
Paper plate puppets
Puppet lending library

A Child's Connection to the World

Math

Math center
Folder and lotto games
Cooking
Counting songs
Finger plays
Unit blocks
Manipulatives

Dramatic Play and Creative Dramatics

Dramatic play center
Home living center
Prop boxes
Dress-up clothes and
costumes
Pantomime

Music and Movement

Moving with props
Songs and singing
Recorded music and
songbooks
Multicultural music
Music center
Instruments

Sensory Centers

Water, sand, and mud
Blocks
Woodworking
Cooking
Manipulatives
Computers

Art

Art center
Tearing, cutting, and
gluing paper
Paints
Crayons, markers, and chalk
3-D art
Play dough, clay,
and goop

FIGURE 10–7 A curriculum planning web worksheet with math activities added.

EXPLORATIONS

1. In writing, develop criteria for the selection of appropriate math activities. Provide a list of materials and supplies necessary to set up a developmentally appropriate math center.

2. Select an early education classroom and observe for at least one hour. List at least ten items in the environment that relate to number awareness, and list at least ten learning materials available in the math center. If you are already teaching, evaluate your classroom and list the items and materials.

3. Select a classmate or colleague as a partner. Share personal incidents in relationship to the math experiences you had as a young child. Think about what or who influenced you. Did you learn math concepts in early education classes or did you have to learn them as an adult? How will this or does this influ-

ence you in bringing math into the early childhood classroom?

4. Select and plan a math activity for young children. Specify which age group this activity is planned for: infants, toddlers, preschoolers, or primary-age children. Write a list of objectives, materials needed, step-by-step procedures for presenting this activity, follow-up activities, and evaluation guidelines. (Use the activity plan worksheet in Chapter 2.)

5. Based on the information in this chapter and on your observations of early education environments, describe how you would introduce one-to-one correspondence, classifying and sorting, patterns, spatial relationships, and other math concepts to a group of preschoolers. Put these descriptions in writing and share them with a classmate or colleague.

REFERENCES

Benson, T. R., & Downing, J. E. (1999, Spring). Rejuvenate math and science—Revisit children's literature. *Dimensions of Early Childhood, 27*(2), 9–15.

Bredekamp, S., & Copple, C. (Eds.). (1997). *Developmentally appropriate practice in early childhood programs.* Washington, DC: National Association for the Education of Young Children.

Brewer, J. (1998). *Introduction to Early Childhood Education* (3rd ed.). Boston: Allyn and Bacon.

Burns, M. (1998, January). Teaching math, thinking math. *Early Childhood Today, 12*(4), 29–35.

Charlesworth, R., & Lind, K. K. (1999). *Math and science* (3rd ed.). Albany, NY: Delmar.

Dawes, C. (1977). *Early maths.* New York: Longman.

Eliason, C., & Jenkins, L. (1999). *A practical guide to early childhood curriculum* (6th ed.). Columbus, OH: Merrill.

Fortson, L. R., & Reiff, J. C. (1995). *Early childhood curriculum.* Boston: Allyn and Bacon.

Gardner, H. (1995, August/September). Howard Gardner on multiple intelligences. *Early Childhood Today, 10*(1), 30–32.

Hinnant, H. A. (1999, March). Growing gardens and mathematicians: More books and math for young children. *Young Children, 54*(2), 23–26.

Meriwether, L. (1997, July). Math at the snack table. *Young Children, 52*(5), 69–73.

Mitchell, A., & David, J. (Eds.). (1992). *Explorations with young children: A curriculum guide from the Bank Street College of Education.* Beltsville, MD: Gryphon House.

Poole, C. (1998, January). The path to math. *Early Childhood Today, 12*(4), 13–14.

Waite-Stupiansky, S. (1995, March). Think math. *Early Childhood Today, 9*(6), 38–45.

ADDITIONAL READINGS AND RESOURCES

Althouse, R. (1994). *Investigation mathematics with young children.* New York: Teachers College Press.

Blake, S. (1997, Spring). Integrating cultural diversity and mathematics. *Dimensions of Early Childhood, 25*(2), 5–10.

Gardner, H. (1999, January). Understanding the theory of multiple intelligences. *Early Childhood Today, 13*(4), 43–45.

Greenberg, P. (1993, May). How and why to teach all aspects of preschool and kindergarten math naturally, democratically, and effectively—part 1. *Young Children, 48*(4), 75–84.

Jones, G. A., & Thornton, C. A. (1993, July). Children's understanding of place value: A framework for curriculum development and assessment. *Young Children, 48*(5), 12–18.

Mills, H. (1993, January). Teaching math concepts in a K-1 class doesn't have to be like pulling teeth—but maybe it should be! *Young Children, 48*(2), 17–20.

Mills, H., & Clyde, J. A. (1992, Spring). Using art and mathematics to tell a story. *Dimensions of Early Childhood, 20*(3), 28–29, 40.

Mogard, S., & McDonnell, G. (1994). *Gobble up math.* Santa Barbara, CA: The Learning Works, Inc.

Monell, S. (1994, February). Math play and projects. *Early Childhood Today, 8*(5), 45–47.

Moore, C. (1995, January). Math assessment: Teaching the language. *PreK-8, 25*(4), 50–51.

Overholt, J. L., White-Holtz, J., & Dickson, S. (1999). *Big math activities for young children.* Albany, NY: Delmar.

Parks, L. (Ed.). (1993, Winter). Math at play. *Texas Child Care, 17*(3). 22–29.

Phillips, D. R., & Phillips, D. G. (1994, February). Beans, blocks, and buttons: Developing thinking. *Educational Leadership, 51*(5), 50–53.

Reiff, J. C. (1996, Spring). Bridging home and school through multiple intelligences. *Childhood Education, 72*(3), 164–166.

Tankersley, K. (1993, May). Teaching math their way. *Education Leadership, 50*(8), 12–13.

Taylor, B. J. (1999). *A child goes forth: A curriculum guide for preschool children* (9th ed.). Columbus, OH: Merrill.

Unglaub, K. W. (1997, May). What counts in learning to count. *Young Children, 52*(4), 48–50.

Van Scoy, I. J., & Fairchild, S. H. (1993, January). It's about time! Helping preschool and primary children understand time concepts. *Young Children, 48*(2), 21–14.

Waite-Stupiansky, S., & Stupiansky, N. (1990, April). Let's take math outdoors. *Pre-K Today, 4*(7), 37–43.

Williams, D. (1995). *Teaching mathematics through children's art.* Portsmouth, NH: Heinemann.

Wilson, L. (1995, January). Names and numbers: When letters really count. *Teaching Pre-K through 8, 25*(4), 60–61.

Wolfinger, D. M. (1994). *Science and mathematics in early childhood education.* New York: HarperCollins.

Science

■ OVERVIEW

The science curriculum in an early childhood environment should shout "Please touch! Please explore!" We must nourish young children's excitement about learning and encourage them to ask "What would happen if . . . ?," then give them the materials to find out the answers. These active encounters help children define basic concepts and stimulate natural curiosity, exploration, and discovery.

As we have discussed throughout this text, all children learn about the world around them through their senses. Infants and toddlers, as well as preschoolers and school-age children, base their scientific knowledge on what they see, hear, taste, smell, and touch. A developmentally appropriate science center expands on this basic fact of child growth and development by stimulating inquiry, interest, and verbalization.

As a teacher, you will also observe, question, predict, experiment, and verify many scientific occurrences along with the children. That is what science in early childhood is all about: setting the environmental stage for finding out about the world. Encourage young children to want to know "What's in *my* environment? What effect do *I* have? What changes can *I* make?" Attitudes are formed early. We should nurture young children's natural curiosity and their need to know *why*, which will, in turn, encourage future scientific exploration and enthusiasm.

As you brainstorm ways to make exploration and discovery take place, you will come to realize that "some 'science experiences' just happen, some you shape, and others you actively plan. Science experiences are different for children at different ages and what you do to encourage their scientific thinking will differ as well" (Jablon, 1992). Part of this encouragement can be to spontaneously and creatively change the physical environment (indoor room arrangement) when the children initiate and motivate the changes, and to take advantage of what is happening in the outdoor environment. Materials that can be manipulated and reconstructed should be included. Plenty of time should be allowed so that questions can be asked, assumptions can be explored, and ideas can be expanded.

Continue to display your own enthusiasm for science and discovery in our world. Ziemer (1987) offers us a stimulating way to do this:

> *When you look up to the highest branches of an oak tree on an early summer morning, you may not be thinking of scientific principles operating to get nurtients from the soil, up the trunk, and out to every newly forming leaf and embryo acorn. But you have an awareness of it, and guiding your small students to be aware also is part of teaching science. Ask wondering questions: "I wonder what makes the leaves so green." "I wonder how long it took this tree to grow so tall." . . . We may not be teaching facts, but we are teaching curiosity.*

■ BASIC SCIENTIFIC CONCEPTS FOR YOUNG CHILDREN

Science is usually classified into two categories: **biological sciences** and **physical sciences.** The biological sciences relate to living things: people, plants, and animals. Physiology deals with the functions of living organisms or their parts (the children and their bodies, for example). **Ecology** is the relationship between living things and their environment and each other.

Physical sciences relate to nonliving materials. These include: physics, the science that explores the nature of matter and energy and their laws, such as gravity and balance (an infant dropping a spoon from a high chair or a child building an unbalanced block tower that falls); chemistry, the science dealing with the composition and transformations of substances, such as those that occur in cooking; geology, the scientific study of the earth, such as rocks and shells; meteorology, the science of weather and atmosphere; and astronomy, the study of the universe beyond the earth's atmosphere, such as the sun, moon, planets, and stars.

Young children enjoy pushing on levers, making bulbs light, working with magnets, using a string-and-can telephone, and changing matter. This is the study of physical science—forces, motion, energy, and machines. . . . Keep in mind that children are growing up in a technological world. They interact daily with technology. It is likely that future lifestyles and job opportunities may depend on skills related to the realm of physical science. (Charlesworth & Lind, 1999)

In trying to understand the world around them (which includes biological and physical sciences), young children form their own concepts. Their thinking about basic science concepts is not the same as our thinking. They perceive the nature of things and events from their own perspective and experiences (Charlesworth & Lind, 1999). As adults, we have the ability "to analyze, form hypotheses, and to make inferences and deductions. Young children are not able to do this. We need to build our science program around children's present ways of thinking and provide the experiences that will foster future development" (Van Hoorn, Nourot, Scales, & Alward, 1999).

Methods of Discovery

Give children many open-ended opportunities to investigate, self-discover, and problem solve. Examples of observation and exploration activities follow.

- Sensory exploration outdoors can include touching the bark of a tree or the grass, seeing the birds building nests or leaves blowing, hearing the sounds carried by the wind or the honking of a car horn nearby, smelling freshly cut grass or the fragrance of flowers, and tasting the vegetables grown in the school garden they helped to plant.
- Investigating the properties of items can be done using a magnifying glass to examine shells, rocks, feathers, or objects discovered on a nature walk.
- Children can problem solve while predicting or guessing which items will float or sink in a container filled with water.

WHY I TEACH YOUNG CHILDREN

One morning, Sammi came bounding across the classroom to me calling, "Come and look!" I followed her across the room, where she pointed to the window. She was bursting with excitement. Expecting to see no less than an elephant on the playground or a hot air balloon caught in the tree, I looked out, and saw nothing different. A quick glance at Sammi told me that it was still there, and I looked again. I saw nothing. She must have realized my inability to share her excitement, and lifted a tiny finger to the window, and said, "There." Then I saw *it.* On the outside of the window pane was the tiniest spider I'd ever seen. Thank you, Sammi, for reminding me about the little things in life.

Janet Galantay

Give children many open-ended opportunities to question, to compare similarities and differences, and to use trial-and-error to try out their theories. Experimentation, verification, and discovery activities follow.

- With a teacher's supervision, children can experiment with cooking and discover how certain foods change through the cooking process as well as what happens when foods are mixed together.
- Tasting different foods gives children a hands-on experience and at the same time enables them to discover the similarities and differences of ingredients such as flour, salt, and sugar.
- Classifying leaves by comparing their color, type, and vein structure offers another way to distinguish the similarities and differences of nature.

Give children many open-ended opportunities to concretely demonstrate their discoveries. Reproducing and reworking what they observe and remember helps the children and the teacher learn together. Recording and communicating activities follow.

- Children's drawings, paintings, tape recordings, and/or discussions can record their scientific experiences.
- Children can mark off days on a calendar as they watch the silkworms go through their life cycles or predict how long it will take acorns that they planted to grow.

■ CREATING AN ENVIRONMENT THAT SUPPORTS CRITICAL THINKING AND PROBLEM SOLVING

Many times, in an early education program, science activities are thrown in as an afterthought. The "science corner or table" has very little to offer children, and materials remain the same for many weeks. It is important for us to look at science as a vital component that encompasses every part of the early childhood curriculum.

Eliason and Jenkins (1999) remind us that "young children think neither logically nor abstractly, but rather in concrete terms." With this developmental factor in mind, opportunities for scientific activities should be part of the theme, lesson plan, and daily life of a classroom. As in other curriculum areas, build on what the children already know. Guide them concretely by involving them in experiences that emphasize sensory awareness, exploring, manipulating, questioning, discovering, and other process skills. "All around the room and across the curriculum, children observe, predict, experiment, and analyze—it's the scientific method in action" (Church, 1998).

In planning science activities, take advantage of the children's real world as you introduce new materials. Remember that young children comprehend many things "in the context of playing with other children as together they use appropriately selected materials and equipment" (Hildebrand & Hearron, 1999). Older children, especially, enjoy working collaboratively or cooperatively on experiments that offer social interaction and collective problem solving. "Critical thinking skills come into play as children break down a whole problem into parts. . . . [S]orting, classifying, comparing predicting, and analyzing are common critical-thinking skills" (Church, 1998).

The following are a few suggestions to get you started.

Investigate Water

- Indoors or outdoors, place water in the water table or a large plastic tub. Let the children select which color they want the water to be. Add several drops of food coloring to the water. Also be sure to have plastic pouring and measuring containers along with funnels and spray bottles.
- Later add boats, corks, sponges, rocks, pieces of wood, large marbles, keys, feathers, and pine cones. What sinks? What floats? Guide the children in making a chart

of what items sink and what items float. Ask the children why they think some things stay above water and others settle to the bottom? For example, the air holes in a sponge make it float. When the children squeeze the sponge under the water they can see bubbles of air come out of the sponge. What happens when they let go of the squeezed sponge? What other items can the children add?

■ What happens to the items that sink or float in water when you add sugar, salt, oil, or sand to the water?

■ Place plain water and one or two eggbeaters in the water table or tub. What happens when the children "beat the water"? Have them add liquid dish detergent, and then beat the water. Now what happens? (The water can then be used to wash the doll dishes from the dramatic play area.)

■ Fill a sink full of water and notice how, when you pull the plug, the water always swirls down the drain in the same *clockwise spiral*. (This is because of the rotation of the earth. South of the equator, it goes in the opposite direction.) This can be fascinating to young children. Follow up this activity by looking at a globe and demonstrating how the world turns.

■ Introduce the children to absorption and evaporation by having them dampen cloth rags and paper towels with water, then hang them in the sun to dry. What happens to the water? Does the cloth or the paper dry faster? Why?

■ Making and blowing bubbles are delightful additions to water investigation. They float on air, glimmer with color, change shape, and pop! Why do bubbles pop? To make bubbles, mix one part liquid dish detergent to five parts water in a shallow tub or pan. Plastic circles on a handle or circles made with pipe cleaners work fine for making bubbles. Let the children experiment with blowing bubbles or moving the bubble ring in any manner they can think of to make bubbles.

■ See how water magnifies pebbles in a glass jar.

- Taste water, then add salt or sugar or both. Discuss what this tastes like. What else will the children want to add?
- Examine how water takes the shape of the container it is in.
- Boil water in a pan on a hot plate (with close teacher supervision). Discuss the steam that forms.
- Guide children on how to change a liquid into a solid, and then reverse the process. First place the water in a small, sealable plastic bag, and then freeze it. Next let them watch the ice melt. Encourage the children to predict how long they think it will take the water to freeze and then how long to melt. Actively discuss the changes in the water.

Review Chapter 8 in this text for additional activities.

Discover Rainbows

- Set the scene for activities relating to rainbows by introducing a prism (a triangular piece of glass that breaks up a ray of light into a colored spectrum). This can be purchased inexpensively. Glass beads can be used as well. (Parents may even have other glass costume jewelry that can be used.) Whatever you choose, tape this "rainbow-making" glass onto a window of the classroom that faces the outdoors to catch the sunlight. Let the children locate the rainbow by themselves. This rainbow will mean more to them if they make the discovery. How many colors do they see? Have they seen a rainbow before? When? Do they remember how many colors it had? Encourage the children to draw the rainbow. What colors do they choose?
- Create other rainbows with the children by taking a shallow bowl of water out into some bright sunshine. Place a drop or two of oil on the surface of the water. How many colors do the children see? Are they the same colors as the prism rainbow? If you stir the water with a stick, do the colors change?
- On a sunny day, you can help children find a rainbow by spraying water across the sun's rays with a garden hose or a spray bottle. The rays of the sun contain all the colors mixed together, but the water acts as a prism and separates the colors. Are they the same colors as the other rainbows the children discovered?

Explore Shadows

- What is a shadow? It is fun to find out what the children will answer. Can they offer suggestions about how to produce a shadow? Try out their predictions. Are shadows created? If they have difficulty, you might guide them by suggesting that one child holds her hand in front of a bright light. (Shade is a dark place that light cannot reach. A shadow is the shape cast by whatever is in front of the light.)
- Let the children experiment with different objects in the room to find out which ones cast shadows and which ones do not. They can make a chart of the items.
- Review Chapter 5 and have the children make shadow puppets and share them with each other.
- Extend "shadow play" into dramatic play or music and movement activities.
- The children can outline their shadows in chalk outside on the sidewalk. They can measure how long or how short their shadows are. Try this at different times during the day. Do the shadows change?
- Take the children on a nature walk and look for shadows that the plants, trees, buildings, or cars make. They can come back and create shadow drawings or write a story of what they discovered during their explorations.
- Here are some suggestions of books to read to the children and then place in the book center:

Cendrars, B. (1982). *Shadows, an African story.* Illustrated by M. Brown. New York: Charles Scribner's Sons.

Gomi, T. (1981). *Shadows.* San Francisco: Heian International.

Hoban, T. (1990). *Shadows and reflections.* New York: Greenwillow.

Keats, E. J. (1964). *Whistle for Willie.* New York: Viking Press.

Extended Science Activities

The following activities extend over a period of time. This will demonstrate to the children that many scientific investigations take time to evolve and that some are unpredictable. These experiments can also offer a concrete way to introduce the children to edible plant parts.

- Roots—Carrots, potatoes, turnips, radishes, and beets are the roots of plants.
- Stems—Celery and asparagus are examples of the stems of plants that connect the roots with the leaves.
- Leaf—Lettuce, spinach, cabbage, and parsley are the leaves of the plants.
- Flower—Broccoli and cauliflower are examples of the flowers of plants.
- Vegetable/fruit—Tomatoes and squash are examples of the "fruit" of plants.

Try the following activities.

CARROT TOP GARDEN

Carrot Top Garden. After cutting the tops off of three or four carrots, the children place them in a shallow pan or dish. The carrot tops should be sitting in ¼-inch water and should be watered daily, a task that could be performed by the "plant helper" of the day. (A child can use a ruler to determine exactly how much ¼ inch is.)

The children can predict how many days it will take the carrot tops to sprout new green foliage. Guide them into making a chart or graph that shows them how correct their predictions were. If some of the tops do not sprout, ask the children *why* they think they did not.

This is a great opportunity to read Ruth Krauss's *The carrot seed* (1988). Illustrated by Crockett Johnson. New York: HarperCollins.

Rooting a Sweet Potato. This is another experiment children enjoy doing. Push toothpicks halfway into a sweet potato. Then place the potato in a glass or jar of water with the toothpicks resting on the top rim. Be sure the end of the potato is immersed in water. The plant helper can be responsible to see that the bottom of the potato is *always* immersed in water. Place the potato where it will receive enough light. (Put another sweet potato in a dark spot of the room so the children can see what happens to the potato's growth without adequate light.) See Figure 11–1 for illustrations of a carrot top garden and rooting a sweet potato.

The children can create a group art activity by drawing the sweet potato and adding to it over the time it takes for roots to grow out of the sides and bottom of the potato and the leaves to grow out of the top. A "before and after" drawing is interesting, too.

SWEET POTATO "EXPERIMENT"

FIGURE 11–1 This illustrates the rooting of a sweet potato and a carrot garden.

Thirsty Celery. This science experience demonstrates how plants get their water. Fill two tall, clear plastic glasses with water. Let the children put a few drops of red food coloring in one glass and drops of blue food coloring in the other. Put a piece of celery into each of the glasses, being careful to make a fresh cut at the base of the celery stalks before you place them in the water. Ask the children to watch the celery and record what happens. They can do this with a drawing or verbally with a tape recorder. Over the next few days, the colored water should travel up the stalk and into the leaves. Ask the children what happened to the celery. Why do they think this happened?

Focus on Nature

For a teacher, it is exciting to share the natural world with young children. They are eager for active firsthand experiences. Wilson (1995) helps us examine nature and young children:

> They can learn about nature as a "resource" to be used; they can learn that air, water, and sunlight are important to all living things; they can learn to divide the world of nature into living and nonliving things. But the most important thing young children can learn about the natural world is that it is full of beauty and wonder.

Air. Can the children taste or see air? Can they feel it? How? On the playground, guide the children to experience how the wind (moving air) can come from different directions. Children can experiment with wind streamers, windsocks, wind chimes, and bubbles. You might read the following book as an introduction or extension to the other activities relating to air: De Coteau Orie, Sandra. (1995). *Did you hear the wind sing your name?* Illustrated by Christopher Canyon. New York: Walker and Company.

Nature Walk. There are opportunities for many discoveries to take place during a walk around the children's natural environment. Before you go for a walk, encourage the children to make binoculars. Tape together two toilet paper rolls. Place holes on one end of the rolls and attach a piece of yarn or string to make a neck strap. Looking for bird nests and watching butterflies or birds fly are only samples of the many things the children can look at through their binoculars (Figure 11–2).

FIGURE 11–2 This illustrates child-made binoculars.

COLLECTION BAG

NATURE BOOK

FIGURE 11–3 These are examples of a collection bag and nature book.

Each child can also make an individual nature walk "collection bag" (see Figure 11–3). Construct it with folded construction paper or tagboard and lace it with yarn that is left long enough to serve as a shoulder strap (Ziemer, 1987). Construct a classroom book with pages made out of sturdy cardboard and fastened together with rings. The children glue or tape items that they found on the nature walk onto the pages. Then place it in the book center for the children to enjoy.

Fresh leaves can be pressed easily by placing them between sheets of newspaper, which are then sandwiched between two pieces of cardboard and secured tightly with rubber bands. After a week, the leaves can be removed and glued into a scrapbook (see Figure 11–3) or displayed in other ways in the classroom. Dried leaves can be ironed between two pieces of waxed paper (with teacher supervision) and then hung for decoration. Children can compare and contrast each leaf (Eklof, 1995).

Grow Grass. Go on a "science search" in which children look for different kinds of grass growing around their environment. In the classroom provide grass seeds for the children to plant. The quickest and easiest way to germinate the seeds is to place a damp sponge in a pie pan of water and sprinkle the seeds on the sponge. These seeds usually grow almost anywhere as long as they are watered regularly and have sunlight. (It is fun to cut the sponges into different shapes and watch the grass grow into a circle, triangle, or heart shape.) This is another way for children to observe nature firsthand. An alternative way to grow grass is to fill a plastic cup (which the children can decorate to look like a face) with dirt or potting soil. Sprinkle the grass seeds on the dirt, then water. The children really enjoy watching "the hair" grow.

Gardens. "Gardening is a wonderful activity for young children. As they plan, plant, and take care of plants, they learn valuable concepts and skills that will help them later in life. They learn science as they observe the life cycle of plants, math as they count and sort seeds, and language as they read seed packets and planting instructions. And there is a sense of pride that develops when children nurture a seed into a full grown plant" (Durkin & Perez, 1999). The children can plant an indoor garden (flowers and/or vegetables) in the sand and water table or in a window box. If there is a protected space outdoors, they can plant a garden there. This activity is another way to encourage children to take active responsibility for living things.

Here are some suggestions of books on nature to read to the children and then place in the book center:

Behn, H. (1992). *Trees.* New York: Henry Holt.

Bunting, E. (1994). *Flower garden.* Illustrated by K. Hewitt. San Diego, CA: Harcourt Brace.

Dorros, A. (1997). *A tree is growing.* New York: Scholastic.

Ehlert, L. (1988). *Planting a rainbow.* San Diego, CA: Harcourt Brace.

Florian, D. (1989). *Nature walk.* New York: Greenwillow.

Gibbons, G. (1991). *From seed to plant.* New York: Holiday House.

Howard, E. (1993). *The big seed.* New York: Simon & Schuster.

National Wildlife Foundation. (1998). *Trees are terrific.* (Ranger Rick's Nature Scope). New York: McGraw-Hill.

■ SUGGESTED SCIENCE MATERIALS AND EQUIPMENT

Many materials in a science center can be donated and many can be recycled. Some equipment can be purchased inexpensively. Figure 11–4 lists suggested materials and equipment that are appropriate for an early education science center. (Only some of the items will be appropriate for infants and toddlers; you will need to be very cautious in what you select.)

■ ECOLOGY IN THE EARLY EDUCATION ENVIRONMENT

Early involvement with the environment will help foster a sense of appreciation and caring in a generation of children who will then make a difference in how our future world is treated. "We should emphasize the environment and the role humans play in consuming or protecting the Earth's riches. Humans affect their environments, and vice versa. Each child's interactions with the world affects not only the child but the world" (Rivkin, 1992).

What are the environmental problems that confront us today? Some of these are air and water pollution, too much garbage, global warming, the depletion of the ozone layer, and the destruction of the forests. Our responsibility as teachers is to guide the children by demonstrating our concern about "sound environmental practices such as recycling, composting and, above all, thrift" (Petrash, 1992).

As defined earlier in this chapter, ecology is the study of living things in relation to their environment and to one another. The environment is everything that surrounds us. We human beings change the environment with our actions and reactions. In addition, everything in nature is constantly changing, and change in one area can cause changes in another.

There are several approaches you can take in your early childhood curriculum planning that will include the changing environment and what we can do to protect it. One suggestion is to select the theme "Things in Nature That Are Always Changing." Using this thematic method, you can introduce the children to changing seasons, specific weather changes, night changing into day, and the changes that take place with the individual child.

Aluminum foil pans	Pipe cleaners
Aquarium with contents and supplies	Plants
Ant farm	Plastic bottles, jars, and trays
Binoculars	Prisms
Bird house and bird feeders	Rain gauge
Collection boxes and collecting net	Rock and seashell collections
Color paddles	Rulers, tape measure, and yard stick
Compass	Scales
Corks, plugs, and stoppers	Seeds and seed catalogs
Dried plants, such as flowers and grasses	Sieves, sifters, and funnels
Eggbeaters and wire whip	Shallow pans
Eye droppers	Soil samples, such as clay, sand, and loam
Feathers	Stethoscope
Flashlights	Sundial
Food coloring	Tape recorder and cassettes
Fossils	Telescope
Garden hose	Terrarium
Instant print camera	Thermometers, both indoor and outdoor type
Kitchen timer	
Magnets, such as bar and horseshoe types	Tongs and tweezers
	Watering cans
Magnifying glasses and tripod magnifier stand	X-rays (Parents who are doctors or veterinarians often will give teachers old ones.)
Pinecones	

FIGURE 11–4 List of science materials and equipment.

We will serve our children well when we turn their attention to the stones, the grasses and flowers, the trees and animals by finding meaningful and creative ways to allow nature to enter our classrooms and play areas, and by bringing our children out into nature as much as possible. A loving relationship with nature will not only promote health for our planet but health for our children as well. (Petrash, 1992)

Some activities that focus on ecology include:

Plant and Garden at Different Times of the Year. In some places it is warm all year round, and plants there grow well at any time. In places where the ground freezes in winter, you will have to wait for warmer weather to garden outdoors, but indoor planting can work well. You can start plants in a collection of cans, grow a tree in a tub, or plant seeds in cracks in the concrete.

Make a Compost Pile. The children can place leaves, plant cuttings, and food scraps in the compost bin or pile. Then they can use the compost when they plant a garden in the spring. This can be a cooperative experience with one or two other classes. Children enjoy participating with other children in the center or school.

Catch Rain Water in a Container and Recycle It to Water the Plants. Filter the rain water through a fine sieve, such as a tea strainer. This will provide an opportunity for

the children to see what pollutants rainwater collects, in addition to providing rain water to water the indoor plants and vegetables.

Adopt-A-Tree or Plant-A-Tree. The children can select a tree on the playground or in a nearby park to "adopt" as their tree to take care of and to observe throughout the year. Sometimes children prefer to plant a tree of their own on the playground or in a tub. Whatever choice is made can lead to an environmental discussion when you ask the question, "What do you think the tree takes from the environment, and what does it give to the environment?"

It is helpful to invite a parent who knows a lot about trees or a professional gardener to visit the class to answer their questions and advise the children in their selections. In addition, a field trip to a garden shop can motivate the children. Giving young children the responsibility to take care of the tree can be a significant factor in encouraging them to take care of the environment.

After they select the tree and identify what kind it is, they can make drawings of it, take photos of their tree in different seasons, and compare it to other trees. They will also find it interesting to examine the bark, leaves, and bugs on the tree with a magnifying glass and observe and identify which birds like their tree. Children enjoy hanging a bird house or a bird feeder in their tree and watching the activity it attracts. (An easy-to-make bird feeder is putting peanut butter and bird seed on a pine cone and hanging it in a tree.)

Recycle and Conserve Materials and Natural Resources. The children can recycle newspapers, other types of paper, aluminum, glass, some plastics, and clothing. Find out about the recycling projects in your community and get the children and their families involved.

Try fixing broken items in the classroom instead of buying new things or throwing old things away. Encourage the children to stop wasting water. Have them turn off the water while brushing their teeth or washing their hands, instead of letting it run.

Create a central storage area in your classroom with labeled bins for recycled materials, such as "boxes," "foam," and "paper." The children can help sort them into the appropriate bins (Drew, 1995).

Grocery Sacks and Newspapers Can Be Placed at the Easels. Provide one or both along with paints for the children to paint on. To make newspaper logs for the block center take a section of newpaper and roll into a tight roll. Use tape to hold the "logs." These can then be used to build towers, fences, etc.

Stress the Importance of Not Littering. Trash should be placed in a trash container. Because littering can be dangerous and unhealthy, the children should be shown how to avoid littering and to participate in cleaning up instead.

Earth Day Is April 22. Make party hats out of newspaper and grocery bags. Bake an Earth Day cake decorated to look like the planet earth. Cut out eco-cookies in natural shapes, such as birds, leaves, and trees. Have the children go on a "pick up trash walk." Celebrate with an environmental musical band. Provide materials for the children to make recycled instruments, and have a parade!

Ask the Children Open-Ended Questions. These will help them think about why it is important to take care of our environment:

> What would happen if everyone threw trash on the ground?
>
> What do you think would happen if we poured polluted water into clean water?
>
> Why do we recycle?
>
> What would happen if we cut down trees instead of planting them?
>
> Why do you think plants are important to us?
>
> What are ways we can help the environment at home?

Special Books. For the younger children, read Anna Ross, (1992). *Grover's 10 terrific ways to help our wonderful world.* Illustrated by Tom Leigh. New York: CTW and Henson Productions with Random House Inc.

For the older children, share John Javna, (1990). *50 simple things kids can do to save the earth.* Kansas City, MO: The EarthWorks Group.

■ ANIMALS IN THE EARLY EDUCATION CLASSROOM

The world of animals inspires wonder and curiosity in young children. Jo Eklof, an educator, songwriter, performer, and wildlife rehabilitator, gives us insight into how to share animals appropriately with children in the classroom. (Many of Miss Jo Productions songs are shared with you throughout this text. She is listed in Appendix B, Teacher Resources.)

You can guide the children into drawing pictures of their experiences with animals, moths, butterflies, and ants. Extend this by making puppets of the animals they draw.

For language development, the children can bring in their favorite stuffed animals and talk about them during group time. Read books aloud and place those books in the book center that relate to animals, moths, butterflies, and ants. For example:

Aliki. (1997). *My visit to the zoo.* New York: HarperCollins.

Carle, E. (1981). *The very hungry caterpillar.* New York: Philomel.

Cassle, B., & Pallotta, J. (1995). *The butterfly alphabet book.* Illustrated by M. Astrella. Watertown, MA: Charlesbridge.

Ehlert, L. (1997). *Color zoo.* New York: HarperCollins.

Flanagan, A.K. (1998). *Buying a pet from Ms. Chavez.* Chicago: Children's Press.

Fowler, A. (1998). *Inside an ant colony.* Chicago: Children's Press.

Horenstein, H. (1994). *My Mom's a vet.* Cambridge, MA: Candlewick.

Martin, B., Jr. (1997). *Polar bear, polar bear, what do you hear?* (Board Book). Illustrated by E. Carle. New York: Henry Holt.

■ SHARING SCIENCE WITH PARENTS

Many of the activities in this chapter can be shared with parents so that science can become a family affair. Help them understand that children are *natural* scientists discovering their world. Send information and suggestions home. Begin with general ideas as to what parents can do with their children, and then show them specific activ-

ities that are ongoing in the classroom. For example, they also can grow a carrot-top garden or root a sweet potato at home with their child, as well as do the following.

■ Look at science experiences all around you. Observe plants, insects, animals, rocks, and sunsets with your child.
■ Go for a walk outside in the park or in the woods and talk about the natural things you and your child see.
■ Feel a tree. Talk about the parts of the tree.
■ Collect all kinds of things—from shells to sticks to rocks. Talk about where they came from.
■ Help your child use his senses—sight, smell, touch, hearing, and taste—to explore the world around him. Look at leaves, smell them, and rub your fingers across their tops and bottoms. Compare one kind of leaf with another, and look for changes over time.
■ As your child begins to talk about plants in her environment, she can observe their growth by taking care of plants at school and at home. Together learn the names of plants, flowers, shrubs, vegetables, and trees.
■ Explain what items you recycle. Share some of these with us at school: plastic containers, egg cartons, paper towel and bathroom tissue rolls, samples and end-cuts from wallpaper, fabric, floor tile, framing materials, and newspapers.

■ TIPS FOR TEACHERS

■ Provide hands-on experiences that make science a part of every child's day.
■ Preserve and value a child's natural curiosity.
■ Avoid "telling" children about a scientific activity that they themselves cannot observe or experiment with. Relying on teacher information *only* is not useful or appropriate for children.
■ If you have difficulty with setting up a science environment, identify an individual interest or area of the real world *you* would like to know more about. Set up your early education classroom so that you can discover and learn things *along with the children.*

THE ANIMALS IN OUR WORLD

As an animal lover and a wildlife rehabilitator, I have come to the conclusion that there are two categories of animals—not good or bad, but rather, touchable and untouchable. Touchable are those we know and with whom we have a relationship. I have spent many wonderful hours with my very special domesticated animals. We have learned to love and trust each other. I have the responsibility to see that all their needs are met.

Untouchable animals are those we do not know, who will probably be frightened of us and will do whatever they need to do to protect themselves. These animals, which are not domesticated, are born to be free. It is not fair to put them in a cage. They deserve to live as nature intended them to live. Because they are not used to people, they will be frightened and potentially very dangerous. They can also have diseases which *you, the children, or your pets* can catch, such as distemper or rabies. Enjoy watching and listening to them, but LEAVE THEM ALONE!

Occasionally, one comes upon an animal that looks as though it needs help; either it is injured or in some way unable to care for itself. It is important to know when and when not to rescue it.

What Not To Do

■ *Do not* "rescue" an animal that does not need help. Most "orphaned" animals are not orphaned at all. The parent is usually hiding nearby, afraid to attend to its offspring when people are present. If you can see a nest from which a baby has fallen, it is best to place the baby back in the nest. Despite myths to the contrary, the scent of human hands will not disturb the parents and they will usually care for their returned offspring.

■ *Do not* be tempted to raise an orphaned animal yourself. Federal and state laws prohibit the possession of most nondomesticated animals—and with good reason. These creatures need special care, far different from domestic animals. Wildlife rehabilitators are trained to provide that care.

What To Do

■ *Do rescue an animal if the parent is known to be dead and the baby is too young to survive on its own, or if the animal is injured or in obvious danger.*

■ Emergency care can be given if you have determined that the animal really needs care. Put on a pair of gloves *before* you touch it. For your safety and the animal's well-being, handle it as little as possible. Place it in a covered box with air holes for ventilation. The box should be just a little larger than the animal. Put the box in a dark, quiet room away from the children (and pets), and free from drafts.

■ Do *not* feed it or give it liquids. The wrong food or wrong feeding method can do more harm than good. These animals have special diets, and as babies, must be fed often. For example, some baby birds must be fed every 20 or 30 minutes during the day and some baby mammals must be fed during the night.

■ *These* babies need to learn from their parents what kind of animal they are and how to take care of themselves (just like human babies). Contact a wildlife rehabilitator *immediately.* A rehabilitator can be found through your state Parks and Wildlife Department or other private organizations in your community. They have been trained to care for these orphans during the early stages of life and to reintroduce them to their natural environment.

CLASSROOM ANIMALS

We, as teachers of the future citizens of the world, have opportunities everyday to instill in our children a love and respect for themselves and for all the people, animals, and plants with whom we share our world.

There are many interesting learning exhibits you can have in your classroom. While visiting classrooms, I have seen some wonderful science centers with plants and animals, but have also, at times, been very saddened by sights of animals being poorly fed or improperly housed. Before you get any animal, be sure you understand and are prepared to meet its needs. Get answers to the following questions:

What kind of enclosure should it have?

What kind of food does it require?

What temperature must it have?

Is there any kind of special light it needs?

Should it be kept with another animal?

Is it safe for children to handle it?

continued

THE ANIMALS IN OUR WORLD continued

Does it need any special veterinarian care?

Does it meet your state licensing requirements? (Some states require documentation that shows animals requiring vaccinations have been vaccinated according to state and local requirements. Some also require that parents must be advised when animals are present in the classroom or school.)

Along with animals that are commonly found in centers and can be displayed safely and effectively (small rodents, such as gerbils and hamsters, frogs, fish, birds, and turtles) you might try some of the following:

■ *Earthworms*—You'll need a large plastic or glass jar, sand or loose moist soil, cloth cover, damp leaves or grass, and a dozen or so earthworms. (You can look for earthworms after a spring rain or buy them from a local bait shop.)

Place a layer of pebbles in the jar, then fill it with sand or loose moist soil. Put in some earthworms. Keep the soil moist but not wet. The children can feed the worms damp leaves and grass clippings. Be sure to cover the container with a dark cloth to shield the worms from light, as they are used to being in the dark ground.

The children can observe how the worms burrow tunnels in the soil. They can also carefully place a worm on a table to watch its movements (with teacher supervision). Note the difference between its back and underside. Using a magnifying glass, count the rings on its body. Notice the worm's reaction to various stimuli: light, sound, types of food, and soil.

After viewing the worms for awhile, the children can return them to their garden or playground. Earthworms are very important for healthy soil. They loosen it so that air and water can get to plant roots as well as fertilize the soil.

■ *Silkworms*—You'll need a terrarium, mulberry leaves, and silkworm eggs or larvae. Many early childhood centers and schools store the eggs laid in one season in a small bottle in a refrigerator until the next

season. When the mulberry leaves are on the trees, these eggs are placed in a terrarium with the leaves. (Network with other colleagues to get your supply of silkworm eggs.)

The silkworm (like all other moths and butterflies) undergoes a complete metamorphosis. *There are four stages of development: egg, larva, pupa, and adult moth.* One female silkworm moth can lay from 300 to 400 eggs. In about 10 days, cream to light green colored caterpillars hatch from the eggs and eat voraciously on mulberry leaves for about 30 days. Be sure you have access to mulberry leaves which have not been sprayed with insecticide. (Many parents can help supply the mulberry leaves.)

A cocoon will then be constructed from a single fiber of silk, which could be up to one quarter mile long! It takes about 3 days to complete the cocoon. Inside the cocoon, the silkworm metamorphoses into a cream colored moth, which will not eat, rarely flies, and lives only a few days. One ounce of silkworm eggs produces 30,000 larvae, which can spin approximately 100 pounds of silk! (As you can see, you need only a few eggs to get started.) Introducing children to silkworms offers a very special way to help them understand what a life cycle is.

■ *Butterflies*—The following companies will ship butterflies directly to your center or school. Butterfly Garden is available from Insect Lore Products, P.O. Box 1535, Shafter, CA 93263, or Let's Get Growing, 1900 Commercial Way, Santa Cruz, CA 95065. Children can watch the metamorphosis of larva to chrysalides to butterflies, then have the fun of releasing the butterflies back into nature.

■ *Ants*—Commercially sold ant farms are widely available in stores selling educational materials. It is fascinating to watch these little creatures dig tunnels, drag food, and interrelate with each other.

—By Jo Eklof

- Allow the children to control the time spent on experimenting with appropriate materials. Children need time to try out ideas, to make mistakes and learn from them, and to learn from one another.
- Select materials and activities that encourage self-directed problem solving and experimentation as well as stimulate children to observe changes taking place (Smith, 1987).
- Choose materials and experiences that allow for differences in abilities, development, and learning styles (Smith, 1987).
- Some adaptations of materials may be necessary to help children with special needs, such as providing additional tactile cues for visually impaired children and helping those with hearing impairments experience sound by feeling the vibrations of tuning forks, guitar strings, or rubber bands stretched across a cigar box (Brewer, 1998).
- Ask open-ended questions, and give children plenty of time to answer questions. This helps children to observe carefully and encourages them to put their ideas into words. (What does a feather look like? How does the sky look when it is going to rain?)
- Model an attitude of respect for nature. Plan a program that shows an appreciation of nature and "consciously teaches children to protect and preserve the best the natural environment has to offer" (Burrell, 1989).
- Allow for across-the-curriculum integration of activities.

■ DEVELOPMENTALLY APPROPRIATE AND MULTICULTURAL/ANTI-BIAS ACTIVITIES

Poetry, flannelboard stories, dramatic play, music, and movement offer additional opportunities for young children to become more aware of the world around them and their place in it. The following poem and songs are creative ways for the children to share their appreciation of the world and each other. (Flannelboard characters for the poem "Seeds" are in Appendix A.)

To introduce a global awareness of the earth to young children, the author recommends the following book:

Temple, L. (Ed.). (1993). *Dear world: How children around the world feel about our environment.* New York: Random House.

This delightful book for kindergarten and school-age children presents a collection of letters and drawings by children from around the world that express their feelings about our environment and the problems facing our natural world. It will encourage the children in your class to write their own letters and draw their own pictures about how they feel their earth should be. Introducing an experience such as this can activate opportunities for child-centered multicultural experiences throughout the year.

Brewer (1998) offers us another reminder: "Teachers should make sure they know enough about the cultures of children in their classrooms that they do not engage the students in activities that will be offensive. For example, people from some cultures would find playing with cornmeal on a sand table offensive. Others would be disturbed by studies of plants or animals that have symbolic meaning in their particular cultures. The key is to understand the various communities of the children well enough that you can avoid offending them."

Visit agencies and organizations in your community that offer resources and information relating to various cultures. As you gather materials and facts, ask the parents of children in your class for specific examples of what would be inappropriate to their culture. Continue to be aware of, and sensitive to, the many elements in each child's world.

Figure 11–5 is the curriculum planning web worksheet with science activities added. This worksheet, with appropriate additions, is included in each chapter.

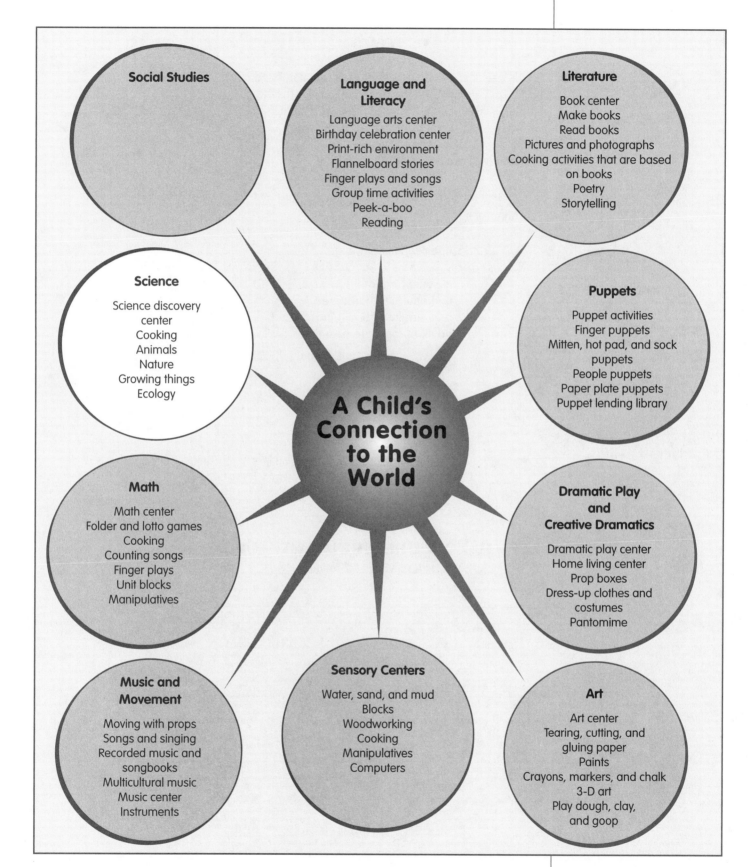

Social Studies

Language and Literacy
Language arts center
Birthday celebration center
Print-rich environment
Flannelboard stories
Finger plays and songs
Group time activities
Peek-a-boo
Reading

Literature
Book center
Make books
Read books
Pictures and photographs
Cooking activities that are based on books
Poetry
Storytelling

Science
Science discovery center
Cooking
Animals
Nature
Growing things
Ecology

Puppets
Puppet activities
Finger puppets
Mitten, hot pad, and sock puppets
People puppets
Paper plate puppets
Puppet lending library

A Child's Connection to the World

Math
Math center
Folder and lotto games
Cooking
Counting songs
Finger plays
Unit blocks
Manipulatives

Dramatic Play and Creative Dramatics
Dramatic play center
Home living center
Prop boxes
Dress-up clothes and costumes
Pantomime

Music and Movement
Moving with props
Songs and singing
Recorded music and songbooks
Multicultural music
Music center
Instruments

Sensory Centers
Water, sand, and mud
Blocks
Woodworking
Cooking
Manipulatives
Computers

Art
Art center
Tearing, cutting, and gluing paper
Paints
Crayons, markers, and chalk
3-D art
Play dough, clay, and goop

FIGURE 11–5 A curriculum planning web worksheet with math activities added.

SEEDS

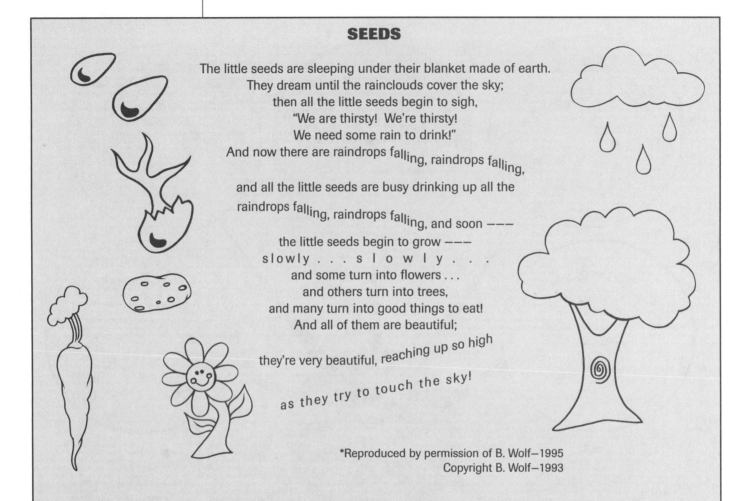

The little seeds are sleeping under their blanket made of earth.
They dream until the rainclouds cover the sky;
then all the little seeds begin to sigh,
"We are thirsty! We're thirsty!
We need some rain to drink!"
And now there are raindrops falling, raindrops falling,

and all the little seeds are busy drinking up all the
raindrops falling, raindrops falling, and soon –––

the little seeds begin to grow –––
s l o w l y . . . s l o w l y . . .
and some turn into flowers . . .
and others turn into trees,
and many turn into good things to eat!
And all of them are beautiful;

they're very beautiful, reaching up so high

as they try to touch the sky!

*Reproduced by permission of B. Wolf–1995
Copyright B. Wolf–1993

LET'S HANDLE OUR WORLD WITH CARE

Words and Music by Jo Eklof

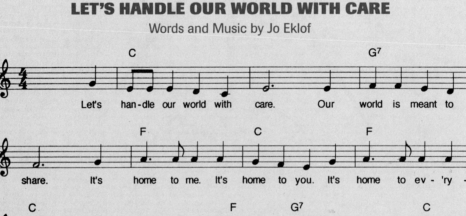

Let's han-dle our world with care. Our world is meant to

share. It's home to me. It's home to you. It's home to ev-'ry-

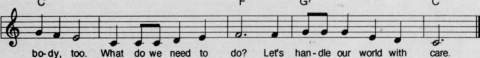

bo-dy, too. What do we need to do? Let's han-dle our world with care.

I'M SO GLAD THAT YOU LIVE IN THE WORLD WITH ME

Words and Music by Jo Eklof

WHAT A LUCKY DAY
Words and Music by Jo Eklof

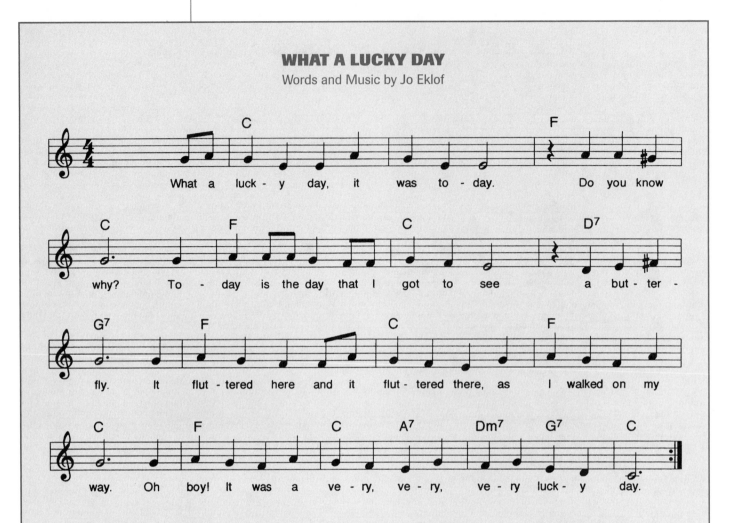

What a luck-y day, it was to-day. Do you know why? To-day is the day that I got to see a but-ter-fly. It flut-tered here and it flut-tered there, as I walked on my way. Oh boy! It was a ve-ry, ve-ry, ve-ry luck-y day.

Additional verses

What a lucky day it was for me. Do you know that? Today is the day that I got to see a cat.
It meow-meowed here and it meow-meowed there as I went on my way.
Oh boy, it was a very very very lucky day.

What a lucky day it was for me.   Please take my word. Today is the day that I got to see a bird.
It flapp-flapped here and it flap-flapped there as I went on my way.
Oh boy, it was a very very very lucky day.

What a lucky day it was for me. Make no mistake. Today is the day that I got to see a snake.
It wiggled here and it wiggled there as I went on my way.
Oh boy, it was a very very very lucky day.

Everyday is lucky. The world is a beautiful place. It's full of wonderful things that put smiles on my face.
I look and learn and listen and then go on my way.
Everyday is a very very very lucky day.

AFTERVIEW

Through science activities, a child

- Enjoys sensory experiences and uses the senses to gain information about the environment
- Becomes more aware of biological and physical sciences
- Sharpens his curiosity, formulates and evaluates predictions, gathers simple data, and draws conclusions
- Investigates and discovers the nature of food, the origin of food, the physical properties of food, and how food changes from one state or form to another
- Observes nature and develops an appreciation of natural beauty
- Learns to care for plants
- Learns to care for animals and develops sympathy and tenderness through association with pets

- Learns that the earth is very special
- Realizes that the earth is our home and that we need to take care of it
- Understands that the earth belongs to all living creatures
- Learns that every living thing must have water to live
- Discovers how growing things enrich the environment
- Realizes that recycling is important to protecting our world
- Learns ways to help clean up litter
- Develops ways to preserve and conserve our natural resources

KEY TERMS

biological sciences
ecology
physical sciences

EXPLORATIONS

1. Select at least two early childhood classrooms. Observe for one hour in each. Describe objectively (factually) in writing how science activities were introduced to the children. Which methods of discovery (as described in this chapter) were used? Explain by giving examples. Which science activities happened indoors and which ones occurred outdoors? Was there a science learning center as part of the room arrangement? Explain. Describe at least four activities you observed. What are your subjective (opinion) thoughts about early education science activities once you have completed this assignment?

2. Find out what materials are collected in your community and how they are recycled. Then, using this information, plan a recycling program appropriate for a preschool classroom. What will you recycle? How will you collect the discarded materials? What are your objectives? What projects can you and the children do to reuse the materials instead of discarding them? Share your plan with another classmate or colleague.

3. With a classmate or colleague, brainstorm science activities appropriate for a group of young children. Use the methods of discovery discussed in this chapter. Explain why you think each of these activities is developmentally appropriate.

4. Select two of the activities suggested in this chapter, such as the carrot-top garden, rooting a sweet potato, thirsty celery, or growing grass, and experiment with them at home. Then plan how you will arrange the environment, what transitions into the activities you will use, and what materials you will supply for the scientific investigations as you set up the activities for a group of young children.

5. Based on the information from this chapter, write a letter on science activities to give to the parents of the children in your class. Be creative. Explain what science projects you and the children are doing. Give suggestions for extended activities the parents can do with their children. Describe other ways to communicate with parents.

REFERENCES

Brewer, J. A. (1998). *Introduction to early childhood education.* Boston: Allyn and Bacon.

Burrell, S. (1989, May). Respecting nature. *First Teacher, 10*(5), 2.

Charlesworth, R., & Lind, K. K. (1999). *Math and science for young children* (3rd ed.). Albany, NY: Delmar.

Church, E. R. (1998, May/June). Seeing science everywhere. *Early Childhood Today, 12*(8), 38–42.

Durkin, L., & Perez, J. (1999, March/April). Gardening activities. *Early Childhood News, 11*(2), 58–59, 61.

Drew, W. F. (1995, February). Recycled materials—Tools for creative thinking. *Early Childhood Today, 9*(5), 36–43.

Eklof, J. (1995). *Animals in the classroom.* Dallas, TX: Miss Jo Productions.

Eliason, C., & Jenkins, L. (1999). *A practical guide to early childhood curriculum* (6th ed.). Columbus, OH: Merrill.

Hildebrand, V, & Hearron, P. F. (1999). *Guiding young children* (6th ed.). Columbus, OH: Merrill.

Jablon, J. (1992). Science in early childhood. In A. Mitchell and J. David (Eds.), *Explorations with young children: A curriculum guide from the Bank Street College of Education,* 189–197.

Petrash, C. (1992). *Earthways.* Mt. Rainier, MD: Gryphon House.

Rivkin, M. (Ed.). (1992, May). Science is a way of life. *Young Children, 47*(4), 4–8.

Smith, R. F. (1987, January). Theoretical framework for preschool science experiences. *Young Children, 42*(2), 34–40.

Van Hoorn, J., Nourot, P., Scales, B., & Alward, M. E. (1999). *Play at the center of the curriculum.* Columbus, OH: Merrill.

Wilson, R. A. (1995, September). Nature and young children: A natural connection. *Young Children, 50*(6), 4–11.

Ziemer, M. (1987, September). Science and the early childhood curriculum. *Young Children, 42*(6), 44–51.

ADDITIONAL READINGS AND RESOURCES

Bullock, J. R. (1994, Summer). Helping children value and appreciate nature. *Day Care and Early Education, 21*(4), 4–8.

Burns, J. (1993, Fall). Classroom gardening. *Dimensions of Early Childhood, 22*(1), 14–17.

Cohen, R. (1994, April). Creatures in the classroom. *Early Childhood Today, 8*(7), 51–57.

Furman, E. (1990, November). Plant a potato—Learn about life (and death). *Young Children, 46*(1), 15–20.

Goldhaber, J. (1994, Fall). If we call it science, then can we let the children play? *Childhood Education, 71*(2), 24–27.

Griffin, S. (1992, Summer). Wondering about trees. *Dimensions of Early Childhood, 20*(4), 31–34.

Halbrook, A. M. (1993, May). The amazing seed. *Educational Leadership, 50*(8), 83.

Harlan, J. D., & Rivkin, M. (1996). *Science experiences for the early childhood years* (6th ed.). Columbus, OH: Merrill.

Hofschield, K. A. (1991, March). The gift of a butterfly. *Young Children, 46*(3), 3–6.

Klein, A. (1991, July). All about ants: Discovery learning in the primary grades. *Young Children, 46*(5), 23–27.

Perry, G., & Rivkin, M. (1992, May). Answering the "wonder" questions in the primary grades: Teachers and science. *Young Children, 47*(4), 9–16.

Redleaf, R., & Robertson, A. (1999). *Learn and play the recycle way.* St. Paul, MN: Redleaf Press.

Ross, M. E. (1995, May/June). Investigating nature. *Early Childhood Today, 9*(8), 40–47.

Taylor, B. (1990). *Fun with simple science: Liquid and buoyancy.* New York: Warwick Press.

Taylor, B. (1991). *Fun with simple science: Color and light.* New York: Warwick Press.

Taylor, B. J. (1993). *Science everywhere—Opportunities for very young children.* Fort Worth, TX: Harcourt Brace.

Vansant, R., & Dondiego, B. L (1995). *Moths, butterflies, other insects and spiders: Science in art, song, and play.* Illustrated by C. Kalish. New York: McGraw-Hill.

Wilson, R. A. (1995, Spring). Environmental education—Let nature be your teacher. *Day Care and Early Education, 22*(3), 31–34.

Wilson, R. A. (1994, Winter). Environmental education at the early childhood level. *Day Care and Early Education, 22*(2), 23–25.

Wolfinger, D. M. (1994). *Science and mathematics in early childhood education.* New York: HarperCollins.

Social Studies

■ OVERVIEW

Social studies in early education has been placed as the last chapter in this text for a specific reason. This chapter is the connecting link to all other chapters in the curriculum chain. The previous chapters have stressed developmentally appropriate environments and activities, the uniqueness of the individual child, and creativity—the self-expressive part of each child. This chapter continues to do this as well, plus emphasizes ways to provide care and education for each child by connecting the curriculum to the child's family, the community, the nation, and the world. The social studies curriculum allows us to do this effectively.

> *The field of social studies is uniquely suited to prepare children with the knowledge, skills, and attitudes they need to participate in, and contribute to, the small democracies of their homes, their preschool or primary groups, and their immediate neighborhoods today, as well as to become functioning citizens of society in general in the future. (Seefeldt, 1997)*

Social studies, like math and science, needs to be experienced firsthand by the children. To have this happen, children need to be taken out into the world of people as well as have the world brought to them in the classroom (Feeney, Christensen, & Moravcik, 1996). Through interactions with children's families and the community, you can assist children in learning about the core of social studies—the **social sciences**. Individually they are the following: anthropology, the study of the way people live, such as their beliefs and customs; sociology, the study of group living, cooperation, and responsibilities; history, the study of what has happened in the life of a country or people; geography, the study of the earth's surface, resources, and the concepts of direction, location, and distance; economics, the study of the production, distribution, and consumption of goods and services; and psychology, the study of the mind, emotions, and behaviorial processes. (Specific activities relating to the social sciences will be discussed as we continue through this chapter.)

Children today are aware at a very young age about aspects of all the social sciences. They are experiencing moving to and living in different places or knowing family members and friends who have. Many travel on a regular basis and have access to television, video games, movies, books, and magazines that introduce them to an ever-changing world.

> *Today's children, who view fighting in Iraq and Bosnia and starving children in Somalia via television, have already had their horizons expanded (or shattered) in starkly dramatic and confusing ways. The challenge for teachers and parents is to help these children make the connections between themselves and the larger world that abruptly enters their homes with each news telecast. Children need concepts that will help them make sense of the strange and complex things they see and hear. (Fortson & Reiff, 1995)*

This is underscored by the fact that teachers daily deal with the problem of violence in our society in their early childhood classrooms through the thoughts, feelings, and behaviors of young children (Slaby, Roedell, Arezzo, & Hendrix, 1995). With this in mind, your role as an early childhood teacher continues to be nurturing, valuing, and accepting of the children in your classroom, both individually and as a group.

■ GUIDING YOUNG CHILDREN AWAY FROM AGGRESSION

Through observing and intervening in conflicts before they escalate, you can guide the children toward mutually agreeable resolutions. Slaby et al. (1995) suggest that additionally you can:

- Help children identify violence and its consequences
- Recognize and talk with children about real-world violence
- Recognize and respond to children's traumatic reactions to violence
- Teach problem-solving skills that relate to reducing aggression
- Help children understand and deal with their strong feelings
- Provide children with practice in thinking of solutions, anticipating consequences, and evaluating the harmfulness of aggressive solutions
- Support families as they help their children cope with violence

■ GOALS OF EARLY EDUCATION SOCIAL STUDIES

"Community begins in the classroom. For most young children, being a 'classmate'—at day care, at a place of worship, or at school—constitutes their first active participation in an ongoing social structure outside the family. The vision of community that the classroom provides can color a child's ideas and expectations about equity, cooperation, and citizenship for a lifetime" (Teaching Tolerance Project, 1997).

The social studies curriculum emphasizes basic goals that encourage children to become self-reliant, contributing members of their society, i.e., the family, the classroom, and the community. These goals encourage children to make choices, act independently, and develop a sense of responsibility and respect for themselves and others. In addition, Seefeldt (1997) believes that in "an early childhood program, children are not just preparing to become members of a democratic society but actually are citizens of a democracy. Within the democratic environment of an early childhood program, children practice principles of democracy."

The following goals help us focus on the core of the social studies curriculum. They are adapted from various sources (Taylor, 1999; Day, 1994; Seefeldt, 1997; Sunal, 1997; and Mayesky, 1998):

- To develop a child's positive self-concept—A child's understanding and appreciation of himself must come first before learning to appreciate and relate to others. From infancy on, a child is learning to adjust and accept himself in the family and the larger community. Curriculum activities to emphasize this goal should relate to a child's developing sense of autonomy and his place in the world.
- To further an understanding of a child's role in the family—As the child learns about herself, she is learning about her family. Knowing about the family history; where family members lived before; and the family's values, attitudes, customs, celebrations, and occupations all contribute to a child's sense of belonging. They, in turn, help her to solidify a positive self-concept. Activities should offer opportunities for a child to talk about and identify things about herself and her family.
- To develop an awareness of a child's own cultural heritage as well as the traditions of others—Continuing in the classroom what the child is experiencing in the home environment requires a teacher to communicate openly and often with the child's family. It also means that a teacher should start where the child is with his language, customs, traditions, and values, and build on his growth toward self-understanding and acceptance.

- To provide a multicultural classroom environment— This should reflect the lives and interests of the children, families, and teacher who live in the immediate environment, as well as foster a respect for people everywhere. Social study activities should blend this diversity into the theme, lesson plans, and daily activities *throughout the year.*
- To understand the need for rules and laws—Starting with the rules of the family, the child begins to understand the limits placed on her within her environment at a very young age. Conflicts often occur as the child's sense of independence clashes

FIGURE 12–1 Social studies activities offer an understanding of people around the world.

with the rules of the home and classroom. To minimize these encounters, the child should participate in setting the rules.

As teachers, we are daily role models for young children. By incorporating the goals for social studies into our activities, we are creating a supportive environment for the children and their families. We are emphasizing an **anti-bias** approach that influences children to respect and appreciate differences and similarities among people. See Figure 12–1. (All chapters of this text extend this philosophy. Review Chapter 2 for additional multicultural/anti-bias considerations.)

■ ACTIVITIES THAT SUPPORT THE GOALS

As suggested at the beginning of this chapter, the social studies curriculum is connected to all learning centers in an early education environment. Rather than create a separate center for social studies activities, the teacher needs to blend these projects into all other learning centers. Many of the activities already described in the preceding chapters can become part of the social studies curriculum. The following are some additional suggestions to get you started:

■ Appropriate *themes* to encourage the development of a positive self-concept are "Magnificent Me" or "All About Me." Extensions of this can be "Me and My Family," "Me and My Friends," "Me and My Community."

■ After making life-size body outlines of themselves, the children can make individual *handprints* and *footprints* with tempera or finger paint.
   This body-awareness activity is time-tested, according to Helen H. Johnson (1994):

   What brilliant teacher first conceived the notion of young children painting their own life-size self-portraits? The activity never fails to capture and hold attention through all its stages: outlining oneself on butcher paper; painting in one's hair, features and clothing; cutting out the final two-dimensional Me.

■ Children can dictate stories about themselves to the teacher or create an "I like" book from drawings and pictures they cut from magazines. These very meaningful activities can be introduced at group time and continued in the language and art centers.

■ Plan for the social studies curriculum to include topics that relate specifically to a child's family. For infants and toddlers, creating an atmosphere that makes them feel safe, secure, and special while they are away from home is most important. Activities for all children can include creating an individual or class scrapbook with photographs of family members and pets, as well as magazine pictures depicting toys and home furnishings. Preschoolers can make craft stick puppets, coloring and designing one puppet for each family member. (Review Chapter 5.)

■ As a teacher, you can help a child to identify his role in the family and understand how families change over time. Placement in the family may change due to adoption, birth, marriage, divorce, or the death of a family member. Some books dealing with these themes that you can share with the children are:

Cooney, B. (1985). *Miss Rumphius.* New York: Puffin Books.

Dorros, A. (1991). *Abuela.* Illustrated by E. Kleven. New York: Dutton Children's Books.

Garza, C. L. (1990). *Family pictures—Cuadros de familia.* San Francisco: Children's Book Press.

Greenfield, E. (1991). *Daddy and I.* Illustrated by J. A. Gilcrest. New York: Black Butterfly Board Books.

Hudson, W. (1993). *I love my family.* New York: Scholastic.

Karkowsky, N. (1989). *Grandma's soup.* Illustrated by S. O. Haas. Rockville, MD: Kar-Ben Copies Inc.

Katz, K. (1997). *Over the Moon.* New York: Henry Holt and Company, Inc.

Kroll, V. (1993). *A carp for Kimiko.* Illustrated by K. Roundtree. Watertown, MA: Charlesbridge Publishing.

Kuklin, S. (1992). *How my family lives in America.* New York: Bradbury Press.

Morris, A. (1990). *Loving.* Photographs by K. Heyman. New York: Lothrop, Lee & Shepard Books.

Ostarch, J. and Nex, A. (1993). *My family.* Los Angeles: Price Stern Sloan Inc.

Scott, A. H. (1992). *On mother's lap.* Illustrated by G. Coalson. New York: Clarion Books.

Williams, V. B. (1982). *A chair for my mother.* New York: Mulberry Books.

■ It is important for children to feel good about themselves and their families. As you continue to prepare your classroom to reflect this attitude, consider the following: What members are in a child's family? How many family members (or others) live in a child's home? What ages are they? What are the roles of family members both inside and outside the home? What do family members do together? What holidays or events do they celebrate? How are they celebrated? What is the family's history and ethnic background? What changes has the family experienced? (Cunningham, 1994). Knowing this about each child's family will help you plan appropriate activities for the children in your class.

■ An exciting social studies theme can be "Homes." Stretch your and the children's interest and creativity by investigating information about all kinds of shelters for humans and animals. What types of habitats do the following live in: birds, rabbits, turtles, dogs, horses, and cows? Think of all the residences people live in, such as apartments, houses, duplexes, trailers, hotels, and tents. What are they made of, besides wood, brick, stone, and ice? Examine what climate and location have to do with determining how a house is built. Gather books and pictures to illustrate concretely what you are talking about. The children can even experiment with building some of these residences with blocks, pieces of fabric, scrap wood, boxes, and other materials.

■ Taking a social studies viewpoint can become a process you can apply to most curriculum themes. Ramsey (1987) suggests a multicultural approach to learning about pets that could include the following activities and topics:

Caring for pets: social responsibility

Cooperative care of a classroom pet

Similarities among all pets

Diversity of pets

Learning about pets belonging to people in the classroom

Friendships, despite differences, between people and pets

Names of animals in other languages

Pets in other places

Communicating with pets

Animals communicating with each other

Protecting the rights of pets

Different ways that animals feed, clean, and care for their young

Working to change conditions that are harmful to animals

This social sciences/social studies approach can also be used with other topics, such as different ways of cooking and eating, types of clothing, kinds of occupations and work roles, weather conditions, and how people in the world are transported from one place to another.

■ Another social studies activity relates to maps or place awareness. The main objective is to introduce children to a map as a picture that shows places and things, where they are located, and how to get from one to another. Young children can usually understand this concept by working with puzzles or by drawing maps of their rooms at home, the classroom, or the playground. Map making is an abstract concept, so the activities should be fairly simple. Keep a globe and other types of maps available to provide visual answers to children's questions about places in the world. Children can use these also as props in their dramatic play activities.

■ Create an opportunity for the children to make a three-dimensional map (model) of the classroom, their bedroom (see Figure 12–2), or the playground. Clear a large space of classroom floor where the children can constuct their map. Place a large piece of cardboard, such as the side of a large box, on the floor. Gather materials, such as pipe cleaners, Styrofoam pieces, small counting cubes, crayons, markers, glue, and various types and colors of paper. The children will let you know what other materials they need during the creative process. They can work cooperatively in small groups to make their map. This activity may take several days or weeks to complete. Let the children make the decision as to when it's time to stop working on and playing with this activity.

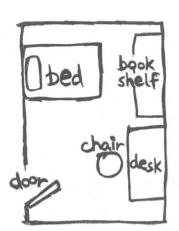

FIGURE 12–2 Map-making opportunities for children are an important part of early education social studies activities.

■ RESPECTING A CHILD'S BILINGUAL, BICULTURAL WORLD

You may now have or eventually will have young children in your classroom who speak languages other than English and whose country of origin is not the United States. "These children contribute a great richness of diversity and cultural heritage to our classrooms, but at the same time they bring considerable challenges" (Schall, 1995).

In meeting the needs of these **bilingual, bicultural** children, you should first try to understand the stages of language acquisition in relationship to limited-English proficient (LEP) children. The following stages are adapted from Hernandez (1995) and Ramsey (1987):

■ *The Preproduction or Silent Stage* A child's initial response to a new language is to listen to or "take in" the language rather than to speak it. The length of this particular stage will vary from child to child. During this period, music, movement, dramatic play, and art activities are appropriate. Reading books aloud to the child can offer a one-on-one experience with a teacher as well.

■ *Early Production Stage* At this stage, children have limited verbalization and growing comprehension. Occasionally asking questions that require a "yes" or "no" answer from the child will give a teacher an informal assessment of what the child is understanding. Speech can also be encouraged by asking questions that ask for the labeling of familiar objects ("What is this?") or finishing a statement ("We are eating. . . ." "The color of this crayon is. . . ."). This can be accomplished easily in informal conversations with the child. Group time, classroom games, outdoor play, and one-on-one activities will provide ample opportunities in which you can guide children through this stage.

■ *Expansion of Production Stage* This is the speech emergence and expansion stage. With this comes increased comprehension and the ability to speak in simple sentences. Encourage the child to talk about his family and friends. Motivate him to describe, using his words, what he is experiencing with his five senses. Finger plays, songs, and rhymes are useful in stimulating the child toward using his new language.

Throughout the process of a child's language acquisition, your role will be to understand the whole child. Give "opportunities to exhibit skills and not assume that because the child doesn't speak the new language that he or she doesn't have the ability to function" (Hernandez, 1995).

Be sensitive and encourage the child to communicate in her own way during social interaction with other children. "Independent play and outdoor play offer excellent opportunities for children to interact with each other in the comfortable language. A caregiver [teacher] must give verbal as well as nonverbal support to LEP children in both languages" (Schiller & Bermudez, 1988). Emphasize the child's strengths, and help to build her positive self-concept.

It is also essential to maintain personal contact with the child's parents. Encourage the parents to participate as much as possible in the center's or school's activities. Invite them to visit the classroom and share their language with all the children. "Instead of the teacher being viewed as the sole expert, there is a reciprocal exchange where parents are valued as resources" (Ramsey, 1987).

■ CREATING PARTNERSHIPS WITH FAMILIES AND THE COMMUNITY

As you establish partnerships with parents, it is important to continuously assess their needs and interests and use this knowledge to involve the parents as active partners in the lives of the children at the center or school. The families of today offer new challenges to early childhood educators. "Frequently, teachers find themselves in situations that were rare only a few years ago. Dealing with a variety of family structures, coping with increased occurrences of family violence, and witnessing strained parental relationships are difficult dimensions of this field" (Stamp & Groves, 1994).

Knowing this, we should relate to the families of our children with a commitment to accept their individual differences. We should acknowledge and respect children's home language and **culture** (NAEYC, 1996). We should maintain positive interractions with them while communicating our goals of a child-centered, developmentally appropriate curriculum.

Get parental input as you plan activities and services. If the parents help to set the priorities and agenda, your planned activities will meet their needs. The following are some examples of how to communicate with parents to maximize their involvement:

- With parents of an infant or toddler you will need to spend a lot of time making them feel comfortable in leaving their child with you. It is most important to build a sense of trust, and this takes time. Show them that you will communicate with them through daily notes and conversations. Let them know that there will be a period of adjustment for their child as well as for them. Explain that during this time, it might be helpful if their child brought a "security" toy or blanket. The parents can also call during the day to check on how their child is doing, if this will help the parents feel more at ease. All these suggestions can open lines of communication between you and the family members.
- Place a parent bulletin board or information sheet on the door of your classroom. For family members who bring and pick up the child each day, this offers a consistent place to look for messages and items of interest. Change materials often.
- Post weekly lesson plans on the classroom door to keep the parents up-to-date on the curriculum. This sends a signal that you want the parents to be fully aware of the daily activities of their children.

- The weekly menu of lunch and snacks should also be posted for parents to see, as required by licensing regulations in most states.
- A newsletter is another way to get parents involved. Some enjoy receiving it, while others are interested in taking the responsibility for writing it or collecting information to be in the newsletter. The teacher can contribute facts about what is happening in the classroom, suggestions for children's books and videos, parenting articles, and children's art.
- Some teachers use audio cassettes instead of newsletters. "Children record current happenings on a cassette tape and several copies are circulated until all parents have heard them. This method allows busy parents to listen on the drive to work or school. Parents who cannot read also have access to classroom news" (Silliman & Royston, 1990). If there are non–English-speaking parents in your class, have a family or community member record or translate the information into their language.
- Have a family breakfast, potluck supper, or picnic on the playground. Food always adds to the welcoming environment of family-school activities.
- An open house or family meeting is a time for sharing with parents what their children are doing and what they are learning. This is an excellent opportunity to talk about the importance of play and other developmentally appropriate learning experiences. Be prepared to answer questions. Give family members an opportunity to take part in some of the activities the children have been doing. Set up materials and supplies in each learning center so that they can "learn by doing" the same as the children. Read a story to the parents or have them participate in a music and movement activity.
- Once or twice a year, plan parent-teacher conferences to discuss their child's developmental progress. Plan both day and evening conferences to accommodate the parents' work schedules.
- Invite family members to share their interests, talents, and occupations with the children in the class. This offers another way to make parent involvement special and unique.

Creating partnerships with community members and resources can be helpful. One of the most important groups of individuals to invite into your classroom consists of older members of the families of children in your class as well as other community senior adults. Intergenerational programs offer many ways to connect young children with the history and family customs of their own or other cultures.

There is much to be gained from contact with elders, yet some children either do not have grandparents and/or great-grandparents or don't see them often enough to understand the joy of listening to their stories. Interacting with older adults teaches children about the abundant wisdom, talent, and love elders possess. (Church, 1994)

After the visit or visits, it is important to keep in touch with the older adults. The children can establish a pen pal relationship, send frequent drawings, or dictate stories on audio cassettes to send to their new friends. Many times the children receive replies that they can share with their classmates.

■ FIELD TRIPS AS CONCRETE EXPERIENCES IN EARLY EDUCATION

Another way of connecting the child to the community is through taking field trips with the children in your class. Such trips are an enriching part of early education curriculum that add a special dimension to classroom learning by providing firsthand experience that books, pictures, or discussions alone cannot provide. Young children

need to see, hear, feel, taste, and touch their world to connect words and ideas to locations and people within their community.

Types of Field Trips

There are different types of field trips to consider. Leipzig (1993), Seefeldt (1997), and Redleaf (1983) suggest the following.

A Walking Trip Around a Familiar Room. This offers infants and toddlers an opportunity to notice and learn the names of everything in the room. This can then be extended to another room until the children feel comfortable exploring and noticing things in the entire building or house.

A Walking Trip Around the Neighborhood. This is the natural extension of the room walk, and there are advantages to neighborhood field trips. They are free, and you do not have to arrange for buses or cars. They are short in duration and less tiring for the children. There is not a rush to meet schedules, so the children can make discoveries, their questions can be answered, and learning can occur. Repeated trips around the neighborhood offer chances to learn something new each time you visit the same places. (First take a walk without the children. Look at things from a child's point of view. Find connections that can be natural outgrowths of classroom activities.)

Taking a Small Group of Children at One Time on a Mini-Field Trip. Once the children become used to taking turns, go on a mini-trip. There are frequent opportunities to do so. There usually is no difficulty in planning trips for a specific purpose with a small group of children.

Specific-Purpose Field Trips. This type of field trip can be as simple as a neighborhood walk to go bird-watching or to record sounds around the neighborhood. It can be a short trip to the grocery store to get carrots and celery to go into the vegetable soup the children are making or down the block to see the new house being built.

Major Field Trips. These are often taken by the entire class to a community location. This type requires additional adults and travel arrangements for a bus, a van, or cars. (This type of field trip is discussed in more detail as you read through the rest of this chapter.)

Planning for a Successful Field Trip

Making decisions about what an appropriate field trip should provide, selecting the site, visiting the location, planning for the trip, taking the trip, preparing follow-up activities, and evaluating the trip are all parts of the *process*. Think about the following guidelines as you plan field trips for young children.

Appropriate field trips provide:

- Opportunities to clarify misconceptions young children have about places and people in the community
- Concrete experiences for the children
- Sensory activities outside the classroom
- Occasions to discover firsthand examples of "real-life" work settings
- Contact with adult work models
- Opportunities to gather information and observe multiple environments
- Reinforcement and extension of concepts already learned, while developing new concepts
- A common core of experiences for play and problem-solving activities

An appropriate site should:

- Be safe for young children to visit
- Be fairly close by so that the children have a short bus ride or car trip
- Not be too fatiguing for the children
- Not be too crowded or noisy
- Offer the children sensory experiences
- Offer genuine learning experiences through participation

Before you step out of the classroom door with the children, you should:

- Visit the field trip site *yourself*
- Talk to the contact person who will be there on the day you and the children visit and call her for verification the day before the field trip
- Explain how many children and adults will be coming and the ages of the children; arrange for a time when the site is not too crowded
- Explain the children's need to be able to explore, see, and touch
- Find out the site's rules and regulations
- Find out where the bathrooms are placed
- Find out accommodations for children with special needs, if applicable
- Determine arrangements for lunch or snack
- Walk around the location and look for dangerous places
- Set up length of visit, date, and time
- Get brochures, posters, and any other information to share with the children during pretrip discussions

Prepare the children for the trip by:

- Giving them an idea of what to expect
- Reading books; showing films, pictures, and posters; and talking about the planned trip
- Involving them in the planning of the trip
- Reminding them of the rules of expected behavior
- Reminding them that during the field trip they are not to talk to or go with anyone other than the people on the field trip
- Selecting a partner or buddy for each child and explaining how important it is to stay with their partner
- Telling them what to do if they get separated from the group

Prepare the parents for the trip by:

■ Having the parent or guardian sign a walking field trip permission form at the beginning of the year, so that you can take the children on spontaneous walks around the neighborhood (Figure 12–3 is an example of a walking trip permission form.)
■ Having the parent or guardian sign a field trip form for major types of field trips a week before the trip is to be taken (Figure 12–4 is an example of a field trip permission form.)
■ Sending information home to parents explaining the field trip, its purpose, and other details
■ Involving parent volunteers to accompany you and the children (One adult for every two or three children is advised. For older children, one adult for every five or six children seems to work well. You will need to decide what child/adult ratio is best for you and the children.)
■ Explaining the emergency procedures and assuring them that all of the adults going on the trip understand the procedures
■ Explaining that arrangements have been made for any child who does not have permission to go on the trip to visit another class during the duration of the field trip

Taking the Field Trip

Consider the following guidelines when you and the children take the field trip:

■ Be sure that the drivers of buses, vans, or cars have a map with simple, precise directions on how to get to the field trip location.
■ Prepare a trip kit containing bottled water and paper cups, a basic first-aid kit, and several wet wash cloths in individual self-seal bags.
■ Keep the most apprehensive children close to you.
■ Take the time to see things along the way.

I give my permission for my child (child's name) to take part in any walking field trip around the neighborhood immediately surrounding the (center or school name). This permission is valid for the entire year (year date).

                    (signature of
              parent or guardian)

                          (date)

FIGURE 12–3 Walking trip permission form.

Dear Parent,

We will be going on a field trip to (name of site) on (day-date-time-return time). We will travel by (mode of transportation).

If you give permission for your child to go on this field trip, please sign this form in the space provided below.

                        (Child's name)

(Signature of parent or guardian)

                                (date)

Cost (if any) to be paid to the center or school by (date) in the amount of (amount).

FIGURE 12–4 Field trip permission form.

- Listen to the children to find out what they know and what they do not know. Talk to them; ask open-ended questions, and answer their questions.
- Count "heads" often throughout the trip.
- It is helpful if the children wear T-shirts or name tags with the center's or school's name on them. It is best not to put the child's name where it is visible. An adult calling the child's name may pull the child away from the group.
- Enjoy the field trip!

Follow-Up to the Field Trip

There should be many opportunities for follow-up activities. Here are a few suggestions:

- Have the children write thank-you notes or draw pictures to send to the parent volunteers and the field site guides or managers who helped make the field trip successful.
- Encourage group discussions with the children on what they liked best or what they remember about the trip.
- Expand lesson plans to include follow-up activities.
- Deepen the children's understanding and recall through follow-up activities: dictate or write stories, draw pictures, create songs and poems, make puppet characters, and draw maps. Add related props and materials to the dramatic play, block, and other learning centers.
- Clarify and build upon what the children have seen, heard, experienced, and shared.
- Get written evaluations from all of the adults participating in the trip. Did the activity fulfill the trip's goals and objectives?

Suggested Field Trips

These are only suggestions. You know your community best and can make the most appropriate selection of places to visit with the children. If you choose not to take any trips outside the center or school, many individuals connected to the organizations or institutions mentioned will make presentations, bring exhibits or animals, and interact with the children. Here are some places to visit:

Airport terminal	Livestock show
Animal shelter	Museum of natural history
Aquarium	Newspaper
Arboretum	Park
Art museum	Pet shop
Bakery	Planetarium
Bird-watching site	Police department
Bottling company	Pottery factory
Children's theater	Puppet show
City hall	Radio station
College or university campus	Restaurant
Dairy	Science museum
Dance studio	Sports field or arena
Farm	Television station
Farmer's market	Train station or museum
Fire department	U.S. Post Office
Florist	Water treatment plant
Garden center	Wildlife sanctuary
Library	Zoo

Teachers find that making a card file of possible field trip sites can be helpful. It is easy to add to or correct. Place the information on an index card, color coding each type of location. After you complete a visit to the site to see if it is appropriate for the children in your class, you can make notations on the card for easy reference. Figure 12–5 is a suggested form to use.

NAME OF POSSIBLE SITE/LOCATION

Address: _____

Phone: _____

Contact: _____

Days and hours open: _____

Length of tour or presentation: _____

What the tour or presentation consists of: _____

_____

Size of group permitted: _____

Ages of children: _____

Adult/child ratio required: _____

How early do reservations need to be made: _____

Special notes: _____

FIGURE 12–5 Index card site form.

■ TIPS FOR TEACHERS

It is helpful to have a checklist to complete on the day of the field trip. This should be filled out completely by you. Not only will this give you an opportunity to "double check" all of your preparations, but it is also written documentation that you are in compliance with state and/or school requirements for taking children away from the center or school (Figure 12–6 on page 308).

■ DEVELOPMENTALLY APPROPRIATE AND MULTICULTURAL/ ANTI-BIAS ACTIVITIES

Connect the social studies curriculum to the theme "Self and Family" to assist children in learning the values, cultural traditions, and history of families.

Family Quilts

An effective way to accomplish this goal is to introduce children to quilts. Throughout the history of many countries, you will find quilting, an ancient craft. In American pioneer days, families and friends got together to make quilts for special occasions, such as weddings, births, and farewells to families moving west. This tradition continues today, and the act of quilting brings many adults together in friendship and sharing.

The term *quilt* "refers to a fabric sandwich made of a top, bottom or backing, and a soft filler [batting] in between. The top consists of blocks arranged in a pattern. Each block may be a *patchwork*, that is—pieces of fabric cut in squares, rectangles, and other shapes and sewn together to form the block" (Parks, 1994).

1. Notification of field trip was posted in a prominent place for the parents to see at least 48 hours before the planned trip. Name, address, and phone number of where we are going was clearly stated. Name of contact person was listed. Time of departure and return was clearly stated.

   Yes _____ No _____

2. Field trip permission forms, specifically for this trip, have been signed by each child's parent or guardian. These permission forms are on file in the director's or administrator's office.

   Yes _____ No _____

3. Only adults, 18 years of age or older, are counted as part of the child/adult ratio. Requirements have been met for the number of adults to accompany the children, including the teachers.

   Yes _____ No _____

4. The medical emergency consent form signed by the parent or guardian for each child is being taken on the field trip, as well as the emergency phone numbers for each child's family and a written list of children in the group taking the field trip. This information should be put in the vehicle transporting the child.

   Yes _____ No _____

5. An emergency first-aid kit is in each vehicle going on the trip.

   Yes _____ No _____

6. There is an adult trained in first aid and another adult trained in CPR going on the field trip.

   Yes _____ No _____

7. Arrangements for lunch or snack have been made. They are the following: _____

   _____

8. The driver(s) of the bus (van or cars) is/are: _____

   The driver's license number of each is: _____

   The license plate number of each vehicle is: _____

9. Names of adults going on trip: _____

10. Names of children going on trip: _____

11. Departure time: _____   Return time: _____

12. Additional information: _____

   _____

   _____

FIGURE 12–6 Teacher checklist for field trip.

Invite a quilter to visit your class. This individual can bring some of the quilts she has made, as well as show the children the three unfinished parts of a quilt—top, batting, and backing.

Your children may enjoy making a friendship quilt of single pieces of fabric or paper. To further illustrate this activity, there are several books that give information about family quilts. These selections offer oportunities for literature-based integrated curriculum. As you read one of the books during group time, pass a quilt around the circle of children. This is a tangible example of the abstract story you are reading. (Older children will be able to read the books by themselves or read them to younger children.)

These books, when shared with family members, stimulate the telling of family stories and, many times, the discovery of family quilts. The stories relate not only to families, but also to the multiple relationships within a family.

Suggested books are:

Bolton, J. (1994). *My grandmother's patchwork quilt. A book and pocketful of patchwork pieces.* New York: Doubleday Book for Young Readers.

Coerr, E. (1989). *The Josefina story quilt.* An I Can Read Book. Illustrated by B. Degen. New York: HarperTrophy.

Flournoy, V. (1985). *The patchwork quilt.* Illustrated by J. Pinkney. New York: Dial Books for Young Readers.

Hopkinson, D. (1993). *Sweet Clara and the freedom quilt.* Illustrated by J. Ransome. New York: Alfred A. Knopf.

Johnston, T., & de Paola, T. (1985). *The quilt story.* New York: G. P. Putnam's Sons.

Jonas, A. (1984). *The quilt.* New York: Greenwillow.

Polacco, P. (1988). *The keeping quilt.* New York: Simon and Schuster Books for Young Readers.

After you read the story, encourage the children to retell the story by acting out the parts in small groups. You can extend the quilt to many learning centers. There are many projects that can promote the development of large and small muscle skills, as well as problem solving, socialization, language, and literacy abilities. The following are suggestions for these extended activities:

- Develop a story or sequencing chart that diagrams the storyline of the book. This can be a way of developing how the story can be re-enacted.
- Ask the children open-ended questions, such as "Do you have a quilt at your house?" "Would you like to make a paper quilt in the art center?" "Do you want to write your story about a quilt in the writing center?" "Would you help me collect fabric to make new squares for our class quilt?" "How do you think we can find the fabric?" "Who should we ask to help us?" "Would you like to make a quilt for the doll bed?"
- Invite a quilter to visit and show the children some of the quilts she has made. Perhaps this will stimulate the children to make their own quilts or quilt squares.
- Place a "quilt box" in the manipulative center containing an assortment of fabric squares (all the same size) with snaps or Velcro on each corner (top and bottom). A child can snap pieces together to make his own quilt, or several children can do this activity together.
- Each child can design and paint a paper square for the classroom quilt. Patch the painted squares together with clear tape. Then place the completed quilt on the wall outside the classroom to share with the parents and other children.
- Put washable paint of several skin-tone colors into individual shallow aluminum pans, and let each child make a single handprint on a piece of paper (white or

yellow). Cut out each handprint and glue it onto a precut, individual square of construction paper. Let each child label her handprint with her name. Make holes in the corners of each square and use brightly colored yarn to lace the squares together. Hang this in the classroom so that the children can daily enjoy seeing their art displayed.

■ "Our Family Quilt" bulletin board can be made by mounting photographs of the children on squares of fabric. Add the children's dictated comments to the squares. A variation of this bulletin board can be to make a "Family Tree," with the photographs added as leaves of a tree.

■ During group time, discuss with the children activities that they enjoy doing with their families. They can draw pictures of what they like to do best with their families.

Making the Class into a Neighborhood

Another more complex social studies theme and series of activities is making the entire classroom into a neighborhood. This can be a creative follow-up to a walking trip around the neighborhood. It requires careful planning with the children to decide on how to do this, which will then indicate to the teacher what supplies, materials, and props will be needed for each area. Each learning activity center can be restructured into a part of the neighborhood, such as a home, construction site, fire station, grocery store, or other business establishment in the community. This all-encompassing plan benefits the physical, intellectual, social, emotional, and language development of all the children. The neighborhood concept connects children to their immediate world and brings about a feeling of community.

Figure 12–7 is the curriculum planning web worksheet with social studies activities added. This worksheet, with appropriate additions, is included in each chapter.

AFTERVIEW

Through social studies activities, a child

■ Learns about his world and his place in it

■ Identifies her family members and the multiple relationships within the family

■ Develops an awareness of his own cultural heritage as well as the traditions of others

■ Learns about other people who live in the world with her

■ Explores the geography, lifestyles, customs, and languages of other people

■ Explores his neighborhood and community and the resources within them

■ Participates in the democratic society of her classroom, school, and family

■ Has opportunities to learn firsthand about differences and similarities of classmates and other people in his world

■ Develops a positive self-concept and an acceptance of others

■ Participates in field trips within her neighborhood and wider community to learn about people, places, occupations, and resources

KEY TERMS

anti-bias

bicultural

bilingual

culture

social sciences

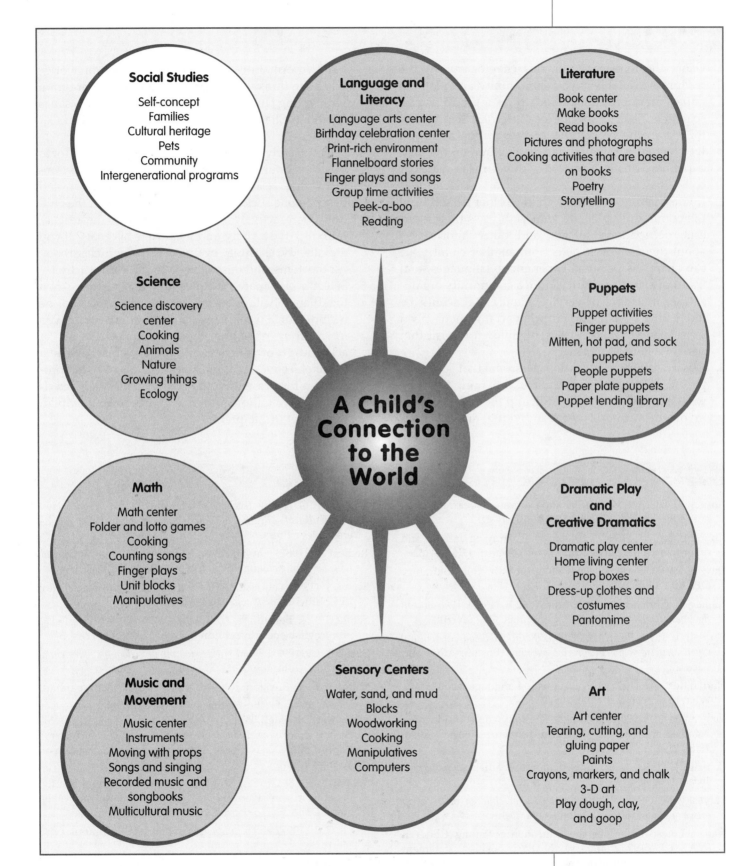

FIGURE 12–7 A curriculum planning web worksheet with social studies activities added.

EXPLORATIONS

1. Using the information in this chapter, survey the resources available in your community, and plan (on paper) an appropriate field trip for a group of preschoolers. Select a specific location, visit the site, and follow all the procedures of preparation as if you were actually going to take the children on the field trip. Share this information with your classmates or colleagues.

2. Invite a parent of a young child or other person from the community to share with your class their interests, occupations, talents, and other information about themselves. If he is from another country, he can share his personal experiences, languages, and traditions. If the person is from a community organization, museum, or service agency that would be interesting to visit, find out what arrangements need to be made to take a group of children to visit that person where he works.

3. Observe an early education classroom that is participating in an intergenerational program. Describe what activities the older adult and the children were involved in. Interview the individual and get first-hand information about how the program works, what she thinks about participating in the program with young children, and what personal goals she is fulfilling. Share this information with the class or colleagues.

4. Select an early education classroom and observe for at least one hour. List at least ten items in the environment that relate to social studies activities, and describe one social studies activity in which the children were actively involved. How did the teacher introduce the activity, and what were his goals? If you are already teaching, evaluate your own classroom, list the items, and describe one social studies activity.

5. Select a classmate or colleague as a partner. Then together develop social studies activities to be included on a weekly lesson plan or curriculum web for a group of young childen. Choose one of the activities from your lesson plan or web and write a list of objectives, materials needed, step-by-step procedures for presenting the activity, follow-up activities, and evaluation guidelines. (Use the activity plan worksheet in Chapter 2.)

REFERENCES

Church, E. B. (1994, November and December). Learning from our elders. *Early Childhood Today, 9*(3), 40–41.

Cunningham, B. (1994, September). Portraying fathers and other men in the curriculum. *Young Children, 49*(6), 4–13.

Day, B. (1994). *Early childhood education* (4th ed.). Columbus, OH: Merrill.

Feeney, S., Christensen, D., & Moravcik, E. (1996). *Who am I in the lives of children?* (5th ed.). Columbus, OH: Merrill.

Fortson, L. R., & Reiff, J. C. (1995). *Early childhood curriculum: Open structures for integrative learning.* Boston: Allyn and Bacon.

Hernandez, A. (1995, July/August). Language acquisition: What to expect. *Instructor, 105*(1), 56–57.

Johnson, H. H. (1994, September). The bodyworks: Inside me—Another approach to alike and different. *Young Children, 49*(6), 21–26.

Leipzig, J. (1993, May/June). Community field trips. *Pre-K Today, 7*(8), 44–51.

Mayesky, M. (1998). *Creative activities for children in the early primary grades* (6th ed.). Albany, NY: Delmar.

National Association for the Education of Young Children (NAEYC). (1996, January). NAEYC position statement responding to linguistic and cultural diversity. *Young Children, 52*(2), 4–12.

Parks, L. (Ed.). (1994, Spring). Make a friendship quilt. *Texas Child Care, 17*(4), 22–28.

Ramsey, P. G. (1987). *Teaching and learning in a diverse world—Multicultural education for young children.* New York: Teachers College Press.

Redleaf, R. (1983). *Open the door, let's explore: Neighborhood field trips for young children.* St. Paul, MN: Redleaf Press.

Schall, J. (1995, July/August). Unbeatable way to reach your LEP students. *Instructor, 105*(1), 54–59.

Schiller, P., & Bermudez, A. B. (1988, Winter). Working with non-English speaking children. *Texas Child Care, 12*(3), 3–8.

Seefeldt, C. (1997). *Social studies for the preschool–primary child* (5th ed.). Columbus, OH: Merrill.

Silliman, B., & Royston, K. (1990, Fall). Working with parents. *Dimensions of Early Childhood, 19*(1), 15–18.

Slaby, R. G., Roedell, W. C., Arezzo, D., & Hendrix, K. (1995). *Early violence prevention: tools for teachers of young children.* Washington, DC: National Association for the Education of Young Children.

Stamp, L. N., & Groves, M. M. (1994, Winter). Strengthening the ethic of care: Planning and supporting family involvement. *Dimensions of Early Childhood, 22*(2), 5–9.

Sunal, C. S. (1997). *Early childhood social studies.* Columbus, OH: Merrill.

Taylor, B. J. (1999). *A child goes forth* (8th ed.). Englewood Cliffs, NJ: Merrill/Prentice Hall.

Teaching Tolerance Project. (1997). *Starting small.* Montgomery, AL: Southern Poverty Law Center.

ADDITIONAL READINGS AND RESOURCES

Allen, P. (1994, Fall). When children speak a different language. *Day Care and Early Education, 22*(1), 38–39.

Alvarado, C. (1996, January). Working with children whose home language is other than English: The teacher's role. *Child Care Information Exchange, 55*, 48–49.

Ball, J., & Pence, A. R. (1999, March). Beyond developmentally appropriate practice: Developing community and culturally appropriate practice. *Young Children, 54*(2), 46–50.

Bennett, L. (1995, July). Wide world of breads in children's literature. *Young Children, 50*(5), 54–68.

Booth, C. (1997, July). The fiber project: One teacher's adventure toward emergent curriculum. *Young Children, 52*(5), 79–85.

Cerbus, D. P., & Rice, C. F. (1992). *Connecting social studies and literature.* Huntington Beach, CA: Teacher Created Materials Inc.

Click, P. (1998). *Caring for school-age children* (2nd ed.). Albany, NY: Delmar.

Foster, S. M. (1994, November). Successful parent meetings. *Young Children, 50*(1), 78–80.

Fung, C. V. (1995, July). Rationales for teaching world musics. *Music Educators Journal, 82*(1), 36–40.

Gestwicki, C. (2000). *Home, school, and community relations* (4th ed.). Albany, NY: Delmar.

Hendrick, J. (1992, March). Where does it all begin? Teaching the principles of democracy in the early years. *Young Children, 47*(3), 51–53.

Kasting, A. (1994, Spring). Respect, responsibility, and reciprocity: The 3Rs of parent involvement. *Childhood Education, 70*(3), 146–150.

Klein, T., Bittel, C., & Molnar, J. (1993, September). No place to call home: Supporting the needs of homeless children in the early childhood classroom. *Young Children, 48*(6), 22–31.

Kupetz, B. N. (1994, Spring). Ageism: A prejudice touching both young and old. *Day Care and Early Education, 21*(3), 24–37.

Lee, F. Y. (1995, March). Asian parents as partners. *Young Children, 50*(3), 4–9.

Lopez, A. (1996, January). Creation is ongoing: Developing a relationship with non-English speaking parents. *Child Care Information Exchange, 107*, 56–59.

McCarthy, T. (1992). *Literature-based geography activities, an integrated approach.* New York: Scholastic.

Morrison, J. W., & Rodgers, L. S. (1996, November). Being responsive to the needs of children from dual heritage backgrounds. *Young Children, 52*(1), 29–33.

Neubert, K., & Jones, E. (1998, September). Creating culturally relevant holiday curriculum: A negotiation. *Young Children, 53*(5), 14–19.

Niffenegger, J. P. (1991, Spring). Introduce map concepts to young children. *Dimensions of Early Childhood, 19*(3), 33–34, 39.

Parsons, C. (1995, Summer). Field trips can enhance family involvement. *Dimensions of Early Childhood, 23*(4), 16–18, 32.

Ross, L. (1995, July/August). Connect with kids and parents of different cultures. *Instructor, 105*(1), 50–53.

Saul, J. D. (1993, Fall). Ready, set, let's go! Using field trips in your curriculum. *Day Care and Early Education, 21*(1), 27–29.

Seefeldt, C. (1993, March). Social studies: Learning for freedom. *Young Children, 48*(3), 4–9.

Starnes, L. B., Hood, B., Selby, K., Moore, C., & Parrison, B. S. (1995, Summer). Plan successful field trips. *Dimensions of Early Childhood, 23*(4), 13–15, 32.

Stipek, D., Rosenblatt, L., & DiRocco, L. (1994, March). Making parents your allies. *Young Children, 49*(3), 4–9.

Studer, J. R. (Winter 1993/94). Listen so that parents will speak. *Childhood Education, 70*(2), 74–76.

Swick, K. J. (1995, Spring). What parents really want from family involvement programs. *Day Care and Early Education, 22*(3), 20–23.

Thomson, B. J. (1993). *Words can hurt you: Beginning a program of anti-bias education.* Menlo Park, CA: Addison-Wesley.

Vold, E. B. (Ed.). (1992). *Multicultural Education in the Early Childhood Classroom.* Washington, DC: National Education Association.

Washington, V., Johnson, V., & McCracken, J. B. (1995). *Grassroots success! Preparing schools and families for each other.* Washington, DC: National Association for the Education of Young Children.

York, S. (1991). *Roots and wings: Affirming culture in early childhood programs.* St. Paul, MN: Redleaf Press.

Appendix A

FLANNELBOARD CHARACTERS, PUPPET PATTERNS, AND LESSON PLAN WORKSHEETS

These sample flannelboard characters and puppet patterns are full-size replications of those mentioned in Chapters 3, 4, 5, 10, and 11.

Use the blank lesson plan worksheets to help you plan appropriate activities for young children in an early childhood setting. Examples of these can be found in Chapter 2.

Lesson plans visually demonstrate the concepts expressed throughout the book. They are only suggestions.

MAMÁ

MARIA

PACO

PAPÁ

APPLE TREE

FALLING APPLE

CAT

SEÑOR WIND

APPLE
CUT IN HALF

SUN

FLOWERS

CLOUD

TREES

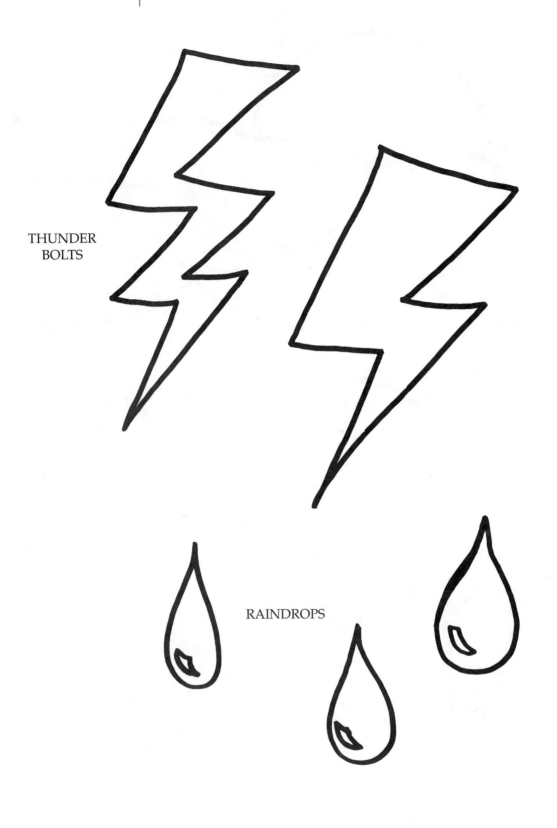

THUNDER
BOLTS

RAINDROPS

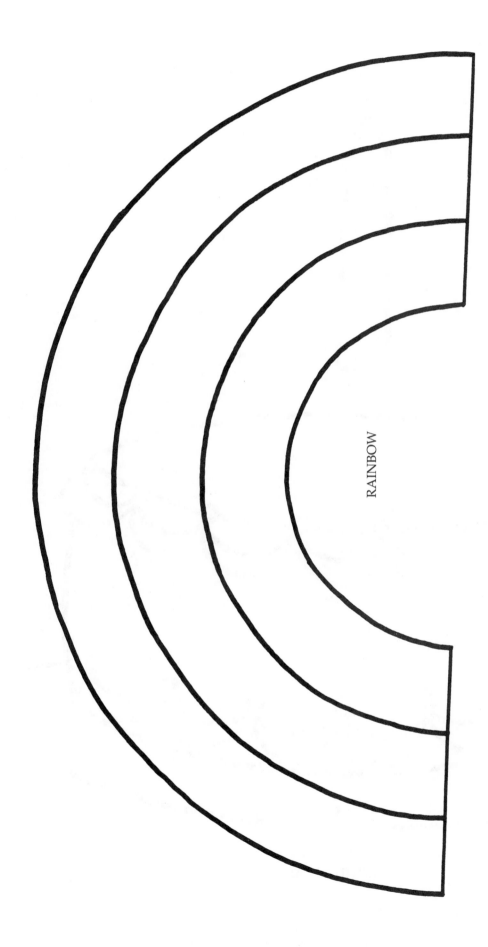

RAINBOW

CANDLE
(MAKE 10)

BIRTHDAY CAKE

SEED

SEED

SPROUTING
SEED

RAINCLOUD

RAINDROPS

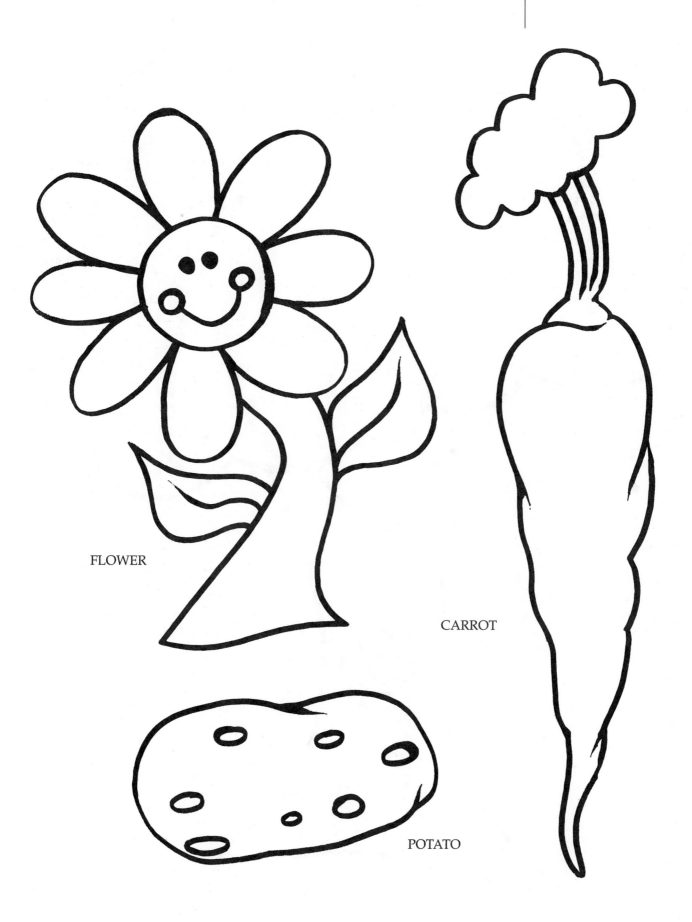

FLOWER

CARROT

POTATO

TREE

FINGER PUPPET PATTERNS

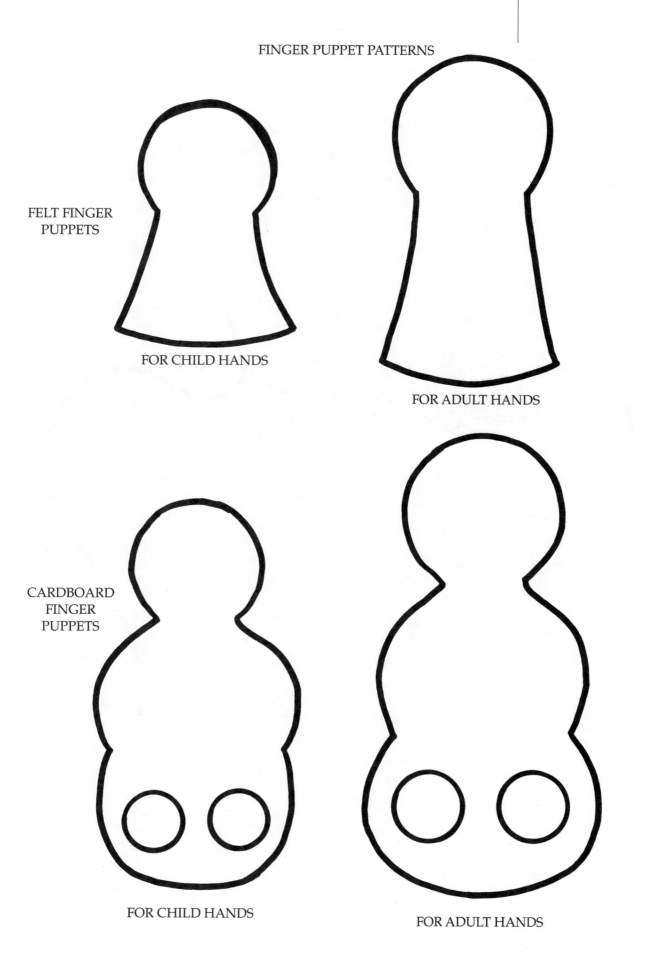

FELT FINGER
PUPPETS

FOR CHILD HANDS

FOR ADULT HANDS

CARDBOARD
FINGER
PUPPETS

FOR CHILD HANDS

FOR ADULT HANDS

HAND PUPPET PATTERN

FOR CHILD HAND
(Can be made larger or smaller to fit different size hands.)

HAND PUPPET PATTERN

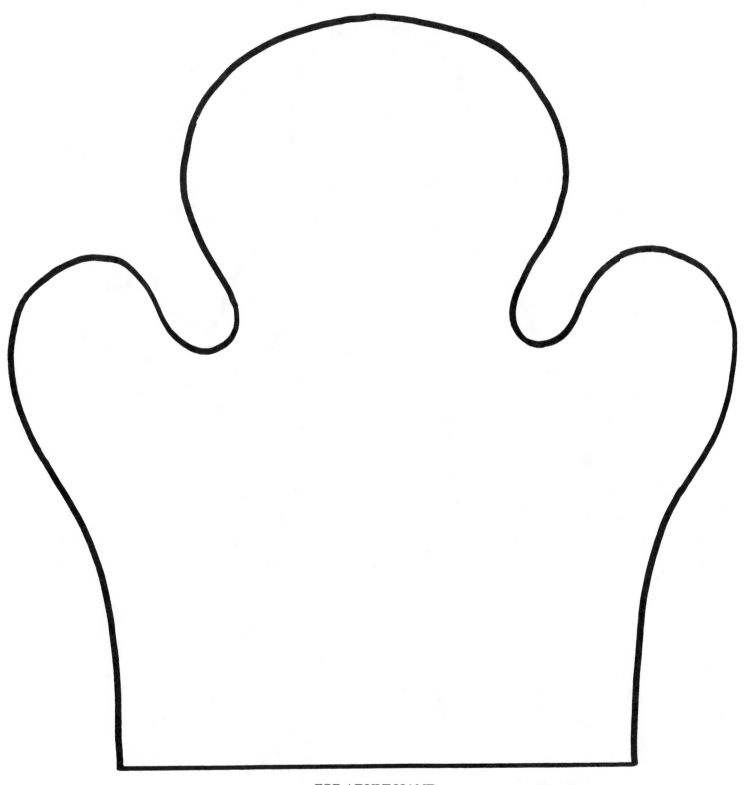

FOR ADULT HAND

PATTERN FOR PEOPLE PUPPETS

INFANT LESSON PLAN

TEACHER(S):   DATES: THEME:

CENTER / ACTIVITY	MONDAY	TUESDAY	WEDNESDAY	THURSDAY	FRIDAY
SENSORY: ART, MUSIC, TACTILE ACTIVITIES					
COGNITIVE & LANGUAGE ACTIVITIES					
SMALL MUSCLE & LARGE MUSCLE ACTIVITIES					
SELF-AWARENESS, SELF-ESTEEM, SELF-HELP ACTIVITIES					
SPECIAL ACTIVITIES					
BOOKS OF THE WEEK					
SPECIAL NOTES					

TODDLER LESSON PLAN

TEACHER(S):

DATES:

THEME:

CONCEPTS:

SKILLS:

DAY	LARGE GROUP ACTIVITIES	SMALL GROUP ACTIVITIES
MONDAY		
TUESDAY		
WEDNESDAY		
THURSDAY		
FRIDAY		

SENSORY ACTIVITIES	DRAMATIC PLAY / HOME LIVING & PUPPETS	MOVEMENT / OUTDOOR ACTIVITIES
MUSIC ACTIVITIES	SELF-AWARENESS, SELF-ESTEEM, SELF-HELP ACTIVITIES	SMALL MUSCLE / MANIPULATIVE ACTIVITIES
ART ACTIVITIES	LANGUAGE ACTIVITIES	TRANSITIONS

BOOKS OF THE WEEK:

ACTIVITIES / NOTES:

PRESCHOOL–KINDERGARTEN LESSON PLAN

TEACHER(S):

CONCEPTS:

DATES:

SKILLS:

THEME:

CENTERS & ACTIVITIES	MONDAY	TUESDAY	WEDNESDAY	THURSDAY	FRIDAY
MORNING GROUP ACTIVITY					
AFTERNOON GROUP ACTIVITY					
LANGUAGE & LITERACY					
ART					
MUSIC & MOVEMENT					
DRAMATIC PLAY					
HOME LIVING					
MATH					
MANIPULATIVE					
SCIENCE & DISCOVERY					

BLOCKS	OUTDOOR / LARGE MUSCLE	TRANSITIONS
SENSORY CENTERS	SOCIAL STUDIES	BOOKS OF THE WEEK

SPECIAL ACTIVITIES & NOTES

Appendix B

■ RESOURCES FOR TEACHERS WITH INTERNET WEB SITE LISTINGS

The following resources offer publications, educational materials, services, and other resources for teachers. They encourage writing to request information about their services. (The resources are listed in association with chapter content.) Internet Web Sites are also listed for many of the resources.

Internet Disclaimer

The author and Delmar make every effort to ensure that all Internet resources are accurate at the time of printing. However, due to the fluid, time-sensitive nature of the Internet, Delmar cannot guarantee that all URLs and Web site addresses will remain current for the duration of this edition.

Chapter 1

- Administration for Children, Youth, and Families
  U.S. Department of Health and Human Services
  www.acf.dhhs.gov/programs/ccb/index.html

- Child Care Information Exchange
  P.O. Box 2890
  Redmond, WA 98073-2890
  (Professional magazine for early childhood administrators and teachers.)

- Early Childhood News
  P.O. Box 49728
  Dayton, OH 45449-0728
  1-800-543-4383
  (Professional magazine for early childhood educators)

- National Association for the Education of Young Children (NAEYC)
  1509–16th Street, NW
  Washington, DC 20036-1426
  www.naeyc.org
  (Write for catalog of publications and membership information.)

- National Association for Gifted Children
  1707 L Street NW—Suite 550
  Washington, DC 20036
  www.nagc.org

- Scholastic Early Childhood Today
  Scholastic Inc.
  555 Broadway
  New York, NY 10012
  www.scholastic.com
  (Professional magazine for early childhood teachers)

- School-Age Notes
  A National Resource Organization
  for School-Age Care
  P.O. Box 40205
  Nashville, TN 37204
  www.schoolagenotes.com

Chapter 2

- Administration for Children, Youth, and Families—Head Start Bureau
  www2.acf.dhhs.gov/programs/hsb

- American Montessori Society
  281 Park Avenue South—6th floor
  New York, NY 10010-6102
  www.amshq.org

- Anti-Defamation League of B'nai B'rith
  Dept. JW
  823 United Nations Plaza
  New York, NY 10117
  (Write for information on teacher resources and audio-visual materials that relate to multicultural education. Many cities have a local office that also has these materials.)

- Association Montessori International/USA
  410 Alexander Street
  Rochester, NY 14607-1028
  www.ami.edu
- Bank Street College of Education
  Broadway at 112th Street
  New York, NY 10025
  www.bnkst.edu
- Council for Exceptional Children
  1920 Association Drive
  Reston, VA 20191-1589
  1-888-CEC-SPED
  www.cec.sped.org
  (Offers comprehensive information and
  publications.)
- Gryphon House Inc.
  P.O. Box 207
  Beltsville, MD 20704-0207
  www.ghbooks.com
- High/Scope Educational Research Foundation
  600 North River Street
  Ypsilanti, MI 48197
  www.highscope.org
- National Information Center for Children and
  Youth with Disabilities (NICHCY)
  P.O. Box 1472
  Washington, DC 20013
  1-800-695-0285
  www.NICHCY.org
  (Publications are free; includes Parent Guide
  and publication list.)
- National Program for Playground Safety
  University of Northern Iowa
  School for Health, Physical Education,
  and Leisure Services
  Cedar Falls, IA 50614-0618
  1-800-554-PLAY
  www.uni.edu/playground
- National Resource Center for Health
  and Safety in Child Care
  UCHSC School of Nursing—C-287
  4200 E. 9th Avenue
  Denver, CO 80262
  www.nrc.uchsc.edu
- Redleaf Press (A division of Resources
  for Child Caring)
  450 N. Syndicate—Suite 5
  St. Paul, MN 55104-4125
  www.child2000.org/REDLEAF.HTM

- Reggio Emilia
  http://ericeece.org/reggio.html
  Reggio Children/USA
  www.cdacouncil/org/reggio
- U.S. Consumer Product Safety Commission
  Washington, DC 20207
  1-800-638-2772
  www.cpsc.gov

Chapter 3

- Council on Interracial Books for Children
  1841 Broadway
  New York, NY 10023
  (Write for catalog of books and filmstrips.)
- The Braille Alphabet . . . FREE!
  Instead of words and letters printed on a page or in
  a book, braille letters and numbers are "bumps"
  embossed on the page. To receive a card with the
  alphabet and numbers in braille, free for the asking,
  send a postcard to:
  American Foundation for the Blind
  11 Penn Plaza—Suite 300
  New York, NY 10011
  (Ask for the Braille Alphabet Card.)
  1-800-232-5463
  www.afb.org
- Internet Public Library
  www.ipl.org
  (The youth section offers references; story hour;
  books and authors; teacher's corner; information
  and activities on art, music, science, math, etc.)

Chapter 4

- Cricket Magazine Group
  Babybug for infants and toddlers
  Ladybug for young children
  Spider for beginning readers
  Cricket for young people
  315 Fifth Street
  Peru, IL 61354
  www.cricketmag.com/home.html
- Highlights for Children Magazine
  P.O. Box 269
  Columbus, OH 43272–0002
- Let's Find Out and My First Magazine
  Scholastic
  2931 East McCarty Street
  Jefferson City, MO 65101-9957
  http://scholastic.com/curriculum/lfo

- Literature Notes: Multicultural Series
Frank Schaffer Publications Inc.
23740 Hawthorne Blvd.
Torrance, CA 90505
1-800-421-5533
www.frank.schaffer.com
- National Center for Family Literacy
325 W. Main Street—Suite 200
Louisville, KY 40202-4251
www.famlit.org
- National Children's Book Week (November)
For information and classroom "streamers"
write to:
Children's Book Council
568 Broadway, Suite 404
New York, NY 10012
www.cbcbooks.org
- Reading Rainbow Gazette
648 Broadway
New York, NY 10003
(Write for information about the books read
on the PBS Television program.)
www.pbs.org/readingrainbow
- Stone Soup: The Magazine by Children
P.O. Box 83
Santa Cruz, CA 95063
www.stonesoup.com
- Weekly Reader
Field Publications
P.O. Box 16630
Columbus, OH 43216
www.weeklyreader.com
(See Chapter 4 in text for other resources on
the Internet.)

Chapters 5 and 6

- Bea Wolf—The Young Ages Festival
A Special Series for Toddlers and Preschoolers
5553 Harvest Hill, Suite 2128
Dallas, TX 75230
(Write for information on performances available
for child-care centers and preschools. The Young
Ages Festival is designed especially for very young
children and features original songs, stories, finger
plays, and puppets.)
- Center for Puppetry Arts
1404 Spring Street
Atlanta, GA 30309
www.puppet.org

(Write for information about the Center for
Puppetry Arts Museum, featuring puppets from all
over the world and their special "Create a Puppet
Workshops.")
- Kathy Burks Marionette Theatre
5553 Harvest Hill, Suite 2128
Dallas, TX 75230
(Write for information on performances available
for preschool and primary-age children, such as
"Carnival of the Animals," "Young King Arthur,"
"Rumpelstilskin," and "The Frog Prince.")
- Mister Rogers' Neighborhood
Child Care Partnership
4802 Fifth Avenue
Pittsburgh, PA 15213
www.pbs.org/rogers
(Write for information regarding training and
curriculum materials.)
- Puppeteers of America
Gayle Schluter
#5 Cricklewood
Pasadena, CA 91107–1002
www.puppeteers.org
(Write for information about their publications.)
- Sesame Street Magazine and Sesame Street
Magazine for Parents
P.O. Box 55518
Boulder, CO 80322-5518
www.henson.com
(Includes link to Sesame Street and other sites.)

Chapter 7

- Aline D. Wolf's "Mommy, It's A Renoir" and four
volumes of accompanying art postcards entitled
"Child-Size Masterpieces"
Write for information to:
Parent Child Press
P.O. Box 767
Altoona, PA 16603
- Barron's Educational Series
250 Wireless Blvd.
Hauppauge, New York 11788
(Write for catalog of creative art books.)
- Crayola
www.crayola.com
(Explore this site. It's full of ideas and information
for stimulating creativity.)

- Children's Press Getting to Know the World's Greatest Artists Series
(Call: Customer service 1-800-621-1115 for information on the 1990–1995 series.)

Chapter 8

- American Academy of Pediatrics
Division of Publications
141 Northwest Point Blvd.
P.O. Box 927
Elk Grove Village, IL 60009-0927
www.aap.org
(Write for "Healthy Start Food To Grow On" brochures.)

- Children's Software Revue Newsletter
Warren Buckleitner, Editor
E-mail Internet address is: buckleit@aol.com.

- "Read It Before You Eat It!"
This free booklet teaches children how to read the new nutrition labels. (1995 FDA). Send self-addressed stamped envelope to:

 S. James
Consumer Information Center-5C
P.O. Box 100
Pueblo, CO 81002
Attn: "Read It Before You Eat It!"

- USDA offers a copy of the Food Guide Pyramid for Young Children booklet. Call the government printing office—(202) 512-1800
www.usda.gov/cnpp

Chapter 9

- Bea Wolf's KinderSongs
Carrot Top Publishers
5553 Harvest Hill, Suite 2128
Dallas, TX 75230
(Write for information regarding KinderSongs Audio Tapes for Young Children. These songs relate specifically to a young child's world and offer songs and song dramas.)

- Center for Music and Young Children
217 Nassau Street
Princeton, NJ 08542
(Write for information regarding materials and instrument catalog and workshop presentation.)

- Dallas Symphony Young People's Concert
"Amazing Music"
Andrew Litton, Host and Conductor

(For information on how to order this video presentation of the Dallas Symphony Orchestra's special performance for children and their parents, call: 1-800-423-1212.)

- Folkway Records
701 Seventh Avenue
New York, NY 10035

- Jo Eklof's "Miss Jo's Picture Book Learning Songs" are read-along and sing-along large print picture books, big books, and musical cassette tapes. These are designed to nurture within each child respect for self, others, and the world around us, while promoting language acquisition and having fun! They are used successfully by teachers of preschool, primary, ESL, and special education. Many of these are now available in Spanish.
Jo Eklof is available to do appearances for child-care centers and schools.
Miss Jo Productions
6131 Royal Crest Drive
Dallas, TX 75230
(Write for catalog and additional information.)

- Music Educators National Conference (MENC)
1806 Robert Fulton Drive
Reston, VA 20191
www.menc.org

- "Music in Motion"—A Music Education and Gift Catalog for all ages
13650 TI Blvd.—Suite 202
Dallas, TX 75243
1-800-445-0649
www.music-in-motion.com

- "Music Together"
Kenneth K. Guilmartin, Director
Center for Music and Young Children
66 Witherspoon Street
Princeton, NJ 08542
(Program for children, infant to kindergarten, and their adult primary caregivers.)

- Thomas Moore Records and Tapes
4600 Park Road, Suite 1000
Charlotte, NC 28209

- West Music
P.O. Box 5521
Coralville, IA 52241
1-800-397-0378
www.westmusic.com
(Write for catalog.)

■ Wolf Trap Institute for Early Learning through the Arts offers workshops for teachers, parents, and administrators. The purpose of the workshops is to introduce performing arts activities that will help early childhood educators teach a variety of physical, cognitive, social, and emotional skills to preschool children. These staff development workshops stress the importance of children creating their own stories, songs, and dances. All of the workshops include material that is appropriate for children with special needs.

For further information about services, fees, and field trips (for early childhood programs in the Washington, DC area) write:

Wolf Trap Institute for Early Learning through the Arts
1624 Trap Road
Vienna, Virginia 22180
www.wolf-trap.org

Chapter 10

■ 3–2-1 Contact Magazine
P.O. Box 2933
Boulder, CO 80322

■ Activities Integrating Mathematics and Science (AIMS) Education Foundation
1595 S. Chestnut Avenue
Fresno, CA 93702
1-888-SEE-AIMS
www.aimsedu.org
(Write for AIMS Programs and Products catalog.)

■ Chickadee: The Canadian Magazine for Children
Young Naturalist Foundation
56 the Esplanade, Suite 304
Toronto, Ontario, Canada M5E1A7

■ Innovative Learning Publications
Addison-Wesley Publishing Co.
Route 128
Reading, MA 01867
(Write for catalog.)

■ National Council of Teachers of Mathematics
1906 Association Drive, Dept. 1-CT
Reston, VA 22091-1593
www.nctm.org
(Write for catalog of resources and publications.)

Chapter 11

■ Audubon Magazine
National Audubon Society
700 Broadway
New York, NY 10003
www.audubon.org

■ Bring Birds to Your Backyard
A number of government-sponsored booklets are offered to children . . . FREE for the asking.
"Homes for Birds" (582Z) is a booklet that describes the characteristics of various birds and tells the best housing for each.
"Backyard Bird Feeding" tells how to attract different species to your house.
Write to:
Consumer Information Center
S. James
Pueblo, CO 81009

■ EPA—United States Environmental Agency (EPA's Environmental Education Center)
www.epa.gov/teachers/index/html

■ Friends of the Environment Foundation—
Earth Day Canada
http://ecokids.earthday.ca

■ National Science Teachers Association
1840 Wilson Blvd.
Arlington, VA 22201
www.nsta.org

■ Nature's Classroom—Environmental Education
75 Harrington Road
Charlton, MA 01507
www.naturesclassroom.org

■ Soundprints—Where Children Discover Nature
353 Main Avenue
Norwalk, CT 06851
1-800-228-7839
www.soundprints.com
(Write for catalog featuring four exciting multi-media series of hands-on experiences for children, available in conjunction with the Smithsonian Institution and the National Wildlife Federation.)

■ The National Wildlife Federation offers several magazines and programs especially for young children. Some of these are:

1. *Your Big Backyard Magazine* (for ages 3–5)
2. *Ranger Rick Magazine* (for ages 6–12)

National Wildlife Federation
8925 Leesburg Pike
Vienna, VA 22184
www.nwf.org
(Explore the Outdoors, Backyard Wildlife Habitat,
Animal Tracks, and National Wildlife Week.)

- "Woodsey Owl" Grab-Bag . . . Yours Free! A great
  way for children to learn all about the environment.
  It is sponsored by the Forest Service in their
  campaign for a clean environment.
  Write to:
  Woodsey Owl Fan Club
  USDA Forest Service
  P.O. Box 96090
  Washington, DC 20090–6090
  www.fs.fed.us/spf/woodsey,
  Conservation Education
  www.fs.fed.us/outdoors/nrce, and
  Nature Watch
  www.fs.fed.us/outdoors/naturewatch

Chapter 12

- Afro-Am Distributing Company
  819 South Wabash Avenue
  Chicago, IL 60605
  (Write for catalog that includes games, puzzles,
  posters, and books for children and adults, with
  emphasis on African Americans and Africa.)

- Foster Grandparent Program
  Retired Senior Volunteer Program (RSVP)
  1100 Vermont Ave, NW
  Room 6100
  Washington, DC 20525
  This organization can help you locate older
  volunteers to work with you and the children.

They, or the following three agencies, may offer
intergenerational programs in your area:
American Association of Retired Persons
National Retired Teachers Association
National Council on Aging

- How to Find an Overseas Pen Pal

  Special information is available for teachers. Send
  $1.00 for postage and handling to:
  International Pen Friends
  Attn: Guidelines for Teachers
  P.O. Box 43904
  Tucson, AZ 85733-3904
  (Ask for: Teachers Pen-Pal Information Package)
  www.pen-pals.net

- National Association for Bilingual Education
  1220 L Street, NW
  Washington, DC 20005-4018
  www.nabe.org

- National Council for the Social Studies
  3501 Newark St. NW
  Washington, DC 20016
  www.ncss.org

- The Native American Authors Distribution Project
  The Greenfield Press
  Greenfield Center, NY 12833
  (More than 250 titles by authors of American Indian
  ancestry are included in this small catalog including
  books for children and adults.)

- United States Committee for UNICEF
  United Nations Children's Fund
  1 Children's Blvd.
  P.O. Box 182233
  Chattanooga, TN 37422
  (Write for catalog of cards and gifts.)

Appendix C

■ PROFESSIONAL ORGANIZATIONS

American Speech-Language-Hearing Association
10801 Rockville Pike
Rockville, MD 20852
www.asha.org

Association for Childhood Education
International (ACEI)
11141 Georgia Avenue—Suite 315
Wheaton, MD 20902
www.udel.edu/bateman/acei
(Publishes *Childhood Education* and *Journal of Research in Childhood Education*)

Canadian Association for Young Children (CAYC)
252 Bloor Street—Suite 12-115
Toronto, Ontario
Canada M5S 1V5
www.cayc.ca
(Publishes *Canadian Children*)

Child Care Action Campaign
3370 Seventh Avenue—17th Floor
New York, NY 10001
www.usakids.org

Children's Defense Fund
25 E Street, NW
Washington, DC 20001
www.childrensdefense.org

Children's Foundation
725 15th Street, NW—Suite 505
Washington, DC 20005
www.childrensfoundation.net

Council for Early Childhood Professional
Recognition (CDA)
2460 16th Street NW
Washington, DC 20009
www.cdacouncil.org

Council for Exceptional Children (CEC)
1920 Association Drive
Reston, VA 22091
www.dec.sped.org
(Publishes *Exceptional Children's Journal*)

Educational Resources Information Center on Early
Childhood Education (ERIC)
905 W. Pennsylvania Avenue
Urbana, IL 61801
http://ericeece.org
(Publishes ERIC/ECE newsletter)

Families and Work Institute
330 Seventh Avenue—14th Floor
New York, NY 10001
www.familiesandwork.org

International Reading Association Inc.
800 Barksdale Road
Box 8139
Newark, DE 19714
www.ira.org
(Publishes *Reading Today* and *The Reading Teacher*)

Learning Disabilities Association
4156 Library Road
Pittsburgh, PA 15234
www.ldanatl.org

National Association for the Education of Young
Children (NAEYC)
1509 16th Street, NW
Washington, DC 20036
www.naeyc.org
(Publishes *Young Children*)

National Association for Family Child Care
525 S.W. 5th Street—Suite A
Des Moines, IA 50309
www.nafcc.org

Save the Children
54 Wilton Road
Westport, CT 06880
www.savethechild.org

Southern Early Childhood Association (SECA)
7107 W. 12th—Suite 102
Little Rock, AR 72215
1–800-SECA (7322)
www.seca50.org
(Publishes *Dimensions of Early Childhood*)

Stand for Children
1834 Connecticut Avenue NW
Washington, DC 20009
1–800-663-4032
www.stand.org

Zero to Three—National Center for Infants,
Toddlers, and Families
734 15th Street NW—Suite 1000
Washington, DC 20005
www.zerotothree.org/professional.html

Glossary

A

aesthetic environment. An environment that cultivates an appreciation for beauty and a feeling of wonder and excitement of the world in which we live.

alphabet books. Simple stories based on the alphabet that present letter identification and one-object picture association.

anecdotal record. A brief, informal narrative account describing an incident of a child's behavior that is important to the observer.

anti-bias. An attitude that actively challenges prejudice, stereotyping, and unfair treatment of an individual or group of individuals.

art. Visual communication through the elements of color, line, shape, and texture instead of words.

assessment. The collection of information or data on young children through observation and recordkeeping of what they do and how they do it as a basis for making educational decisions.

associative play. An activity of a three- or four-year-old child playing with other children in a group, but he drops in and out of play with minimal organization of activity.

B

beat. An accent of sound or a continuing series of accents.

beginning-to-read books. Predictable books that are easy to read and present words that are simple and repetitive.

bias. Any attitude, belief, or feeling that results in unfair treatment of an individual or group of individuals.

bicultural. A term used to describe an individual from two distinct cultures.

big books. Oversized books that present extra-large text and illustrations.

bilingual. A term used to describe the use of two languages as part of the learning process.

biological sciences. These sciences (physiology and ecology) relate to living things (people, plants, and animals).

board books. First books for infants and toddlers made of laminated heavy cardboard.

C

case study. A way of collecting and organizing all of the information gathered from various sources to provide insights into the behavior of the child studied.

checklist. A record of direct observation that involves selecting from a previously prepared list the statement that best describes the behavior observed, the conditions present, or the equipment, supplies, and materials available.

classifying and sorting. Grouping objects by a common characteristic, such as size, shape, or color.

cognitive development. The mental process that focuses on how children's intelligence and thinking abilities emerge through distinct ages. Type of development relating to children making art forms that represent and clarify how they see the world; finding new ways to problem solve with art materials and supplies; experimenting with cause and effect; comparing sizes and shapes; and predicting outcomes through their involvement with art activities.

concept books. Books that present themes, ideas, or concepts with specific examples. They also identify and clarify abstractions, such as color or shape and help with vocabulary development.

concept development. The construction of knowledge through solving problems and experiencing the results, while being actively involved with the environment.

constructive play. Play which helps children understand their experiences. Involves planning or manipulation of objects or people to create a specific experience.

cooperative play. This type of play is organized for some purpose by the four-year-old and older child. It requires group membership and reflects a child's growing capacity to accept and respond to ideas and actions not originally her own.

crayon resist. A type of art for older children that involves drawing a picture in light-colored crayons then covering the picture with watercolors or thin tempera paint. The paint will cover all but the crayon drawing.

crayon rubbings. Duplicating an object of texture by placing it under paper and rubbing over it with a crayon.

creative dramatics. The improvised drama of children, age five or six and older.

creativity. The process of doing, of bringing something new and imaginative into being.

culture. The sum total of a child's or family's ways of living: their values or beliefs, language, patterns of thinking, appearance, and behavior. These are passed or learned from one generation to the next.

curriculum. A multileveled process that encompasses what happens in an early education classroom each day, reflecting the philosophy, goals, and objectives of the early childhood program.

curriculum web. A visual illustration or process that integrates various learning activities and curriculum areas.

D

developmentally appropriate practice. The curriculum planning philosophy expressed by NAEYC that recognizes that each child learns and develops differently in physical, intellectual, cultural, emotional, and social growth.

dramatic play. A type of creative, spontaneous play in which children use their imaginations to create and dramatize pretend characters, actions, or events.

E

early childhood education and early education. The curriculum, programs, and settings that serve young children, from birth through the eighth year of life.

ecology. The study of living things in relation to their environment and to each other.

environment. In an early childhood setting, the environment represents the conditions and surroundings affecting children and adults.

evaluation. The process of determining if the philosophy, goals, and objectives of the early childhood program have been met.

F

flannelboard. Used as a prop to tell or extend a story effectively.

folk literature. Tales that come from the oral tradition of storytelling that appeal to the child's sense of fantasy.

functional play. Play that occurs when a child takes on a role and pretends to be someone else.

G

games with rules. Children's spontaneous physical and cognitive play that occurs during Piaget's concrete operations stage of development (seven years and older).

goals. The general overall aims or overview of an early childhood program.

H

hand puppet. Puppets that come in many types and varieties and are easy for young children to make and manipulate.

hardware. The physical components of the computer system, such as monitor, keyboard, mouse, and printer.

hollow blocks. Wooden blocks larger than unit blocks and opened on the sides.

I

inclusion. Reflective of the blending of practices from early childhood education and early childhood special education.

informational books. Books that offer nonfiction for emergent readers by providing accurate facts about people and subject matter.

interaction books. Books used to stimulate imagination by using some device for involving young readers, such as pop-ups, fold-outs, scratch and sniff, pasting books, puzzle pictures, humor, and riddles.

L

language. Human speech, the written symbols for speech, or any means of communicating.

language development. Developmental process of a predictable sequence which includes both sending and receiving information. It is related, but not tied, to chronological age.

learning centers. These curriculum centers (sometimes called interest centers or activity centers) are well-defined areas where materials and supplies are combined around special groupings and common activities.

lesson plan. An outgrowth of theme selection, brainstorming/webbing, and selection of projects and activities. This involves making a series of choices based on the developmental stages, learning styles, and interests of the children; the goals and objectives of the program; and the availability of materials, supplies, and resources.

literacy. The ability to read and write, which gives one the command of a native language for the purpose of communicating.

literacy development. A lifelong process that begins at birth and includes listening, speaking, reading, and writing.

literature. All the writings (prose and verse) of a people, country, or period, including those written especially for children.

locomotor movement. The ability to move the whole body from one place to another.

M

manipulative movement. Large (gross) motor movements demonstrated by pulling, lifting, throwing, or kicking an object.

manipulatives. Toys and materials that enable young children to gain the fine motor control they need to accomplish tasks important to their growth and development.

marionettes. Puppets controlled by strings that offer an extra range of expression and full body movement.

melody. A sequence of tones of varying pitches organized in a rhythmically meaningful way.

Mother Goose nursery rhyme books. Books passed from generation to generation and known by children all over the world. These are often a child's first introduction to literature.

multicultural books. Books that develop awareness of and sensitivity to other cultures. They also help to increase positive attitudes toward similarities and differences in people.

N

nonlocomotor movement. This occurs when the feet remain stationary (as in standing, kneeling, or sitting), while other parts of the body move.

O

objectives. The specific purposes or teaching techniques that interpret the goals of planning, schedules, and routines. These objectives are designed to meet the physical, intellectual, social, emotional, and creative development of young children.

one-to-one correspondence. The pairing of one object to another object or one group of objects to another group of equal number.

onlooker play. The play of young children introduced to new situations that focuses on an activity rather than the environment.

P

pantomime. The art of conveying ideas without words.

parallel play. Observable play in the older toddler and young three-year-old that emphasizes being near another child while playing with an object rather than playing with a child.

pattern. A sequence of colors, objects, sounds, stories, or movements that repeats in the same order over and over again.

perceptual development. Type of development in which children use their senses to learn about the nature of objects, action, and events.

philosophy. In an early childhood program the philosophy expresses the basic principles, attitudes, and beliefs of the center or school or individual teacher.

phonics. The phonetic method of teaching reading, as it relates to the study of the production and written representation of speech sounds.

physical development. Type of development involving children using large muscles, manipulating small muscles, developing eye-hand coordination, and acquiring self-help skills.

physical sciences. These sciences (physics, chemistry, geology, meteorology, and astronomy) that relate to nonliving materials.

picture books. Books written in a direct style that tell a simple story with illustrations complementing the text.

pitch. The highness or lowness of a tone on a musical scale.

play. A behavior that is self-motivated, freely chosen, process-oriented, and enjoyable.

poetry. A form of literature that contributes imaginative rhyme, rhythm, and sound.

portfolio assessment. An evaluation method based on a systematic collection of information about a child and the child's work gathered by both the child and teacher over time from all available sources.

practice play. During Piaget's sensorimotor play (infancy to two years), infants explore the sensory qualities of objects and practice motor skills.

predictable books. Books that contain familiar and repetitive sequences.

prejudice. An attitude, opinion, or idea that is preconceived or decided, usually unfavorably.

project. An in-depth investigation of a topic.

prop box. A collection of actual items related to dramatic play activities that focuses on a specific theme or lesson plan.

puppetry. The art of making or operating puppets or producing puppet shows.

R

realistic literature. A form of literature that helps children cope with common, actual experiences by offering positive solutions and insights.

rebus chart. Visual pictures, such as signs, illustrations, and directions, to help children make sense of any activity.

reference books. Books that emphasize individualized learning through special topic books, picture dictionaries, and encyclopedias.

reflective log or diary. A teacher or administrator's record of the most significant happenings, usually made at the end of the day or during an uninterrupted block of time.

rhythm. A sense of movement and patterns in music created by beats, the duration and volume of sounds, and the silences between sounds.

routines. The events that fit into the daily time frame of an early childhood program.

S

schedule. The basic daily timeline of an early childhood program.

sensory experiences. Experiences that offer opportunities for free exploration in a variety of curriculum areas.

series books. Books written for primary-grade children and are built around a single character or group of characters.

shadow puppets. Puppets held from rods against a translucent screen lit from behind. These puppets offer a visual dimension that other types do not.

social and emotional development. Type of development consisting of children developing positive images of themselves; expressing personality and individualism; representing imagination and fantasy; establishing enjoyable relationships with others and expressing feelings.

social sciences. The core of social studies: anthropology, sociology, history, geology, economics, and psychology.

software. A set of instructions used to direct a computer to perform some activity.

solitary play. Independent play behavior of a child without regard to what other children or adults are doing.

spatial relationships. Comparisons that help children develop an awareness of the relationship of objects in space, such as, exploration using blocks and boxes.

stereotype. An oversimplified generalization about a particular group, race, or sex, often with negative implications.

stick or rod puppets. Puppets controlled by a single stick, such as a tongue depressor, dowel rod, paper towel roll, craft stick, or ice cream stick.

string painting. A type of painting that involves moving string dipped in paint around on paper to make a design.

symbolic or dramatic play. This type of play allows the child to transfer objects into symbols (things that represent something else) and images into people, places, and events within his experiences. Symbolic play occurs during Piaget's preoperational stage (two to seven years). Superhero fantasy play is considered a type of symbolic play for a young child.

T

teacher- and child-made books. Books made by the teacher or child that encourage self-esteem, creativity, and the sharing of ideas. They also encourage children to articulate experiences.

tempo. A sense of slowness or rapidity in music.

theme. This is a broad concept or topic that enables the development of a lesson plan and the activities that fit within this curriculum plan.

three-dimensional art. Any art form that has three sides. Play dough and clay are examples of three-dimensional materials.

timbre. The unique tone quality of a voice or musical instrument.

tone. An individual musical sound.

transitions. Activities or learning experiences that move children from one activity to another.

U

unit. A section of the curriculum based on the unifying theme around which activities are planned.

unit blocks. Hardwood blocks used in early education environments, especially in block center play.

unoccupied behavior. Refers to a child (infant or toddler) who occupies herself by watching anything of momentary interest.

V

volume. The softness or loudness of sound.

W

whole language. A view of literacy and learning that builds on what children already know about oral language, reading, and writing while emphasizing meaningful language rather than isolated skill development.

wordless picture books. Books that tell a story with visually appealing illustrations. These books promote creativity by encouraging a child to talk about experiences and use his or her imagination.

Index